KEN RUSSELL'S FILMS

by
Ken Hanke

The Scarecrow Press, Inc.
Metuchen, N.J., & London
1984

Library of Congress Cataloging in Publication Data

Hanke, Ken, 1954–
  Ken Russell's films.

  Includes index.
  1. Russell, Ken, 1927–   . I. Title.
PN1998.A3R7734 1984   791.43'0233'0924 [B] 84-5483
ISBN 0-8108-1700-4

Copyright © 1984 by Ken Hanke

Manufactured in the United States of America

CONTENTS

Acknowledgments		v
Preface		vii
Foreword, by Richard Chamberlain		ix
Chapter 1:	Introduction: The Amazing Journey-- An Overview of Russell's Work	1
Chapter 2:	On Russell and Religion: "All My Films Are Very Catholic"	10
Chapter 3:	Training Ground: The BBC Films	15
Chapter 4:	Two False Steps: French Dressing and Billion Dollar Brain	42
Chapter 5:	The First Controlled Feature: Women in Love	51
Chapter 6:	The Breakthrough: The Music Lovers	75
Chapter 7:	Finding a Voice: The Devils, The Boy Friend, and Savage Messiah	118
Chapter 8:	The Mature Films: Mahler, Tommy, and Lisztomania	220
Chapter 9:	Toward a New Horizon: Valentino	326
Chapter 10:	Intermission: Clouds of Glory	348
Chapter 11:	A Summing Up in Hollywood: Altered States	397
Chapter 12:	The Medium of the Future: Madama Butterfly	416
Chapter 13:	The Influence of Russell	428
Filmography		433
Index		447

ACKNOWLEDGMENTS

Special thanks must go to Ken Russell, not only for his great kindness to me in helping with this book, but for going so far as to virtually perform the function of proofreader, catching several errors and making helpful suggestions all round. He never took issue with my value judgments or interpretations. For this and for making these films in the first place, I am forever in his debt.

Thanks are also due to a number of people who helped, in one way or another, in the creation of this book:

- Dick Blodgett, Ken Russell's agent.
- Rev. Gene D. Phillips, S.J., who helped get things underway.
- Michael Gallagher, U.S. Catholic Conference Film Dept. for his assistance.
- Robert Littman.
- Barbara Humphreys, Library of Congress.
- Robert W. Pohle, Jr., for his hours of reading the manuscript, making suggestions, and just listening at all hours.
- Greg Pitt, for invaluable research.
- Reginald A. Gaulle, Jr., research.
- Steve Pugh, photographic assistance.
- John and Robbie Roberts, bed and board in Washington, D.C.
- Julie J. Haffner, bed and board in New York.

This book is dedicated to my wife, Shonsa: constant companion, sometime proofreader, and perhaps the only person living who would not have objected too violently to being dragged 125 miles to see Mahler, sixty-five miles to a porno house (!) for a midnight show of The Devils, and, the crowning indignity, being convinced that we should catch "just one more showing" of Tommy when it happened to be playing in the town where we were spending our honeymoon. I thank you.

This book is also for John Roberts, who has believed --perhaps feared--that I would do something like this since we were in tenth grade together, longer ago than either of us would care to remember.

PREFACE

I came late to Ken Russell's films. It was not until 1975 with the release of Tommy that Ken Russell was ever anything more than a name to me. It is not even now perfectly clear to me why I saw Tommy as I had never been a fan of the original album by The Who, but after two tries at the long lines outside the theatre it became a point of fierce importance that I finally see the thing. The third time proved the charm, and despite a load of misgivings and being prepared to thoroughly dislike this film that had already caused me so much annoyance in just trying to get in, I was almost immediately a complete convert. By the end of the following week I had reacquainted myself with the film several more times, finding new things to admire in each successive viewing. (To this day, even after studying and writing extensively about it, I am always discovering new things about Tommy --indeed all of Russell's work--when I revisit it.)

Naturally, it soon became necessary to fill in the gaps in my Russell knowledge--The Devils, The Music Lovers, Women in Love, The Boy Friend, Mahler, and, of course, the new releases of Lisztomania, Valentino, and Altered States. Universities, art house theatres, and many miles of traveling eventually paid off, though it took every bit of five years until I finally saw the last piece of the puzzle, Savage Messiah, which had stubbornly refused to show up on any program.

Somewhere along the way the idea was born that I should write about these films. I had long had the desire to do this, but it was not until film-historian Robert W. Pohle, Jr. started badgering me on the subject that I took up the task in earnest. I sincerely believe that it was his hope that if I started writing about Ken Russell, I might stop talking about him all the time. I'm sure Mr. Pohle would be the first to admit that in this hope he failed, but he did succeed in getting me to write the book in any case!

When I started writing this book, it was largely my idea that it would be successful if it managed to convey even a part of the excitement and admiration I feel for the films it encompasses. I hope that I have been fortunate in this respect. I never dreamed, however, that the book could have made the impression it did upon Ken Russell, who, upon reading the manuscript, said, "It has certainly helped me--which, I guess, was furthest from your mind when you set upon what would be to me, at least, a very daunting undertaking." If this book has in any way been of a help to its subject then it has succeeded far better than I ever hoped. Moreover, if, as Russell also states, it gave him new insight into his biographical films and filled him with a desire to carry on with them, nothing more can be asked.

FOREWORD

My first visions of Ken Russell's work were two of his legendary series of films for BBC-TV in England during the late 1960's. The first was Delius: A Song of Summer and the other Isadora with Vivian Pickles. Both knocked me out. They were films of such sure style and psychological depth, such pictorial beauty and eccentric verve that I, being American, could hardly believe I was watching television.

A mysterious facet of Ken's genius at that time was his ability in television to exceed feature films made with much vaster budgets. Ms. Pickles' "Isadora" captured that great dancer's extravagant and rather funny sensuality much more vividly than did the concurrent feature film.

Ken's sustained success in television lifted him out of that medium into the realm of feature films, a dubious but irresistible advancement.

I like to think of Delius and Isadora as part of Ken's Classical period in that his powerful attraction to the excesses of his subjects was held in balance by a strong style rooted in the best of European cinema. This controlled style extended into the harrowing drama of his splendid feature film Women in Love. Ken and his superb actors served D. H. Lawrence brilliantly and his transition into the hazardous world of cinema was triumphant.

Around this time I was living in London and Ken asked to see me about possibly playing Peter Ilyich Tchaikovsky in his next film, The Music Lovers. Ken's immense love of music and his fascination with lives of obsession and excess had drawn him towards the composer. As he told me about Tchaikovsky's tortured life I was completely won over by both the story and Ken's soft-spoken intensity. Ken can be articulate, charming and urbane, as he was through our rehearsal period and the early days of shooting. Then other aspects of his creative method surfaced. A volcanic, dangerous brooding which, though few words were spoken (except "Again, Again, Again!"), electrified the set and made the most grueling demands seem bearable--even exciting. Ken likes to rehearse on film, which means playing each scene full out as many as 20 or 25 times. This process was mesmerizing and could lead to unexpected emotional heights. It was also utterly exhausting. Ken likes to keep the camera in near constant movement creating intricate mazes of choreography through which the actors must move with seeming naturalness, not easy for us to do but most exciting to watch.

The Music Lovers was the beginning of Ken's Baroque period. Floods of unbridled fantasy and emotion began to test the seawalls of restraint. Yet even the most bizarre scenes seemed to me to express unforgettably Tchaikovsky's state of being. And the film's central theme that the avoidance of truth leads to insanity was deeply felt.

Ken gleefully crashed through the seawalls with a mighty storm of fantastic images and sound with The Devils and Tommy. The Devils, which featured a splendid performance by Oliver Reed, reveled in the chills and thrills of religion gone mad, while Tommy celebrated the pleasures of chaos.

Altered States, the last of Ken's films I've seen, was a carefully conceived flight through the astonishing layers of perception which lie beneath our ordinary awareness. In this film Ken found a new balance between his earlier thoughtfulness and his more tempestuous urges.

Ken Russell's films have taken us on an astonishing variety of journeys, often into exotic territories we would not otherwise have dared to trespass. I'm grateful for these adventures and eagerly anticipating his next improbable excursion.

Richard Chamberlain

CHAPTER 1

INTRODUCTION

<u>The Amazing Journey--An Overview of Russell's Work</u>

To some extent the study of the films of any filmmaker constitutes a journey, but in the case of Ken Russell this journey takes on additional significance. With Russell we do not have simply the journey from the films made with youthful enthusiasm to the works of a mature filmmaker in complete control of his medium, or even just the more personal move from a creator of British television films to a filmmaker of international importance. In addition to these more traditional journeys, the films of Ken Russell present the picture of a journey from darkness into light.

The earliest Russell films--those made for television--are an interesting mixture of the positive aspects of humanity with the negative aspects. The overall feeling, however, is one of a negative attitude. Russell may indeed allow Isadora Duncan's fantasy of dancing with hundreds of school-children to the "Ode to Joy" from Beethoven's Ninth Symphony to become reality at the moment of her death, but his final judgment is to present her contorted, dead face, thereby undercutting the fulfillment of the fantasy. Russell's first full-blown theatrical masterpiece, <u>The Music Lovers</u>, is even more negative in approach and summation, but with his very next offering, <u>The Devils</u>, the attitude takes an immediate upward turn. Astonishingly, every film since then has advanced this progression of attitude, which finally finds its culmination in the overpoweringly positive climax of <u>Altered States</u>. This journey toward a positive outlook is perhaps Russell's greatest attribute, and one of his most distinctive, as a filmmaker.

Unlike many of the serious filmmakers working today, Russell has learned that there is no intrinsic greatness in the downbeat, in the hopeless, in the use of tragedy for its

own sake. In itself this likely accounts for a great deal of
the critical neglect and downright hostility to which Russell
has been subjected. Critical analysis has always tended to
attach--at least when dealing with contemporary works--
greater significance to supposedly serious treatments of serious subjects. This is why a film like Edmund Goulding's
Grand Hotel (admittedly a quite good film) was originally considered 1932's best film over such obviously superior works
as Rouben Mamoulian's Love Me Tonight and Josef von Sternberg's Shanghai Express. To say that Mamoulian and von
Sternberg were ahead of their time is an oversimplification,
though on a purely stylistic level this is true. More importantly, however, they just did not have the proper approach
on a broader thematic level. Had the train in Love Me Tonight run down Jeanette MacDonald, or had Clive Brook and
Marlene Dietrich not reconciled at the end of Shanghai Express, it is likely that either film would have been taken
more seriously. Much the same is true of Russell's work.
Despite critical protestations of Russell's self-indulgence and
his supposedly hysterical approach to history, the end feeling
is more that it is difficult to come to terms with him as a
serious artist because his outlook is not bleak enough.

  At the same time it would be quite impossible to overlook the fact that many critics are uncomfortable with Russell's approach to history. Surely it is no accident that the
Russell films that have received the least critical abuse
(Women in Love, The Boy Friend, Tommy, and Altered
States) are also the films that are based on works of fiction. The difficulty in coming to terms with Russell's historical or biographical films is largely an outgrowth of simple complacency. The Russell views of historical persons
and events are shocking not so much due to the outrageousness of their design, but because they challenge comfortable
preconceived notions. In order to accept Russell's basic
premise, it is necessary first to accept the fact that they
are as much essays on Russell's reactions to the characters and events as they are biographical or historical. It
is not Russell's desire to tell a life story, but rather to
capture the essence or spirit of the character being portrayed. Most importantly it must be understood that this
essence is subjective, so much so that the spirit of Tchaikovsky which permeates The Music Lovers is what Russell
personally perceives as that spirit. In a very real sense it
is necessary to leave personal preconceived notions in the
theatre lobby, and only later weigh Russell's judgments
against those notions. Without taking this approach the

Introduction 3

reaction to a Russell film is likely to be far more hysterical than any hysteria presented by the filmmaker himself.

Significantly Russell's detractors have completely missed the fact that his interpretations are openly subjective. To take a more neutral example, consider Russell's film The Boy Friend. The credits of the film themselves indicate Russell's stance: "Metro-Goldwyn-Mayer presents Ken Russell's Talking Picture, The Boy Friend, based on a musical play by Sandy Wilson." The film is first and foremost, "Ken Russell's Talking Picture," and the play on which it is based is purely secondary. Exactly as in the historical films, The Boy Friend is as much about Russell's reaction to the play as it is a film of the play. The inclusion of a self-parody in the form of an outlandish movie director, De Thrill, brings this idea into even sharper focus. "Ken Russell's Talking Picture" is not even really a film of The Boy Friend at all. (In one respect at least, De Thrill's decision not to make The Boy Friend in favor of making Singin' in the Rain is indicative of Russell's decision not to film Sandy Wilson's play.) In consideration of this, charges of his being unfaithful to the source material or being historically inaccurate have little bearing on the evaluation of this or any other Russell film.

Russell's use of symbolism has posed an almost equally thorny problem for reviewers, for though there are recurring symbols in Russell's work these symbols are never accorded fixed meanings. Chief among Russell's symbols are fire, water, mountains (and the Lake District), and trains. These are all fairly common symbolic devices, but in Russell's case they achieve new power, not in the least because of the ambiguity with which they are applied.

Fire runs rampant in Russell's work, but any attempt to ascribe an affixed value on it is hopeless. In Women in Love, fire frequently indicates the inner warmth of a situation and at the same time the need for outside warmth for one who lacks inner warmth and is spiritually dead. When dealing with Rupert and Ursula fire is a positive element, but when associated with Gerald or Gudrun it is a destructive, negative force. In The Devils, Grandier's death by fire destroys him physically, but allows him to transcend his physical limitations by its very purification. When "Gosh" Boyle-Smith firebombs a mailbox as a revolutionary act in Savage Messiah, the fire is an apt symbol of her own very potentially dangerous and volatile inner nature. In

Mahler, fire is a destructive force in the burning of the lakeside hut, but the destruction of the hut is not important in itself, instead it is the death of innocence and hope. (In much the same way the burning of the wheatfields in The Music Lovers is the death of a dream.) In Tommy, fire is again destructive, but its destruction of the Holiday Camp takes on the significance of Grandier's death by fire as this destruction leads to Tommy's salvation. In Lisztomania, fire is used in two very different manners. It can destroy innocence, as in the burning baby carriage, but it can also destroy evil, as in the destruction of Wagner. Everything depends on the use to which it is being put.

In the use of water imagery Russell forces us to place the symbolic value within its text. Water destroys in Isadora and Women in Love, and Tchaikovsky attempts to drown himself (and indeed dies from contaminated water) in The Music Lovers. In The Devils, Savage Messiah, and Mahler, however, it is always associated with well-being, calmness, and being at momentary peace. In Tommy this is taken even further and water takes on a completely new dimension as the source of creation and purification. Even in Lisztomania, where water plays a relatively insignificant role (unless we include Liszt's false faith in Holy Water), the one use of water as such is at the point where Liszt is celebrating his freedom from having to marry Princess Carolyn out of gratitude.

Then, too, there is the question of Russell's mountain imagery and with it his continual use of the Lake District for his films. Joseph Gomez feels that this recurring setting is a minor fault with Russell's work. Flaw or not, there is no getting around the repetitive use of the Lake District. So much does it appear in Russell's work that it is tempting to call Russell the Lake Filmmaker, especially after his two-part TV film on the Lake Poets. In all honesty there would be some justification in calling him this, since he keeps a home there, and there is little doubt that Russell draws inspiration from the area. His continual use of it as a setting for his films is something more than a personal trademark. Symbolically the Lake District embodies the overall elemental earth, air, and water imagery that pervades his work, and amazingly this use of the very same area of the Lake District takes on the self-same ambiguity that marks his other symbols. The best example of this comes in the back to back use of the same lake in Mahler and Tommy. Geographically the lakeside hut in Mahler rests against the very shore of the lake that can be seen from the mountaintop in Tommy. The-

Introduction 5

matically speaking, however, they are worlds apart. In
Mahler the setting is idyllic and tranquil (the more so for
the contrast of the violent explosion of the hut into flame that
opens the film). In Tommy the setting is used more for the
awesomeness of its beauty, not for the idyllic intimacy of
Mahler. It is clear that Russell's use of the Lake District
is neither arbitrary, nor is it born of economy. Much as
if the District itself were a thematic entity, Russell uses it
again and again to capture all the nuances of the broad range
of feelings it can evoke.

    Drawing on the great heritage of film, Russell has
also made extensive use of trains in his films. Historically
speaking, trains have always held a fascination for filmmakers. Even one of the very first of the Lumière Brothers' films consisted of nothing more than a train racing up
to and past the camera. Since that time trains have figured
prominently in any number of films. Alfred Hitchcock got
more use out of trains than any other filmmaker, but Preston Sturges, Ernst Lubitsch, Howard Hawks, Josef von Sternberg, Rouben Mamoulian, and Carol Reed have also made
good use of trains. In keeping with this heritage, Russell
has prominently featured trains in six of his ten major features. Typically, Russell has not been merely satisfied with
carrying on a great tradition, but has turned that tradition to
his own end. As with other Russell symbols, the train is
not used arbitrarily, nor is it given any fixed meaning. The
trains in Women in Love rather obviously evoke the machine
age with which Gerald Crich is taking over the colliery from
his father. More than this is the fact that while depending
on those very machines, it is a train that serves in the sequence where Gerald tries to subjugate his horse. For Gerald the symbol of the train is not only progress, but a way
of bending natural forces to his will. The train in The Music Lovers is never actually seen. All that appears on
screen is the cramped sleeping compartment, and here it is
the claustrophobia, the incessant swaying and the inevitability
of the unstoppable movement that is important. Most impres-
sively there is the train in Mahler. Here Russell has structured an entire film around a train journey, which serves as
the literal equivalent of the metaphorical, interior journey
being experienced by Mahler. While the train--and by implication Mahler's life--moves forward to a predestined end,
Mahler sifts backwards and forward in a counter journey of
memories, dreams, guilts, and premonitions, trying to make
some sense of his life and his relationship with his wife before reaching that end. The trains in Savage Messiah, Tom-

my, and Lisztomania serve somewhat lesser functions--a false idea of freedom and a force against creativity in the first; a powerful physical force, separating husband and wife in the second; and as an evocation of the bound-and-gagged style silent serial film in the last--but ever here their inclusion is something more than a mere predeliction for trains. (Certainly a fondness for trains enters into this, and trains have always held a certain cinematic value, as a feeling of movement, and of plot and action being pressed forward by the very movement of the train. Nonetheless there is something more important than this in Russell's utilization of trains. Were it simply a desire to use trains for no other reason than just because they appeal to him, there would be no reason for their exclusion from The Boy Friend, Valentino, or Altered States--particularly Altered States, which includes a scene where Eddie and Arthur start to enter a subway, at which point Russell cuts away from the scene. In these instances the inclusion of a train would have served no function, and so the supposedly self-indulgent filmmaker does not indulge in them.)

In the final analysis, Russell's use of symbolism is unique, and when understood helps to clarify much about his approach to filmmaking. Unfortunately, his insistence on the viewer reading each symbol according to its context has perplexed more than one critic, but ultimately this will likely come to be recognized as one of his greatest strengths. In this manner Russell's symbolism, personal as it is, never reaches the level of shtick as much of the symbolism in Fellini's films does. Russell's use of fire, water, the Lake District, and trains never simply signifies (as Fellini's obese women, actors staring into the camera, and exotic black women all too often do) that this is a Ken Russell film.

Much has been written in the defense of Russell's films on a purely technical basis, and this line of reasoning is at least partly sound. Few filmmakers possess his technical mastery. Who but Russell could have shot a complex film like Mahler in a scant seven weeks, given the current state of the film industry? Nonetheless, championing Russell on purely technical grounds is a left-handed compliment at best, as it robs the films of their greater significance. For that matter a concentrated inspection of his work will reveal that he will gladly forego sheer technical achievement in order to capture the far more important feeling of a scene. In Tommy there are a number of minor imperfections left in the final cut of the film because the scenes themselves are

Introduction

so good. Some of these are not immediately discernible, but in the "Acid Queen" sequence, the shadow of Russell and the cameraman is clearly visible in one of the tracking shots. A similar shadow appears in the junkyard sequence, and a minor break in continuity (as concerns the phallic pillow) occurs in Nora's baked-bean fantasy. All of these are exceptionally small mistakes, but Russell's decision to overlook such "flaws" in favor of the overall rightness of the take suggests a concern for something far beyond the technical.

John Baxter has noted that Russell is "eaten up with the IMAGE,"[1] a judgment that stresses his great visual flair, but visual flair is only part of the package. In a much broader sense Russell has a filmic flair that transcends a preoccupation with the image. Virtually alone among modern filmmakers, Russell seems to revel in film for the pure joy of film. In many areas he lacks the great technical polish of, say, Stanley Kubrick, but with Kubrick (and with many other highly acclaimed filmmakers of recent vintage) there is always a niggling feeling that the filmmaker does not particularly like films. A far too great number of contemporary films which have fared well on a critical basis share the common bond of appearing to have been made by people who do not like movies for people who don't like them either. No such feeling hangs over any Ken Russell film. Russell's films are alive with the joy of filmmaking, the joy of fusing--as film ought to do--the elements of every art form into the only art form that can encompass them all. More than this is the strong sense of a love and feel for the history of film itself. It is not by accident that Russell's work frequently includes evocations of films from the past, salutes to the films that have had an influence on his filmmaking. Much of this comes from "respectable" sources--Citizen Kane, Potemkin, The Searchers, The Informer, Siegfried, and similarly recognized masterworks, but there is another side to Russell's filmmaking which is at least as important and maybe more so. It is the influence of the vibrancy of the more commercial cinema, the influence that might well be expected to come through from the young man who continually "broke bounds" to see Carmen Miranda musicals while at school. As a result Russell's films abound with echoes of the Marx Brothers, Laurel and Hardy, Al Jolson, Crosby and Hope, Douglas Fairbanks, etc. These elements, so misconstrued by Russell's detractors, are essential to Russell's approach to filmmaking. Beyond their value as a worthy link to a glorious past, they serve to bring much of Russell's point home in an allegorical way more readily accessible and comprehensible to the modern viewer. This in no way supports Pauline Kael's assessment of Russell as a "compulsive Hollywoodiser," who "unintentionally cheapens everything he touches."2 Aside from the singular misapplication of the word "compulsive," which implies an unconscious act, Russell's evocations of Hollywood are not simple idolatry. Russell loves much about the films of the past and the state of mind that is the Hollywood legend. (Hence, the legend of Hollywood remains unblemished in Valentino although specific instances and occurrences are attacked.) His utilizations of these quotations and evocations always occur with his eyes wide open, fully realizing the limitations of his sources. Far from cheapening his films, these aspects serve to deepen them, to give them an added historical perspective.

On a similar level Russell is almost alone in keeping certain "fun" traditions alive in filmmaking. His works abound in "guest stars"--Glenda Jackson in The Boy Friend, Oliver Reed in both Mahler and Lisztomania, John Justin in Lisztomania and Valentino, Ringo Starr and Rick Wakeman in Lisztomania, assistant musical director Peter Greenwell in The Boy Friend, and Russell's own appearances as an invalid in Tommy and as Rex Ingram in Valentino. There is also a tendency toward "in" references to Russell's own earlier works, best exemplified by Iza Teller as Madame von Meck and Georgina Hale as Alma Mahler cropping up as groupies in the concert scene in Lisztomania. The outrageousness of these in-jokes poses a problem for the critic who does not realize that Russell's films are supposed to be entertaining. Once more it is the question of approach, and while Russell openly admits to preaching about things in which he believes with his films, he adamantly insists that his films are designed to be entertaining.3 Perhaps the clearest equivalent to Russell's attitude is filmmaker Leo McCarey, though stylistically they are basically unrelated. In examining Russell's attitude about making his point by entertaining rather than by forcing ideas on people, one finds the rough equivalent of this position in a scene from McCarey's Going My Way, where Father O'Malley explains that in his approach to religion there is no need for heavy-handedness and unnecessary somberness. It is a scene that neatly sums up Russell's own approach to the subjects he takes seriously. Significantly, it comes from a filmmaker who shared a similar sense of fun. (Consider McCarey's inclusion of an in-joke reference to Ginger Rogers' films with Fred Astaire in his comedy-drama Once upon a Honeymoon, in which Cary Grant admonishes Miss Rogers to stand still so that he might remember her, "just 'The Way You Look Tonight.'") Still, for many this again denotes a lack of seriousness on Russell's part, which prevents them from taking the films seriously enough to give them the attention they deserve (and indeed require) so that they might be appreciated.

No better argument for the sheer contagious enthusiasm with which Russell approaches filmmaking can be found than that represented by a several-second piece of film which appears in the "Pinball Wizard" sequence of Tommy. At the very beginning of the three-part edit that makes up the action of Keith Moon frantically kicking over his drums, there is a quick glimpse of Russell himself filming from behind the action. (Dressed appropriately for the scene, he generally goes unnoticed, taken for one of the technicians ostensibly covering the championship for television.) As the action begins to peak, Russell is so involved in the excitement of the moment that an assistant begins pulling him out of harm's way. When the filmmaker himself is so mesmerized by the events taking place before his camera, there can be little question of his own interest and belief in his creation. Such an episode may not be a guarantee of the quality of the finished product. It is even doubtful that it will affect anyone's opinion of the filmmaker, but it does bear out Russell's outlook on art, expressed by Henri in Savage Messiah: "Art is alive. Enjoy it. Laugh at it. Love it or hate it, but don't worship it. You're not in church." In the same way Russell's work is alive; love it or hate it, there can be no serious question about the sincerity of its creator. Were he anything less there would be no reason for his own enthusiasm and his open subjectivity, qualities that are indicative of the inner fire that burns within every great artist.

NOTES

1. Baxter, John. An Appalling Talent: Ken Russell. London: Michael Joseph, 1973.
2. Kael, Pauline. "Hyperbole and Narcissus," New Yorker, 48 (November 18, 1972): 225-232.
3. Barnes, Richard, and Townshend, Peter. The Story of Tommy. Middlesex, England: Eel Pie, 1977, p. 96.

CHAPTER 2

ON RUSSELL AND RELIGION

"All My Films Are Very Catholic"

Few, if indeed any, modern filmmakers are as preoccupied with religion in a positive manner as Ken Russell. Three of his films--The Devils, Tommy, and Altered States--are unreservedly religious in tone, and the bulk of his work is concerned with religion in one way or another. It is therefore necessary that any attempt to understand Russell's work must effectively deal with Russell's religious outlook.

A Catholic convert, who has since drifted away from the Church, Russell nevertheless considers his work to be that of a Catholic filmmaker with a Catholic viewpoint. To a large extent the films bear this out. Admittedly, Russell's Catholicism is of a very personal nature, but the overriding factor is decidedly Catholic, particularly as concerns the element of forgiveness that pervades the films. Even the great mystic poet (and this appellation could well be applied to Russell as well) William Blake found an inherent appeal in Catholicism because of its belief in forgiveness, which in consideration of Russell's work and its presentation of this belief is understandable. Of course, there can be no forgiveness without the recognition of sin, and much of Russell's work is concerned with the ability of his protagonists to understand and come to terms with their sins and failings in order to attain this level of forgiveness. The curious thing about all this is that a quick scan down the general run of criticism of Russell's work reveals little of this. In fact, the mainstream of film reviewers would suggest that, at best, the filmmaker is a scandal-mongering pornographer, dedicated to the corruption of society. Nothing could be further from the truth, as a study of his films proves, but this is the overall impression to be gained from the critics. At the other end of the scale there is the question of the stance of the church (that he self-avowedly represents in his films) on the films themselves: Does the religion itself recognize the moral viewpoint at work in Russell's films?

To find the answer to the question it becomes necessary to go to the U.S. Catholic Conference's Department of Communication--the modern day equivalent of the old Legion of Decency which once effectively emasculated motion pictures as an art form in 1934. The present version of the Legion of Decency is considerably more broad-minded than the old one. Surprisingly enough, only two of Russell's films have ever been awarded the infamous "Condemned" rating, which has since ceased to exist. Less of a surprise is that one of the two is The Devils, though the rating has nothing to do with the film's attack on a corruption of the religion. The other film to receive the "C" certificate is, less understandably, Valentino. (Unfortunately, the Department's Catholic Film Newsletter is not very specific regarding the logic behind this decision; unlike the other Russell films, Valentino is not dealt with in any depth.) The remaining Russell films run the gamut from "A-1" (the equivalent of a "G" rating) to "B," which means the film is termed "morally objectionable." Most surprising of all in these ratings is the inclusion of The Music Lovers, Mahler, and Tommy in the "A-IV" category, which indicates that although some reservations are held about the work, it is still considered acceptable viewing for adults. (It should be remembered that these value judgments are merely guidelines and not censorial in the accepted sense.)

Actually, the bare-bones ratings themselves are an unfair way to assess the Department's stance, as a "C" rating does not necessarily indicate that a film has no merit, nor does an "A-I" indicate quality. Because of this it is necessary to look at the individual reviews in the Newsletter. A prime example of the reasoning behind the inadvisability of accepting the ratings at face value emerges if we compare the "A-IV"-rated Tommy with the "B"-rated Lisztomania. The Tommy review is one of the Newsletter's more disappointing efforts (perhaps because of the film's heavily mystical leanings) in that it fails to really get at the core of the work, mistaking much of the symbolism for "ridiculously excessive satiric jabs at organized religion," which is a misreading of some import. The critical methods applied to the seemingly more censurable Lisztomania are something else again. Newsletter editor Michael Gallagher, who wrote this review, has here delved more deeply into the film than any mainstream critic. The review shows a keen insight into the film and into Russell. In discussing Russell's excesses, Gallagher notes, "To accuse Russell of excess when he is working in this area, however, is very much like accusing Rubens of sensuality. Russell does go too far in his sexual imagery, and he does it fairly often, but defect though this be, one is always aware of an immense and, yes, wholesome talent at work." Gallagher then concludes with, "There is much that is good, then, in Lisztomania, much that is funny and on-target. So much so that one regrets the moral and aesthetic flaws--those excesses of 'excess'--that make a recommendation of it impossible." Of course, a separate moral and aesthetic judgment is impossible given the nature of the Department's intent, but it should be apparent that this is as much carefully considered criticism as it is a moral decision. (Considering the incomprehensible critical raves for the work of such morally dubious filmmakers as Sam Peckinpah and Brian De Palma, this alignment of aesthetic and moral judgment may not be that unwelcome.)

The Newsletter also scores on other levels of understanding Russell's work. The review of The Music Lovers indicates a firm grasp on the method employed by Russell in structuring his work.

> Russell has used the same daring and boldness [that he had used in Women in Love] to create rather than translate or merely interpret, a film about the tortured life of the nineteenth-century Russian composer Peter Illyitch Tchaikovsky. This film, based on a collection of letters between the musician and his patroness, goes far beyond the limits of artistic interpretation and mere translation and into the realm of invention.

As might be expected Russell is castigated for his excesses once more, but the review manages to keep the overriding viewpoint in mind at all times:

> Yet despite all this, the film grips. Russell is so consistently and consciously a film-maker, not a storyteller, that it is possible to become absorbed by the lush cinematic effects themselves. Russell experiments along the border separating realism and surrealism, for example, and succeeds in a surprising number of instances. Scenes of such inconsequential subjects as sun-dappled woods come alive under his direction of Douglas Slocombe's

color camera in a way that startles in its discovery of beauty in ordinary things.

Such an assessment is not without its flaws (especially as Russell is a surprisingly better storyteller than is generally supposed), but it indicates a grasp of his style and the personality of his films. More importantly, the review is an indication of an attempt to understand the reasoning behind what many would condemn out of hand.

The Catholic Film Newsletter also presented the earliest indication of an understanding for the major reasons behind the current assessment that Women in Love (rated "B") is a lesser Russell work: '[The actors'] greatest handicap is being forced to mouth Lawrentian dialogue, which on screen is clearly out of sorts and strained." Further, the review notes: "All of this is too beautifully photographed by Billy Williams, a circumstance which further undercuts the effect of the movie." Both of these are undeniably major problems encountered in Women in Love, yet the latter difficulty in particular went largely unnoticed by most critics in 1969. This is not to suggest that the review is the last word on the film. Indeed the reviewer's judgment that the wrestling match "has none of the importance that it had in the book," is curious and ill-conceived.

By far the most successful understanding of Russell and his work is shown in the Newsletter's review of Savage Messiah. Although granting the film a "B" rating, the understanding of the film is profound:

> As a director, Russell has himself often been accused of creative prodigality (The Music Lovers, The Devils). In Savage Messiah, he has for the most part kept a strict check on his weakness for bizarre imagery and excessive camerawork. These elements are there, of course, but only as a natural reflection of the period. The several times that Russell does stray over the edge (as in the Vortex Club scenes or in depicting at great length the crass vulgarity of a naked society girl), the fault is really not so much a lack of control as a failure to achieve what he had really intended.

It is easy to question the label of "failure," but impossible to ignore the essential rightness of approach at work here. Similarly, there is a deep understanding at work in the assessment that "Russell has a deep sensitivity for the interior life of the artistic world and in depicting it, he takes chances few other directors would hazard" and in the review's summation of Russell's success on both his depiction of the artist at odds with the world in the period of the film and in his allegorical implications: "Russell has captured this tension very well and, for those who see the comparisons, has made this conflict seem very much linked to our own age and its own artistic malaise."

The very fact that Michael Gallagher notes that Russell's is "an immense and, yes, wholesome talent" is an indication that, on some level, there is keen perception of the filmmaker's intentions, and this recognition echoes much of Russell's own sentiments about the Catholic nature of his work. The reviews themselves are not always successful, nor do they tell the whole story, but in comparison with the usual poorly considered bile poured out on Russell's work by acknowledged film critics, they emerge like an oasis of rational thought. Many of our supposed film authorities would do well to take a lesson or two from the <u>Catholic Film Newsletter</u>.

CHAPTER 3

TRAINING GROUND

The BBC Films

Ken Russell's works for BBC Television--at least the more mature ones--are very probably the most universally respected films ever done for that medium. Three of those films have performed the not inconsiderable feat of becoming standard theatrical art house fare. It is not at all an uncommon sight to see a triple bill of Isadora, Dante's Inferno, and Song of Summer. Unfortunately, except for Isadora, which has been trotted out on a number of occasions to entice viewer dollars on PBS pledge weeks, the films are largely lost to those not living in a major metropolitan area. Through a curious quirk of fate, however, Isadora turns out to be a most felicitous choice if we are to have but one of these films before the general public. Overall it is less ambitious than Dante's Inferno, and not quite the film that Song of Summer is, but for anyone interested in tracing Russell's development as a filmmaker, it is the essential BBC offering. In dealing with Russell's formative period at the BBC it is this film on which we shall concentrate, for brilliant as much of this work surely is, it is the work of a developing filmmaker, not yet a truly great one. Further, the films are just too numerous and diffuse to be dealt with adequately here. In truth they deserve a book of their own, which they will, it is hoped, one day receive. Were they to be undertaken as they need to be in this volume it would necessitate the serious pruning of the chapters on the later works, and this would be ill-advised because there is little that Russell has done in the BBC films that he has not done better in his theatrical and later television work.

* * *

The story of Ken Russell's entry into the BBC via his short amateur films is well known, and there seems little

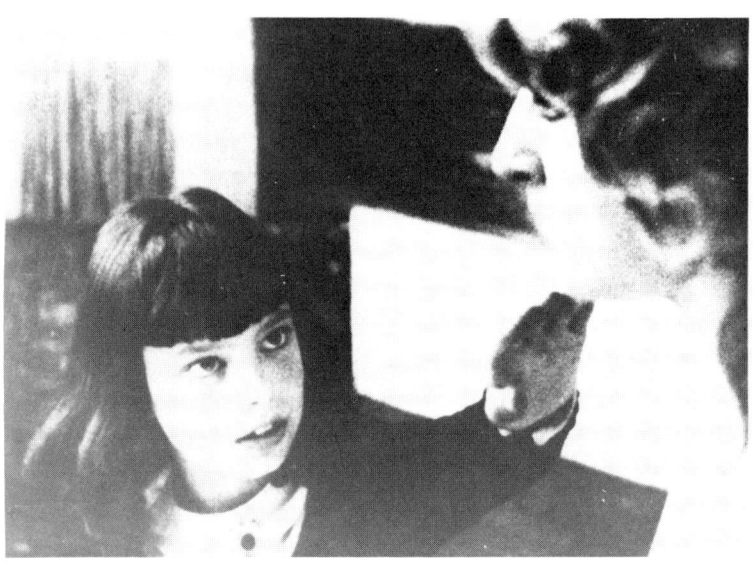

Mercedes Quadros as Amelia in Russell's second amateur film, Amelia and the Angel. (Courtesy of Ken Russell)

point in doing more than covering the bases in discussing the events. There is more than a little prophetic irony in the fact that Russell went out of his way to make a documentary film on Lourdes to use as his portfolio for the BBC and was hired instead on the strength of his allegorical fairy tale, Amelia and the Angel. (Interestingly, it is this film that was chosen to represent Russell for the 1983 New York salute to Great Britain.) It would not be very long before his documentary work for the BBC tended toward this kind of presentation.

From the beginning it is apparent that many of Russell's mature concerns were already very much in evidence. Amelia and the Angel, for example, deals with a young girl who does exactly what she is not supposed to do, suffers the consequences, and then is redeemed through those sufferings. Having ignored her teacher's advice about her angel wings for the school play, Amelia loses them and finds that her teacher was quite correct in her assessment that there is not another pair to be found "this side of heaven." Through perseverance and luck, or guidance, she chances upon a

Training Ground

In this film within a film, Oliver Reed, Audrey Searle (center), and Elna Pearl are actors portraying Debussy, Madame Vasnier, and Debussy's daughter in <u>The Debussy Film</u> (BBC-TV).

house where the beautiful music issuing from inside entices her to go in, and there she finds an artist working on a religious painting. Upon hearing of her situation the artist climbs up an impossibly long ladder and returns with a new pair of wings for her. Small the film may be, and relatively crude in a number of ways, but the story and the approach are purest Russell, concerned as it is, in a minor way, with sin, guilt, and redemption, and with overtones on the sacred/magical position of art and the artist. It even includes the typical Russell ambiguities, i.e., from where does the artist obtain the new wings, and who is the angel of the title, her character in the school play or the artist? One might also note that it is also typically Russell in its penchant for being slightly fantastic. It therefore should come as no surprise that Russell's earliest films for the BBC were the ones that veered, however slightly, toward the bizarre figures and places in the art world, e.g., Spike Milligan and the Old Battersea House. Being the BBC's expert on the outré seems a promising beginning for the man who would one day become a fantastic controversy himself.

Engaging though many of these little projects are, it was in 1962 with the much longer film biography Elgar (the first film in which Russell was allowed to use actors impersonating historical characters) that he finally made his mark. Enormously popular, it is the first film to represent something like the mature Russell. Today it is a disappointment, and Russell is the first to admit this, because a "speak no evil" air of compromise hangs heavily over the work. (Russell has often expressed a desire to do a film on Elgar as a theatrical feature, but as of this writing nothing has come of it.)

The real ground-breaker came with The Debussy Film, an ingeniously structured work in which the biographical aspects of the production are countered by the film's framing story about making a film on the life of Debussy. In this way Russell was able to make a critical as well as a historical evaluation without incurring too much wrath. The idea of making a film on these grounds, so that the idea that the film is a film is never lost, and of offering the filmmaker an on-screen incarnation paid off even more when Russell later adapted the idea (using Vladek Sheybal once again as his alter ego) for The Boy Friend. (The technique was also used by Karel Reisz and Harold Pinter years later in their adaptation of The French Lieutenant's Woman, but much of the impact was lost through poor construction and the fact that their parallel filmmaking structure really had nothing to say.)

Always on Sunday, a film about Henri Rousseau, and Don't Shoot the Composer, a work about Georges Delerue, who had scored French Dressing and would later score Women in Love, followed. Next was Isadora, a film which seemingly just could not succeed due to the insurmountable problem that the Hakim Brothers owned the rights to nearly every scrap of literary work on the dancer. Russell was therefore constrained by being able to utilize only facts about the dancer that were in the public domain. As a result of this the director has always felt that the film is not what it might have been. This is an understandable attitude, but one in which he fails to take into account that this situation forced him to extend himself as an artist. Had it not been for the necessity of creating fictional bits that captured the essence of real situations it is likely that Russell would have taken far longer in developing his now recognizably unique approach, for with Isadora it becomes clear that fiction firmly rooted in fact can be more persuasive than the fact--and somehow more "true." A quick comparison with the feature film made by Karel Reisz from all those books gathered up by the Hakims bears this out. Even in its final bastardized form (the studio recut Reisz's film after the fact) the theatrical film drags badly, burdened with innumerable irrelevancies. Worse, it captures almost none of the magnificently vulgar spirit of the woman herself. Vanessa Redgrave's performance is full of boldness and bravado, but there is no underlying feeling of the compulsive artist. The gaucherie and self-indulgence are not lacking, but the fire, the genuine need to create, the divine spark of personal genius are lost. In the Reisz-Redgrave Isadora all is eccentricity and little art. There is no gulf between Isadora's reality and her dream of artistic perfection because the dream has been lost along the way. Russell and his Isadora, Vivian Pickles, are another matter altogether. Not only is the artistry of Isadora kept in full view, but the gap between her ideal and reality is at the very heart of the film. There is no loss of eccentricity or outrageousness--things which both thwarted and made Isadora-- but the interest is in the woman and and her art. Reisz's film comes much closer to being a version of what is described in the narration of Russell's film as Isadora's status late in life of being "good copy for a journalist hard up for a story."

Russell's Isadora is a many-sided complex work, sometimes as outrageous as its subject, and it may therefore seem odd that the film has found such ready acceptance. It is indeed difficult to fathom the rationale behind welcoming Isadora with open arms, and damning the bulk of Russell's theatrical biographies, all of which are more factual even at their most stylized, as in Lisztomania. There is really only one major difference that is readily noticeable and it should cast serious doubt on the critic who believes that the film is more authoritative because of Sewell Stokes' narration. It is true, of course, that this narration lends an air of the documentary to Isadora, but it does not turn it into one by any means. Truth to tell, Stokes' narration is the weakest point in the film, not because it is bad per se. Rather, narration is a tricky business at best, and all too often becomes the filmmaker's crutch as far as construction is concerned. After all, a clear-cut narration can be made to smooth over almost any sort of narrative leap that one might care to make. Russell does not really fall into this trap with Isadora, but on occasion (as in the South American sequence) he comes perilously close.

Richly photographed by the quintessential Russell cinematographer, Dick Bush (along with Brian Tuffano), Isadora is the most beautiful of Russell's black and white works, and along with the similarly Bush-photographed Song of Summer, stands as a perfect example of the range of tonalities that can be captured and the moods that can be evoked through the intelligent manipulation of the black and white format. The harsh, high-contrast image of Isadora on the river bank holding her private funeral for her drowned children, and the misty greyness of her woodland encounters with Yessenin are images that long remain in the mind.

Musically, Isadora still remains one of Russell's most innovative and daring works, as he plays pop tunes off classical music in a way that mirrors the same sort of duality inherent in his main character. The score runs the gamut from Beethoven to Tchaikovsky to Debussy to Wagner to Satie to Prokofiev to such ditties as "The Sewing Machine," "Thanks for the Buggy Ride," and "Bye, Bye, Blackbird." Diversification without point can be just as deadly as stagnation, but in Isadora this blending of music is completely successful because nothing is left to chance. There is every bit as much thematic justification for "Bye, Bye, Blackbird" as there is for the Beethoven Ninth Symphony within the text of Isadora.

Russell opens his film with a newsreel presentation of Isadora's life à la Citizen Kane, in which, as Russell says, one can find the historical/legendary Isadora. One might also note that it is also where one can find most of the later elements in the film put forth in an abbreviated fashion. Russell tantalizes the viewer with a barrage of outrageous incidents culminating in Isadora's death. Too good a showman to tip his hand this early in the film, no mention is made of the manner of her death. Instead, Russell interjects a note of mystery to the proceedings as the announcer tells us that Isadora was "strangled at Nice," and we see a man being hauled away by the police, proclaiming that he has killed Isadora. Of course a greal deal of the reasoning behind opening the film in this way is based on keeping the television viewer's attention so that the channel is not switched, and there is little doubt that few viewers are going to change channels when confronted with the image of a naked woman being pursued around a stage by a policeman. The scene is definitely a grabber, but Russell's designs are more far-reaching than this. He first gives us a shorthand, sensationalistic view of Isadora, so that he can more fully explore these episodes as the film progresses. The majority of the sequences--the nude dance, the suicide attempts, Yessenin's suicide, the wild parties--are presented undercranked, conveying a sense of both a newsreel quality and of Isadora's rushing headlong to her own destruction. It was a fast life and a sensational one, and the opening of Russell's film captures this feeling perfectly.

Unfortunately, the subsequent "interview" with Sewell Stokes is a letdown, and seems scarcely necessary to the film, despite any claim to authenticity that might be read into his presence. All that the Stokes' interview in the graveyard at Chelsea Old Church really accomplishes is to distance us from the film as it begins, which is not harmful, only superfluous. This transition leads us to a series of excerpts from Leni Riefenstahl's _Olympia_, intercut with a little Russell footage. By doing this Russell first takes us to the ideal of Grecian perfection, which Isadora sought to follow, before contrasting the real Isadora with it. As a depiction of the Greek Ideal it works wonderfully well, but one cannot help but wish that Russell had created his own footage here rather than slipping in these excerpts. (Of course, this is partly an economic move and partly just typical BBC, as are the later bits of stock footage that crop up in the film. The effect this has had on Russell is not immediately apparent as it does not show on the screen, but as recently as _Tommy_, one finds notations calling for stock footage in the screenplay, an obvious hangover from the BBC days.) Even so, Russell goes far beyond mere counterpoint in his introduction of the real Isadora. Utilizing a straight cut to Isadora as the music on the track swells to a crescendo, he first shows her with her arms outstretched reaching heavenward, a clear metaphor for her search for transcendence. She is rather grotesque and slightly absurd, but there is real magic in the sudden transformation, and she is somehow more entrancing than Riefenstahl's sanitized ideal, if only because she seems so real by comparison. Here is Isadora, "warts and all, " a bit too large and a bit too foolish, but in Russell's presentation touched with an indefinable spark of inner divinity. For Russell, however, Isadora is also a doomed woman, and this becomes apparent as this scene leads into two further scenes of her dancing with children. At the climax of the series of dancing scenes, she boldly jerks her head back in a manner that comes to have great significance upon consideration of the film as a piece.

This section of the film, concerned as it is with setting up a background, also sets up the basic symbolism for the film, as in the aforementioned head-thrust-back motif. First there is the heavy linkage of Isadora with children. Of course, children and Isadora's dream of inspiring children through dance are central to the historical personage, but in the film this takes on the added meaning of associating Isadora with children. As presented in the film Isadora is herself something of a spoiled, overgrown child--with a child's capacity for wonderment and enjoyment. One suspects, judging by Russell's subsequent work, that it is this very childlike quality which most appeals to him in Isadora, and indeed this aspect of her personality runs throughout the entire film. No matter how dissipated or self-indulgent or outwardly world-weary she becomes, Russell's Isadora remains an innocent at bottom. The narration suggests that her great passion for a "school of dance, for her a school of life," was based in part on fulfilling some emptiness in her own life, viewing the children as an extension of her own family. Russell's images again stress a familial feeling in the accompanying visuals of her relations with the children.

As if to directly contradict this innate innocence the next scenes depict what is outwardly quite a different side of Isadora Duncan. Quickly executed in one deft sketch she is presented as an incongruous madonna-like model for one artist, while another sketches her in verse, and a musician on a platform above her and the poet becomes the unwilling musical accompanist for their ensuing romantic tryst. It is significant that Russell handles the scene more for its humor than for any sensationalistic purposes, because as the film unfolds it becomes increasingly clear that this sort of promiscuity is of itself borne of the basic innocence of the woman. For Isadora all artists of any form are sacred and she is immediately drawn to them. (Note how she responds at once to Yessenin upon discovering he is a poet even though she has never read a single word of his poetry.) Russell is careful, though, not to lose sight of the fact that, naive as this attitude may be and as charming as it undoubtedly is because of that naivete, it is nevertheless a weakness, and in the following scenes with Paris Singer, Russell details its destructive effects.

The relationship with Paris Singer is possibly the single oddest event in Isadora's life, both historically and in the film. Russell is quick to establish the fact that this is not one of Isadora's artistic compulsions in a brief scene in which Isadora embraces a Singer sewing machine and purports to be in love with "Paris Singer, the millionaire." From the onset it is clear the attachment is due to his status as a millionaire and has little if anything to do with Paris Singer the man. Russell is curiously nonjudgmental on Isadora's fortune-seeking foray at the expense of Singer. This is likely due, at least in part, to the fact that Singer's motives, though less monetary, do not appear to be appreciably more honorable. Singer's intention seems to rest largely on the idea of "collecting" Isadora as a piece of exotica. True to this idea the first thing he does is remove her from public life and install her at his home in South Devon. The narration refers to this house as "a fascinating mausoleum of commerce and bad taste," and the film bears this out. Singer's inaugural gift to Isadora of a golden box containing lady harpists is certainly in this mold, and Isadora's decision to dance her gratitude ... all night, much to Singer's dismay, quickly establishes a basic incompatability. The beautiful economy of cutting from Isadora's tossing a glass of champagne into the sleeping industrialist's face to Singer splashing around in his swimming pool forms a smooth bridge for the transition from the early excitement of the relationship to Singer's "settling back into his hypochondria and his water cures."

    Early on it is obvious that Singer cares little for Isadora's art and so it comes as no surprise that she should start seeking out more sympathetic companionship. Unfortunately, the effect of being isolated by Singer in South Devon (where even the statuary is made to look disapprovingly at Isadora at one point) makes it necessary for her to create this companionship from material at hand. Resultantly, Isadora proceeds to find hidden talent in a footman she finds reading "The Owl and the Pussycat" to her daughter. Making the staggering leap from this storybook reading to the idea that this man should be an actor is no problem for her, and rather than worry over it, Singer agrees to her demands. The situation is obviously inspired by Isadora's romantic attachment to an incredibly unattractive pianist Singer had hired, reasoning she could not possibly take up with someone so physically unappealing. (With typical resourcefulness Isadora found the beauty of the man's soul and did exactly what Singer had assumed inconceivable.) This story, alas, was part of the material owned by the Hakim Brothers, and so was unavailable to Russell. Comparing the Russell-Stokes invention with the more factual representation of the same basic situation in the Reisz film, one is immediately struck by the fact that the fabrication tells more about the deadliness of her situation with Singer than does the reality (or possibly Reisz's uninspired handling of the reality).

Singer's eventual retaliation for this uneasy threesome comes when he refuses to pay any more of Isadora's actor's bills. Accosting Singer in his therapeutic swimming pool (it is difficult to tell to what extent the noises on the track are made by Isadora and which are made by the whining, luckless Afghan Hounds she has in tow), she accuses him of embarrassing her protégé into running away. Singer chooses to ignore the situation and simply dives out of earshot. Enraged by his lackadaisical attitude, she flings the unpaid bills at him and Singer merely bobs around in the water, surrounded by them (something which finds a visual reworking with her love letters later in the flim, and which we find an echo in <u>Mahler</u> with the <u>Kindertotenlieder</u>). The entire affair is little more than a temporary setback for Isadora, who immediately latches onto yet another servant. This time she finds a young man playing a toy flute. "Have you ever thought of becoming a musician?" is her ominous question to him. The young man turns toward the camera and Russell says all that need be said by introducing the first four notes of the Beethoven Fifth Symphony on the track. As the narration notes, "Thus a pattern was set up that was to blight their relationship," and indeed the stark finality of those four notes has all the impact of a door abruptly closing on the relationship. Significantly, we never see Paris Singer again.

The next portion of the film is in direct counterpoint to the satirical scenes with Paris Singer. Commencing with footage of a young Isadora dancing on the beaches, Russell moves in on the present after establishing the recurrent head-pulled-back image. There is an eerie starkness to the scenes of Isadora dancing with her children in a cavernous room, and this is amplified by the piano version of Satie's "Three Gymnopedies" on the soundtrack. In a daring move, Russell creates a hallucinatory flow of images, where the dancing, the departure of the children on their fatal automobile ride, and their subsequent death by drowning, all appear to be occurring at the same time. In doing this their deaths become a ritualistic occurrence as well as a symbol of Isadora's own death of hope, and, to some degree, innocence. Russell cleverly heightens the impact of the scene by moving from the Satie piano score to Debussy's orchestrated version of the composition halfway through the sequence and by further stressing the effect on Isadora by including a shot of the dancer herself drowning. It comes across finally as one of the most chilling scenes on the death of children in any film, and yet Russell was to one day surpass it in <u>Mahler</u>. (The comparison of the two scenes is apt, but should not be extended to the scenes of grief which follow in both cases. Isadora's rather flamboyant and theatrical private funeral service by the river is as much in keeping with her character as the subdued sadness of Mahler's mourning is in keeping with his, and although the scene in Mahler is the more effective by its simplicity and restraint, Russell was right in his respective choices of presentation.)

The effect of the deaths of her children plunges Isadora into a despair which finds its outlet in her already considerable self-indulgences. This Russell most clearly depicts in the film's South American sequences where we find Isadora dancing "in a small-time brothel where they didn't give a damn." Her self-indulgence in this instance, and in several later ones, serves to turn Isadora into a mockery of herself. Like so many future Russell protagonists, we have here the spectacle of the artist trapped in his or her own myth.

Even so, the South American section is perfunctory at best. No such reservations need be made about the sequence which follows, however, where Russell shows Isadora's struggles to start the school again. He begins the sequence with a stage presentation of Isadora dancing to the "Marseillaise," the meaning of which he conveys to the viewer by opening up the scene so that Isadora's movements become reactions to the intercut footage of the devastations of war. This is one point where there can be little quarrel with the use of stock footage, though to compare this scene which parallels the war with Isadora's personal struggle with herself to a later sequence designed along similar lines, but which substitutes a flood of personal memories and experiences for the war footage, does cause this one to pale. Russell's decision to intermingle Isadora's dance with visions of war and, late in the sequence, with her experiences in trying to reestablish her school is a bold and instructive move. In so doing Russell attempts what Karel Reisz never does in his Isadora film: to find the reasons for the dances, to touch on their underlying meanings, and to touch on the greatness of Isadora Duncan. It is just not enough to dress an actress in Duncan styled clothes and have her traipse around a stage, partly because the actress is just not Isadora, whose curious genius by its very nature could not live beyond her own life span except in the spirit.

At the climax of her dance (incidentally, the date given this sequence just happens to be Russell's birthday), Isa-

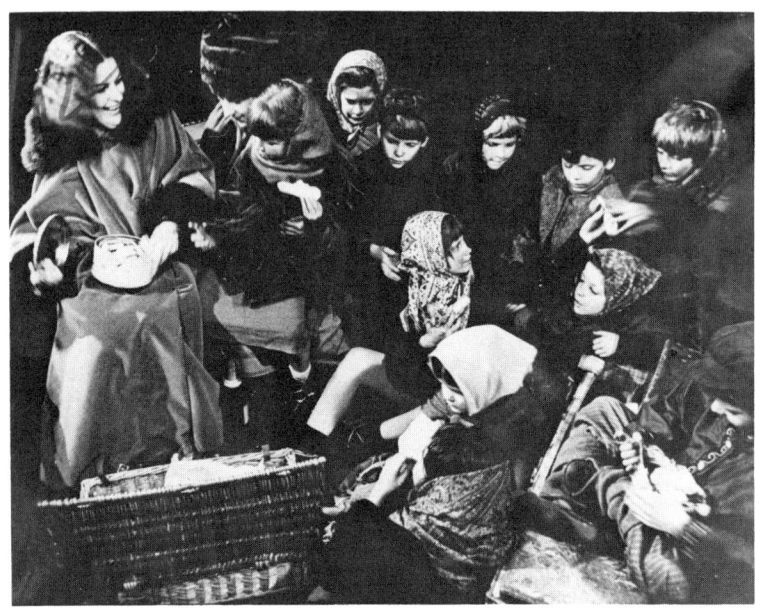

Isadora surrounded by starving children in the Moscow train station upon her arrival in Russia. (From Isadora.) (Courtesy of Ken Russell)

dora makes a plea to the French for money on which to found her school. Her great threat that should she fail to receive this money she will be "forced" to go to the Soviet Union provokes some mild shock, but no money. Resultantly, the dancer resolves to accept the offer from Russia to give her a school.

As the narration comments, the Russians never really thought Isadora would accept such an offer. Russell's use of stock footage to convey Isadora's fantasy of what her reception by the Russians will be like is here a masterstroke because the footage is just as worn and shaky as the hopes that will soon be dashed. Starting on a big close-up of Isadora, Russell pulls back as she makes her speech in what turns out to be a huge, empty railway station. The fervor with which Isadora delivers her greetings to the people of Moscow, however, indicates that though this is not what she had expected, she has not the slightest intention of giving up

her dream. The mood of the scene is in no way defeatist
since the sudden throng of hungry children who surround
Isadora (thankfully equipped with a Fortnum and Mason hamper of food) is in many ways far more heartening and certainly more apt than any reception committee. After attending to their physical needs, Isadora puts on a scratchy gramophone record of, ironically, Sousa's "Stars and Stripes Forever" and leads the children in an impromptu dance along
the train tracks. It is a joyous, good-humored moment, and
as its magic takes hold, Russell switches from the worn
record to a full-bodied orchestration, indicative of the power
of the music underneath and an implication of the very real
power of Isadora to communicate her response to the music
to others.

The Russian sequences make up the single longest
stretch of Isadora, and as such the film seems a little heavy
around the middle, but the sequences are generally strong,
to the point, and invariably engaging. In quick succession
Russell details Isadora's efforts to build a school out of an
abandoned palace, her meeting with a group of new Soviet
elite artists during which she proves herself more revolutionary than the revolutionaries ("Even the dead whose possessions you stole would have made tougher revolutionaries,
you Goddam bourgeois usurpers. You're just a lot of bloated
fish and you stink! Communists? My sweet ass!"), and ultimately her meeting with the poet Yessenin.

The meeting of the dancer and the poet is splendidly
conceived and executed. As Isadora works with her pupils
to a pianist drubbing out Tchaikovsky's Fifth Symphony, she
is suddenly interrupted by a man who dances into the room
accompanied by an accordion player. No more fitting introduction is possible for the man who will be one of the major
disruptions in Isadora's life. His obvious contempt for her
teaching as he leaps about the room, dancing on the furniture,
is, however, more apparent to the viewer than to Isadora,
who falls into Yessenin's arms as soon as she learns he is
a poet.

Thanks to a combination of elements ranging from a
remarkable visual structure to Stokes' dryly acid narration
to the inspired use of Prokofiev's "Lieutenant Kije" on the
track, the courtship of Isadora and Yessenin strikes a delicate balance of mockery and understanding. While Stokes
runs down a list of Yessenin's good and bad qualities--with
the accent on the bad ones--Russell stages the playing out of

the scene so that at first the two of them are shown in separate shots or with a large space between them. Stokes recounts the fact that "no less a person than Maxim Gorky" had declared Yessenin to be the "new Pushkin," but also notes that, among other things, the man was also "an epileptic, a drunkard, a lecher, a layabout, and a thief. Isadora found him irresistible." Russell counters the biting tone of this assessment by visually representing the idea that it is not so much a language barrier that poses a problem for the two as it is that each is so involved in himself or herself that they take little notice of the other. Both Isadora and Yessenin are engaged in playing out love scenes with themselves. Isadora has a fantasy poet, and Yessenin has a fantasy benefactress. (It is therefore especially fitting that the music on the track should be about an imaginary character, Lieutenant Kije, who ultimately has to be "killed off" and given a sham funeral so that his lack of existence is no longer a burden to those who invented him.) It should be clear to us by this time that once Isadora has made her mind up about something or someone that is the way she will find it (e.g., her reception at the Moscow station), no matter how damning the evidence might be to the contrary.

Russell next moves his film to cover Isadora's disastrous American tour. Structured in three basic episodes, Russell first examines the professional aspects of the tour in a brief sequence in which Isadora dances to the "March Slav" while, unbeknownst to her, Yessenin tries recruiting for Communism from the balcony of their hotel. The application of music to the scene is skillfully accomplished, but it is only a slight indication of the full brilliance with which Russell imbues the far more intricately designed second such occurrence. Sandwiched between these scenes is a sequence in which Russell examines their rapidly disintegrating personal life. Russell tends to view this situation as two strongly opposed intellectual viewpoints colliding head-on in an outburst of childishness. Given the pattern of their courtship, the tour is quite literally the first time that the couple have had to consider their respective ideologies. Reisz's film contains a similar scene, though one which takes place in Moscow, but in many respects Reisz makes a distinctly different point. In Russell's film the crushing blow in which Yessenin smashes a framed photo of Isadora's children (an image Russell re-uses to greater effect in Tommy with the photo of Captain Walker) during a fit of ill-tempered egotism signals the destruction of the marriage itself. Reisz's film on the other hand stages this occurrence early in the relationship.

In Russell's film we never see the two of them together again. Oddly both filmmakers have chosen to present the actions as those of an overgrown child--only Reisz's film presents a rowdy schoolboy, and Russell's gives us a spoiled brat. Both are therefore instrumental in establishing a basis for our understanding what Isadora sees in the man, considering her affinity for children. Only the Russell film, however, really uses the episode to its full potential, managing to suggest a reason for the existence as well as the end of the relationship at the same time.

   It is similarly interesting and instructive to notice that the following sequence (which in the Russell film fleshes out the first tour performances) is common to both works, but where Russell opts for an organic denouement with the trouble coming as much from within as from outside pressures, Reisz concentrates on the outside forces undermining the performance. Where Reisz introduces the hell-fire and damnation ravings of Gospel Billy (seemingly based on evangelist Billy Sunday) in his tirade against Communism, Russell heads straight to the more personal heart of the matter: Yessenin. In a thrillingly edited barrage of intercutting, Russell moves from Isadora's dance onstage to Yessenin's antics, which range from his kleptomaniacal attempts at robbing his own wife, the rape of her maid, and yet another Communist doctrine harangue. As built by Russell the flow of the images perfectly matches that of Tchaikovsky's "March Slav," so that while Isadora's professional world is crumbling onstage, her private life is falling apart off-stage. The timing of the intercut sequences is marvelously assured with Isadora's rejection by the audience occurring at the same time as Yessenin is being overtaken by the police. Yessenin, however, can only struggle vainly with his captors, while Isadora decides to upbraid her audience for what she considers to be their repressed attitude. Instead of simply stalking off the stage when she is greeted with catcalls instead of applause, Isadora challenges her audience: "What the hell is the matter with you?" Her tirade ends in the famous breast baring ("This ... this is real!") and along with Yessenin's escapades earns them a deportation. Russell has played the sequence for all its power, consistently utilizing the symbolism he has designed for the film (notably the head-thrust-back imagery as both commentary on Yessenin and the hostile audience), in a way that fully conveys the importance of the event in Isadora's mind. As the narration later makes clear, the most killing aspect of her downhill slide was rejection by her own country. Like the main character in Citizen Kane, the film from which some of the inspiration for Isadora was drawn, Isadora also considers herself "First, last, and always--an American." Her cries of "You were once wild here! Don't let them tame you!" are the cries of one suffering from the horror of the passing of what she perceives as the American spirit, not the ravings of a rejected performer.

Back in Russia things have gotten worse financially, and though Isadora has managed to shed herself of Yessenin, there is virtually nothing left over from the American tour, due largely to paying for the trail of smashed up hotel rooms the couple left in their wake. It therefore becomes necessary to undertake a new tour, this time in Russia, in order to save the school. Saddled with a sullen impressario, and a surly chauffeur (played by Russell, who is first glimpsed holding up the trip while he relieves himself in the bushes by the roadside), the trip promises to be a nightmare from the onset. As Isadora herself notes in a letter, the only ones who appreciate her dancing have no money and those with money "cordially detest us." In a particularly poignant scene

Isadora dances to Tchaikovsky's "March Slav" onstage, expressing the spirit of Russia to a hostile American audience, while offstage her personal life collapses. (From Isadora.) (Courtesy of Ken Russell)

Isadora and her entourage sit in the car next to a field while a gramophone cranks out "Oh, Bury Me Not on the Lone Prairie." The atmosphere is harsh and desolate. Stokes' narration entails the financial disaster of the trip to the point that Isadora is considering selling her love letters. Sorrowfully looking through the trunk which contains them she gets into a tiff with the driver, who, while Isadora's back is turned, cruelly throws a large portion of the letters into the air. Russell switches from the sound of the gramophone record to a very mournful orchestral version of the same song as Isadora realizes what has happened. In a rush of emotionalism Russell sums up the desolation of failed dreams and promises that fall short of their full potential in this one image of Isadora faced with the seemingly impossible task of gathering up these little bits of the past.

    The tour having been a disaster Isadora attempts to curry favor with the Russian government in an effort to obtain the finances to keep her school open. Like everything else Isadora does this is approached with good-hearted enthusiasm and a child-like naivete, e.g., "In my heart I've been a Communist all my life. I'm the Queen of Communists." Failure on the bureaucratic front drives her to the people of Russia in a scene which parallels her "Marseillaise" dance for the French. Here, of course, she dances to the "Internationale" with her pupils before making one final plea for help. "Art," she tells them, "is so much greater than government," putting forth an idea one finds constantly resurfacing in Russell's work.

    Her pleas go for nothing, however, and Isadora leaves Russia forever. Russell telescopes the next section of Isadora's life into a few vignettes, indicative of the level to which she has descended. He pictures her in a shabby hotel room in Germany, engaged in applying far too much make-up in order to hide her diminishing physical attributes, frying a piece of roast beef over a spirit lamp, and, in narration fashion, answering a letter. Both the images and the letter reflect the sadness and disillusionment of the dancer, but Russell is very careful to illustrate that the spirit is far from dead. In part this is inherent in the letter in which, speaking of Yessenin's suicide, Isadora writes, "I'm often tempted to follow his example--only I'll walk into the sea. Now, in case I don't do that, here's a plan for the future," and in conclusion she strikes on the up-beat note, "We will dance to the Ninth Symphony yet!"

In the following sequence where Isadora attends a tea party recital in her honor Russell leaves us no doubt that the indomitable spirit of la Duncan is still very much alive. Upon being given a cup of tea, Isadora immediately, much to the shock of the others, puts in her request for--and gets --champagne. This point settled, a young woman maneuvers next to her and asks if she minds if she calls her Isadora. "You can call me anything you like," is the brusque response. Then there is the recital itself--an impossibly bad display of exactly the sort of thing that Isadora had fought against in her dancing. The recital is over-planned, clumsy, and worst of all the tunic clad stumble about the lawn to the strains of a mocking version of "Narcissus" as it becomes obvious that they have not made the slightest connection with the music itself. When Isadora is presented a bouquet of flowers by one of these young dancers she can only comment, "I lay this wreath on the grave of my hope," and walk away. She might deign to attend such a function, says Russell with this scene, but she is not going to take anything off anyone--from a cup of tea to the insulting mockery of a betrayal of her art.

Russell brings the two elements of her decision to "walk into the sea" with "the grave" of Isadora's hopes in the next sequence--a fantastic blending of every aspect of the dancer's life and dreams set to the "Liebestod" from Tristan und Isolde. Beginning with a close-shot of Isadora gulping down a glass of champagne, Russell's images cascade across the screen: a dance in which Isadora seems to be thwarted at every turn by images from her past; a hysterical ride in a fast car ("Faster! Faster! This is the way to die!"); her suicide bid, which as she walks into the sea conjures up images from the idealized Riefenstahl sequences. It is a fabulously emotional sequence, though one that is not without its satirical side, not in the least because her suicide is prevented by Captain Patterson (played by Russell), a one-legged man on crutches.

"Isadora landed on her feet in Nice," Stokes' narration tells us, and in a jaunty scene we are shown her lifestyle there. The combination of the slightly pathetic older woman being squired around the dance floor by a young man who obviously wants to be able to say that he danced with Isadora Duncan, and the sense of her refusal to be defeated by life is wonderfully balanced.

The press conference in her studio that follows is used as a summation of the good and the bad, the sublime and the

Isadora in the after-the-fact fantasy fulfillment of her dream to dance to the Beethoven Ninth Symphony with hundreds of children. (From Isadora.) (Courtesy of Ken Russell)

vulgar qualities of Isadora Duncan. Her statements are a
fairly even mixture of her philosophy on art and the dance
and of sheer nonsense. That she has become somewhat tiresome--as is evidenced by the increasing boredom of the
newspaperman--matters little, for when she at length becomes
swept away by music, her enthusiasm is infectious. Admittedly, the pop tune, "Bye, Bye, Blackbird," scarcely qualifies for inclusion in the group she calls for, "Beethoven,
Wagner, Brahms, one of the immortals!" Nonetheless, its
use here strikes just the right note with its jauntiness expressive of Isadora's own unbeatable spirit and its commercialized quality stressing her vulgarity at the same moment.
After dancing around the studio, knocking over potted palms,
and just generally enjoying herself, Isadora sets out with her
"Buggy boy," still in high spirits. No sooner does the Bugati start to pull away from the front of the studio than her
long scarf becomes tangled on the knock-off hub of one of
the car's wire wheels and Isadora is killed instantly as her
neck snaps. This, by the way, is closer to the actual occurrence than Karel Reisz's approach. Russell opts for the
reality of the sudden shock, whereas Reisz plays the scene
out for suspense.

Here Russell grants Isadora a beautiful tribute as, at
the moment of her death, he abruptly cuts to a lovely slow-motion sequence of the dancer as we saw her in the early
portions of the film, fulfilling her dream of dancing with
hundreds of school children to Beethoven's Ninth Symphony.
It is presented as if her soul has been released, and it is
a very positive and moving sequence, but, as if to underline
the fact that it is only the director's rendering of Isadora's
dream, Russell cuts back to her disfigured, dead face in the
head-thrust-back position we have become so accustomed to
seeing at the end of her performances.

As Joseph Gomez has noted Isadora represented a
real breakthrough for Russell, containing as it does most of
the elements that one finds in his later works. In the end
Isadora can be seen as something of a blueprint for the films
to come, but it should not be judged on this basis alone. As
comparatively crude and formative as many of its aspects
are, Isadora has much to be said for it on its own merits.
Individual sequences like the drowning of the dancer's children
and "Liebestod" section of the film are quite as good as anything Russell has ever done. Russell's use of music within
the film is also notable on its own grounds, especially as concerns his application of patriotic themes--e.g., when Isadora

appeals to the French she dances to the "Marseillaise" and when she appeals to the Russians it is the "Internationale"-- but in her personal scenes she leans toward distinctly American music like "Stars and Stripes Forever" and "Bury Me Not on the Lone Prairie."

* * *

The year 1967 brought the release of Russell's second theatrical venture, Billion Dollar Brain, and the elaborate BBC film Dante's Inferno. In this feature-length examination of the Pre-Raphaelite painter-poet Dante Gabriel Rossetti, Russell was able to go beyond the boundaries determined by Isadora, achieving an even greater sense of freedom and experiment. From the film's very first image Russell's visual imagination never falters, and the film's heavy usage of fire, water, and mountain symbolism bespeaks of much that is to come, especially the mature Clouds of Glory films in 1978. Perhaps the single most important aspect of Dante's Inferno, though, is Russell's use of the overt fantasy in a way that cuts through many layers at once reaching a truth in a refreshing and powerful manner, i.e., the unearthing of Rossetti's wife in order to retrieve the book of poems he had buried with her in a fit of remorse. In actual fact Rossetti did not disinter his wife himself, and, of course, her decaying corpse did not rise up in outrage (Russell does not present it as an actual occurrence), but presented thus in the film we have the full sense of desecration, guilt, and terror that is inherent in the action even though the actual work was done by others.

The most completely successful and mature of Russell's BBC output, though, is surely 1968's Song of Summer, Russell's film on the composer Frederick Delius, or more correctly his film on the relation between Delius and his amanuensis, Eric Fenby. It is an intricately designed little film, frequently cited as an example of Russell's ability to work in a restrained manner if the subject matter calls for it. Gene D. Phillips calls it a product of the same creative burst that produced Women in Love, and while this is probably true it would be unwise to consider the two films as similar. Women in Love suffers too much in comparison if one tries to place the two side by side. At any rate Russell's concerns in the two are too different to allow for direct comparison.

Much as in the Isadora Duncan film Russell has the

Lizzie Siddal posing as Ophelia for Millais' painting in Dante's Inferno. (Courtesy of Ken Russell)

Training Ground 37

advantage of working with someone who actually knew the subject of the film, but with Isadora this really did not matter very much. With Song of Summer it is only through Eric Fenby that the film exists in the manner in which it was made. Russell was neither overly fond of Delius as a man or a composer, and it is only through forcing himself to view Delius and the story through Fenby's perception and as a drama centering on Fenby's own love and sacrifice for Delius that Russell was able to make the film at all. Perhaps because of this there is a unique feeling of a growing understanding at the core of Song of Summer that makes it one of the director's most pleasing works. Russell may not respond to Delius as a man, and he might only occasionally admire the music, but because he is sympathetic to Eric Fenby and Fenby's sacrifice he must come to terms with Delius as well or Fenby comes off as a dullard whose sacrifice is for nothing. In this respect Song of Summer is the earliest Russell film where the filmmaker has been forced to stretch his own understanding and compassion. In doing so Russell manages to give us a picture of Delius as an egomaniacal tyrant of a man who is somehow still lovable. With the composer's death at the end of the film we are quite aware that as limited as Delius undeniably was as both a man and an artist the world is somehow the worse for his passing.

Russell's approach to Song of Summer is in some ways unique. This is most readily apparent in the fact that where in other films Russell tries to convey a feeling of shared emotional response between his protagonist and the viewer in certain sequences and for relatively short periods of time, here he does this for the bulk of the film. The reason for this is not hard to fathom as the intimacy of the film--there are not more than a handful of characters in the entire work--allows for an almost microscopic inspection. Because of this Song of Summer becomes more of an experience that we share with Eric Fenby than it is a film about Fenby and Delius. The first half of the film is in many ways as suffocating an experience for us as the enclosed and rather bizarre Delius ménage is for Fenby. This is so beautifully achieved and conveyed that the sudden arrival of Percy Grainger at the halfway mark in the work has quite a liberating effect. So accustomed have we become to largely static compositions within the stifling environment that the high spirits of Percy Grainger and the wild tracking shot, set to his "Country Gardens" composition, as he runs around the yard pushing Delius' wheelchair seem like a reprieve.

In tackling Song of Summer as the story of a relationship rather than as a straight biography of Delius, Russell illustrates an interesting point about creativity. Approaching his material in this manner allows him to turn what would otherwise have been a project of lesser importance to his filmography as a whole into one that is at the core of his concerns. We find the idea of the artist's unfortunate need to debase himself and his art in the sequence with Fenby working as a musician in a cinema house. We find the idea of the sacrifice of the lesser talent (Fenby) to the greater talent (Delius) in the relationship of the two men. We find Fenby's faith in his newly acquired Catholicism sorely tested in both his visit to the local church where he finds the priest (a bit by Russell) seducing a parishioner, and in his relations with Delius who urges him to "throw off those Catholic blinders." All of these elements are very much a part of Russell's overall concerns, and all of them rely on the presence of Fenby for their place in the film.

In Delius himself the only typically Russellian aspect --aside from an engagingly eccentric personality--is the obsession with nature. This is most clearly illustrated in the film's most famous set piece where Percy Grainger and Jelka Delius laboriously carry the crippled composer to the top of a mountain so that he might see the sunset from this vantage point one last time before his eyes give out completely. Told to Fenby in flashback it is a perfectly achieved scene, deftly capturing both Delius' love of nature and the unreasonable demands he makes on those around him. It should be remembered, though, that there is not the slightest bitterness in the telling of the story, and it is quite apparent that this is a sacrifice that both Grainger and Jelka undertake willingly, out of love for the composer.

Even though it is within the second half of the film-- beginning with the sharp contrast between Grainer's exuberance and Fenby's growing malaise--that Fenby is most affected by Delius' inhumanity (to the extent of having to leave for a time at which point he suffers a psychosomatic paralysis), this is also the part of the film in which we begin to sense something in Delius beyond his peevishness and bad temper. Little by little Russell--aided by the brilliant playing of Max Adrian--reveals Delius' more human side, his own sense of frailty, his need for other people, his fears, and, perhaps most importantly, his thirst for life. In the scene between the doctor and Fenby in which Fenby is informed of the syphilis which is surely and steadily killing

Delius, Fenby's initial response to the doctor's verdict of death is disbelief because, "Mr. Delius is so alive." This is an assessment of no little weight when one considers the totally helpless state in which Delius lives without sight or movement, but despite the fact that Delius as an invalid is completely reliant on outside help (he is even carried from room to room slung over people's shoulders like a sack) he holds his world together by the sheer force of his will.

The climactic scene of the film in which Fenby and Jelka strew rose petals over Delius' corpse in their private sorrow while the film's focal point of the Fenby-Delius collaboration, "Song of Summer," plays on the radio in memoriam is a splendid summation of Delius the composer and Fenby's self-sacrifice in devoting his life to helping Delius complete the work that his own body would no longer allow him to do. Topping this off are the film's ending credits themselves, which represent an eclipsing sun in reference to the passing of Delius and the mountain journey earlier in the film. The eclipse imagery itself will come to have greater significance as a Russell symbol in later films, notably Lisztomania and Altered States, but here says much about Delius and, in light of Russell's next projects, would seem to have a bearing on the filmmaker's state of mind, for the three films which follow Song of Summer--Women in Love, Dance of the Seven Veils, and The Music Lovers--are the darkest edged, most pessimistic works in the Russell canon.

There is so much about Song of Summer that is good that one can overlook its few flaws, though it is impossible not to wish that Russell could have found a clip from an actual Laurel and Hardy silent film for Fenby's tenure as a cinema pianist, rather than pressing a clip from 1937's Way Out West into service. This, however, is a very small, atypical error and it in no way detracts from the central issues of the film.

* * *

That there should be no available outlet through which to see Russell's final, and only color, BBC offering, Dance of the Seven Veils, is something of a tragedy as concerns fairly assessing the frame of mind in which he left the BBC. It is apparent that although hampered by budgetary restrictions the film is stylistically ahead of its time even for Russell. The no-holds-barred approach to Richard Strauss of the film would seem more at home with the approach one finds in

Mahler and Lisztomania, and yet it is obvious that on a thematic level Dance of the Seven Veils is perfectly suited to the time of The Music Lovers.

Designed in part as a reaction to the sort of film that generally passes as being historically accurate on the basis of the fact that the characters wear the appropriate clothing for the time period of the film, it was Russell's intention to do it "in a totally unreal way, but make it more real than ever."[1] Unfortunately, Russell's approach coincided with his personal distaste for the subject of his film and the resultant film proved too strong (much as The Music Lovers would do on a theatrical level) for viewers expecting another Song of Summer. Because of the furor over Russell's admittedly justifiable attack on Strauss, Dance of the Seven Veils was only transmitted once and has since drifted more into legend than fact. Generally held up as being cut from the same cloth as Lisztomania (an aspect with which we will deal in the chapter on that film), but more controlled and better executed (a point it is difficult to refute except on thematic grounds owing to the inaccessibility of the film), Dance of the Seven Veils remains for most of us a tantalizing enigma.

In essence Dance of the Seven Veils deals with the life of Richard Strauss as viewed by Russell in terms of a comic strip format (the film's full title is Dance of the Seven Veils: A Comic Strip in Seven Episodes on the Life of Richard Strauss). It is Russell's contention that Strauss betrayed himself and his art through his lack of personal responsibility, e.g., hiding himself and his family away so that they might pretend the First World War does not exist; currying favor with the Nazis during the Second World War. Not surprisingly, although the interpretation is certainly a personal one, Russell has done his homework and the facts--presented in a stylized manner--bear out this approach.

At the time of the film's airing the most strenuously objected to sequences involved Strauss' conducting of his Rosenkavalier and exhorting his musicians to play louder and louder so as to drown out the screams of Jews in the audience being tortured by S.S. men, and the staging of the "Domestic Symphony" to Strauss and his wife making love with their climax mirrored by the orchestra. Both of these sequences are certainly used for symbolic effect, but it is interesting to note that in the first one Russell has drawn on musical legend for the basic premise (Strauss is said to have urged an orchestra to greater volume in this manner to overwhelm a singer he disliked). In so doing Russell manages to capture something of a real situation within his allegory.

One cannot but regret the inaccessibility of the film and the attendant loss of performances by Christopher Gable as Strauss and Ken Colley (so memorable as Modeste Tchaikovsky in The Music Lovers) as Hitler. Particularly upsetting, though, is missing the spectacle of Russell himself as a wild-haired sub-Stokowski orchestra conductor in the "Domestic Symphony" sequence.

It seems extremely unlikely, considering the film's last image of Russell in orchestra conducting garb bowing and walking away from the camera for his directorial credit, that the director was unaware that Dance of the Seven Veils was his BBC swan song. The feeling is certainly one of a last grand gesture before the move to theatrical filmmaking.

NOTE

1. Cited in Baxter, John. "The Television Films: Poet's London to Dance of the Seven Veils," Ken Russell, edited by Thomas R. Atkins. New York: Simon and Schuster, 1976, p. 35.

CHAPTER 4

TWO FALSE STEPS

"French Dressing" and "Billion Dollar Brain"

Russell's two first attempts at crossing over from television to theatrical filmmaking show little of either the promise of the BBC films or the greatness of his later features. The first of these, French Dressing, fails in part because the screenplay--a sort of All at Sea (GB Title: Barnacle Bill) meets the British youth film hybrid--is not especially funny and in part because Russell just was not all that skilled with actors at the time. The basic premise of a film festival at a seaside resort and the presence of pleasant players like Roy Kinnear and Bryan Pringle were just not enough. The film suffers by being too early to benefit from the Richard Lester inspired new-look youth films started with A Hard Day's Night and too late to fit comfortably into the Ealing niche. Considered inexportable at the time of its release, French Dressing has been relegated to film limbo, existing mostly as a title in a list of films.

Another false step in Russell's attempt to cross over into theatrical films, Billion Dollar Brain is one of the most irritating films in Russell's filmography. The film irritates mainly because it is not good enough to be seriously considered with the main body of Russell's work, and yet it is too good for off-hand dismissal.

Coming as the third and final entry in the Harry Palmer spy series--the ostensible "thinking man's James Bond" --Billion Dollar Brain is at least something of an improvement over its immediate predecessor, Funeral in Berlin. Nonetheless, the final film more than bears out the assertion that neither Russell nor screenwriter John McGrath could make much sense out of Len Deighton's novel, and instead of actually adapting it, they simply opted for bits of it that either appealed to them or just appeared intrinsically cine-

Two False Steps   43

James Booth explains his plan for a film festival for Gormleigh-on-Sea to mayor Bryan Pringle in Russell's first theatrical outing, French Dressing. (Cinema Bookshop)

matic.[1] It is obvious that somewhere along the way they were able to make out something of a plot-line, but the end result is kind of a fantastically complex jigsaw puzzle that was not worth the effort of putting together. To be sure, Billion Dollar Brain does not have the structural complexity of Mahler, Tommy, Lisztomania, or Clouds of Glory, but in those films the structure has direct bearing on the film as a whole, where Billion Dollar Brain's structure and its incipient complexity do not. It is merely confusing. Worse, it is confused.

From time to time Billion Dollar Brain is dragged out of the closet and broken down into a few supposedly creative fragments where Russell's hand can be discerned. That may be a kind gesture, but much of what is being lauded as

Russell's handiwork owes more to the time in which the film was made than it does to Russell. The oft-cited example of the "shock" cut from the assassin's rifle to Françoise Dorleac's screaming face, which turns out to be, in the superseding cuts, her reaction to a hockey game, has far more in common with the work of Richard Lester and Michael Winner than with Russell. For Winner in particular this kind of effect was absorbed into his cinematic vocabulary, but for Russell its inclusion seems gimmicky and too clever. Similarly, the reworking of Eisenstein's "Battle on the Ice" from Alexander Nevsky in the film borders on being crackpot filmmaking. Thrillingly shot and edited, it is an exciting scene, but to what end? There is a certain justification in terms of the futility of General Midwinter's attack, which grows naturally from the overall atmosphere of the film, but the sequence never really transcends being any more than a "touch." Unlike other Russell film-inspired sequences in later works, this homage to Eisenstein stubbornly refuses to integrate with the film on any level--structural, symbolic, or thematic.

Indeed, most of what might be pleasing in passing to the confirmed Russellphile are a number of little touches scattered throughout the film, ranging from an in-joke reference to Carol Reed's The Third Man to Miss Dorleac scraping away at "None But the Lonely Heart" on a cello, to a snatch of a Shostakovich symphony at a concert, to marvelously corrupt Latvian "revolutionaries" listening to contraband Beatle albums. In all this there is much to please those familiar with Russell's mature works, but at best they remain snippets of the complete work. Viewing Billion Dollar Brain in this light makes it appear like a two-hour trailer for promises that will be fulfilled at a later date.

There is a more positive side to the film--one that can be appreciated for its own sake, and one which may actually be a product of Russell and McGrath's inability to come to terms with the novel. Billion Dollar Brain has a curious atmosphere of futility and entrapment to equal the grimly incomprehensible and hostile world of the best of Edgar G. Ulmer's dark films, especially The Black Cat, Detour, Bluebeard, and Ruthless. Like Ulmer's protagonists the major characters in Billion Dollar Brain exist in a world with no choices, where motives, when they exist at all, are so vague as to be of no value. It is a black, hopeless universe in which the characters simply move from one uncontrolled and uncontrollable encounter and event to the next.

Two False Steps

On this level Russell has succeeded admirably. To some extent this attitude is inherent in the spy film sub-genre, but even within the Harry Palmer series itself, which is certainly defeatist in tone, it is not taken to the extremes we find here. Resistance, in fact, is not only possible in the other series entries, but it forms the cornerstone of the first film, <u>The Ipcress File</u>. In <u>Billion Dollar Brain</u> resistance is worse than futile, it is deadly.

In evaluating <u>Billion Dollar Brain</u> on any level other than those few touches that qualify certain aspects of it as "Russellesque" or as a botched spy movie, the only sensible and rewarding approach is to look at the film from this aspect of a vision of a hostile and hopeless universe. With this in mind, <u>Billion Dollar Brain</u> can be seen to have more relevance to Russell's work on the whole than is generally supposed. Apart from the fact that Russell obviously cares very little for his characters in this case--an apathy which he transmits to the viewer--<u>Billion Dollar Brain</u> is the thematic forerunner to <u>The Music Lovers</u>. It is only the lack of directorial and audience empathy that makes it appear any less black. This is not meant to suggest that there is any actual connection between the two films, nor that <u>Billion Dollar Brain</u> is any kind of unsung masterpiece, but the two films are quite similar in outlook.

In Russell's view of the characters in the film we find two separate and distinct groups. The first group is made up of those characters who have ceased to struggle with the world: Harry Palmer, Anya, Colonel Stok, and Colonel Ross. The second group consists of the idealists, those who believe they can resist: Leo Newbegin, General Midwinter, and Dr. Eiwort. Regardless of the warped perception of Russell's idealists, they accurately reflect the same sort of thought that blights the existence of the characters in <u>The Music Lovers</u>. They are the romantics of <u>Billion Dollar Brain</u>. Similarly, all of their idealism is tainted by perverse or selfish notions. Thus Leo is only looking out for himself though ostensibly fighting for freedom; General Midwinter is blissfully unconcerned with any idea of "right" other than his own--the Latvians are to rise up and overthrow their oppressors whether they want to or not; Dr. Eiwort is out for personal vengeance and is a notorious war criminal in the bargain. It is their inability to accept the hostile world for what it is that brings about their destruction. Leo disobeys orders and does not kill Anya as instructed, an act of defiance which ultimately causes his own demise. General Mid-

General Midwinter in his fanciful and rather pointedly anti-Communist target range in Billion Dollar Brain. (Courtesy of Ken Russell)

Two False Steps   47

winter refuses to believe the truth about his proposed Latvian
uprising and so perishes under the ice.

   On the other side of the scale, the realists are able
to survive because they have given up any idea of effective
resistance. Harry Palmer may not understand the world
around him, but apart from some very token resistance, he
knows better than to challenge it. The only thing that sets
Harry apart from Anya, Colonel Stok, and Colonel Ross is
the fact that he is not himself manipulative, whereas they
are. In essence he is manipulated by them, but the implication is clearly that they too are manipulated by some unknown force higher than they. In Anya's case this higher
force comes to be known as Colonel Stok, but there is still
someone controlling him, as is evidenced by the fact that in
offering Harry protection he is careful to warn that there is
a limit to his abilities in this. Colonel Ross is quite obviously under higher control. His own open antagonism toward
Harry would otherwise preclude his dogged persistence in re-
instating Palmer in British Secret Service.

   Completely in keeping with the atmosphere of an im-
movable, hostile environment is the film's insistence that
nothing is what it seems. This is evident from the film's
pre-credit sequence in which an unknown man is seen burgling
Harry's seedy private eye office. As it turns out, it is not
a burglar. Rather it is Colonel Ross, who has come to persuade Harry to return to the Service. It is a fascinating
pattern which is continually repeated throughout the film.
Hence, a bellboy in Harry's hotel room is revealed as Colonel Stok, and the trays of food he carries actually contain
his real clothes; the Latvian revolutionaries are only a few
of Leo's hand-picked black marketeering relatives; the "big
wheel" at which Harry is to meet his contact is not the
Third Man-like giant we expect but only a children's toy
with four seats; General Midwinter's ideas of "freedom" and
"Americanism" are in reality fascism under another name as
borne out by the swastika-looking "MW" emblems festooning
his soldiers and trucks--the trucks themselves look like oil
tankers, but are really troop transports; and so on. Perhaps
the best reversal of all, though, is the double reversal at
the film's end. The all-important virus-carrying eggs are
returned by Stok to Harry and Colonel Ross, but when the
container is opened they prove to be real eggs which have
hatched in the meantime, leaving the British with half a dozen
baby chicks. In this instance eggs that we have found are
not eggs in the normal sense turn out to be eggs after all,
so our original reevaluation has to be reevaluated.

Billion Dollar Brain, quite apart from its uniquely unappetizing title, is neither a good film, nor is it particularly important to Russell's development as a filmmaker. Among other more obvious flaws, it suffers from an acute case of the late 1960's. Unlike any of Russell's other work, Billion Dollar Brain is not placed in a specific period of time. Where Russell's other films attain a level of universality by working in an allegorical fashion within a determined frame of time, Billion Dollar Brain makes the stultifying error of attempting to be up to the minute modern. At the same time there is no attempt to depict this concept of modernity as indigenous to 1967, and the result is a film that must have appeared dated within a few months of its release. This is apparent in the gimmicky presentation of a number of scenes, in the disposable looking Carnaby Street styled fashions of Françoise Dorleac, the then obligatory Maurice Binder title designs, even the spy film format itself. Had Russell chosen to use these devices to make a point about 1967, the results might have been something quite different, but as it stands the film's insistence on being "now" is totally to its detriment.

That Billion Dollar Brain is a misfire is undeniable, but Russell's statement that this is in part due to the fact that he is "more at home in the past,"[2] explains very little in light of his films of Tommy and Altered States. Nonetheless Billion Dollar Brain is a prime example of misplaced talent. Billion Dollar Brain was not a good subject for Russell, and not because of its overly intricate nature, or its modern setting, or its fanciful spy yarn. In fact the major problem of Russell's participation in the subject stems from the fact that the film is not fanciful enough. Harry Palmer is too everyday ordinary--his dreams and ambitions too narrow. Harry is not a seeker after truth or beauty. He is completely uninvolved in transcending his limitations. In short, the character is too plain and uninvolving to kindle Russell's interest. Is it therefore any wonder that it is the film's atmosphere that is more noteworthy than the film? That the lovably roguish Colonel Stok receives greater attention at Russell's hands than his supposed hero? That the film only really springs to life in the bizarre fascist rally presided over by the big thinking, albeit wrong-headed, General Midwinter? Russell may not, as he claimed, have known what a Texas millionaire or an American fascist was like,[3] but he certainly can recognize and identify with flamboyance over drabness, regardless of how morally repugnant that flamboyance may be.

Two False Steps

No matter how charitable a view one takes of Billion Dollar Brain there is no way around the fact that if it were not made by Ken Russell no one would bother discussing it at all. This fact alone relegates it to a lower position than any of Russell's subsequent features, all of which are films meriting discussion apart from their inclusion in Russell's filmography. In retrospect, Billion Dollar Brain, much like Women in Love, is of less importance as a film than it is as a stepping stone in Russell's career. For reasons that will never fully be comprehensible United Artists were favorably impressed with Billion Dollar Brain (heightened by its abuse in the United States because of its alleged anti-American bias in that its two major American characters are unsympathetic and unwholesome, while the Russian Colonel Stok comes off as a likable, if peculiar, figure). Whatever the reason, it was their attitude on the film that helped in the decision that Ken Russell was the very man to bring Women in Love to the screen.

Inauspicious a debut into international filmmaking though it may seem, Billion Dollar Brain should be viewed with the atmosphere of its creation in mind. Though it is true that filmmakers as such were beginning to come into their own by 1967, it was still the last gasp of the studio system as such. Russell's work on the film is largely that of a contract director--a position that, for better or worse, would soon become virtually extinct. His stance at the time, and with Women in Love for that matter, was that he could return to television until he could have the same kind of control on features that he enjoyed at the BBC, an attitude that stresses Billion Dollar Brain's studio film status. Had Russell made such a film in the days when the studio system was flourishing--when it was common practice to thrust a project at a director regardless of his suitability for the subject (consider William Wellman, a director noted for his toughness, trapped in the mawkish ersatz-Capra drivel of Magic Town in 1947)--Billion Dollar Brain would not seem all that odd. Russell himself explains it this way: "The reason I did Billion Dollar Brain: Saltzman promised me Nijinsky if I did it. He said it would give me 'experience,' and I fell for it. Actually, Mike Caine saw The Debussy Film and felt I had possibilities."[4]

NOTES

1. Gomez, Joseph. Ken Russell: The Adaptor as Creator. London: Frederick Muller, 1976, pp. 78-79.

2. Cited in Phillips, Gene D. *Ken Russell.* Boston: Twayne, 1979, p. 81.
3. Ibid.
4. Personal correspondence with Ken Russell, September 1983.

CHAPTER 5

THE FIRST CONTROLLED FEATURE

<u>Women in Love</u>

After two unsuccessful efforts to break into the mainstream of feature filmmaking, Russell finally made the transition with his landmark adaptation of D. H. Lawrence's complex novel <u>Women in Love</u>. The reasons for its success are not hard to fathom. <u>Women in Love</u> has the look and feel of its period setting. It is extremely visual (perhaps too much so). It takes full advantage in the best sense of the relatively new-found censorial freedom of the late sixties. Best of all, perhaps, it at least has the illusion of being a faithful adaptation of Lawrence's novel. Even today the film is probably the most admired of Russell's theatrical films--at least by people who do not much admire any of his other theatrical films. Whenever someone goes on record as appreciating Russell's work and cites <u>Women in Love</u> as an example of this appreciation, chances are good that they dismiss the larger body of "purer" Russell films out of hand. Among serious Russell scholars <u>Women in Love</u> has taken on a decidedly lesser status. In his article on Russell, Jack Fisher calls the film "constrained,"[1] and Joseph Gomez is careful to warn the reader that it would be a mistake to place too much emphasis on <u>Women in Love</u> and its relation to Russell's work as a whole in his book.[2]

For anyone coming upon <u>Women in Love</u> for the first time today, after years of more mature Russell works, the film almost invariably disappoints. It seems overlong, too lyrical, impossibly mannered, and even somewhat stilted by comparison. Like many complex films a good deal of this first impression is dispelled on a second viewing when one knows where the filmmaker is going and can examine the subtleties of the film in a more leisurely frame of mind. Still, one is disturbed by the frequently pointless artistic camera of Billy Williams, by some of Russell's too clever scene transitions, and by a final third that tends to drag (though this last problem is found in Lawrence's original as well). The odd fact is that the major feeling against the film--that it does not represent Russell at his boldest and most originally experimental--does not hold water if the film is really examined. Far from being a picture book version of Lawrence's novel, Women in Love is a brilliantly interpretive reading of that novel, its author, and its implications. The few dissenting critical voices at the time of its release, who felt that the film betrayed the novel or who felt that the film proved the novel should not be filmed, were probably objecting to this very fact, though they were seemingly unaware of just exactly what had bothered them about the film.

Russell begins his film just slightly before the opening of the novel, and in doing so illustrates much of the economy of establishment for which we now know him. Beginning his film on the image of Mr. Brangwen placidly working at a piece of leather craft, while Mrs. Brangwen sets the dinner table in the background, he presents an enclosed world of perfect order. The sound of chirping birds and the monotonous tapping of Mr. Brangwen's hammer make up the only noise on the soundtrack until the sudden introduction of the clatter of the Brangwen girls, Ursula and Gudrun, whose running down the stairs breaks this rhythm. In this manner Russell conveys the sense of their inability to fit into their ordered surroundings. They are noisy, disruptive, bumptious, full of youth and high spirits, and this is established before they are even onscreen. Once they appear they bear out this promise by actually disrupting their parents' plans as they only pop into the room to inform them that they are going to go to see the Crich wedding instead of staying for lunch.

Once out on the street Russell picks up the novel from its literal start with the notable change of the location of the girls' conversation upon the merits of marriage. Lawrence stages this scene inside the Brangwen home, whereas Russell places it in the street. In making this minor change he is able to communicate a sense of time and place that would otherwise be lacking. This attitude of the importance of background is very much central to Women in Love as a film, because, somewhat against Lawrence's own desire (in the "Foreword" to the book Lawrence says, "I should wish the time to remain unfixed so that the bitterness of the war may be taken for granted in the characters"[3]), Russell has given his film a fairly concrete time frame. Where Lawrence wanted "the bitterness of the war," Russell has chosen more

The First Controlled Feature 53

to settle upon the malaise of the post-war period. This is not mere cussedness on the filmmaker's part as we shall see, for Russell intends his film to be as much about the novel as an adaptation of it.

    The aspect of the period brought about by the First World War becomes apparent during the film's opening credits, which shows the girls' trip to the wedding. Even the music on the soundtrack, the pop song "I'm Forever Blowing Bubbles," is indicative of the time and the feelings of the characters. Russell's use of music here is a blueprint for the rest of the film. All of the music in Women in Love aside from Georges Delerue's score, which serves quite a different function, issues from sources within the film, and all of it is used in a manner that communicates the actual effect of the music on the characters as part of the background that helps to explain their actions. In this case the music issues from a scruffy street band of beggars, who appear to be victims of the war, and the irony of this jaunty tune coming from such a source is not lost on Russell, nor is the commentary nature of the song on the dreams of the girls.

    At the conclusion of the opening credits Russell's camera zooms back from the girls taking their places in the churchyard among the tombstones (from which they can watch the wedding) to the gathering wedding party itself. It is in this section of the film that one notices what at first may appear to be a flaw in Russell's presentation. In this case it is with the introduction of Gerald Crich. As we first see him Russell appears to arbitrarily glide his camera down from the stone edifice of the church to a fairly tight close-shot of Gerald, and for anyone used to Russell's mature films this strikes rather a false note. Russell's characters generally move--sometimes burst--into the frame rather than having the frame move to encompass them in this fashion. One is tempted to write off this kind of camera move with its overly formal appearance as, at best, due to Russell's relative inexperience or, at worst, as a bad borrowing from Fellini, who uses such an effect with frequency, e.g., the spa scene in $8\frac{1}{2}$. The problem with either approach is evident. The first falls apart because such an approach to camerawork is not found in Russell's BBC films, and the second seems too much at odds with the overall film. If, however, we follow the methods Russell utilizes in introducing the other characters, it becomes apparent that within the introductions Russell is delineating the personalities of his characters by the physical structures of the introductory shots. Hence we have the very formal and stiff introduction of Gerald (further strengthened by the move from the cold stone of the church), Hermione Roddice barges into the frame as befits her pushy character, and Rupert Birkin is first seen, in a more typical Russell fashion, rushing into the frame in a brisk run with the bridegroom. Instead of the camera moving onto a motionless composition like that of Gerald, it must pan with Rupert just to keep up with him. Later within the same sequence it is Birkin's entry into the frame that necessitates the tracking shot toward the church with Gerald and him. Similarly, in the intercut flashbacks to Ursula's memory of the visit by Rupert to her classroom in his capacity as a school inspector, Hermione's "barging" into the room is mirrored with perfect visual logic by her crowding into the frame (i.e., Ursula's field of vision) with Rupert after the wedding. Russell uses this kind of visual patterning throughout Women in Love, so that it should become clear that much of what might appear to us as overly mannered and stiff is actually thematically sound. (However, this by no means is the case with the entire film, which contains the most artificial and arch camera work in some instances to be found this side of Luchino Visconti.)

Alan Bates and Jennie Linden prepare for the classroom scene on the set of Women in Love. (Courtesy of Ken Russell)

The First Controlled Feature

By far Russell's single greatest accomplishment in these early scenes of <u>Women in Love</u> is his ability to present the viewer with <u>more information</u> than seems possible. Basically these are expository scenes establishing the setting and the characters of the film, and yet Russell treats them in such a manner that there is never the feeling of sheer establishment for the sake of aligning the audience with the basic premise. Unlike Lawrence, who has the benefit of stopping the action dead in its tracks in order to explore the situation, Russell must adapt his visuals to accomplish the same end, while relying on the judicious selection of Lawrence's dialogue to create the impression of whole characters. As we have already noted, Russell has done this through the visual patterning in the introduction of the characters from the off-screen arrival of Gudrun and Ursula to Rupert's running introduction into the film. Combining this with the carefully worked out application of sound, music, and background, and a well-balanced sense of editing, which is used to suggest the future connections between Ursula and Rupert, and Gudrun and Gerald, Russell is able to reduce many pages of novel into a few minutes of concise screen time. It would be foolish to say that nothing of the book is lost in this kind of translation, but the film, after all, is not the book, nor does it pretend to be, but Russell's economics preserve much of the feel and character of the original.

Having so carefully set the stage for the proceedings Russell now plunges headlong into the actual storyline of the film in a sudden shift to Hermione's country weekend party to which the major characters have all been invited. Linking the opening of this scene to the wedding is the fact that as we find the Brangwen girls preparing for the weekend they are discussing Hermione's intrusion into Ursula's classroom. Ursula dismisses this with the thought Hermione "loves to dominate everything. I think she'd like to dominate us." The following scenes do much to enforce this aspect of Hermione's character.

Moving directly to the famous fig-eating dinner table scene on the girls' arrival at Hermione's country "cottage" (like the small lodge in <u>The Music Lovers</u> this kind of deliberate "oh-this-old-thing" downplaying is less an indication of the owner's common touch than of a lack of a sense of proportion) Russell begins experimenting with the type of approach he is taking with Lawrence's novel. There never was any secret about the fact that <u>Women in Love</u> is a thinly veiled account of Lawrence's own circle, so that the novel

has a decidedly autobiographical slant to it. The problem
with this aspect of the novel is that it is by no means an
autobiography, but might best be classed as a quasi-autobio-
graphical wish-fulfillment fantasy. The characters, though
firmly rooted in reality, are at best Lawrence's subjective
representations of them either as he saw them or would have
liked them to be. This poses a thorny problem for a filmmaker who wishes to take on this side of the novel, and it is
doubly difficult for a filmmaker who insists on presenting
his or her own truth. Typically, Russell tackles the idea
head-on, and the results are sometimes brilliant, sometimes
disappointing, and sometimes baffling, but never uninteresting.
The end product is not at all unlike the two films which flank
it--Song of Summer and The Music Lovers. In the former
there is a sense of actual growth on the part of the filmmaker as his ideas about Delius are influenced by those of
Eric Fenby. In the latter there is the conflict within Russell
himself as he tried to balance the things he admires in Tchaikovsky's music with a growing distaste for the man. Unfortunately, this tension which actually helps to hold the other
films together, threatens here to pull the film apart by the
force of two sometimes opposing strong viewpoints.

Whether consciously or not, Russell has chosen to illustrate the gap between Lawrence as he really was and the
alter ego he invented for himself in Rupert Birkin. Russell
remains faithful to Lawrence's basic portrait of himself as
Birkin (which has its share of dubious self-castigation), but
he enlarges upon it as it relates to Lawrence as Russell
sees him. In many ways Birkin, for all his outward charm
and wit, is one of the least likable of Russell's heroes--cer-
tainly one of the most stubbornly dream obsessed. For all
of Birkin's talk about spontaneity and "acting on one's im-
pulses," he is not really very spontaneous at all. His concern about being spontaneous leaves him little room to actually practice it. Russell first conveys this aspect of Birkin in this luncheon table sequence, where he interjects Lawrence's poem, "Figs," as part of the dialogue. Birkin
achieves his desired effect in that his words delightfully
shock those around him, but the use of the poem makes it a
very deliberate move and not really spontaneous in the least.
To some extent this is inherent in Lawrence's original where

[Opposite:] A beautifully detailed production shot of Gudrun
and Ursula arriving at Hermione's "country cottage," in
Women in Love. (Courtesy of Ken Russell)

Birkin, who overanalyzes everything, spends the better part of a page of the novel agonizing over whether he has said something untoward by accident or on purpose, only to arrive at the conclusion that he said it "accidentally on purpose." Russell takes this further than Lawrence, however, so that the film of Women in Love is expanded to a point where it becomes more biographical than the novel. In all fairness Russell has the advantages of an historical perspective from which to work, and the lack of any personal relations with the characters in question, which allows him to be, if not more detached (which he is not), then at least more levelheaded. It is a daring move, but one which is performed so deftly that it never seems at odds with the original except on those occasions where the Russell-Lawrence viewpoints are too much at odds. There is certainly nothing wrong with Russell's attempts to expand his rendering of Women in Love to something beyond a simple novel to film translation, anymore than in so doing does he betray Lawrence or the novel. The point and thrust of Lawrence's concerns remain intact in Russell's final film.

The second great set piece of the country weekend sequence is, of course, Hermione's "entertainment in the style of the Russian Ballet," popularly known as the dance with the wheat. Hermione's rather ridiculous sub-Isadora Duncan dance, partly performed to Liszt's "Marche Funebre," is the ultimate in Russell's depiction of the woman's ludicrous need to dominate and control things. To some extend the scene has its roots in the "Narcissus" dance in Isadora, but Russell's control here is more masterful. Instead of concentrating on the ineptitude of the dancers as in the earlier film, he concerns himself with the burdensome over-planned look of the dance and the fact that only Hermione is unaware of its inherent tackiness and stupidity. The heavily choreographed camera movement and rhythmic editing in itself are used to convey the complete lack of anything approaching surprise in the performance, and the heavy-handedness of atmosphere it generates make the liberating force of Birkin's having the pianist switch over to a mocking ragtime tune free the viewer as well as the characters. Russell's camera mirrors this liberation as he switches from the plodding preconceived movement to a series of freestyle pans and infectiously jumbled editing. Significantly, everyone who was either bored or appalled at Hermione's dance is only too ready to join in the ragtime dance, and Hermione, having lost her control of the situation, can only stand by and fume. Russell shrewdly incorporates "I'm Forever Blowing Bubbles" into the fabric

Hermione tries to crack Rupert's skull with a paperweight in Women in Love. (Courtesy of Ken Russell)

of the dance music so that its reflection on the state of dreams ("Then like my dreams they fade and die") aptly comments on Ursula's state of mind as Rupert deserts her to go apologize to Hermione.

The ensuing argument with Hermione, which starts out as a half-hearted apology and explanation, is used not so much to point up Rupert's spontaneity contrasted with Hermione's obsession for control, as it is to establish the inherent dangers in this spontaneity. "If one cracked your skull," Rupert tells her, "maybe they could get a spontaneous reaction out of you." At this point, in a purely spontaneous reaction, Hermione picks up a heavy paperweight and attempts to do just that to Rupert's skull, precipitating his escape into the natural world outside.

Rupert's flight into the woods is a splendid piece of filmmaking. The feelings of terror, confusion, and release are all there in the presentation as Rupert staggers down the house steps and runs into the woods, the close-shots of him shifting in and out of focus as he runs, photographed with a telephoto lens giving the scene a dream-like running in place atmosphere. The latter portion of the scene where Rupert is stripped of his clothes which represent the trappings of civilization, is a little poem of naturalism, as Russell eschews Delerue's thundering score in favor of the sounds of nature. The twittering of the birds on the soundtrack stands out in marked contrast to the cawing of a crow on the track behind Hermione's words at the luncheon table earlier. For Rupert, like most of Russell's protagonists, nature is a healing force, putting forth a timeless sense of beauty and wellbeing that just cannot be found within the confines of civilization.

Civilization and the specter of World War I resurface in the following scene where Ursula runs into Rupert at the unveiling of a war memorial. Here Rupert appears to be a wonderfully embarrassing person to know as he launches into a tirade against the hypocritical words of the vicar conducting the ceremony. "In the name of righteousness and love ye shall have hate," he rails, "Ye shall throw down nitroglycerin bombs and ye shall kill your brother." It is a charmingly ironic scene with the sounds of Elgar's patriotic music on the soundtrack. In the main, however, the purpose

Gerald, in one of his attempts at controlling nature, races the train to the crossing in Women in Love. (Courtesy of Ken Russell)

of the scene is to put the actions of the previous scene into words and to better establish the beginning of a relationship between Rupert and Ursula. In this first case there is an unfortunate air of too much explanation such as is found in no other Russell work, and the scene is slightly redundant because of this. Still there is a good sense of the birth of a relationship between Rupert and Ursula--a strong feeling of each testing the other to see what they are made of, and in this respect the scene is very important. Similarly, the scene is indicative of the fact that Rupert has a need to dominate, not unlike Hermione. At the luncheon table he had sarcastically commented, "We all struggle so, don't we?" and in his own way Rupert is very much among the strugglers, and part of that struggle is for the power to control. Not that Rupert's struggle is unhealthy per se. Certainly his destruction of Hermione's entertainment was far healthier than the entertainment itself, and his points about love are frequently valid, but in both cases it is undeniable that Rupert Birkin is asserting himself, dominating the situation.

    Russell continues in this examination of the need to dominate found within the characters of the film in his first close-up portraits of Gerald Crich. The first of these occurs in the scene where Gerald subjugates his terrified horse at a train crossing to the horror of Ursula and the fascination of Gudrun (a scene which we find counterpoint to late in the film with their reactions to Loerke's horse statue). Unlike Rupert, Gerald is a completely un-natural man. Gerald does not find himself at one with nature by any stretch of the imagination. Instead, nature as symbolized here by the horse (not surprisingly--considering the proliferation of white horses in Russell's films--changed to white from the red horse of the novel) is something to bend to his will. As we have already gleaned from the dialogue, Gerald is a very modern man, a man of and for change, a man for the machine age.

    The scenes examining his working at his family's coal mine indicate his modernity. Where his father ran the colliery like a "charitable institution," keeping men on beyond their usefulness to the firm and giving free coal to the widows of mine workers, Gerald is hard and business-like. It becomes increasingly clear in the course of the film that he is his mother's son. His attitude toward the miners is very like hers minus the half-insane ravings. At the same time there is more than a little truth in his statement to his father that he had "made a fortune exploiting them, and now you

want to ease your conscience by slipping them a few pennies."
For a man of the people, as Mr. Crich obviously likes to
think of himself, there is more than a tinge of incongruity
in the shot which closes the mine sequence of Gerald and Mr.
Crich riding off in a glistening white Rolls Royce through a
blackened mob of miners.

    The humorous scene where Russell begins delving into Gudrun's character as she prowls the seamier sections of the town at night serves an additional purpose as it sets up the situation (the Crich picnic) that will bring the four main characters together, and it provides an opportunity for Gerald to come to Gudrun's aid, establishing a link between them. When Gerald fortuitously appears after Gudrun has gone too far in leading on a miner, her reaction to his intervention serves much the same function as Ursula's reaction to Rupert's speech, placing the relationship on a level of a game of power. This game runs throughout the relationships in the film, and in fact is central to the relationship of Gudrun and Gerald. His aid to Gudrun is the logical extension of his character, as it is less out of concern for her than it is because she is being harassed by one of his miners for whom Gerald feels responsible. Russell's handling of the physical movement and atmosphere of the scene raises it far beyond the level of facile transition, which could have easily been the case. The tracking shot as Gudrun walks along the meat vendor stalls with the miner, Palmer (an in-joke reference to the working-class spy hero of Billion Dollar Brain?), is timed like a bit of choreography so that Palmer finds himself confronted with a large slab of meat at the exact moment Gudrun tells him that she wants "to drown in flesh--hot, naked, animal flesh." The soundtrack, too, is of interest because of the integration of "Oh, You Beautiful Doll" into the film, which Russell uses as a symbol of the baser side of his protagonists' lives, just as he uses "I'm Forever Blowing Bubbles" to represent their unattainable dreams.

    In the picnic scene at the Crich's huge estate, Shortlands, which follows, Russell alternates the two songs on the track as part of the music heard during the festivities. The character vignettes sprinkled throughout its opening are sharply drawn and telling--Rupert playing at a dart game, tossing darts in rapid succession; Mr. Crich lording over a table of miners like "one of the boys"; Mrs. Crich staring distastefully down on a miner from the safety of a window; Gerald taking charge of everything, being certain all goes smoothly and safely. Again, as in the film's opening, Ursula

The First Controlled Feature   63

and Gudrun do not fit in with their surroundings and so in
this case they convince Gerald to let them take his canoe to
a deserted shore where they can have a private picnic.

The girls' private party is at first an idyllic set-up,
containing a bit that manages to be satiric and altogether
lovely at the same time as Ursula sings "I'm Forever Blowing Bubbles" in a charming, clear voice, while Gudrun does
a mock Hermione interpretive dance. The easy grace of the
scene is quickly dispelled by the arrival of a menacing herd
of cattle. "Aren't they lovely?" Gudrun nervously asks Ursula. When asked if the cattle will "do anything" to them
Gudrun replies that she is sure that they will not, and, in
a moment of curious desperation mingled with cold fear, she
begins to dance to them. Russell plays and photographs the
beginning of this for all it is worth in terms of both humor
and danger as the at first bemused and then startled cattle
respond to Gudrun's dance. Delerue's score is used to good
advantage here as it moves from a mockingly weird theme
into full hysteria as Gudrun begins to enjoy her power over
the cattle at length sending them into a run. The arrival of
Gerald and Rupert breaks the odd spell Russell has conjured
with the cattle dance. Rupert rushes up to Ursula singing
"Oh, You Beautiful Doll," and jumping part way up the trunk
of a tree (much as he had earlier done clambering up a column in making a rude gesture upon Hermione's departure
after he had upset her entertainment). The allusion to the
earlier scene is quite apt as their arrival puts a stop to this
dance in much the same manner. Unfortunately, the scene
between Gerald and Gudrun, while important, is overburdened
by Russell's use of dissolves linking their dialogue. It is
obvious that his intention here is to create an almost dreamlike state in their strange and feverish encounter, but the
end product in this instance is more stilted than anything
else. The sequence looks altogether too thoroughly rehearsed
and mapped out as Gerald declares his love for Gudrun.
Even so there is one very fine moment at the end where she
strikes him on the face. "Don't forget," he warns her,
"You struck the first blow," and, as a portent of things to
come she replies, "And I shall strike the last!" her words
resounding eerily in the open air.

Russell thoroughly recovers his grip on the film in
the boat journey back to the main party and in the drowning
of the young Lupton couple that accompanies it. The film
captures perfectly the splendid coolness of the early evening
with the Japanese lanterns playing on the water, and setting

up a sense of well-being that is almost immediately spoiled by the drowning. The drowning of Gerald's sister and her husband (for which we have been, to some extent, symbolically prepared by the graveyard and the photographer accidentally smashing the photographic plates at the wedding) is used by both Russell and Lawrence mostly to reveal Gerald's character. In this moment of crisis, which, significantly, comes right on the tail of Gerald revealing his emotions to Gudrun, he is anything but the clear-headed modern in-charge business man. Not only does Gerald completely lose control of himself in his blind panic to attempt to put right something that cannot be put right, but he reveals himself as essentially a superstitious primitive in his assertion that once something has gone wrong for himself and his family, everything will go wrong. Worse, he has done the one thing that seals his doom in his relationship with Gudrun--lost his carefully established mastery to the extent that his father is able to take over the situation and send Gerald home like a child.

The hopelessness and despair of the attempts to save the couple prove a quite curious and yet completely understandable catalyst for the emotions of Rupert and Ursula. The horror of the drowning gives way to a desperate lovemaking between the two of them in a refreshingly erotic scene which takes place on their walk back from opening the floodgates that will drain the lake. (It is significant within the overall text of Russell's work that Tibby and Laura Lupton should drown in a lake that is held in by man and not nature.) That the release of their sexual tension should bring them a momentary respite from the events of the drowning is beautifully conveyed, but the altogether too artful cut from the bodies of the drowned lovers to Rupert and Ursula in exactly the same position is a questionable move on Russell's part. One could argue a certain thematic soundness on the basis of Ursula's future desires to domesticate Rupert to an extent that is neither possible nor desirable, but there is no way of getting around the fact that the move is far too clever for the film's own good.

At this juncture Women in Love reaches its most famous set piece, the nude wrestling match--a scene about which so much has been said that it sometimes seems as if the rest of the film might as well not exist. As a single piece of filmmaking ripped from its text and discussed on its own the scene will probably plague Russell to the end of his days in much the same manner as Hitchcock was never able to shed the shower murder in Psycho. As part of the overall film the wrestling match works very well and is so central to the story that its excision is unthinkable. Russell himself has tended to cloud the issue of the wrestling match and its implications in his statements avowing that Rupert is in no way pleading for a homosexual relationship with Gerald.[4] If what Russell means by this statement is that Rupert is desirous of a romantic, and possibly sexual, relationship in which the distinction of sexual boundaries do not enter, then his words make sense. On the other hand, however, the evidence of the novel--especially the expurgated introductory passage in which it is flatly stated that Rupert had always felt more attracted to his own gender than to women[5]--and of Russell's own film precludes much chance of taking his statement on the scene in a strictly literal sense. Russell could easily have shot the scene to avoid sexual implications since there is nothing intrinsically erotic in two nude men engaging in Japanese style wrestling. He has assuredly not filmed the scene in an erotic manner, but it is done in a very romantic tone. Russell stresses the similarity to the love-making act of Rupert and Ursula in the way he films the latter portions of the scene, and even goes so far as to utilize the same Delerue theme on the soundtrack. Beyond this the scene of the two of them lying sweaty and winded in the floor at the conclusion of the match is markedly like the aftermath of sex. The point of the scene and the film itself is blunted and made incomprehensible if we take Russell's words at face value. It would be just as great a mistake, though, to read the scene as an act of homosexuality pure and simple. Again if this is the case why link it to the scene of Rupert and Ursula in the woods? The linkage here is undoubtedly romantic because of the implications about the release of civilized tension through a physical encounter. Hence the scene's nudity is a prerequisite and not a sexual charge. "We are mentally and spiritually close," Rupert tells Gerald, "Therefore we should be physically close as well. It's more complete." The depth and complexity of the emotions involved herein which allow for dropping off the orderly, even sterile, existence of the two characters, to cut below the glossy patina of civilization to the essence of the human being underneath, carries such a wealth of stylistic and thematic soundness with the entire film (indeed with Russell's whole output) that there is little wonder that the director might bristle over the idea that this is simply a veiled homosexual love scene. That Gerald cannot accept Rupert's desire that the two of them should "swear to be true to each other all our lives without any chance of going back on it" is by no means the rejection of a homosexual pass. Instead

Gerald clearly is unable to go along with the idea because he cannot bring himself to make a commitment as a human being on any level. Gerald does not even function as a human being. Stripping him down to his elemental essence he is nothing, a dead thing. He only exists as Gerald Crich of the Crich family, head of the Crich mining empire. Inside Gerald is as cold as the stone church front to which Russell visually linked him at the film's opening. The very fact that Gerald shatters the mood by symbolically reasserting his modernity in switching on the electric lights is the key to understanding that without the trappings of his world Gerald is lost.

Gerald's "responsibility" and his position in the world are reinforced in the scene which follows where Gudrun visits Shortlands to investigate the possibility of giving Winifred, Gerald's youngest sister, drawing lessons. Gudrun's arrival just happens to coincide with that of a small delegation of miners upon whom Mrs. Crich looses the dogs in a fit of pique. (Gerald's later description of his mother as a "strange lady" scarcely does her justice.) Gudrun can only stand back in vague horror and watch as the dogs attack the miners much to the delight of Mrs. Crich. The arrival of Gerald sets things right as he undertakes the job of calling off the dogs and soothing everyone's feelings except those of his mother. The quirky humor of the scene obviously appealed to Russell's sense of the bizarre as he lingers over Mrs. Crich's reactions to her sport and cuts away to Winifred wheeling her father crazily through the garden in the midst of the proceedings.

The underlying feeling that there is something mildly dangerous in associating with the Crich family is underscored in the next scene drawn from Lawrence's chapter called "Rabbit." Lawrence spends far more time on the rabbit episode than does Russell, but the end result is much the same. What Lawrence conveys in words, Russell conveys in simple imagery, when at the climax of the scene Gerald holds the rabbit, Bismarck, in his powerful hands and strokes it while staring at Gudrun. The implication of Gudrun as something to be caught and held by power is unmistakable. It is also this very point of view that will be Gerald's undoing. Again we have the contrast of the natural and the unnatural. Where Rupert would like humanity "swept away," leaving nothing but the "tall grass and the rabbits," Gerald holds a rabbit in his hands, controlling it.

The First Controlled Feature

Cross-cutting to the more superficially open relationship of Ursula and Rupert, Russell stages a scene in the "tall grass" where the two of them are having a picnic. Things go smoothly enough for them until Rupert reveals his intention to have dinner at Shortlands in order to say goodbye to Hermione. This admission prompts a barrage of abuse from Ursula, and many of her points about Rupert's "spiritual mess" are well taken. The scene, however, has none of the murky undertones found in the scenes dealing with Gerald and Gudrun. Where Rupert and Ursula might have a lively knock-down argument, Gerald and Gudrun rarely even speak to each other, and then it is usually noncommittal and indirect when they do. Therefore Russell feels himself at complete liberty--and rightly so--to play up the comedic aspects of Lawrence's chapter here with the extraordinarily polite cyclist and Rupert's momentary inability to find Ursula so that he appears to be being assailed by a disembodied voice. The healthiness of such an open emotional situation is further strengthened by the fact that once the argument is over things are easily set to rights as Ursula comes up to Rupert holding out a peace offering, "See what a flower I found you." At the same time there is a suggestion of problems to come in the relationship because of the inability of the pair to find an intellectual-emotional meeting ground.

Russell points to the idea that they are living something of a fantasy relationship in the slow-motion pastoral sequence which follows their wedding plans, designed to look very deliberately like a television advertisement. Russell has very smoothly integrated this image into the fabric of the film, moving from an over-under shot on Rupert and Ursula into the side-wise view of them in the field, but even though his intentions are obviously satirical of this "perfect" idea of a relationship, the whole business of flipping the camera on its side is too smart-alecky for the text of the film. The end result carries the feeling of a director who has become bored with his material, and is reminiscent of von Sternberg's brief tenure at MGM in the late twenties where he is supposed to have aimed his camera at the studio rafters because he found them more interesting than the action he was supposed to film.

Moving back to the enclosed world of Shortlands finds Gerald and the family waiting for Mr. Crich to die. Russell places the words of Gerald's opening remarks to Gudrun over images of the sick room, thereby covering two areas at once.

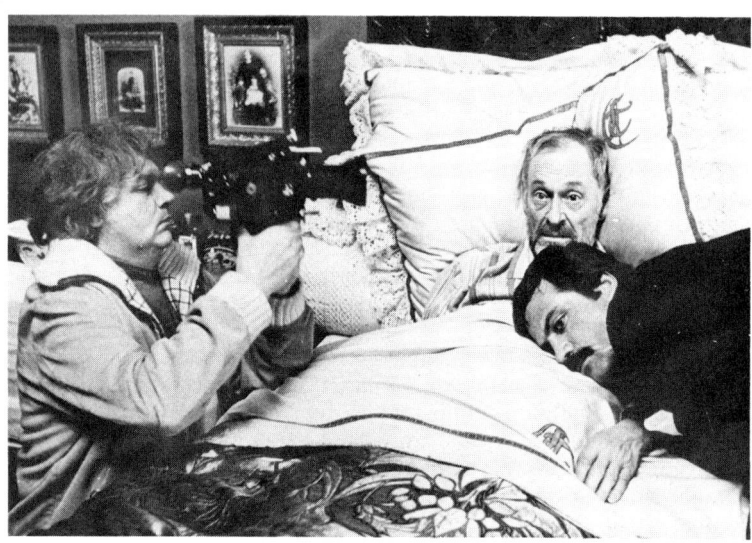

Russell preparing to film the death of Mr. Crich in <u>Women in Love</u>. (Courtesy of Ken Russell)

Gerald is in the grips of the same inherently superstitious frame of mind in which we found him after the drowning, and as we find he is talking to Gudrun it is apparent that he is again placing his weaker side in her full view. Far worse, however, is that Gudrun is here exposed to Mrs. Crich's pronouncements on her son, which, considering her own mental state, are surprisingly insightful. When Gerald tells her that his father's approaching death has to be seen through, her response is that it will "see itself through. Why should you take it on yourself to see it through?" Her realization that Gerald has done this in order to be important, to take on the responsibility, is quite apt. As Gerald views things he is himself responsible for the drowning of Tibby and Laura since he was responsible for the waters in which they drowned, and as this has had a bearing on his father's health, Gerald's sense of responsibility is extended to include this.

It is out of the despair over the situation with his father that Gerald makes his first attempt at making love to Gudrun, much as Rupert and Ursula had done after the drowning.

Gudrun is quite a different person from her sister, though, and instead of yielding to his desires she teases him as she had done with the miner and then deserts him. Significantly, the action is staged in a tunnel where earlier Gudrun had watched miners in trysts with their girlfriends. This psychological use of the location is in itself suggestive of a far more base and unhealthy desire than that displayed in the encounter between Rupert and Ursula.

With Mr. Crich's death and its nightmarish comic funeral service in which Mrs. Crich accidentally drops her trowel into the grave with its layer of earth (an action which she finds monstrously funny), Gerald has reached the end of his tether and seeks comfort with Gudrun. Everything about the situation is unwholesome. His trip into the graveyard and his impotently angry gathering up of a handful of mud link the entire sexual process to come with death and dirt. The experience itself is very off-hand and brutal. Gerald is not responding in any way to Gudrun as a human being, but only as a device by which he might drive out his personal demons, represented by the recurring image of his mother laughing. The furtive nature of their actions only adds to the general atmosphere of confined spiritual illness. Obviously the scene counterpoints the earlier love-making with Rupert and Ursula, where Rupert never lost sight of Ursula as a human being. Gerald is only interested in achieving a kind of oblivion through a sensual act.

Russell follows this brilliantly conceived contrapuntal scene with one of his more thematically dubious moves in a scene where Rupert and Gerald discuss the relative merits of marriage (as the girls had done at the film's opening), and whether Gerald and Gudrun should "rush into marriage" along with Rupert and Ursula. Admittedly the scene is dialogue heavy, and Russell's decision to circumvent the potential tedium of a scene that is nothing but talk by the clever manipulation of the mirrors in the room is understandable. Unfortunately, there seems little point in any of his elaborate framings other than just to add visual interest, which he undeniably does do in this manner. In a lesser filmmaker one might be content to appreciate the sheer cleverness of the staging, but in Russell it seems a waste of time and talent. Only at the very end of the scene where Rupert is framed side by side with his mirror image and Gerald is seen in a single-faced close-shot does the approach seem thematically sound.

Control and a sense of immediacy and soundness of purpose are restored in the scene where Rupert and Ursula visit the "jumble market." The screenplay makes a considerable departure from the novel in its presentation of the purchase of an old chair. In the novel Ursula is at first as charmed by the chair as is Rupert, but in the film she does not want it from the onset. This change from the novel is a fine example of slightly shifting the structural emphasis of a scene so that much the same point can be made in the required condensation of screen time. Russell's film conveys the same point as Lawrence's prose. The entire thrust of the scene in both cases is to raise the question of Ursula's ability to adapt to Rupert's view of the world--his desire for something additional to marriage, something more fulfilling than an enclosed world of man, wife, and family. Classically, the problem faced by both of them is that of any two people about to embark on a relationship where each hopes that in time the other will change or adapt.

There is a brief and unreservedly symbolic scene separating the jumble market from the trip to Switzerland in which Gudrun and Ursula discuss the coming trip. The scene works almost entirely due to Russell's staging of it. The dialogue itself counts for very little beyond the requisite information to get us to Switzerland, but the two very separate activities in which the girls are involved is another matter. On the one hand, Ursula is engaged in making herself a piece of toast and generally behaving in a very domesticated manner. Gudrun, however, is working at her art, and more significant still is the fact that she is sculpting Gerald--molding the man in the image she fancies. The sculpture itself is a hulking, slightly Neanderthal creation, and Gudrun's actions are those of someone taking out her hostilities on an effigy of the real item. The climax of the scene where she suddenly stuffs one of her tools into the mouth of the sculpture is a deadly harbinger of the events to come.

In a direct cut Russell moves us to Switzerland for the final portion of the film. The exciting zoom back shot from the horses drawing their sleigh and Delerue's sprightly music perfectly capture the high spirits with which the section opens. The activities themselves are also free and unrestrained as the two couples "let go" and happily indulge in a free-for-all snow fight played out with great oversized boulders of snow. Once the scene switches to the dark, candle-lit interior of the inn in which they are staying the mood alters abruptly, especially with the introduction of

Loerke, a strange figure hovering in the background whose attention is immediately drawn to Gudrun. Russell carefully prefigures the events to come as Gudrun and Gerald end up changing partners during the second dance.

In order to effectively telescope the events of the novel into a tenable screen time, Russell relies quite heavily on symbolic shorthand to capture the essence of these last scenes. After discontent begins settling into the characters, he stages a scene between Rupert and Gerald in which Gerald discusses the pain he feels in his relationship with Gudrun. Russell underlines the helplessness and hopelessness of his situation by continually inserting flash close-shots of Gudrun as he talks in the same manner in which he had earlier done with shots of Mrs. Crich during Gerald's nocturnal visit to Gudrun's bed. Gudrun has now become a reminder of his spiritual impotence and his physical inability to affect things as he would wish. Perhaps the most singularly telling and shattering moment about Rupert's character comes at the end of this scene, where, in response to Rupert's reminder that he has also loved Gerald "as well as Gudrun," Gerald snaps, "Have you, Rupert? Or do you just think you have?"

Gudrun's relationship with Loerke has symbolic overtones to her relationships with both Gerald and Hermione. As previously mentioned the situation with Loerke's horse statue in which he speaks of having had to subdue the model by "beating her harder than I have ever beaten anything in my life" in order to execute his work of art (the line is left deliberately ambiguous so that it is not clear as to whether he is in reference to the horse or to the woman on the horse) is not dissimilar to both Gerald's subjugation of his horse at the train crossing and his attempted "taming" of Gudrun. Then, too, his artistic thoughts that "art should interpret industry" are also very modern, civilized notions, not out of keeping with Gerald's own approach to his colliery. Loerke is, of course, quite different from Gerald in other respects, and some of these reflect much of Hermione's character. He is remarkably pretentious, and despite anything he says about art or passes off as his creation, the only actual piece of work we see him execute is a crude crayon drawing of Gudrun. In the big set-piece where he and Gudrun act out the wedding of Tchaikovsky and Nina, we find the scene opening with Loerke making up Gudrun's eyes in the same manner they were made up for Hermione's wheat dance. (Even the dialogue about Cleopatra "harvesting" the essential from a man, and then throwing away the "husk" supports this.) Loerke is not really an alternative to the life-style and situation to which Gudrun has become accustomed, merely a reworking of it and an ironically bisexual tool with which to finally emasculate Gerald.

The complete disintegration of the relationship between Gerald and Gudrun really occurs at the point where, in a variation on all of their encounters in the film, Gudrun leads Gerald on to a point in the bedroom and then proceeds to cut him off dead. His brutal rape of her at this moment rephrases their first sexual bout in her bedroom, but it is obvious that he has nonetheless lost out because she has defeated him into an admission of love ("Fancy, your actually having said it."). Where earlier he had used Gudrun to try and destroy the phantoms of his own mind through sex, he now tries to destroy her through the same means.

Failing this he next tries to literally destroy her in a confrontation with her and Loerke in the snow. Loerke's surprise at seeing him--"You came like a ghost"--is wonderfully evocative of the fact that Gerald is in actuality already dead. Slugging Loerke and then half-strangling Gudrun, Gerald ultimately wanders off into the snowy wastes ("I want to sleep") to freeze to death. It is, after all, a small step for Gerald from oblivion through sexual release to oblivion through death. The horrors of his own making and his inability to interact on a human level drive him to his death, and significantly it is the forces of nature which finally claim this modern, unnatural man.

"I did not want it to be like this," says Rupert, standing over Gerald's body, which lies frozen on a bed at the inn, "He should have loved me." Russell stages this scene so that Rupert stands on one side of the bed separated from Ursula on the other by the dead Gerald, who, like "this eternal frozen place" of which Rupert had complained, is now himself eternally frozen. Symbolically, Gerald will always come between Rupert and Ursula and the idyllic relationship she so believes in.

The last scene in the film, taken directly from the novel, restates this shot in words. Back in England Rupert and Ursula discuss his need for Gerald and "two kinds of love." When Ursula tells him at length that he cannot have both kinds of love, that his idea is impossible, Rupert simply says, "I don't believe that." It is very instructive to compare the diverse conclusions about this scene as reached by

Gene D. Phillips and Joseph Gomez. Phillips concludes his statement on the scene with the thought on the final line, "nor one infers does Lawrence,"[6] whereas Gomez points out that the freeze frame of Ursula on which the film ends "tends to reinforce her position."[7] Essentially both points of view are correct. Phillips is perfectly right about Lawrence, and Gomez is similarly on the mark about the film. Neither sentiment goes quite far enough, however, as Russell's final image goes considerably beyond a visual reinforcement of Ursula's position. It is far more shattering than that since it indicates the first horrifying moment of realization for her that Rupert is not going to become what she would like, that his belief in the separate man to man relationship did not die with Gerald, that life with Rupert will never be like the slow-motion pastoral fantasy of her dreams. Lawrence certainly subscribes to Rupert's line of thought in the novel, but Russell's concluding visual points to the filmmaker's own rejection of Lawrence's belief. In a small way this final departure underlines Russell's approach to the film as being about the novel as well as being an adaptation of it.

Flawed though much of the film is, Women in Love is a sound start for Russell's theatrical film career. In it he explores many new facets of filmmaking and he can scarcely be blamed that not all of them quite come off. The film has much to recommend it, and even some of its dead ends are of interest to anyone studying Russell's overall work. That there is a dichotomy of viewpoint between Russell and Lawrence is undeniable, but there is also much similarity in their shared concerns over natural man. In no way was it Russell's intention to undermine or distort Lawrence, merely to comment. If there was no level on which the two met intellectually it seems unlikely that Russell should have spent much of his recent energies in attempting to get his script of Lawrence's The Rainbow, which is a kind of "prequel" to Women in Love and one of the writer's most ambitious works, produced. In the end, however, Women in Love's greatest importance lies in what it allowed Russell to achieve in theatrical film by opening the door for him and giving him the power to make the films as he wanted.

NOTES

1. Fisher, Jack. "Three Paintings of Sex: The Films of Ken Russell," Film Journal, 2 (September 1972): 32-43.

2. Gomez, Joseph. Ken Russell: The Adaptor as Creator. London: Frederick Muller, 1976, p. 93.
3. Lawrence, D. H. Foreword to Women in Love. New York: Penguin Books, 1978, p. vii.
4. Cited in Phillips, Gene D. Ken Russell. Boston: Twayne, 1979, pp. 83-84.
5. Cited in Hahn, Emily. Lorenzo. Philadelphia and New York: J. B. Lippincott, 1975, p. 136.
6. Phillips, Gene D. Ken Russell, p. 82.
7. Gomez, Joseph. Ken Russell: The Adaptor as Creator, p. 93.

CHAPTER 6

THE BREAKTHROUGH

The Music Lovers

This, the first full-fledged Ken Russell film, is a complex, many faceted work, the importance of which cannot be underestimated in any assessment of Russell's work. A good understanding of The Music Lovers is essential to anyone interested in the director's output as a whole. The Music Lovers not only represents Russell's first theatrical attempt at dealing with an overtly biographical subject (Lawrence must be exempted on the grounds that Women in Love is a largely fictional story peopled with real characters), but it also contains the seeds for virtually everything to come in terms of style, content, and intent.

Perhaps no later film so well represents a prime paradox about the filmmaker. Although the work sets out to debunk the myth of Romanticism and its destructive power, it is equally apparent that Russell is himself drawn to this very Romanticism. The implication here being that Romanticism is all well and good so long as one knows where to draw the line, which the characters in The Music Lovers most assuredly do not. The film damns Romanticism and celebrates its very real beauty and attraction at the same time. No more clear-cut denunciation of the Romantic Ideal could be imagined than the absurdist pastoral fantasy set to the first piano concerto, or Tchaikovsky's pathetic belief that Nina's letter to him is a case of life unconsciously imitating art and his subsequent acceptance of this imitation as the genuine article. On the other hand it is difficult to imagine a more deliriously Romantic image than Tchaikovsky and Madame von Meck seeing each other from a distance (for the first and only time) as her coach passes him on the road, or his gift to her of the Fourth Symphony. For that matter the sequence in which Madame von Meck basks in the aura of Tchaikovsky's having been in her house--caressing the chair where he sat, handling

and tasting the peach he has left half-eaten--is a case where
Russell achieves a delicate balance of both attitudes. The
sequence is at once heartbreakingly Romantic and, at the
same time, carries an undertone of a true sickness of the
spirit in its inverted sexuality. To be sure, it is a paradox.
It is a love-hate relationship--a relationship which runs
through the bulk of Russell's work, but, perhaps, never so
clearly nor so aptly illustrated as in The Music Lovers. For
Russell is not only of two minds about Romanticism in general, but also about Tchaikovsky in particular, whom he feels
represents the worst qualities of the Romantic Ideal. Russell is undeniably sympathetic toward Tchaikovsky, and admires his music, but he is similarly aware of the many failings of the man as a human being and is hard pressed to
reconcile one aspect with the other.

This is not to say that Ken Russell is putting himself
in the position of sitting in judgment on his character, except
to balance his personal acceptance. The point here being
that Russell is concerned with coming to terms with some
very primary problems about art and the artist--specifically,
can the man transcend his limitations and can the art transcend the man? Essentially Russell is (probably unconsciously) subscribing to the philosophy of a filmmaker with whom
he shares certain stylistic traits, Rouben Mamoulian, who
said, "Art hasn't got to be just life: it must transform it;
it must speak the whole truth. A profile isn't the whole face.
I want to recreate the face of man, and to show it all."[1]
That Russell's truth is by nature subjective, and that his recreation of the "face of man" is not always pretty is quite
beside the point. Russell presents the viewer with a series
of scenes designed to illuminate the artist and his art and
how the two relate. From these scenes come the questions
about the limitations of the artist and the balance between his
worth as a creator and a human being. The final judgment,
however, rests as much with the viewer as with Ken Russell.
Above all else, Russell wants the viewer to think, to respond, to look at the subject through new eyes.

The Music Lovers is Russell's most supremely negative statement on an artist, and resultantly the most terrifying. It could be argued that his representations of Richard
Strauss in the TV film Dance of the Seven Veils and of Wagner in Lisztomania are more overtly critical, but there Russell is dealing in a different area altogether. It is far easier
to deal with Strauss and Wagner because Russell finds them
to be little more than figures of fun, with very little, save a

The Breakthrough

certain regard for sheer nerve and artistic boldness, to admire in these men. This is not the case with Tchaikovsky. Among other things it is Russell's contention that Tchaikovsky is, at least, free of debasing his talents by perverting them with corrupt ideals in the manner of Strauss and Wagner. Even though Russell finds very little to admire in Tchaikovsky as a human being, he also finds it impossible not to empathize with the man on some level. Indeed, it is this very empathy that makes The Music Lovers such a black vision.

Russell's problem in coming to terms with the gap which separates the man and his music forms the crux of the film. Just as Tchaikovsky hopes that he can make life imitate art, Russell would like to feel a little less betrayed by the same type of discrepancy inherent in Tchaikovsky. Unfortunately Russell can no more reconcile this difference between creator and human being than Tchaikovsky can, and this is central to the film. It is one of the many aspects of Russell that makes him unique as a filmmaker, for not only is dramatic tension derived from the events on the screen, but from the very attitude of the film's creator. This, in part, explains the overwhelming emotional response many viewers have to Russell's work. As David Sterritt would later say about Mahler in his Christian Science Monitor review, Russell's film "throbs with life," and Russell is an integral part of that life. It is impossible to remove the filmmaker's own inner conflict over his characters from the film, and there is no evidence that Russell would have it otherwise. It is an inherent part of the role of any truly subjective filmmaker.

Thematic qualities aside, The Music Lovers is the first of the feature films that physically resembles Russell's mature works. Women in Love, though a very handsome film in every way, fails to capture much of the intensity and aptness of color and composition which graces the later films. The Music Lovers is very much more in this mold of the films to come, even though cinematographer Douglas Slocombe is not really a Russellian photographer. Photographers like David Watkin, Peter Suschitsky, and, most importantly, Dick Bush are better suited to Russell as they seem more attuned to his sense of immediacy. This is not meant to detract from Douglas Slocombe's photography on The Music Lovers. His work here is outstanding, beautifully rendering some of Russell's finest and most powerful images, but there is an undercurrent of kinship lacking between Slocombe and Russell--

Ken Russell and cinematographer Douglas Slocombe (left) discuss a shot on the set of The Music Lovers. (Courtesy of Ken Russell)

a kinship that exists with Russell's later cinematographers. The Music Lovers occasionally looks too good, too polished, though, thankfully, without the camera moves which continually seemed ahead of the action and marred parts of Women in Love.

    As is the case with any major work of art, be it film, painting, music, literature, what have you, The Music Lovers cannot be fully appreciated in one sitting. (This fact has probably accounted for more misconceptions and dubious judgments in film criticism than any other single factor, since most critics see a film only once before passing sentence on it.) It demands to be seen several times, so that the true substance and subtle nuance of the film can be fully evaluated and digested. Russell's intentions are not those of a film-maker wanting to be completely understood on a one-shot basis. Rather the desire is that the film-goer should be sufficiently intrigued by the work to want to see it again. All of Russell's work is geared toward this idea, but The Music Lovers presents a particularly good case for study. In his

The Breakthrough

book on Russell, Joseph Gomez notes that the opening of the film is especially well designed and describes it in some detail, as concerns the fact that in this one sequence we are introduced to all the major characters in the film with the exception of Rubinstein. Further, he remarks that the careful construction may not be apparent on the first viewing. True enough, but that really is not the point. One of Russell's primary reasons for the switch from television to motion pictures was that films are shown time and time again, as opposed to television's now-you-see-it-now-you-don't manner of presentation (fine for most TV, but galling for the serious artist). Therefore, it seems safe to conclude that Russell expects his work to be seen more than once. A detailed examination of the opening sequence quite clearly reveals that it would be virtually impossible to take in the incredible array of detail and character development with which Russell has endowed his completely visual scene in a single viewing.

The Music Lovers veritably bursts onto the screen from the first frame. With a cymbal crash and a blast of Tchaikovsky's "Dance of the Clowns" from The Nutcracker the viewer is thrust headlong into the film as Tchaikovsky and his lover, Count Anton Chiluvsky, romp on a sled ride at a Shrovetide carnival in Moscow. Their subsequent crash into the snow gives Russell a tidy blank space into which he can insert the very singificant title sequence: "Ken Russell's Film on Tchaikovsky and The Music Lovers." Not, it should be noted, The Story of Tchaikovsky, nor The Life of Peter Tchaikovsky, but "Ken Russell's Film on Tchaikovsky," stressing the personal interpretation to follow. Moreover the actual title, The Music Lovers, makes it clear that the film has as much to do with those in Tchaikovsky's sphere as it has with Tchaikovsky. The Music Lovers never purports to be the definitive account of Tchaikovsky's life. It is one man's view of the composer and those around him and must be judged on those grounds. Any attempt to comprehend, let alone judge, The Music Lovers on any other basis is doomed from the onset, and this remains true and consistent throughout the entirety of Russell's work.

From this brief break, Russell returns to introducing and delineating his characters. We have seen Tchaikovsky, now let us see "The Music Lovers" themselves. One by one, Russell parades them past us and set up the dramatic tension of the film. Tchaikovsky's future wife, Nina, is seen moving along to keep her vantage point on a young lieutenant whom

she has decided to pursue, ultimately lobbing a snowball at
him. In this simple manner, with its overtones of aggression and eccentric behavior, Russell has laid the groundwork
for Nina's later nymphomania and general mental instability.
Tchaikovsky's sister, Sasha, and her family pass by Tchaikovsky and Chiluvsky, who are concealed in large papier-mâché heads. Tchaikovsky is torn between following after
them and staying with Chiluvsky--a decision Chiluvsky makes
for him by pulling him along in the opposite direction. Once
again, Russell has presented a simple scene, which will
take on added significance. Russell's depiction of Sasha, confused, a bit disgusted and harried, reflects the smug, self-satisfaction with her cocoon-like existence and her rejection
of anything that does not fit in with this life. In this instance
it is a rejection of the thronging life-filled crowds at the
carnival, but the implication will extend to greater areas of
intolerance, specifically her brother's homosexuality, which
she decides not to notice. (In the same manner she quite
overlooks not only Tchaikovsky's incestuous attraction to her,
but, unconsciously, encourages it--not because she reciprocates, but because such things are not possible in her world.)
Tchaikovsky's indecision about following his family or Chiluvsky also has a bearing on the incestuous nature of his relationship with Sasha, as it puts him in the position of weighing her against his lover. Finally, there is Chiluvsky's
position of making the decision for him. This move not only
establishes Chiluvsky as the stronger of the two and the dominant character in their relationship, but it also asserts his
need to be in control of the situation.

    Also in the scene are relatively brief glimpses of
Madame von Meck and Tchaikovsky's brother, Modeste.
Madame von Meck is presented as a figure in black (invariably she dresses in black), solemn and completely disassociated from the activities around her. This is underscored
by her brightly dressed charges, who are laughing at some
performers. This isolation is perfectly consistent with the
character's development--isolated and bored. Modeste, on
the other hand, is far from bored, but too conscious of public opinion to really enjoy himself. He is with his pupil,
Koyola, and protectively ushers him away from a scene where
some soldiers are pouring wine down a dancing girl's throat.
It is obvious that Modeste is less appalled by these actions
than by the chance that anyone might see him watching them.
This is an apt bit of characterization for a man who will
shortly advise his brother of the disaster of the world at
large discovering his secret--"your music will never be
played."

The Breakthrough   81

Having established his characters and laid the groundwork for their personalities, Russell ends the opening sequence on the same frolicsome note with which it began, as Tchaikovsky and Chiluvsky dance drunkenly in the snow with torches before staggering into Chiluvsky's house and collapsing on the bed. If any part of The Music Lovers can be said to present Tchaikovsky as a relatively normal human being--a whole man--it is surely the film's very opening shots (up to the credits) and these scenes which end the overall sequence. It is the only instance in The Music Lovers where Tchaikovsky, through inebriation or high spirits or both, allows himself to be himself outside of his music. Russell's point is not to celebrate Tchaikovsky's drunkenness, but to give the viewer a vital glimpse of the human being that remains buried beneath the generally troubled composer. This is a glimmer of the Tchaikovsky who might have existed had he come to terms with his sexuality; had those around him supported him rather than turned a blind eye, or cautioned him about public outcry--the Tchaikovsky who might have been had he not chosen instead to mask himself in self-delusions and the aura of the Romantic Ideal.

Technically, Russell's sequence is apparently inspired by the opening of William Dieterle's The Hunchback of Notre Dame (1939), which it physically resembles. A later direct quotation from the Dieterle film (Modeste swinging on a giant bell à la Quasimodo in the "1812 Overture" fantasy), tends to support this inspiration. It is not altogether surprising that Russell should choose to quote from Dieterle, as Dieterle is perhaps best known for his Warner Bros. biographical films of the mid and late 1930's. Strictly speaking, The Hunchback of Notre Dame is not a biographical film, but it does deal with historical characters, and in a very subjective manner, not unlike Russell's film. These quotations, like subsequent ones in this film and others, serve Russell in more than one respect. They stress his desire to present his subjective truth in a slightly unreal yet appropriate manner with which the movie audience can readily come to terms. It is, after all, likely that more of the audience have seen Dieterle's film than have read Herbert Weinstock's Tchaikovsky biography, or even the film's own source book, Beloved Friend, even if it is presuming too much to picture the average movie-goer watching The Music Lovers and exclaiming, "Ah! Dieterle!" It is, however, not unreasonable to assume that the familiarity registers on some level if the source does not. Russell's quotations also serve to enforce the strong feeling of the legacy of film history which runs throughout his films. Perhaps no other director is quite so aware of the tremendous debt owed to the work that came before him, and certainly no other is so willing and happy to acknowledge that debt. Aware of and attuned to his influences Russell's quotations are the grateful homages to those influences and a testament to his inimitable joy of filmmaking--a factor quite lacking in the majority of present day filmmakers. (Consider the case of William Friedkin, who, when asked about the possible influence of The Devils on his film, The Exorcist, immediately asserted that he was not influenced by Russell or anyone else--a ludicrous notion at best, not entirely borne out by the ineptitude of his film, but partly supported by it. A little influence from some other source might have helped.)

To some extent Russell's use of quotations has posed part of the problem many critics have had in coming to terms with his work. Russell has himself noted that as a general rule people involved in music are more sympathetic to his aims than those involved in film. This idea does indeed seem to hold true as a general rule. Aside from the very obvious fact that Russell is drawn to music and utilizes it in ways not dreamed of by other filmmakers, there is the similarity of the structure of a Russell film to a musical composition. Beyond Russell's use of continuing visual motifs, which find their counterpart in music, there is this question of the inclusion of quotations from earlier films and other art forms, e.g., the Dieterle references here, the "Birth of Venus" in The Devils, the passages from Isaac Babel in Mahler, etc. Musicians are used to this kind of quoting. It is done in music all the time. Fundamentally Russell's quotations are no different than the inclusion of the Dies Irae in the fourth movement of Tchaikovsky's Third Orchestral Suite, or Bruckner's Wagner quotations in his Third Symphony, or even John Corigliano's utilization of "Rock of Ages" in the score for Russell's own Altered States.

The second major sequence in The Music Lovers occurs at the premiere performance of Tchaikovsky's First Piano Concerto. Once again detail is presented in an almost breakneck fashion, and the viewer need be prepared to pick up a good deal of information on the run. A brief conversation between Prince Balukin and Nicholas Rubinstein concerning "all this gossip" about Tchaikovsky's sexual preferences; Tchaikovsky admonishing Modeste to spirit the family away after the performance in the event that Rubinstein attacks his composition; Nina, still in pursuit of her lieutenant, clumsily

Richard Chamberlain, a remarkably sensitive and intelligent Tchaikovsky, and Russell's daughter, Victoria, in the First Piano Concerto fantasy in The Music Lovers. (United Artists)

colliding with Tchaikovsky--all these are seemingly tossed off, yet these random events help to create the tensions which hold the sequence together. Indeed the entire segment is designed to build on this tension until the atmosphere is choked with it, released at the last moment by the music and Russell's visual equivalent of it.

The only flaw with the sequence is one which Russell himself has expressed some misgivings about: namely, the insistence on attacking the advertising world's notion of slow-motion pastoral beauty. As a statement against this prefabricated world of specious and unattainable beauty, the sequence works only if Russell's intentions are known beforehand. The irony and underlying sickness of the sequence comes through, but Russell never quite achieves the "cigarette commercial" look for which he strives, largely because he is too good a filmmaker. Once it is known that the sequence parodies the ad man's vision of beauty being accepted as a true sense of aesthetic values, it is possible to see where the images fit into the television commercial world. Russell the consummate filmmaker, however, prevents the tackiness of the TV commercial from showing through. His mastery of the medium of film and his powerful ability to utilize clichés as if they were almost fresh concepts undermines his stated intent. (His much later and more pointed jab at television advertising in Tommy works better because it is presented in the more aggressive, hard-edged manner of the genuine article.) In reflection, the pastoral scenes in the segment though undeniably beautiful do carry an undertone of absurdity, but the lasting impression of the inverted, incestuous relationship just beneath the surface takes precedence over the satire. Taking the entirety of The Music Lovers into consideration it is not a bad thing that Russell falls somewhat short of his aims. As it stands the sequence is more at one with the film, especially since, thematically, the incestuous relationship has more bearing on the overall film.

Important though the fantasy sequences are to the scene at hand, it is really the tension created by placing the collective group of "Music Lovers" in one room that makes the scene work, as well as establishing a continuity with the opening sequence which had already utilized and characterized the same set of people. (Again there is the similarity to musical composition with re-stated and embellished motifs.)

Russell's placement of his characters within the room

The Breakthrough 85

is in itself masterful. Those most immediately important to Tchaikovsky at this point in the film--Sasha, Modeste, Davidov and Rubinstein--are seated closest to him, whereas Nina, who is not even in his sphere yet, is at the back of the theatre. Also in the background is Chiluvsky, who, as an indication of his social inappropriateness, stands apart from the audience. Madame von Meck is disassociated from the audience as well, but on a higher level both figuratively and literally, as she hovers above Tchaikovsky in her private balcony. Dressed in black feathers like some wild Josef von Sternberg creation, Madame von Meck resembles nothing so much as a vulture perched over Tchaikovsky. Physically, she is removed from both Tchaikovsky and the audience. Through skillful manipulation of his camera in a series of immaculate zoom shots, Russell brings the collective tension of these characters to bear directly on Tchaikovsky by placing him at the very center of this series of shots. The effect becomes positively claustrophobic by the point where the music stops dead just prior to its climax and Russell inserts three large, breathlessly rapid close shots of Sasha, Nina, and Madame von Meck. Having reached the peak of this tension, the camera careens crazily past the violinists and along the keyboard to Tchaikovsky for the final outburst of the lush music. Joseph Gomez has noted that these immaculate keyboard shots would be "the envy of Hollywood's Charles Vidor," but it should be noted that Russell's use of this kind of technical panache is streets ahead of Vidor. Beyond providing a perfect visual that reflects the music, this shot, as much as anything in the film, underlines Tchaikovsky's ability to escape the real world through his music, coming as it does just when the tension becomes unbearable.

There has been a good deal of quibbling about the historical accuracy of the sequence just described, most of it resting on the fact that Madame von Meck was not present at this particular performance, and that there is no evidence that Nina attended any performance whatsoever, though Catherine Drinker Bowen muses that she might have in the text of Beloved Friend. Not only does this argument rest on the untenable assumption that Russell is telling a life story in the strictest sense of the biographical form, but it also denies the overwhelming subjectivity of the film as a whole. Russell has stated that no piece of music is arbitrarily injected into The Music Lovers, that it is all there for a purpose. What, then, we must ask is the purpose of this piece of music in the context of the film? Why not use the performance of the violin concerto which Madame von Meck did attend? To find the answer it is necessary to bring the question of subjectivity into the foreground. In so doing we are reminded that Russell is not a purveyor of dry historical facts--for him these are real and very vital people and issues. Gene D. Phillips has noted that it was this piece of music that had first attracted Russell to music in the first place. Significantly it was the second movement of the Concerto which Russell had found "unbearably beautiful."[2] It is also this movement in which Russell has staged the central fantasies of the sequence, as if to purge himself of the great difficulty of balancing Tchaikovsky the composer against Tchaikovsky the man. Russell is neither able nor willing to put the man in one pocket and the composer in the other. The outrage he feels over the failings of the man cannot be denied, and no better example of this discrepancy exists for Russell than the First Piano Concerto. For that matter, if a filmmaker or any artist is to succeed he or she must believe in and be able to relate to the subject. Having been captivated by this piece of music himself how better might Russell understand the effects on Madame von Meck and Nina? Nothing is arbitrary.

Russell follows his first big set-piece with a series of vignettes depicting the instability of the falsely romantic world of Tchaikovsky's music, as one by one the characters' illusions are shattered by the real world: Rubinstein attacks the work as "bad ... vulgar ... woman's stuff"; Nina, lost in her fantasies, cracks her head against a low doorway (reminiscent of Gypo in John Ford's The Informer); even Madame von Meck finds herself besieged by her family to join in their Christmas celebrations. The only exemptions from this emotional let-down are the film's two major realists, Modeste and Chiluvsky, and the ever sheltered Sasha, who is ushered away immediately after the performance so that in no case might she brush against reality.

By this point in the film, scarcely twenty minutes into the overall one hundred and twenty-two, Russell has established every major character in the film and can now begin to fully explore those characters for the bulk of the film. Despite the amount of incident with which the film is fleshed out, these character studies are at the center of The Music Lovers. Unfortunately, these studies have been glossed over, ignored, simplified, or misunderstood far too often by far too many people attempting to come to terms with Russell's vision.

The major, and most common, simplification concerns the relationship of Tchaikovsky and Nina. While it is undeniable that Tchaikovsky did her a nasty turn by marrying her in the first place, it is going altogether too far to suggest that he destroyed her or is solely responsible for her mental deterioration. As presented by Russell, Nina is already unstable long before she becomes involved with Tchaikovsky. Nothing in her character suggests that happiness or even a reasonable amount of normalcy was ever within her grasp with or without Tchaikovsky. In no degree does this lessen Tchaikovsky's guilt in the situation, since he surely served as a catalyst, and the selfishness and wrong-headedness of his actions are the same regardless of the outcome. It does, however, remove Nina from the traditional role of a completely sympathetic character. In fact she is monumentally unsympathetic, though she, like Tchaikovsky, is certainly pathetic. Her actions are far from admirable, as unhealthy in their own way as Tchaikovsky's.

At the same time there is a tendency, reinforced to some degree by Russell's imagery, to view Chiluvsky in an entirely unsympathetic light. In a way it is possible to view Chiluvsky's relationship with Tchaikovsky as the rough equivalent of Tchaikovsky's relationship with Nina. Similarities abound: as a member of the aristocracy Chiluvsky is in a social position one step higher than Tchaikovsky, just as Tchaikovsky is one higher than Nina; as Chiluvsky is generally cleverer than Tchaikovsky, so Tchaikovsky is cleverer than Nina. As concerns the characters' relative levels of perceiving reality, again we find the downward progression from the coldly realistic Chiluvsky to the less realistic Tchaikovsky to the totally unrealistic Nina. The primary difference between the two characters in this respect is that while the viewer must, by the evidence presented on the screen, come to the conclusion that Chiluvsky is governed by genuine emotion, Nina is not. However undesirable and selfish Chiluvsky's feelings for Tchaikovsky may be, they are the genuine article. Nina's emotions on the other hand are specious at best. Certainly she is not motivated by a love of Tchaikovsky the man, nor is she motivated by a love for the composer, as Madame von Meck is. Instead she is only taken with the idea of being the wife of a famous composer. Even at his most unsympathetic, when he denounces Tchaikovsky to Madame von Meck, Chiluvsky is acting upon his real emotions, and not, as Nina or Tchaikovsky might act, on the emotions he would like to have. There is no way around the viciousness of his actions, but they are far less reprehensible than the inverted logic of those of Tchaikovsky, Nina, and Madame von Meck. If nothing else, and apart from the implication of genuine emotion involved, Chiluvsky's actions are firmly rooted in the reality of the situation. He, like Modeste, can take reality and turn it to advantage, while Tchaikovsky can only escape from it through his music, Nina can only withdraw into her madness, and Madame von Meck can only create a phantom image of someone to love by reading her own confused emotions into the music.

At this point in the narrative Russell offers some insight into why Tchaikovsky is the way he is. It is the evening of the performance and Tchaikovsky's nerves are already frayed from the emotions of the afternoon. Further pressures from Chiluvsky trying to induce Tchaikovsky to join in the party going on outside his workroom, and the noise of the party itself prevent Tchaikovsky from finding escape in the fantasy world of his music. With no means of escape from his advanced nervous state, Tchaikovsky regresses into childhood upon hearing a woman singing in the distance. The sound triggers the memory of his mother singing Mozart's "Porgi Amor," and his sense of reality and of past and present becomes distorted, so that when he finds the woman who is singing in a steaming bath, he cannot differentiate between this and his mother's death in a tub of scalding water as part of a last ditch, kill or cure, treatment for cholera. The distinctions between the memory and the present are so blurred that Tchaikovsky suffers a breakdown and has to be restrained from pulling the woman from the bath.

On one level this sequence merely serves to further the destruction of the high spirits engendered by the Piano Concerto, but this is purely a surface reading. Russell establishes several points here, as well as furnishing the viewer with a key visual motif for the film: the emphasis on Madame Tchaikovsky's feet as she is dragged off to her death. Hereafter this image serves as a symbol indicating a loss of control over one's destiny--a death of hope. More than this Russell shows the seeds of the relationship with Sasha, based on the excessive attachment to his mother, later characterized by Tchaikovsky as "the only woman I ever remember loving." Historians (who, perhaps, lack the psychosocial expertise for such judgment) are pretty much unanimous in viewing Tchaikovsky's unnatural attachment to his mother as the foundation for his homosexuality, and Russell's depiction of the trauma of her death enlarges upon this. In truth, Tchaikovsky was not present at the time of his mother's death,

The Breakthrough

but by placing him physically in the scene Russell not only better delineates the trauma, but implies certain reasons for Tchaikovsky's aversion to women in general. Tchaikovsky last sees his mother as a grotesque creature, her face marked with sores and drawn with fever, a dead thing--presented in a manner that effectively foreshadows the image of Nina in the floor in the train carriage. The youthful Tchaikovsky's cries of "Don't die" indicate an early inability to grasp reality, and create the impression that he believes subconsciously that the only woman he remembers loving betrayed him by dying.

Similarly the glimpses of his sheltered hot-house environment suggests that reality has always been an unknown commodity for Tchaikovsky. (Sasha's attitude toward life bears this out.) It establishes the pattern for Tchaikovsky's entire life, based on arrested development. First his mother creates an environment for him, then Rubinstein, later Madame von Meck, and finally Modeste will do the same. At no point does Tchaikovsky exist on his own. He is never allowed to even try to do so.

Thus far Russell's primary concern in the film has been to establish the setting (on an emotional and psychological level) in which the major drama of The Music Lovers could exist. Having so prepared us he proceeds to unfold this drama. This results in a series of relatively short scenes which culminate in the Eugene Onegin letter sequence. Brief though many of these scenes are, each is done very deliberately. Nothing is simply tossed off or thrown away as mere exposition or transition. As Nina writes her letter to the dashing Lieutenant, her high flown phrases and statements of virtue are sharply undercut by tawdriness of her surroundings and her general demeanor. When Rubinstein comes to see Madame von Meck, who wishes to put forth her strange proposal of supporting yet never meeting Tchaikovsky ("He can write to me if he considers it worth his time"), Rubinstein acquiesces to her wishes, but cannot resist pushing himself forward at the same time by offering to play one of his favorite Tchaikovsky pieces, "the 'Romeo and Juliet Fantasy,' arranged by myself." Russell then shrewdly connects this scene to the following one. As Madame von Meck leans back to invent the man who wrote the music Rubinstein is playing, Russell knocks the supports from beneath the fantasy by counterpointing it with the real. The music changes from Rubinstein at the piano to an orchestral rendition as Russell shows us the result of Nina's encounter with the Lieutenant who has drunkenly and brutally raped her.

This is the first of several occasions where Russell uses Nina and Madame von Meck contrapuntally, with von Meck as the dream and Nina as the reality. Continually he wants to stress, to allow us not the slightest chance of forgetting, that while the dream world of Romanticism is outwardly beautiful--how otherwise could it be dangerous?-- there is a dreadful reality that cannot be reconciled with this dream.

The method of contrasting or equating one character or situation with another, which is vital to the film, presents another problem for the viewer expecting a simple reading of the facts. Even though it is likely that most anyone could accept the occasional parallel between the same two characters, the complexities of The Music Lovers do not allow for this. It is impossible to look at the film and say that Madame von Meck is meant to parallel Nina and leave it at that. At this point in the film there is some truth in the statement, but this line of reasoning will not hold water throughout the length of the film. It is much the same as with Russell's use of symbolism. The meaning of the symbol is only clear within its context; no fixed meaning is applied. In the instance of the analogies between characters in The Music Lovers the shift in identification carries a further implication. Linking Nina to Madame von Meck, Nina to Chiluvsky, even Nina to Tchaikovsky himself is by no means fuzzy thinking on Russell's part, nor is it an indication of an inability to reach a conclusion. Rather the unsettled identification which characterizes the analogies and parallels serves a sound thematic function, which enforces the film's stance on Romanticism. The characters in The Music Lovers who follow the Romantic Ideal, either by choice or association, are all related. They are all dying of the same disease.

The actual letter scene itself, and those scenes which directly lead into it, bear some examination. Essentially, this is the most misunderstood part of the film. The general run of criticism would have it that it is Russell who is trying to make Tchaikovsky's life fit his art, which is an argument completely at odds with the film. True enough, Russell has seized upon the startling similarity between the opera and the situation between Tchaikovsky and Nina, but it is not his desire to present the similarities as actually mirroring life. In fact Russell is doing his utmost to do the opposite. Again it is by juxtaposing the Romantic Ideal (in this case the opera) with its real-life counterpart (Nina's letter writing) that he stresses the immense gulf between the

Nina works on the newest version of her standard letter, this time with the naive Tchaikovsky as its target in The Music Lovers. (United Artists)

two. The viewer is already aware that Nina is somewhat unbalanced. Similarly Russell has demonstrated that she has no actual interest in Tchaikovsky, but that she has merely transferred her affections to him on the basis that he happened to be the first person who popped into her mind when her efforts with the Lieutenant proved so disastrous. The impression is not that life is really imitating art, but that someone of Tchaikovsky's mental attitude would eagerly accept this occurrence as such, and that all Nina is going to do is continue to write the same letter again and again until she happens upon someone who will take her up on it. Russell's use of the opera on the soundtrack only serves to illustrate this very point. The absurdly romantic phrases, "No one on earth is here to help me.... No one but you can set me free.... How can you let me be.... How can you let me be alone," only bring forth the hollowness of Nina's emotions and her letter.

If Russell had been content to let the scene rest on the foundation presented above, there might have been far less misunderstanding. It would also not have been the truly great work that it is now by virtue of the other areas that the sequence touches upon. The scene starts building at the moment Tchaikovsky prepares to enter his new home, courtesy of Madame von Meck. It is here that the film's narration, made up of bits and pieces of the actual correspondence between Tchaikovsky and Madame von Meck, begins. The excerpts chosen by Russell and screenwriter Melvyn Bragg are particularly well applied, even when removed from their original context. Aside from providing a very useful counterpoint to Nina's letter writing, the von Meck-Tchaikovsky correspondence serves successfully to magnify the characters, increase a sympathetic attitude toward them, and still undercut the absurdity of their Romantic stance. Madame von Meck's statement about the intensity and greatness of Tchaikovsky's music culminating in the ludicrous thought, "one should like to die experiencing it," conveys the slightly comical, slightly sick aspect of the characters far better than any invented dialogue might have done. Russell's initial use of this narration is likewise well judged. At the best of times narration can easily seem false, and an altogether too facile manner of patching the holes in a film's narrative structure. By avoiding the traditional form of narration Russell greatly minimizes this problem. When Tchaikovsky begins, "My dear Madame von Meck, however can I repay such generosity? Such gifts? And the greatest gift of all--being able to work again? I shall remain forever in your debt," the viewer is not being presented with any new information, only an amplification of known facts. This is so far removed from more standard narrations like Kubrick's "There was me, that is Alex, and my three droogs. That is, Pete, Georgie and Dim" in A Clockwork Orange, or even the unfortunate Chayefsky narration, "The tank itself was unusual..." which mars the opening of Russell's own Altered States, that there is really very little relation. Beyond this, Russell's placement of the narration--Tchaikovsky's words are heard while we see von Meck and Rubinstein sitting in a carriage outside Tchaikovsky's new home, and von Meck's words are heard while Tchaikovsky and his entourage are busily engaged in decorating the flat--helps to convey the sense of a true correspondence rather than a simple device.

Russell then provides a smooth transition from one situation to the next as Madame von Meck's letter ends, "Soon the whole world will worship you. Let me be the first to show it," and Tchaikovsky proposes a toast "to the woman who will change my life." Leaving this line deliberately ambiguous, Russell cuts directly to a close-shot of Nina at the beginning of her fantasy in which she transfers her interest from the Lieutenant to Tchaikovsky. Set to the climactic portion of the fourth movement of Tchaikovsky's Second Symphony, the fantasy is designed to correspond with her fantasy during the Piano Concerto where she dreamed of a romance with the Lieutenant. Significantly, all of Nina's fantasies depicted in the film are of a pathetic and laughable nature, and are executed to music that is all sound and fury with little inside. The similarity to the first fantasy helps establish the impossibility of her dreams, as much as the idea of Tchaikovsky turning into her proud champion within the text of the fantasy does. Having already witnessed the difference between her original fantasy and reality, we know all too well the outcome of the second before it happens.

It is then left to the letter scene itself to tie these sequences together and effectively conclude what can best be viewed as the first act of The Music Lovers. In purely theatrical terms--and this is decidedly the most overtly theatrical of all Russell films--The Music Lovers does divide neatly into four acts. Stressing this feeling of theatricality is the fade-out which climaxes the letter scene, and the first act--a device notably absent in any other Russell film--used here in much the same manner as Peter Medak would later utilize a lengthy fade-out to divide the two acts of his masterpiece of theatre on film, The Ruling Class.

Apart from its thematic attributes, the letter scene is also one of the single best illustrations of Russell's outlook on film in terms of choreographic movement. Viewing this scene, Pauline Kael's later criticism that Russell's editing shows he has no feeling for music or rhythm,[3] seems incomprehensible. Every cut, every movement of the actors or the camera are all interlocked into a cinematic ballet, and not one which is simply a great technical achievement, but one that has direct bearing on the film as a whole.

Starting from a slightly satirical viewpoint as Tchaikovsky says, "she's a wonderful creature, warm and tender, devoid of all artifice," while we watch Nina, Russell immediately proceeds to bring all the divergent elements into play. Tchaikovsky introduces the letter scene to Sasha, who reacts in her typically ill-conceived, unconsciously incest-inspiring manner, as she prostrates herself in a fit of emotion and generally engages in all manner of posturings which feed her brother's fantasy. All the while Nina is writing her version of the opera's letter and Madame von Meck is rhapsodizing over a piano score of the opera that Tchaikovsky has sent her--"You see, he sends me the music the minute he writes it, and what feeling is in it now! This is love, my sons, real love!" These varied scenes are held together by Russell as a piece through the continuing thread of the music, and Russell's first visual link of Tchaikovsky and Nina, as he continually dissolves from a close-shot of Tchaikovsky to one of Nina.

The constant paralleling of actions, the mounting emotional tension between Tchaikovsky and Sasha as the aria reaches its conclusion, played against Nina's nervously delivering her letter, further help to solidify the structure. Then, too, in a move linking the overall sequence with every other musical set piece in the film, there is the tumultuous liberating climax which breaks the tension, as Tchaikovsky, Sasha, Alexei, and Olga Bredska celebrate the performance of the aria with an impromptu dance set to a fully orchestrated version of the music, while Nina, relieved at having delivered her letter, dashes happily through the rain. Best of all is Russell's final shot which choreographically works Tchaikovsky, Sasha, and Nina into the same piece of film. The camera follows Tchaikovsky and Sasha down the street, stops suddenly and slowly zooms in through the passersby to a close-shot of Nina watching from a sidewalk cafe. Aside from the technical verisimilitude of this shot, it carries an emotional punch of no little power, thanks, in part, to Glenda Jackson's brilliant playing of Nina. As the camera zooms in on her, a variety of emotions play across her face, ranging from elation to hope to fear and uncertainty, and finally to just the merest hint of evil. It is on this note of unbalanced evil that Russell chooses to fade-out and the first act of <u>The Music Lovers</u> closes.

The second act of the film is concerned with Tchaikovsky's actual relationship with Nina as a physical presence. As strongly theatrical as the rest of the film, it is set apart from the work as a whole in having only one strong set piece --the controversial train carriage sequence--which acts as a center structure for the middle of the film.

The action begins as Tchaikovsky reads aloud from Nina's letter to Modeste, who is less than receptive to Nina's supposed sincerity. Tchaikovsky, of course, is convinced that it is fate, while Modeste is not only convinced otherwise, but concerned that Tchaikovsky will foolishly jeopardize his position with Madame von Meck. Realistically, Modeste

The Breakthrough

tells his brother, "Eugene Onegin is a fictitious character and so is the girl of your dreams." The argument, though, is largely pointless because Tchaikovsky is going to believe exactly what he wants to believe. It is the most dialogue-conscious part of the film, and the only part where the dialogue deals with the differences between fantasy and reality on such an overt level. Tchaikovsky's conclusion, after talking it over with Modeste in this manner, that if he does not answer the letter he knows he will always regret it, is evident from the first. What is not evident are the lengths to which his Romantic self-delusions will take him.

In the scene which follows, where he drags Sasha into the debate, after having already sent his reply, the blatant stupidity of his attitude is brought home by having Sasha saw away at "None But the Lonely Heart" on a cello (recalling Françoise Dorleac in Billion Dollar Brain) in a hearts-and-flowers manner. We now know, at least, that Tchaikovsky has been extremely foolish in his reply to Nina and his delusion has progressed to the point where he feels compelled to see her.

This much we are prepared for, but Russell's real shocker comes as Nina reads his letter in which his plans for a meeting are revealed--"He says he might love me!" Wisely, Russell does not leave the viewer to speculate on this point long enough for a complete loss of sympathy for the man. Instead he underlines Nina's own instability by recalling the moment where she walked into the low doorway by having her clumsily burn herself as she grabs a hot pan off the fire without thinking. Here, however, he enlarges upon the incident by establishing a visual motif for her progressive mental deterioration as for the first time she sits rocking herself back and forth.

The meeting itself is a tiny masterpiece of theatre, ranking with the best of James Whale and Jean Renoir at their most theatrically evocative, and utilizing theatrical lighting in a manner that again foreshadows Peter Medak's similar technique in The Ruling Class. It should be born in mind, however, that like Whale, Renoir, and later Medak, this theatrical aspect is achieved without compromising cinematic values in the process. Tchaikovsky's apartment in itself has something of the atmosphere of a stage set, and this is apt, not in the least because effectively it is a stage--one on which a preconceived drama is to be played. The theatre of The Music Lovers is by no means arbitrary. It is directly related to the film's theme and structure. The attitudes, words, posturings, and ideas of Russell's Romantic protagonists are in themselves little more than play acting, and it is this fact that has dictated the theatrical style of the film. Nowhere is this brought more clearly into focus than in this particular scene.

As the scene opens, Tchaikovsky is quite literally setting the stage for the meeting with Nina, as he carefully arranges flowers and checks over every detail. The fragility of such a position is illustrated by the untimely arrival of Chiluvsky--"News of this remarkable coincidence between life and art has traveled"--who neatly sums up the sheer artifice of the situation by bringing in a dose of reality. The effect of his bearing, his manner, and his words ("Not all women are satisfied with a spiritual relationship") is not unlike the experience of rehearsing a difficult conversation with one's self, only to have the other person say the wrong thing after the first remark during the actual encounter. Tchaikovsky's delicate fantasy crumbles immediately, plunging him into gloomy despair, which Russell enlarges upon in a boldly theatrical move by having the set around him fade into darkness. It is through this darkness that Tchaikovsky first sees Nina. Only it is not the real Nina whom he sees, but rather his own projection of what she will be. As she enters calling "Cooee," in the same way she did with the Lieutenant, Tchaikovsky turns to see her and she transforms from her rather drab self into the vision she has of herself (her clothing and hair are the same as in her fantasy), which is the vision that Tchaikovsky is expecting and wants to accept. Reality only intrudes when he speaks her name and the vision drops, revealing an insecure woman in the place of the glamorous beauty who crossed the room.

The marriage ceremony, set to the famous theme from the Fifth Symphony, is pictured as a satirical forecast of the future. The hopeful words on the soundtrack, from a letter explaining the situation to Madame von Meck, have less the effect of convincing her of the soundness of this move than of Tchaikovsky convincing himself. Further, the entire marriage ceremony is established as something of a mockery in its use of the same actor in the role of the priest who was previously seen in Nina's fantasy where she married the Lieutenant. The opening shot of the sequence, Christ pictured on the ceiling of the church, seems arbitrary at first, but when contrasted with the painting of the two lovers which hangs over Tchaikovsky and Nina's marital bed at the beginning of the next scene takes on the visual equivalent of Chiluvsky's phrase, "Not all women are satisfied with a spiritual relationship."

The honeymoon contains two splendid sequences. The first of these, in which Tchaikovsky takes Nina to an outdoor performance of Swan Lake, is particularly adroit, in some ways surpassing the more famous train carriage sequence. The scene brings a number of the points of the film together and serves to help humanize Tchaikovsky to some extent and make him considerably more likable. The very fact that, left to his own devices in choosing how the two of them might spend the day, he should decide to take in a performance of one of his own works is refreshingly confident. Beyond this, Tchaikovsky here demonstrates a bit more cleverness than heretofore in his outmaneuvering Chiluvsky, who happens to be at the performance and attempts to tag after the couple. It comes at just the right time in the film to prevent Tchaikovsky from becoming tiresome, as his ingenuousness and simplicity could very easily topple over into simplemindedness.

The sequence is also notable for equating Nina with Chiluvsky, partly through the simple device of dressing them in like colors--Nina in a red shawl and Chiluvsky in a red coat. Symbolically, this is yet another tie with Rouben Mamoulian, reversing, as it does, the action of a scene in Blood and Sand. In the Mamoulian film, Rita Hayworth plays a scene where she becomes, quite literally, a "scarlet woman" by dropping her shawl and revealing her red dress beneath it. In The Music Lovers this action is reversed. During the preceding scene, Nina's red shawl was casually draped over the back of her chair. In this scene she has pulled it on as if to indicate that she and Chiluvsky are romantic rivals.

Technically flawless, the scene is another example of Russell's instinctive feel for choreographed action, especially the cut from the action onstage to Chiluvsky taking his seat beside Nina. Characterization is likewise astutely handled. Our worst fears about Nina are confirmed when she gauchely offers, "My husband wrote this music, you know." Chiluvsky's explanation of the events onstage are an insightful reading of his own values onto the characters of the ballet--an interesting comparison of the realist's ability to turn art into a version of reality to suit his own ends, with the growing inability of the Romantic to achieve this end. Significantly,

Tchaikovsky is prompted to a brief realization of the actual situation by Chiluvsky's words. Whereas Chiluvsky is reading himself into the role of Prince Siegfried's real love, Tchaikovsky's mind glimpses beyond this into something even more real and terrifying as he fancies he sees Sasha dancing the part of the Prince's true love. Visually, this simply restates and magnifies Tchaikovsky's statement to Sasha about the aria, "What a pity you can't sing on the stage. It's you I think of when I write." On a broader level, it is one of the few times when Tchaikovsky perceives the reality of his life, and acknowledges the sort of love he has for his sister.

The second sequence of particular merit in this section of The Music Lovers, the train carriage sequence, is one of Russell's most controversial, and the most discussed in Russell's entire filmography. Detractors will go on at great length about Russell's overstatement in this scene. Supporters will counter with statements about the scene's technical virtuosity and power. On a purely technical level the scene is of particular interest for the way in which it was created. The fact that the entire scene is made up of the image coupled to the music makes it natural to assume that it was carefully structured to this music, though such is not the case. The sequence was actually filmed to a playback of a Shostakovich work, but the final soundtrack is a mixture of Tchaikovsky's Sixth and the Manfred Symphony. The Shostakovich piece was used only to establish a visual rhythm for the scene. An examination of the relation of the Tchaikovsky pastiche to the sequence clearly reveals the method behind this procedure. While the Shostakovich work provides the structure of the movement, the Tchaikovsky music is not applied so that it necessarily matches this rhythm, except for a few uses of musical exclamation points. Instead of blending in a perfect balance, the music and image grate against each other as was Russell's intention. This, as much as the claustrophobia of the camera angles, creates a unique sense of discomfort which becomes almost unbearable. To speak of this scene is one thing. To actually witness it is something else again. It is impossible to get used to the scene; impossible to become steeled against its power. True enough this is a far from traditional use of music in the Max Steiner Mickey-Moused manner, but it is a valid experiment in a new application. Emotionally and thematically the scene does much to contradict the idea that The Music Lovers is an attack on Tchaikovsky since the sequence places the viewer very much in the Tchaikovsky point of view. It is his horror we are experiencing, not Nina's.

The Breakthrough 99

The question remains, is the scene valid and accurate? Accurate to what extent, and valid to what? To The Music Lovers? To Beloved Friend? To Tchaikovsky in a completely historical sense? As concerns the scene's accuracy, it is only marginally accurate as a documented fact, built as it is from Tchaikovsky's description of the nightmarish train journey with Nina on their honeymoon. The core of the sequence has its origin in truth, but how to dramatize this nightmare? Moreover, how not only to detail the growing repulsion Tchaikovsky feels toward his wife, but to communicate that repulsion to the audience? Russell's sequence provides the answer, and in that respect can only be judged as valid not only to the film, but to Beloved Friend and to history.

The scenes which build up to the climax of the second act are more or less expository in nature, concerned primarily with detailing the disintegration of any sort of relationship between Nina and Tchaikovsky. Coming right after the train carriage scene these scenes are somewhat anticlimactic and the least effective in the film. Worse, they momentarily disrupt the flow of Russell's narrative. Even so they contain several nice touches, including a reinforcement of Nina's clumsiness when she breaks a bust of Beethoven while dancing around the room. Skillful as the construction and development of these scenes are in themselves, it is something of a relief when Chiluvsky shows up bearing gifts for Nina and her mother. The tone is humorous as Nina's mother makes faces in a mirror trying on hats and Chiluvsky offers his pronouncement that a hideous feathered hat is "more dignified" than an equally attrocious fruit and flower one. This lightness of tone is not only enjoyable in itself, but sets the audience up by not preparing them for the powerful emotions which will quickly follow.

Tchaikovsky's reaction to Chiluvsky's invitation to the opera is a foregone conclusion. What is not foreseen is Tchaikovsky's single most cruel use of Nina, as he tenderly lays his hand on her shoulder, not from any emotional response, but merely to point out his status as a married man to Chiluvsky. The pathetic look of hope that creeps into Nina's face when he does this is one of the most heart-breaking moments in the film.

That hope is short lived, for once Chiluvsky and Nina's mother depart for the opera (mother proving worthy of daughter with the line, "I've never seen opera. Well, not grand

opera") Tchaikovsky stages a scene in which he informs
Nina that their marriage has failed, "I can't change. I think
you know why." Russell's handling of the scene stresses the
theatricality of the situation. As Tchaikovsky makes his
speech to Nina he makes extensive use of props and bits of
stage business, giving the impression of an actor onstage.
Instead of his melodramatic presentation having the effect of
crushing Nina, his words only serve to infuriate and turn
her from a timid creature into a fury. When Tchaikovsky
goes too far by dramatically exclaiming that nothing lives in
him, Nina flies into a rage, screaming, smashing bric-a-
brac, and very nearly raping Tchaikovsky. Neither he nor
the audience are prepared for her outburst. It is the nightmare of the train carriage come to life, and, instead of facing the situation, Tchaikovsky retains his theatrical attitude
by pronouncing, "I might as well be dead" and running from
the room. Nina, huddled on the floor, can only withdraw
further into herself, rocking back and forth even more violently than before. Unlike Tchaikovsky, she cannot escape
into indulgent theatricals, nor into music, and must therefore drift into her growing insanity. Where Tchaikovsky has
been playing a scene that he has deluded himself into believing real, Nina is neither playing nor deluding herself.
This is her reality.

    Tchaikovsky's suicide attempt which shortly follows is
yet another bravura theatrical move on his part. Based on
fact--Tchaikovsky did wade into a cold river in the hope of
contracting pneumonia and dying of seemingly natural causes--
Russell uses Tchaikovsky's suicide attempt as an extension
of his theatricality rather than a desire to end it all. In
the film Tchaikovsky jumps into the river and the water barely covers his knees. It is a sublimely ridiculous moment.
Considering that it would be perfectly possible to drown in
this much water, and the fact that Tchaikovsky's every move
is done so as to avoid slipping and falling as he ostensibly
searches for a deeper spot, it becomes abundantly clear that
it is not the actual suicide that is important to him. The
important thing is the acting out of jumping into the river.
The results are purely marginal. Russell, however, refuses to let us hold onto the conclusion that the man is a fool
by the simple addition of a spectator. The sudden appearance
of the woman in white walking a dog (calling to mind the Russian film The Lady with the Little Dog) increases the humor
of the situation, while, at the same time, placing the viewer
in a position where it is difficult not to empathize with Tchaikovsky's embarrassment.

The Breakthrough   101

Tchaikovsky's subsequent return home and his attempted
strangulation of Nina is fully as tense as the previous scene
had been absurd. Not because of the violent murder attempt,
since it is no more sincere than the suicide. The scene's
tension comes from the rapidity with which Tchaikovsky's
theatrical gestures and scenes are coming. Nina has retreated into her own mind by this point in the narrative, and
Tchaikovsky is beginning to handle every situation as if it
were on stage. With his response to any given situation becoming more and more fantastic and theatrical, Tchaikovsky
is coming perilously close to losing what little grasp he has
on reality and drifting into a complete fantasy like Nina.

It is during these scenes of the disintegration of the
Tchaikovsky marriage that Russell makes some of his best
and most far-reaching, as well as uncomfortable, observations on human nature. These are not achieved through the
melodramatic play-acting of Tchaikovsky, nor through Nina's
mental collapse, but through two brief scenes with Madame
von Meck. As she listens to her son read a letter from
Tchaikovsky on the horrors of his marriage, in the first of
these scenes, she clucks solicitously and mutters, "Poor boy,
he's martyrizing himself." Seconds later she is on her feet
proclaiming that she feels, "better than I have done for days."
The natural inference to be drawn here is, of course, that
she feels better because the marriage which distances Tchaikovsky from her is failing. In essence she is reveling in
Tchaikovsky's misery, enjoying his suffering. Before any
hasty condemnation is made of Madame von Meck on this
basis, it is necessary to consider how guilty of this same
feeling is the spectator. The viewer of the film is certainly
guilty of this, as is any "music lover" who has ever enjoyed
one of Tchaikovsky's tortured, autobiographical compositions.
Admittedly there is some considerable difference between our
situation and that of Madame von Meck, but the overall feeling of deriving enjoyment through someone else's misery is
there nonetheless.

In the scene that climaxes the second act of The Music Lovers--a scene which, by its very tone is a sweet natured parody of countless similar scenes in countless biopics
of the past--Madame von Meck appears to be all kindness and
benevolence. Upon being told of Tchaikovsky's fragile mental
state and his need for rest, she offers to let him stay at the
"small lodge" near her house at Brailov. (Historically this
is slightly specious as she actually lent Tchaikovsky the house,
not the fictional small lodge, but here Russell and Bragg have

merely telescoped the Brailov interlude with an arrangement the two shared in Italy.) Closer examination of Madame von Meck's kindness will reveal that it is of a very self-serving variety. She is placing Tchaikovsky even further in her debt than before, and at the same time cleverly removing him from society, and temptations like Nina. No situation could be more felicitous from the widow von Meck's point of view. She has Peter Ilich Tchaikovsky just where she wants him--completely to herself and on her terms.

The third act of The Music Lovers opens as Tchaikovsky and Modeste and Alexei arrive at the small lodge. Right away the tone of the act is set. A broad sweeping backward zoom perfectly complementing the excerpt from The Sleeping Beauty on the soundtrack as their carriage drives up to the lodge, establishes the third act as the brightest, best-humored section of the film. The act itself supports this attitude. It is a beautifully conceived resting point between the horrors of the first two acts and those yet to come in the fourth. Interestingly, it does not, however, appear out of place with the rest of the film, nor does it cause the pace to falter as had the dialogue scenes toward the end of act two. Russell has kept this under control here by constantly reminding the viewer that this idyll is far removed from the real world. For while Tchaikovsky, through his natural gifts and through privilege, improves in this make-believe existence, Nina, who is devoid of either gift or privilege, is growing steadily worse.

The Romantic images which grace this section of The Music Lovers are among the most beautiful ever filmed, and Russell is well aware of this. He wants them to be powerful and heart-stopping, but he wishes the viewer to never lost sight of the fact that this is an unattainable dream, a beautiful falsehood, the misery and horror that lie just beneath the surface of the seemingly attractive. Much like Eddie Jessup in the later Altered States, we find something dreadful if we go deep enough. This theme has already been expressed by dialogue earlier in the film when Chiluvsky explains the ballet, "He thinks she's the pure Swan Woman of his dreams, but she's a cheat. She'll destroy him. You'll see it happen in a few minutes," and, in fact, only echoes Rupert Birkin in Women in Love, "No, it's the lie that kills." Here, though, film being what it is, and Russell being who he is, the message is brought to bear more forcefully than any amount of dialogue might do.

The Breakthrough

It is this section of the film which contains the scenes referred to at the beginning of this chapter. The first of these scenes, in which Tchaikovsky and Madame von Meck see each other as her coach passes him on the road, is of particular interest as it tells us much about Russell the film-maker and his ambiguity toward Romanticism.

Again it is an incident based in fact, and once more the fact is merely a starting point. In reality Madame von Meck and Tchaikovsky passed each other in open carriages during the sojourn in Italy, unlike the film where it is only Madame von Meck who is riding. The real life situation was neither as kind to the protagonists, nor as electrifying, for Madame von Meck had two flaws which prevented the scene as envisioned by Russell from taking place--nearsightedness and vanity. The first of these would have necessitated glasses and the second ruled out the glasses. They did pass each other, but Madame von Meck had no idea who was in the other carriage. If, as is often contended, Russell's sole intent was to make Tchaikovsky and Madame von Meck into buffoons, the reality would have served him far better, especially as concerns the terror and dread which Tchaikovsky suffered over the encounter. Not knowing that she had not recognized him, he feared that this mutual sighting might make a difference in their relationship. Instead, Russell wishes the viewer to experience the strong rush of emotion that such a meeting might have provoked. His method of presentation is consistent with the earlier scene where Madame von Meck perched on the balcony above Tchaikovsky at the concert (and will subsequently be consistent with her position at the birthday celebration). By placing Tchaikovsky on foot and Madame von Meck in the carriage, Russell effectively distances them in terms of position. As her coach passes they both become transfixed, staring at each other, unmoving, except for the necessary turning to keep the other person in view as long as possible. Russell has photographed and edited the sequence in such a manner as to present the sighting in a symbolic way. Not only does the coach in which she is riding cause their views of each other to slowly increase in distance, but trees between them momentarily block the line of vision every so often, thereby placing a natural barrier between them.

The second scene in this part of the film to present such a boldly Romantic and dramatic viewpoint is, in many respects, even better. The presentation of the Fourth Symphony to Madame von Meck is, on the surface, a relatively simple scene. Certainly it lacks swirl of motion and the dynamic editing pattern of their meeting on the road, but it still achieves a similar level of emotion by virtue of its remarkable restraint and the judicious application of the music. This is one of those intensely quiet scenes which Russell's major detractors like to pretend do not exist within the body of his work.

Quite simply, the scene consists of Tchaikovsky delivering the newly completed Fourth Symphony to Madame von Meck. What dialogue there is amounts to no more than a muffled exchange between Tchaikovsky and the footman to whom he gives the manuscript. Otherwise the soundtrack consists of a combination of Tchaikovsky's letter narration and a particularly magnificent passage from the second movement of the Fourth Symphony. Visually, the sequence is designed to present the relationship of the two in a bittersweet manner, suggesting the impossibility of any true relation between Tchaikovsky and Madame von Meck. Tchaikovsky is presented in the cool blueness of the night, whereas the von Meck home is glowing with warm light. This light only falls on Tchaikovsky at two points in the scene: the first when the servant opens the door to receive the symphony, and the second when Tchaikovsky watches Madame von Meck accept the gift from the servant. In the first instance, Tchaikovsky is immediately plunged back into darkness as the door is closed. In the second, he is separated from her world by the window through which he watches. Russell's slightly satirical pan from a decorative painting of two lovers to Tchaikovsky at the window only emphasizes the unreality of the relationship with Madame von Meck.

These two scenes, however, are actually building up to the first of two major set pieces which occur in the third act. At the core of this section of the film--indeed of the film as a whole--we find the sequence in which Tchaikovsky visits Madame von Meck's house while she is away, so that she may return and feel his presence. Thus far The Music Lovers has been made up of two isolated modes of thought, which are seemingly contradictory: the first two sections of the film dealing with the destructiveness of Romanticism, and the early portions of the third section detailing the fragile beauty of Romanticism. It is left to this one key sequence to bring these divergent points of view together. This Russell accomplishes by creating a scene in which both points of view mingle and blend to become one. In this manner Russell poses his central problem for the viewer. Is it possible

The Breakthrough

to reconcile these differences between the beauty and the horror? Can the beauty justify the horror?

The sequence itself, inspired in part it would seem by the famous bedroom stroking scene in Rouben Mamoulian's Queen Christina, is again simple. Tchaikovsky comes to the house, eats, gets slightly drunk, and passes out in one of the bedrooms. Madame von Meck returns, runs her hand along the chair in which Tchaikovsky was sitting, touches the things he used, carresses a half-eaten peach with her lips, and, finally, lies next to Tchaikovsky on the bed. The similarities to the Mamoulian film are obvious, but in calling them to mind, it is necessary to note that the earlier film is only a springboard for the sequence, especially as concerns Russell's intent. Whereas Mamoulian wants us to sympathize with Christina, Russell wants us to empathize, almost against our will, with Madame von Meck. Christina's actions in the Mamoulian work are graceful and very delicate (Mamoulian choreographed the scene with a metronome), where Madame von Meck's are almost a grotesque parody in The Music Lovers. (At her most intensely personal moment, when she tastes the peach, she is interrupted by her sons.) In Queen Christina we are moved because Christina is such a sadly beautiful figure, suffering from an actual impending loss. In The Music Lovers we are moved for quite different reasons. It is possible to identify with Madame von Meck, but Christina is too otherworldly for any such transgression. Also, Madame von Meck is creating a situation out of whole cloth. Not only has she not lost Tchaikovsky, but she has never really known him in the first place, only her own projection of him. This does not keep the viewer from experiencing the powerful emotions of the scene, but neither does it allow us to forget the underlying sickness of the entire situation.

Then, too, there is the question of Russell's selection of the "Love Theme" from Romeo and Juliet to accompany the scene. Intrinsically there is nothing wrong with this piece of music. On its own merits, as Russell deftly demonstrates on several occasions in the scene, it is a perfectly acceptable composition. Unfortunately it is also a work which we are no longer able to judge on its own merits. Having been subjected to the various uses, misuses and abuses that the "Love Theme" has suffered at the hands of filmmakers since sound began (even The Jazz Singer utilizes the piece in its music for the non-dialogue sections of the film), it is a composition that can no longer be taken quite seriously. In fact it has frequently been used for comic ef-

fect, even in Russell's own Valentino. In The Music Lovers this very over-familiarity is used to advantage, as it renders the scene slightly ridiculous--an effect enhanced by the (once again) Mamoulian influenced use of commentary paintings which are intercut throughout the scene. Beyond this, the tone is such that on the occasions where Russell chooses to play it completely straight, creating images of such power that the music transcends the joke nature to which it has descended, we are even less prepared for this effect than we might otherwise have been were a less familiar piece of music used.

The beauty of this scene in particular is likewise tarnished by the intercut shots of Nina and her lover (a man whom her mother, who as Nina's protector and procurer-- especially in consideration of Chiluvsky's present to her of a feathered hat not unlike Madame von Meck's at the concert--is to Nina something like Madame von Meck is to Tchaikovsky in helping feed her fantasy while benefiting from it, has palmed off on her as Rimsky-Korsakov). The placement of these shots within the portion of the overall scene where Madame von Meck lies next to Tchaikovsky, barely daring to touch his hand, produces the effect of not only contrasting the very sedate von Meck-Tchaikovsky fantasy relationship with the gritty, near hysterical one between Nina and "Rimsky-Korsakov," but also of reminding the audience of the price Nina is paying so that Tchaikovsky can indulge in his safe relationship. For Tchaikovsky, the sequence ends with Madame von Meck's twins carrying him outside under a tree by a stream, literally unconscious to the sufferings of Nina back in Moscow, laughing maniacally as she descends further into madness.

The third act of The Music Lovers ends in a manner that foreshadows the great multiple climaxes we find in the mature Russell films (Tommy, Lisztomania, and Altered States in particular). In this instance Russell has positioned his two climaxes so that they occur just prior to the film's final act. Though the reasoning behind this placement may not be readily apparent, it does serve a thematic and structural function in that the film's fourth act is almost completely divorced from the first three, if only because a majority of the characters are disposed of for this final act.

[Opposite:] Dancers cavorting in the fireworks display during Madame von Meck's birthday celebration for Tchaikovsky in The Music Lovers. (Courtesy of Ken Russell)

The first section of Russell's double climax is the birthday celebration, a wonderfully complex and lovely scene which works on a number of levels at once. The scene works as a plot device, as a blast of reality into the fantasy world of both Tchaikovsky and Madame von Meck, and as an interesting contrapuntal commentary on Tchaikovsky's music. The least interesting of these aspects, the plot device, is only of importance in that it serves to move the film toward its inevitable conclusion and to force Tchaikovsky out of his fantasy world.

The necessity of coming face to face with reality for both Madame von Meck and Tchaikovsky comes from the reappearance of the film's primary catalyst, Chiluvsky. As his appearance just prior to Tchaikovsky's meeting with Nina served to push Tchaikovsky even more toward accepting Nina on her own word and his own hopes, and his appearance at the already strained Tchaikovsky household helped bring about the Tchaikovsky breakdown, so his appearance here serves to bring about the dissolution of the Tchaikovsky-von Meck relationship, and, more importantly, the fantasy of that relationship. Chiluvsky's role in this instance has often been cited, half-correctly, as Mephistophelean. This is true in so far as it goes, though it is rather like trying to affix the guilt for the crucifixion of Christ on one group or another, when it was a preordained situation in the first place. Russell's use of the "Fate Theme" from the Fourth Symphony says as much. If Chiluvsky must be read as a purely symbolic character, then he needs to be viewed as destiny, not the devil.

First he accosts Tchaikovsky, telling him, "I believe that our friendship is as important to you as it is to me." Chiluvsky's attitude here, along with Tchaikovsky's rebuttal in which he protests that he is "a married man--a respectable married man for all the world to see," is an almost exact recreation of the earlier scene where Chiluvsky urges Tchaikovsky to "accept what you are." Indeed it is quite a blast of reality, so much so that it is the first time in the Brailov sequence that Tchaikovsky has acknowledged the existence of Nina or his marriage. In telling Madame von Meck of Tchaikovsky's sexual predeliction, Chiluvsky effectively damages her fantasy image of the great composer. The scene between them is played without dialogue, because it does not matter what Chiluvsky is telling her. All that matters is that her fantasy has been touched by reality and therefore ruined.

The Breakthrough

Again, Russell proves that the music is not chosen arbitrarily. His utilization of the "March Miniature" from Tchaikovsky's First Orchestral Suite, which readily evokes the ultimate superficial fantasy that Madame von Meck has helped create for the composer, is a perfect counterpart to the injections of the "Fate Theme" that accompanies Count Chiluvsky. The "Fate Theme" rises on the track and veritably overpowers the "March Miniature," or on another level, reality overpowers fantasy. In this respect Russell is similarly making a statement on the music itself. The ability of the more serious composition to overcome the frivolous one is implicitly Russell's most positive assessment of Tchaikovsky's art. Accordingly it is possible to assume that Russell feels that Tchaikovsky was indeed a great composer, when he dealt head-on with the reality of his life, and that these great works overshadow the mediocrity of his trivial and/or commissioned works. Even so Russell holds some reservations about this ability. Just as the greatness of Tchaikovsky's best work cannot totally purge the shortcomings of Tchaikovsky the man, neither can the serious work completely overtake the more trivial. It is always there, undermining the greatness that might have been. The "Fate Theme" never obliterates the little march, which persists just beneath the surface, and even remains after the theme stops.

At the conclusion of the birthday party we know more about the problem caused by Chiluvsky than does Tchaikovsky. He will not, in fact, learn of the dissolution of his union with Madame von Meck until the act's second and final climax. He still exists in the fantasy world of Brailov. How firmly he has become entrenched in this dream is demonstrated by his attitude in the conversation with Sasha which bridges the birthday celebration with the final scene of the act. Sasha has called him home to discuss his responsibilities to the abandoned Nina. For her pains she is accused of having "dragged me down here to talk about Nina" and told the "truth" of the situation--namely, that he cannot possibly go back to Nina. Tchaikovsky concludes by remarking that his "truth doesn't seem to interest you anymore," thereby effectively distancing the person once closest to him. Tchaikovsky's attitude, born of the idealized life of the Brailov dream, also helps to increase the effectiveness of the act's final scene, where he will learn the truth about that dream.

The final scene then entails Tchaikovsky's return to the dream, only to find it destroyed by reality, cut-off to him forever. Russell again creates a sequence with which the viewer can empathize and not sympathize. As the house is barred to him and he stands amid the burning wheat fields (recalling the wheat fields in the idyllic fantasy of the Piano Concerto) we cannot help but share Tchaikovsky's heartbreak. Nonetheless we cannot also help but realize that this heartbreak has little, if anything, to do with the loss of Madame von Meck. Instead Tchaikovsky is a man crying out against the death of a dream, not wanting to have to return to the world and face any sort of reality. We can feel the loss and the hurt, but we also know the pain is far from admirable. So, as Modeste leads Tchaikovsky away past the burning wheat, Russell underscores the artifice of Tchaikovsky's emotions by bringing the "Love Theme" from Romeo and Juliet back up on the track, and the third act concludes.

The final act of The Music Lovers begins without a break in the continuity, unlike the preceding acts, removed from the third act only by the finality of the walk across the burning field, and the difference in tone which is immediately apparent. The ever realistic Modeste is quickly picking up the pieces of his brother's life for him and reassembling them to suit himself as he urges Tchaikovsky to put the past

Tchaikovsky learns that his "beloved friend," Madame von Meck, never wishes to see him again in The Music Lovers. (United Artists)

The Breakthrough

Tchaikovsky conducts while his brother, Modeste, manages things in this scene from the 1812 Fantasy in The Music Lovers. (United Artists)

behind him and take up conducting his own works. Already disassociated from Sasha and Madame von Meck, Tchaikovsky is shown how he needs no one but Modeste. In Modeste's words, "We don't need anyone ... it's all set, like a bonfire, it just needs the final touch and whoosh!"

A blast from a cannon introduces that very controversial Russell scene, the 1812 Overture fantasy, certainly the most outrageous of all Russell creations up to this point. As Jack Fisher notes in his dissertation on The Music Lovers, the scene must indeed be a shock "to anyone who is expecting José Iturbi to appear in this part of the movie and play 'Tonight We Love.'"[4] Shock or not, it is a terribly proficient bit of filmmaking, surprisingly economical and apt, in consideration of the vast amount of time and incident compressed into its relatively short screen time. Basically the sequence depicts Tchaikovsky's emergence into the real world and his subsequent destruction of the forces of fantasy (with Modeste's assistance). "The Music Lovers"--Madame von

Meck, Sasha, Alexei, Chiluvsky, even Modeste's deaf and dumb pupil, Koyola, are unceremoniously "executed" by blasts from Modeste's cannon. (In all fairness it should be noticed that this does not occur until after they have attempted to do the same to Tchaikovsky.) Modeste's dispelling of these ghosts, however, has its price in two respects. It necessitates a certain amount of selling-out to commercialism on the part of Tchaikovsky (hence the musically specious, but phenomenally popular 1812 Overture). Beyond that Modeste cannot get rid of Nina, and his attempt to do so only causes her to become more prominent. It is as if by exorcising the other phantoms Modeste has only increased the presence of the worst of them all. In the end, Tchaikovsky is turned into a grey statue, frozen into position as a conductor--a position that has nothing to do with Tchaikovsky's dreams, and even less to do with reality. With Modeste's help Tchaikovsky has become a prisoner of his own myth, the kindly old "Uncle Petia" of Catherine Drinker Bowen's madly purple prose in the narrative sections of Beloved Friend.

The remainder of The Music Lovers, largely structured to the fourth movement of the Sixth Symphony, deals with the similarities of the fates of Tchaikovsky and Nina. In a series of parallel scenes Russell analyzes these fates, playing one against the other.

As Tchaikovsky notes that with the death of Sasha he is alone, "of all those alive then, there was only her left," Modeste sarcastically reminds him of Nina. Immediately Russell plunges the viewer into Nina's situation at the madhouse. The setting is sombre and grey (recalling the symbolic prison of the Tchaikovsky statue), and the tone is that of a glimpse into hell. Nina's rocking motion has progressed to such a state that she now pops in and out frame during her conversation with her mother. Still, Nina holds onto the fantasy that Tchaikovsky loves her, and pathetically she is still trying to make him jealous by proclaiming, "I have so many lovers ... so many ... so many ... so many." Russell is unflinching in showing the depths to which Nina has been allowed to sink. This is the main point that Russell is here stressing--that Nina has been allowed to reach these depths. "Her mother says she's very well looked after," Tchaikovsky tells Modeste, "God knows I send them enough money." Accepting Nina's mother's word for anything seems dubious at best, but even at that Tchaikovsky is not viewing her as a person at all. Nina has become an item on an expense account. If he will only "send them enough money,"

The Breakthrough

he won't have to deal with her at all. For that matter he has further reduced Nina to a Romanticist notion, which is the only other level on which he can relate to her. In his argument with Modeste as to why the Sixth Symphony should be called "The Tragic," Tchaikovsky says, "Of course, it's tragic. Look at me ... think of her." By relegating Nina to this symbolic position as an embodiment of Tragedy, Tchaikovsky has removed her (and himself) from any existence as a person. Modeste is correct in his assertion that the symphony should be called "'The Pathetic,' if it really is all about you. That's so much more fitting than 'Tragic,'" because Tchaikovsky is pathetic. Not in the sense of his transgressions against those around him, but in his complete inability at any stage of the film to perceive truth. Even at this late date Tchaikovsky is out of touch with reality.

The very last scenes in The Music Lovers, which follow the naming of the symphony, interrelate so delicately that it is almost impossible to separate them. Russell's finish is designed so as to create a dramatic tension between the events transpiring with Tchaikovsky on the one hand and Nina on the other, and also to tie the entire structure of the film into a cohesive whole.

"See how many lovers I have." Nina in the madhouse in The Music Lovers. (United Artists)

Tchaikovsky accepts Modeste's suggestion of calling the symphony "the 'Pathetic,'" and drinks the glass of cholera-tainted water that will kill him. Russell's decision to depict Tchaikovsky's actions as deliberate suicide does not come from a universally accepted fact, but neither is it unique to The Music Lovers. It is, however, essential to The Music Lovers. Taking the film as an entity, the suicide is the Romantic glorification of death, as well as the final grand theatrical gesture of a man who has been living his entire life as if it were a play. This theatrical aspect of his gesture is stressed by Russell's filming the shot where Tchaikovsky reaches for the glass in a manner that is reminiscent of Madame von Meck's reaching for Tchaikovsky's hand in the earlier scene. The sequence also carries overtones of the film's first fantasy where Tchaikovsky took the lemonade from Sasha in the wheat field and downed it with rather absurd overstatement. In this instance the overstatement is not absurd. It is sad, and once again, pathetic. It is as if by drinking the contaminated water Tchaikovsky can somehow recapture his innocence of that earlier time--or at any rate his dream of innocence.

There follows a brief sequence where Nina wanders about the exercise yard in the insane asylum. As she walks about aimlessly, she continually mutters, "I'm Madame Tchaikovsky from Moscow. My husband he really did love me." Suddenly the harsh light of reality falls upon her as she begins shrieking, "No he didn't. He hated me! He hated me!" Reality has penetrated the world she has created in her own mind and the shock is too much for her. Her mental disintegration is so complete that she has to be restrained by the attendants. As they place her in a straitjacket and drag her off to her cell, her feet trail along the ground in the same manner as Tchaikovsky's mother's feet in the childhood fantasy sequence. This is not to link Nina with Tchaikovsky's mother as such, but to reinforce the fact that Nina has now absolutely lost control over her own destiny. The guards strap her down to the bed, much as the attendants had plunged that earlier Madame Tchaikovsky into the hot bath. A case could be made that the hot bath treatment and Nina's treatment in the asylum are roughly similar in the total lack of effectiveness, even destructiveness, of both; however, Russell is not particularly inclined to this sort of social comment. Therefore a more tenable analysis of the paralleling of events rests on the actual end product of the treatment--physical death for Madame Tchaikovsky, and the terrible living death to which Nina is subjected. Of all the characters in The

Music Lovers who live off dreams, Nina is the only one who, through circumstances, has to ultimately come face to face with stark reality. Ironically, Nina is also the one character least equipped to deal with it.

While this is happening to Nina, the cholera germs of the contaminated water are having their effect on Tchaikovsky. As Modeste and the doctor are preparing to subject Tchaikovsky to the "hot water treatment," Tchaikovsky, even in his delirium, is unable or unwilling to let go of the dream, still insisting, "I tried to love her. Nobody would help me then. Nobody." In one respect he is correct in his ravings when he states that at least Nina had cared for him (if only as her famous composer husband) since Modeste, typically, is more concerned that the doctor keep quite about the suicidal aspects of the case, "It wouldn't do if it were known. It would upset people," than he is about his brother's impending death. This, too, is remarkably consistent. Modeste is every bit as unshakable in his allegiance to the real world and the keeping up of appearances as Tchaikovsky is in his Romanticism.

Tchaikovsky is dragged off to the treatment just as his mother and Nina were dragged off, and then plunged into the scalding water, which triggers a dying flash of memories --his mother's death, his fantasy of Sasha dancing Swan Lake, the idealized Nina, Chiluvsky at the birthday celebration, etc. This is of particular interest on two levels. First, because of the mixes of actual events and fantasies, which illustrate that even at the moment of his death, Tchaikovsky is still dodging reality. Second, the sequence is of great interest because it is the only instance of Russell actually attempting to depict the "dying flash," that moment at death where an entire lifetime passes before one's eyes in a matter of seconds--a notion which is at the very center of Russell's approach to story-telling in general, and biography in particular. It is Russell's contention that his films attempt to create something of this same effect in encompassing a person's life in two hours or less of screen time. In effect what he is doing here is depicting the dying flash of a dying flash-- a distillation of the entire film. Remarkably this distillation, far from being a bit of self-justification, captures much of the feeling of what has gone before, so judicious is the selection of scenes included, and so finely integrated are they into the fabric of the film. Nonetheless, it is the closest Russell has ever come to injecting an effect into a film purely for its own sake, and it is just as well he has never attempted a literal depiction of the dying flash again.

One simple, heart-breaking shot remains. It is the image of Nina, who lives on in the asylum, peering out from the bars of her cell. Just as Modeste could not dispose of her in the 1812 fantasy, neither can Tchaikovsky's death have any power over her. She lingers on, her face horribly expressionless, shut off from the world which she has never understood. For Russell she is the specter that blights Tchaikovsky's music, eternally preventing it from absolution on its own merits as an abstract art form. Silently, she, and Russell, restate the film's central question: Can anything, no matter how wondrous or beautiful it might be in itself, justify this kind of suffering?

In the final analysis The Music Lovers can only be viewed as Russell's most horrifying view of life, black and terrible. The Music Lovers represents the abyss, and it is from this point that Russell starts his journey toward a more positive outlook. Considered as such, it is something of a prologue to the films that follow. It is not an entirely successful work. Some of the images in it seem left over from Women in Love, and the film is a bit overlong. Occasionally, as in the dialogue scenes following the train carriage sequence, it can even be somewhat tedious. There is no denying, however, that for the most part The Music Lovers is a remarkable film, far exceeding Women in Love and Russell's earlier works. Its complexities extend far beyond the boundaries of those films, and, indeed, of most films. Already the concern for achieving a spiritual rightness--a reality not dependent on conventional realism--is evident. Russell's utter lack of concern over believable looking effects (e.g., the offhand acceptance of the headless dummies splashed with red paint for the corpses in the 1812 fantasy) has fully emerged. At the age of forty-three Russell finally arrived as a master of filmmaking on the big screen--the first real breath of fresh cinematic air since the great innovators of the early sound era.

Unfortunately neither Russell nor The Music Lovers were readily comprehensible to the bulk of the critical population, though the damnation of both man and film was considerably less universal than is generally supposed. Alas, even a number of critics who had liked the film had not completely understood it, much less Russell's intent. Just how completely off the mark much of this criticism had been became far more apparent upon the release of Russell's next feature, a film many consider to be his masterpiece, The Devils.

NOTES

1. Higham, Charles, and Greenberg, Joel. *The Celluloid Muse*. Chicago: Henry Regnery, 1969, p. 143.
2. Phillips, Gene D. *Ken Russell*. Boston: Twayne, 1979, p. 93.
3. Kael, Pauline. Review of *Lisztomania*. *New Yorker*, 51 (November 24, 1975): 171-172.
4. Fisher, Jack. "Three Paintings of Sex: the Films of Ken Russell," *Film Journal*, 2 (September 1972): 32-43.

CHAPTER 7

FINDING A VOICE:

"The Devils," The Boy Friend," and "Savage Messiah"

Ken Russell's film adaptation of Aldous Huxley's The Devils of Loudun and Charles Whiting's play The Devils occupies the unique position in his filmography of being the most highly praised and the most hotly denounced of all his work. At the time of its release the film was almost universally damned as "outrageous," "overheated," "pornographic," and Judith Crist went so far as to call it "a grand fiesta for sadists and perverts."[1] Since that time, however, the film has come more and more to be recognized in many quarters as a genuine work of art--a belief that finds its apothesis in Joseph Gomez's book on Russell's work. The former school of thought, although still very much with us, has tended to cool down somewhat as admiration for the film has steadily grown. There is an inherent danger in either viewpoint, though, for The Devils is neither the pornographic monster it has been painted as, nor is it the "major achievement" of its creator. (This last, however, is to a large extent a subjective judgment.)

In some ways the film's major supporters are over-reacting to the harsh judgment meted out by those who did not understand the film or Russell's intentions in making it. The general run of the criticism at the time of its release dealt with the work's so-called lack of balance, and the fact that unlike The Music Lovers, The Devils did not alternate its horrific moments with "beautiful" ones. Not only does this illustrate a failure to grasp The Devils, but it also indicates to what extent The Music Lovers had been misunderstood. Considering the two films side by side The Music Lovers is by far the bleaker of the two. Where it is hopeless, The Devils is hopeful; where it is about a man's limitations, The Devils is about transcending those limitations. In The Music Lovers Tchaikovsky is a pathetic figure. In The

Devils Urbain Grandier is elevated to the level of the truly tragic.

Apart from the danger of overreacting in dealing with The Devils, the film's supporters tend to view it as if it were uncompromised, and this, sadly, is not the case. There are two major thematic parts to The Devils. The first and more important of these themes is the aforementioned transcendence of limitations as personified by the case of Urbain Grandier, and this emerges intact and brilliantly accomplished. The film's secondary theme--that of the perversion and misuse of religion--is somewhat less successful due to the interference of the studio and the censor. In Russell's original cut of the film this was to climax in a symbolic scene referred to as "The Rape of Christ," but the scene proved too strong and was removed prior to the film's release. As it stands now the theme is not fully developed, and the scene which was to have carefully led up to the "Rape" appears anticlimactic. Beyond this the scene which follows--carefully designed as counterpoint to the full hysteria of the "Rape"--is awkwardly introduced and no longer works on the same contrapuntal level. This brings up the question of whether a film can or should be judged by intent rather than result. It is all very well to excuse the fact that the film has been tampered with, and that Russell is not to blame, but this does not alter the fact that The Devils never appeared in its uncompromised form. In the end what we are left with is the film as it finally emerged. We may regret that this falls short of its potential because of abuse at the hands of others, but it is difficult to reach a valid conclusion by judging the film as if this had not happened.

Equally troublesome as concerns Joseph Gomez's dissertation on The Devils is the careful delineation of the film's sources. For Gomez the film is at its best when a direct parallel can be found between it and those sources. Hence he is skeptical of the film's purely Russellian inventions to a degree that does a disservice to the film as a whole. It was not Russell's desire or intention to mirror either Huxley's book or Charles Whiting's play in the strict sense of traditional notions of adaptation. That Russell, Huxley, and Whiting are all working within a history as allegory format and are all reaching similar, albeit not identical, conclusions is interesting, but little more. The very idea of creating allegory applicable to the time of the work's creation precludes any possibility of achieving a universal viewpoint when Whiting's play is separated from Huxley's book by nearly ten years, and Russell's film removed by another ten. Russell's concept of The Devils is as a film of and for its time, not of Huxley's time. Many of the concerns of 1952 are not interchangeable with the concerns of 1970. When these concerns are inappropriate Russell takes full liberty in departing from them in creating an allegory more applicable to the time of the film's creation, e.g., the radical hippie styled Father Barré. Gomez's objections to Russell's interpretation of Father Barré seem to be borne of the gap between this interpretation and that of Huxley--scarcely a valid criterion if we assume The Devils as a film to be a separate work of art. Huxley's reading of the events of 1634 is conceived to have a direct relevance with its time frame. Russell's approach to the material is designed for the audience of 1970--an audience so jaded by constant overexposure to the horrors around them via the evening news that they have to be jolted out of their complacency; to be made aware that something is amiss within themselves when dinner is served to the accompaniment of a news broadcast of war, murder, and torture (complete with graphic visuals) and no one is put off their food, or even thinks anything of it. This is far more central to Russell's film than is the relationship of Huxley and Whiting. It is the factor that made The Devils such a modern work in 1970, and, as we have become, if anything, more jaded and complacent in the intervening years, just as modern today.

Unfortunately, the reasoning behind Russell's shock-effect allegory was generally not understood at the time of its release. (It should be noted that Russell was not alone in his concern about the effect of real horrors on the minds and attitudes of the television audiences. Joseph McGrath's only partially successful film The Magic Christian, released the previous year, shared many of these same concerns, and even included a scene in which a character complaining of "all this violence" following an ugly incident at a dog show is relieved by switching over to footage of riots and the infamous street execution in Viet Nam.) One of the very few areas in which Russell's intention was perceived was--oddly and appropriately enough--the Catholic Film Office, where, despite their condemnation of the film's excesses, a major reservation was that Russell's stylized horror was no match for the real horror to which it was supposed to be analogous.

Indeed it is difficult for anyone who has seen the film more than once to completely grasp the abuse that was heaped upon it. Russell uses his shock effects rather sparingly throughout the film, as a visual punctuation to rouse the audience into feeling something. For the most part The Devils relies on the audience to supply the more graphic details. Even the hotly debated clyster (enema) scenes are done largely through suggestion. Sister Jeanne's initial examination by the surgeon and the chemist is singularly horrifying though it consists of nothing more than a woman behind a screen screaming, followed by the reappearance of her examiners with a smattering of theatrical blood smeared on their hands. Just what happened behind that screen can only be supplied by the viewer, and since the viewer knows considerably more about his or her personal fears and terrors than does the filmmaker the scene is all the more effective. Curiously a large number of the film's detractors in their mad rush to catalogue Russell's excesses and horrors added scenes and images that just simply were not in the film in the first place, which may well be the single greatest tribute to Russell's success in communicating horror to the audience.

Russell begins his film with King Louis' rendition of Botticelli's "Birth of Venus"--a singularly bizarre drag act that sets the tone for much of the film. Not content to merely represent the sheer outrageousness of the scene, Russell builds this into a very important occurrence that establishes a norm for the film. Admittedly, it is a reality that does not exist per se outside the film, but in failing to grasp the events which open the film as being familiar and commonplace for that reality the viewer cannot hope to fathom the film as a whole. Russell's sense of satire is very much in evidence here. When Venus' shell rises from the cut-out waves it creaks and groans ominously, utterly destroying the illusion by showing it up as the tacky stage farce that it is. (Surely, it is not entirely coincidental that some of the intentionally tatty stage productions in The Boy Friend call this opening to mind.) At the same time the reactions of the audience are all-important, particularly that of Cardinal Richelieu, whose boredom and scarcely stifled yawns make it all too clear that, though this seems pretty strange to us, it is old stuff to him. For Richelieu the "Birth of Venus" only represents an avenue through which he can express his own desires to "assist" Louis in "the birth of a new France, in which Church and State are one." The final act in the pre-credit sequence--Richelieu crossing himself to the words, "And may the Protestant be driven from the land," indicating that this desire is on equal footing in his mind with the Holy Trinity--firmly establishes the film's concern with the perversion of religion.

Russell follows this scene with the first of his startling shock cuts, perfectly complemented by Peter Maxwell Davies' dissonant score, as he switches from Richelieu and Louis to a close-shot of a maggot-ridden skull. Beyond jolting the audience into a sense of awareness, this image symbolically links Louis and Richelieu with death. As the camera observes the rotting corpse from a greater distance which includes in the frame Richelieu's chief henchman, Baron de Laubardemont, he is also connected with death, as are the mysterious looking, bulky pieces of equipment he is having pulled toward a city--Loudun--on the horizon. The pieces of equipment, it turns out in due course, are machines for pulling down the city's protective walls, and Russell is quite correct in symbolically aligning these with death. Not only do the machines represent the death of Loudun as it exists at the beginning of the film, but, as we shall see, the death of Father Grandier since he is equated with those walls.

Russell is quick to establish the connection between Grandier and the walls of Loudun in the following scene,

Grandier argues for the preservation of Loudun's walls with Baron de Laubardemont while Rangier, Ibert, and Legrand look on in <u>The Devils</u>. (Warner Bros.)

where the priest is presiding over the funeral of the town's governor, Sainte-Marthe. The speech he makes quickly turns from eulogy to a political statement about the significance of the walls which allow the city to be "self-governing" --a fact of more than passing interest to Grandier as the death of Sainte-Marthe has left him acting governor, a position of power which a man of his pride and ego would certainly welcome. It is this pride and his difference as an individual that causes his downfall. Grandier is an independent man. Loudun is an independent city because of the unique feature of its walls. When Grandier refers to those walls as "still standing, proud and erect," the implication extends to include him as well. It is significant that when Grandier dies the walls will be torn down, and equally significant that his destruction must be brought about before this can happen. In a larger sense both must be destroyed because they do not conform.

The surface logic of Russell's narrative construction is impeccable as one scene leads gracefully into the next through a series of thematic, symbolic, or even geographical progressions, i.e., from Louis' court to the skull to Laubardemont on the way to Loudun to the funeral oration of Grandier in Loudun, and now via the funeral procession itself to the Ursuline Convent and the introduction of Sister Jeanne of the Angels. Her first appearance is skillfully designed. The fact that she has entered the room because of the ruckus created by her charges jockeying for better positions to view the passing funeral entourage makes it originally seem as if her head is tilted to one side out of curiosity. It is only when she advances toward the camera with her head in that fixed position that we realize this is a deformity, and her first words--"Satan is always ready to tempt us with sensual delights," followed by a maniacal, cackling, humorless laugh--immediately convey the fact that her deformity is not limited to her physical appearance. At the same time (despite the singularly odd notion that watching a funeral is a "sensual delight") Sister Jeanne's reprimand to the other nuns is not undeserved. Here a pattern begins to emerge in the structure of power as portrayed on the screen, progressing from the broad-based power of the King and Richelieu to the more intimate power of Grandier to the enclosed power of Sister Jeanne. That the broad power of the court finds a reflection in Jeanne's enclosed power is no mistake. Both types of power come from a similar source--an environment that shuts out reality and produces a warped perception. Throughout the film Russell links Louis and Jeanne: each

has a controlling force--in Louis' case Richelieu and in
Jeanne's, Laubardemont; both appear frequently to be quite
insane, but each has moments of extremely lucid thought;
neither takes his or her respective vocation with any degree
of real seriousness or commitment. Jeanne's corruption
through power is immediately demonstrated by her unnecessarily harsh punishment on Sister Agnes and by virtue of the
fact that having broken up the gathering, she proceeds to
watch the funeral herself.

For those familiar with The Music Lovers the method
of presentation of Sister Jeanne watching the funeral procession through the bars of the convent takes on added significance as it mirrors the closing shots of the insane Nina peering through the bars of her cell in the asylum. Without that
foreknowledge of the earlier film, the metaphor of her isolation from the real world by placing her behind these bars
still works, which makes this one of the first examples of
Russell's ability to draw upon an existing source so that it
enhances and enlarges upon a scene for the viewer familiar
with the source material, but which does not depend on that
familiarity in order to be comprehensible.

It is in this scene, too, that Russell introduces the
first of Sister Jeanne's two fantasy sequences. Like the
structure of the film itself the integration of the fantasy element is very shrewdly conceived, making a transition from
the incense smoke from the funeral procession to the mist
that pervades much of the fantasy. However much one may
admire this aspect of smoothness in the transition, it is this
very artful quality that helps mark The Devils as more formative than mature Russell. (Admittedly the similar approach
in the second fantasy is far more successful because of the
intermingling of reality and fantasy giving the transition real
point.) That this is something of an experiment is evidenced
by the lack of any such device in The Music Lovers, and the
fact that it does not recur in any subsequent Russell creations. Looking at the transitions within the text of the overall Russell filmography the effect is more clever than creative, more decorative than useful. The fantasy itself is quite
another matter, fulfilling as it does a number of needs at
once within a far shorter time than would be possible using
more conventional techniques. There is a visual pattern in
the fantasies (the only scenes to present Grandier and Sister
Jeanne together apart from their brief encounter just prior to
his execution) that has been established by and grows out of
the presentation in the narrative proper. Almost invariably

Jeanne is placed in the position of looking up at Grandier so that his presence is heightened in her mind, which is consistent with her view of him from her ground level window in the funeral procession. Further, in both fantasies Grandier is presented as a Christ figure, an aspect which has a curious pertinence to both Sister Jeanne's image of him and to his eventual martyrization. In this first respect the image of Grandier as Christ helps to explain much in Sister Jeanne's later actions (as a nun, a spiritual "Bride of Christ," her view of him in this manner makes her subsequent lashing out at him for his failure to reciprocate her affections perfectly consistent). Not only does this link indicate that she feels Grandier belongs to her already, but her failure to attract his attention seriously undermines her already shaky faith, broadening the implication to extend to a loss of God as well.

The film returns from the fantasy through the device of the mist as it had begun. Shocked and appalled at the workings of her own mind Jeanne attempts to pray, but much in the manner of Richelieu's mock "blessing" ("And may the Protestant be driven from the land"), her prayers are a mockery. Once again Russell has her link Grandier with Christ. As Sister Jeanne prays to be delivered to Christ-- "Let the blood flow between us, uniting us"--she follows this desire by calling out Grandier's name. At this point she seeks solace in reciting the "Hail Mary" with her rosary, which leads to a young woman, Phillipe Trincant (already glimpsed at the funeral), lying naked atop Grandier reading Latin verse.

Unlike the clever artifice of the incense smoke leading to the mists of the fantasy, there is a genuine purpose in this transition. Not only do the words she reads have a definite bearing on Sister Jeanne's state of mind, but Grandier's request, "Translate as you go," has a direct significance on Jeanne's use of the "Hail Mary" as a kind of meaningless, numbing mantra. In essence the scene is expository, but it also contains the first hint of Grandier's potential for self-transcendence, as well as providing keen insight into the fact that, unlike Sister Jeanne or Cardinal Richelieu, Father Grandier does not deceive himself into believing his own abuses of power and religion are anything else. Certainly he uses his status as priest to secure a comfortable position for himself (significantly Grandier's house is the only example of architecture in the town not made of white brick and sharp angles with its cool tones and gracefully curving lines)

as well as relying on this position to help out in his conquest
of attractive lady parishioners. Grandier even takes advantage of his role as a learned man in seducing Phillipe, whose
father has sent her to Grandier for instruction in Latin. At
no time, however, does Grandier attempt to rationalize his
excesses in the manner of Richelieu or Jeanne. Similarly
he is able to maintain a division to some extent between
Grandier the man and Grandier the priest--quite the opposite
of Richelieu, who cannot even conceive of Church and State
as separate entities. As the scene opens he is Grandier the
lover, but upon Phillipe's confession of her pregnancy by
him, Grandier assumes his priestly functions. This is not
done coldly and cruelly, however, except where his pride enters into the situation. Rather it is done with a sense of
dignity and respect for his vocation over his own desires.
The summation of the entire scene comes when, in response
to Phillipe's pleas for help, he asks her, "How can I help
you?" in a manner indicating that his position as priest prevents him from doing the "honorable" thing. This proves,
though, not to be the case as he stretches out his hand to
her, and after she touches it he remarks that it is "like
touching the dead." This is a key element in the character
of Grandier. He feels himself to be dead, or like the dead.
He knows he is sinful and weak, and these are the very qualities that separate his tragic character from Tchaikovsky's
pathetic one in The Music Lovers. Tchaikovsky (and to a
large measure Rupert Birkin in Women in Love) cannot attain Grandier's level because of self-delusion. In some respects Rupert Birkin is the worst of the lot; he tends to
blame everyone and everything other than himself for his inability to achieve his goals. Tchaikovsky, though realizing
that much of the fault is in himself, hopes to find salvation
through adopting the outer trappings of normalcy, and failing
this, escapes into a world of dreams of his own making. At
no point does either character actually attempt to come to
terms with the reality of his situation. On the other hand--
in part through circumstances--Grandier does make that attempt, and he is the first of Russell's protagonists to really
do so.

Grandier's likening himself to the dead goes a long
way toward explaining his more than usual bravery in the
face of death as illustrated in the following scene where he
visits a plague-infested section of Loudun. The plague, heretofore only alluded to in the dialogue, is an often overlooked,
very important, aspect of The Devils. As Russell himself
noted in the production film, "Director of Devils," "There

was a great feeling of death in the air, and of death not mattering." It is this feeling that helps define the atmosphere of the town and makes it clear how the succeeding events would be possible. Much like the court of King Louis, Loudun has degenerated to a point where the unthinkable has become the norm. Grandier's walk through this hell on earth is the entry of sanity into an insane world, and the foreshadowing of his death by fire in the shot where he shields himself from a fire with his cape points up an overlooked facet of Russell's characterization of the priest. Considering the film apart from Huxley's book it becomes obvious that Grandier does not so much seal his fate by his misdeeds as by the nobler side of his character, hence the link to his death as he enters this hell in order to comfort the sick and dying, and just prior to meeting Madeleine de Brou, the woman through whom he might find salvation. This is a complete departure from Huxley who is at pains to catalogue the transgressions against others which lead to Grandier's death with little regard for transcendence.

For a film as truly horrifying as The Devils there is a great deal of not altogether healthy humor present, and a good deal of that humor comes from Ibert, the chemist, and Adam, the surgeon. Drawn both from Huxley's account and the Whiting play (from which a large part of their dialogue comes), the final creations in terms of approach and sound resemble nothing so much as a pair of impossibly unwholesome music hall comics. There is also more than a passing similarity to Peter Brook's production of Peter Weiss' Marat/Sade--an influence that in truth hangs over the entire film. Huxley describes the pair as, "At once absurd and pretentious, solemn and grotesque, the apothecary and the surgeon were predestined butts."[2] This is indeed true of Russell's presentation, but it is this very position that causes them to be horrifying and funny at the same time. We laugh at them only because there is nothing else to be done. For them the plague is a game in which they are free to experiment and torture all in the name of a science that is a good deal like black magic. (One could form a not inconsiderable belief that Russell is profoundly skeptical of the medical world in consideration of the proliferation of unflattering portraits in his films, e.g., the hot water treatment in The Music Lovers; the grotesqueries of the insane asylum in that film and in Mahler; Adam and Ibert here; the unhelpful, money-mad, lecherous specialist in Tommy; the inept diagnosis of the doctor on the train in Mahler; even the false science of reason as pictured in Altered States.) Consistent

with the film's presentation of Grandier's salvation through
suffering, Adam and Ibert become the instruments through
which he meets Madeleine, as they are practicing their craft
on her mother, which causes Madeleine to call out to Grandier. Remarkably complex in its implications the scene is a
tiny encapsulation of the entire film--the moment of tenderness and peace as Madame de Brou dies, turning her face
"towards God," effectively foretelling the film's climactic
moment of transcendence and release through death for Grandier. At the same time the film offers a hope that Grandier's
enemies might defeat themselves through their ineptitude, as
symbolized by Ibert's stuffed crocodile, which, tossed out the
window in disgust by Grandier, becomes the weapon with
which he fends off the attack by Phillipe's father, M. Trincant. Indeed, on a greater level than whether or not Grandier's enemies succeed in removing him, it is their similarly superstitious use of witchcraft as the vehicle for that removal that gives Grandier the spiritual and historical victory
over them.

    The scene which follows at the mass burial pit goes
even further in the establishment of Grandier and Madeleine
as the only normal characters in the world of the film. As
bodies are dumped into the communal grave Grandier and
Canon Mignon offer up last rites. It is not so much the
grotesquerie of the situation itself that appalls here as it is
the off-hand manner in which Canon Mignon decides to strike
up a conversation with Grandier--"My cousin tells me his
daughter is pregnant." Beyond the obvious inappropriateness
of the situation and the markedly callous attitude toward
death, this also casts severe doubt on the sincerity of Canon
Mignon's approach to his position. Even when Grandier responds to Mignon's questions he does so in clipped, abrupt
phrases, and despite the suicidal implications of his remarks
("I have a great need to be united with God") there is nothing
of the petty, personal squabbling that marks Mignon's speech.
Grandier as priest is consistently seen doing his level best
to uphold his office at the expense of Grandier the man. At
the same time Madeleine's presence as the sole mourner at
the services indicates that, unlike the rest of the populace,
she has not come to accept death as an unimportant and commonplace occurrence. The climax of the scene, where Grandier and Madeleine's eyes meet across the burial pit, reflects the same point of view found in Grandier's visit to
Madame de Brou's deathbed--life reaching out to reclaim the
spiritually dead Grandier in the person of Madeleine.

Finding a Voice 129

That Madeleine is not like Phillipe--not like the kind of woman Grandier is used to--is made clear in the next scene, where, having been too attracted to the priest, she attempts to enter the convent. Once again Sister Jeanne is separated from the world by bars, and her insincerity is even greater than before. True, Madeleine is altogether too much of an innocent, and the things that Jeanne tells her ("Most of us are here because we were unmarriagable or a burden to the family") have the stamp of truth. For that matter Sister Jeanne is uncomfortably close to the truth of the situation in wondering whether this woman with "the face of a virgin martyr in a picture book" can really be as good as she appears. There is more than a little irony in the fact that it is Sister Jeanne's harsh and unenlightening attitude that causes Madeleine to seek out Grandier's advice. Bringing Grandier and Madeleine together is the last thing Jeanne would want to do.

Jeanne's visit to Grandier's house to seek his advice is an astonishing little scene shot in a series of circular movements, panning with Grandier as he walks, alternating with shots circling Madeleine as she turns to keep him in view. The effect of this is twofold. The structure of the shots becomes the visual equivalent of Grandier's smooth, even shrewd dialogue ("I'm not surprised that Angela Merici's book of sanctimonious claptrap confused you. Most religious believe that by crying 'Lord! Lord!' often enough they can contrive to enter the kingdom of heaven. A flock of trained parrots could just as readily cry the same with just as little chance of success") as he circles Madeleine like a bird of prey. At the same time the reflective shots in toward Madeleine seem to draw Grandier ever closer to her as something more than a sexual target. (This is implied also by the fact that Grandier is speaking directly to Madeleine in a serious and non-condescending manner, unlike his earlier philosophical musings with Phillipe where he was talking to himself.)

The confession scene which follows further delineates the difference between Madeleine and Phillipe. Interestingly, though this is in part possibly due to the Whiting play which telescopes the characters of Madeleine and Phillipe into one, Russell uses Huxley's description of Phillipe's confession (especially the slip of referring to the mythical lover as "you" instead of "him") as the basis for Madeleine's confession. As structured by Russell the scene runs so that Phillipe utilizes the service as an opportunity to upbraid Grandier, angrily crying, "You should know!" when, in his capacity as

Father Confessor, Grandier asks the name of the man responsible for her condition. Madeleine on the other hand is sincerely, if somewhat humorously ("Sister Jeanne of the Angels provoked me and I wished her ... elsewhere"), there for confession, and it is only due to her slip of the tongue that the situation turns out otherwise. After having Grandier send her back to his house to wait for his return, Russell closes the confession scene on a playful note as a lady parishioner who is there less to confess than to be near Grandier cannot remember of what sin she is guilty. "If you have forgotten, perhaps God has forgotten as well," Grandier tells her.

There follows a remarkably tender scene between Grandier and Madeleine which crystallizes his relation to her. Meeting in the chapel of his home, in front of the cross, where he finds her praying, he explains his feelings on physical love. Placing this scene in the chapel as Ruseell has done he underlines the spiritual nature of Grandier's love for Madeleine, and Grandier's climactic words, "God help me, I love this woman," are the first instance of his spiritual reawakening as he calls on something outside of himself.

Contrapuntally Sister Jeanne's crucifixion fantasy follows this scene. As previously noted the interpolation of this fantasy is a good deal better designed than the earlier one. In contrast to the actual spiritual nature of the scene between Grandier and Madeleine, Sister Jeanne mechanically recites the "Mystery of the Crucifixion" in very graphic terms so that the images become mixed and confused in her mind until reality and fantasy become interchangeable for her. This Russell conveys by simply intercutting close-shots of the nails being driven into Christ's hands with Jeanne's prayers, until reason totally gives way and she views herself as Mary Magdalene at the crucifixion. Her religious zeal, however, is overcome by her own desires and Christ transforms into Grandier, who comes down from the cross to Jeanne. Jeanne kneels before him and kisses the wounds in his hands, before embracing him and tumbling to the ground. As the fantasy ends Jeanne finds she has ground the crucifix on her rosary into the palm of her hand. Jeanne has reduced the crucifixion to a purely physical experience. Her words, "Think of his most beautiful body torn by the nails," the visual realization of those words, the kissing of the wounds, even her self-inflicted mockery of the stigmata, all combine to point toward a sick sensual experience. Jeanne is not a fool, however. The intercut shots of her horror as

Christ becomes Grandier and she looks to the crucifix on the convent wall as if to assure herself that this is not so, indicate that she recognizes the unbalanced side of her mind though she can do nothing about it.

Neither as exciting nor as colorful (obviously, since the fantasy itself is in sepia tone) as the "1812" Fantasy in The Music Lovers, this is nonetheless, in terms of construction, placement, development, execution, and symbolism, Russell's most accomplished fantasy sequence up to its time. The additional bonus of the evocation of DeMille's King of Kings via the sepia-toned footage and the emphasis on Mary Magdalene makes its own point in a carefully unobtrusive manner. King of Kings, brilliant though much of it is on a technical basis, and sincere though certain aspects of it may be, was at best a pseudo-religious epic of the kind in which DeMille specialized after the advent of the Production Code in 1923. Finding that it was permissible to indulge in sensuality, violence, torture, murder, and sex if they were dressed up to resemble edifying religious creations, DeMille proceeded to follow this path in maintaining all the elements of his pre-code modern dramas without offending the censor. The parallel here works on two levels--the similarity between Jeanne's perversion of religion and DeMille's, as well as the fact that DeMille was engaged in turning the religious film into a kind of respectable pornography, while Russell is engaged in creating a truly religious work of art. It is ironic, though not incomprehensible, that the audience for King of Kings would likely be appalled by The Devils, even though the latter film is by far the more devout and well-intentioned.

All of what has occurred on the screen thus far has been to a large extent developmental, establishing character and atmosphere. The stage has been effectively set for the central dramatic conflict of the film. In keeping with the careful construction of the film with one situation or scene either reflecting or growing out of or opposing the preceding scene, Russell follows Jeanne's fantasy with another quiet, rational encounter between Grandier and Madeleine. Simply shot and leisurely paced, it is in this scene that they decide to marry. Madeleine is slightly skeptical about marrying a priest, but ultimately Grandier's arguments win out. ("Nowhere in the Bible is it forbidden for priests to marry.") Again Russell paints a picture of extreme contrasts as concerns Madeleine, who is the only woman character in the film with whom a conversation such as this would be possible.

The idyllic nature of their arrangement is almost immediately shattered by a commotion from outside, which, upon examination, is caused by Laubardemont's machines beginning to tear down the walls. The juxtaposition of this occurrence with the decision to marry, and coming directly after the onset of Grandier's spiritual rebirth, strengthens the relationship between Grandier and the walls, and foreshadows his own destruction. (This is consistent with the presentation of Grandier as a man more destroyed by his attempts to reform and set things to rights, than as a man destroyed by his weaknesses.) This is the first of Grandier's encounters with Laubardemont, and it is interesting that it is this enemy who represents the film's only intellectual equal (apart from Madeleine) of Grandier. Grandier's ability to forestall the destruction of the walls as acting governor of Loudun and the King's promise to the former governer is a minor victory in his game of wits with Laubardemont. It is a deadly game, however, and Laubardemont, in his mental superiority to Grandier's other enemies, is the first person to take it on who could win. In part it is Grandier's pride that allows this. He is so accustomed to beating the likes of Ibert, Adam, Mignon, and Trincant that he does not recognize any other sort of opponent. To balance this, however, one needs to consider the basic innocence of the man in contrast to his superiority and pride. He cannot believe, originally, that the court or the citizens of Loudun could or would seek to destroy him through "the ravings of a crazy nun." He trusts in "the King's good judgment," which to anyone other than an innocent would seem ill-advised, to say the least. Even at his arrest he does not see Jeanne's accusations as intrinsically vicious, or even of her own doing, i.e., "She has been broken by the priests." And these attitudes as much as anything else, including Grandier's pride, contribute to this destruction.

At this point in the narrative Russell begins structuring the film less as a series of scenes and more as a long series of intercut sequences, which seem to flow across the screen, finally erupting into the climactic scene. To firmly establish this pattern of intercutting--intercutting in a more literal sense than the previous method of playing one scene off another--Russell begins with an elaborate sequence crosscutting between Grandier's speech to the townspeople and Richelieu's attempt to convince the King that the walls of Loudun need to be torn down. Russell's handling of these two scenes at once is masterful, not simply because the viewpoint of Grandier is made the more noble by the obvious

treachery of Richelieu as contrasted with it, but also due to
the curiosity he rouses by not letting us see the object of
the game that Louis is playing as he half-heartedly listens
to Richelieu's plans. It is not until the end of the two scenes
that we are allowed to see that Louis is shooting at Huguenots
who have been dressed up to resemble blackbirds and forced
to run along a target range to their deaths. Basically, this
is merely an extension of the "Birth of Venus" drag show,
which opened the film. Now, however, the madness and
decadence of the earlier scene have blossomed into more
concrete action, as Louis quite literally removes "the Protestant from the land." Having the Protestants dressed up like
blackbirds restates the theatrical motif from this first scene
also, and further points up the unreality of the world in which
Louis lives. The blackbird idea also helps to bring the scene
forward in time to the racial problems of our own age, and
Louis' final line, "Bye, bye, blackbird," tends to reinforce
the allegorical nature of the presentation.

On a functional level as narrative the intercut scenes
of Grandier warning of the destruction of the walls with
Richelieu's appeal to the king is well judged. Bringing the
divergent beliefs together in this manner, Russell clearly
states the case for the dramatic conflict of wills, which
serves as a storyline through which the previously stated
themes will be explored. The portrait of Louis, though it
is in this scene as in his later visit incognito to the exorcisms that we catch a glimmer of a shrewd mind beneath
his facade as vicious idiot-King, helps establish the instability of his judgments and, as such, the extreme likelihood of
a turnabout in policy on the walls of Loudun.

Russell's transition from Louis' laugh at his own "Bye,
bye, blackbird" joke to Jeanne's laugh as she composes her
letter asking Grandier to be the nuns' new Father Confessor
with the passing of Canon Moussant helps to underline the
similarity between the enforced closed world of the convent
and the fantasy world of the court. The approach to letter
writing is another link with Nina in The Music Lovers as
Jeanne's request for a new priest, with its ulterior motives,
is markedly like Nina's empty protestations of love and virtue. The scene is structured like the previous one as it is
broken into pieces in order to reflect and comment on the unorthodox, but deeply felt, marriage ceremony between Grandier and Madeleine. The obvious implication of this structure
is that Jeanne's introversion of her sexuality breeds insanity,
while Grandier's sexual honesty--regardless of the Church's

stand on the matter--is a healthy experience, one which has the potential for achieving salvation and transcendence.

This is further brought forward by the succeeding intercuts from the marriage ceremony to Jeanne's masturbation and self-flagellation scenes. Here, too, Russell introduces a parallel the point of which is not entirely clear. While Jeanne's activities are being spied upon by Sister Agnes, Grandier and Madeleine are being watched by Ibert and Adam. Admittedly Sister Agnes has every reason to feel about Sister Jeanne much as Ibert and Adam feel about Grandier, but at the same time nothing comes of her spying and the parallel seems drawn for no reason. Ibert and Adam's spying, on the other hand, leads directly into the following sequence where Richelieu and Laubardemont are researching Grandier's background for a way of undermining his power; as such, it is consistent with the air of foreboding which taints even Grandier's most hopeful scenes.

The library scene itself, designed to appear frighteningly modern with its row upon row of files where information is stored that might be used by a corrupt government to help destroy an individual at will, is significant in that it firmly establishes the sort of attack which Laubardemont plans to launch against the priest. Richelieu, in musing about Grandier's Jesuit background, recites the firmly held belief, "You know what they say--give us the first seven years of a man's life and you can have the rest, you'll never break him." "I, too, have a maxim, Eminence," counters Laubardemont. "Give me seven lines of a man's hand-writing and I will hang him with it." This line, followed by his cry of "Doors!" is given added significance by the huge red cross which adorns those doors and which swings into place after them. Grandier is to be destroyed by the same sort of perversion of religion that places "And may the Protestant be driven from the land" in the realm of "sanctified" religious doctrine.

This is followed by the acting out of the marriage of Grandier and Madeleine by the nuns in the convent, presided over by Sister Agnes. Again Russell emphasizes the gap between Grandier's ideal and the reality of the situation. The convent is an enclosed order, cut off from the world, but word of the marriage has come to them, or more specifically to Sister Agnes, through gossip from the outside world, and their mockery of the event is certainly in keeping with that world's view of the self-performed marriage of the priest.

Sister Agnes, of course, has somewhat stronger reasons for
her part in the charade, as it is an agency through which
she can get back at Sister Jeanne, who, in a reversal of
situations, stands out of sight of the others as she listens to
the proceedings with mounting horror. In a final gesture,
consistent with her confused prayer after the first fantasy
and her self-inflicted stigmata by her crucifix during the second, Jeanne thrusts the crucifix into her mouth to prevent
herself from screaming aloud--one more effort to subjugate
her feelings to a religion that is steadily becoming more confused and warped in her own mind.

  That Jeanne's state of mind has descended to a point
where her personal feelings and her duties as prioress of St.
Ursula have become blurred is made clear in the very next
scene, where, quite forgetting herself, she attacks Madeleine, who has come to return the book which Jeanne had
loaned her. Interestingly, the structure of this scene, plus
its outcome (Jeanne's claim of possession by devils), is repeated almost exactly by Russell at Grandier's arrest. Her
subsequent rationalization that none of this would have happened if Grandier had seen her first is yet another similarity
to Nina in The Music Lovers ("Oh, please, God, just let him
see me. Just let him see me, God, please"). Such a rationalization does no good, however, when upon racing to
meet the new Father Confessor instead of Grandier, she finds
the unprepossessing figure of Canon Mignon. As in every
earlier instance where the burden of her personal emotions
becomes too great, Jeanne immediately retreats into religion
--only this time she begins to actively involve someone else:
Grandier. Sister Jeanne's claim that she is bewitched may
sound ludicrous to our modern minds, but would have been
considered far less outré in 1634, and such a claim is completely in keeping with her earlier actions. Her attitude
about Grandier as a man was originally so unthinkable to her
that her mind worked him around to a Christ figure, and now,
in denying her salvation as she views it by fobbing Mignon off
on her, it is completely natural that he should take on the opposite role for her. It is unimportant in her mind that Grandier has never met her. This is a drama that she is acting
out in her mind, like one of Louis' court entertainments. It
should be remembered at all times that Russell is in no way
using Sister Jeanne as the villain of the film. Even her claim
to possession is not so much an attempt to attack Grandier--
it is for others to turn it into that--as it is an attempt to
place the blame for the problems in her mind outside of herself.

[Left to right:] Conspirators Trincant and Father Mignon with Grandier's supporters, Rangier, Legrand, and Madeleine in The Devils. (Warner Bros.)

Russell reinforces the impact that this claim has on Grandier by countering this scene with the image of Grandier and Madeleine lying peacefully in bed. The tender softness of the scene, which rests as a balance point between Jeanne's claim of possession and the conspiracy scene in which it is decided how to put that claim to use, further underscores the fact that it is less Grandier's sins that are his physical undoing than it is his spiritual rebirth.

The conspiracy scene is one of the most skillfully designed in the film. It is more than a little unclear just exactly where this meeting is taking place--it resembles nothing so much as a disused corner of hell--but the scene is obviously based on the town meetings against Grandier that were held in Adam's apothecary shop. The three major conspirators, Laubardemont, Trincant, and Mignon, aided by the professional advice of Adam and Ibert (none too helpful on occasion as they offer up an explanation of Sister Jeanne's possession--"Known it to happen before, spasmodic swelling of the belly, sense of false pregnancy ... nothing to do with the devil ... wind") are gathered to decide the best method of attack on Grandier. Laubardemont declares at length that since it will be difficult for them to prove that Grandier is responsible for Phillipe's pregnancy, it would be wisest to pursue Sister Jeanne's claims of devils. Once again the proceedings quickly degenerate to a kind of game as Mignon, Trincant, Adam, and Ibert all fall over each other in promising professional advice within their respective specialties, taking care that no one is left out. "Conjecture is useless," concludes Laubardemont. "We need a professional witch-hunter. We must send for Father Barré."

A professional witch-hunter sounds like a rather unsavory calling under the best of circumstances and the entrance of Father Barré bears out our worst fears in this matter. His appearance is that of a college campus radical right down to his ersatz John Lennon eyeglasses, and as such he is sociologically interchangeable with thousands of hypercommitted young men, who have not taken the time or the trouble to actually consider to what it is they are committed. He has a relation, too, to a certain stripe of wild-eyed Christian convert, who has absorbed nothing of Christianity except the false notion that it makes him or her not only better than, but somehow above others. To be sure, Father Barré is a ridiculous figure, and nothing he does in his first minutes on-screen does anything but reinforce this, but, like Ibert and Adam, it is his absurdity that makes him even more dangerous as it allows for the manufacture of fact and logic to suit as he goes. (History is, after all, full of this sort of absurdity. Senator Joseph McCarthy was absurd; Napoleon was absurd; and surely Adolf Hitler was the most absurd of all.) Jeanne herself cannot quite believe in Barré, and as he takes her head in his hands and mutters, "Are you there? Are you there?" she even laughs at him outright. Her examination by that learned pair, Adam and Ibert, is similarly dubious, but implicitly more horrific--a horror that is greatly increased by the jovial attitude of her examiners as they saunter in, nodding inanely, muttering pleasant greetings. The upshot of the examination is that Sister Jeanne is indeed in need of exorcism. This exorcism, historically accurate, is no Hollywood movie priest doing Latin incantations over a recumbent figure, but a vicious, violent, and quite physical approach involving a procedure known as clystering, which is nothing more nor less than a vaginal enema of boiling holy water. When the table with its bubbling water and clyster equipment is wheeled into view, Jeanne immediately tries to recant her claims, but Barré will have none of it. Typically, Jeanne attempts to turn to her religion for aid, but the altar to which she runs becomes the table on which she is held and the enema administered. Public opinion is divided on the method of treatment, but the overall feeling is one of an amused populace, recalling the audience at Louis' court entertainment. Laubardemont's purpose, however, is not entertainment. He wants a public accusation against Grandier as a sorcerer, and he gets one.

Much discussed and frequently cited as one of the prime examples of the supposed sickness and depravity to be found in The Devils, the exorcism scene is a good deal more restrained than might be imagined. Like the examination that immediately precedes it, the overall effect is achieved through suggestion and reaction more than through graphic presentation. It is, however, an intense scene and that intensity may not be entirely in its favor as it tends to obscure another key element within the scene concerning Russell's characterization of Sister Jeanne. Up to this point Jeanne has been presented as a pathetic, but far from likable or sympathetic, character. It is difficult to conceive of her having an actual friend, and yet at the moment of her torture there is a strong outcry from the other nuns suggestive of a feeling of sympathy that one might well have thought impossible. This is the first occasion in the film where it seems that someone outside herself might care what happens to Sister Jeanne, and it is also the beginning of a deeper exploration of her character than has occurred previously in the film.

Russell balances the exorcism with a brief scene of Grandier and Madeleine in bed. It is in this scene that Grandier's sense of duty to the people of Loudun and his inability to perceive the gathering evil begin to tell significantly. That he will not, as Madeleine suggests, stay in Loudun and quell Sister Jeanne's accusations is simply another enforcement of the film's insistence that Grandier's reformation is central to his destruction.

Immediately the situation at the convent with Father Barré resurfaces as we find the nuns who called out at the abuse of Sister Jeanne during the exorcism about to be executed for this heresy. The execution is prevented in the nick of time, however, when Barré has a revelation that these "good sisters" are themselves possessed by Grandier,

Finding a Voice 139

and as long as they agree to act the part ("You will scream!
You will blaspheme! You will no longer be responsible for
your actions!") they will be spared. What is unclear about
this scene, which in color and composition looks astonishingly like a satire of pre-Raphaelite painting, is whether or
not this revelation of Father Barré is a foregone conclusion.
Laubardemont's reaction to it--that under the circumstances
the nuns would not be the first "to see the light"--seems to
indicate that this is so, but such a conclusion would, of
necessity, also indicate that Father Barré is consciously
fraudulent and this just does not seem practical, given every
other aspect of the characterization. Another approach to
the material, though, might be that Laubardemont is here
being developed further as a power to be reckoned with and
that he immediately grasps the possibilities of the situation
as it presents itself. Utilizing this more workable hypothesis,
Laubardemont can be seen to be something of a prototypical
character for Frank Hobbs in Tommy, who is blessed with
a similar adaptability.

    Having thus set up the film's primary situation of
Grandier's destruction by his enemies while he is away,
Russell begins to embark on the most concentrated sequence
of cross-cutting in this or any of his films, though, as previously noted, the bulk of The Devils following the establishment of the characters and atmosphere is largely a matter
of cross-cutting. In one respect this more traditionalist use
of film technique with which The Devils is structured tends
to give the film the appearance of being Russell's most completely cinematic work in a textbook sense. At the same
time, however, it makes the film something of a betrayal of
Russell's own unique vision. In eschewing the literary cum
biographical experiments of Women in Love or the operatic
theatricality of The Music Lovers, Russell has limited the
range of his expressiveness to such an extent that The Devils
very nearly threatens to become structurally commonplace in
the process. Russell's statement that he merely finds himself working in the style in which he is working as dictated
by the type of film he is making does not really apply here
in the question of structure. The type of structure utilized
in The Devils significantly never reappears in Russell's work.
Even the relatively straightforward presentations afforded
Valentino and Altered States (though the former does make
use of symbolic counterpoint) are blessed with more adventurous structures than The Devils. This is one of the aspects that so clearly marks the film as being as much
formative as formed. True, Russell had earlier learned a

good deal of his art in the BBC films, but in The Devils--
as well as the earlier features and to a certain extent The
Boy Friend and Savage Messiah--there is still a great deal
of formal development as concerns structure and approach.
In pushing toward a fusion of a number of art forms at one
time--creating a synthesis approaching a kind of all-art--
certain attitudes common to general film criticism do not
apply easily or correctly in dealing with Russell's work, and,
resultantly, calling The Devils Russell's most purely cinematic work is rather a backhanded compliment.

The contrapuntal set-up of the cross-cutting is, however, markedly effective, especially since Russell is not content merely to play the exorcism scenes of horror against a
series of idyllic scenes simply to achieve a sense of balance.
The counterpoint works on an altogether more profound level
because it not only shows the gap between the mockery that
the exorcisms have become contrasted with Grandier's simple
spirituality, but because we realize that Grandier's spiritual
regeneration cannot save him. Further, the degeneracy of
the exorcisms (including the King's incognito visit as the Duc
de Condé, which adds a note of uncomfortable satire to the
proceedings as his attitude bespeaks of a foregone conclusion
regardless of the fact that he makes a fool of Barré) stands
out in sharper relief because of the contrapuntal scenes. Unfortunately, as discussed earlier, this is the section of the
film that never reached the screen as Russell intended, and
the deletion of the "Rape of Christ" seriously damages the
structure on which Russell has built the sequences.

Continuing in the cross-cutting pattern, Russell quickly delineates Grandier's arrest on charges of witchcraft.
Here again, Russell builds on the destruction through regeneration motif as it is only when Madeleine (the instrument
of Grandier's regeneration) cries out to protest the spiritual
validity of their marriage that Sister Jeanne blurts out her
accusation of his sorcery. The modernity of the situation in
terms of allegory is also brought into the forefront here as
the two people, Rangier and Legrand, brave enough to speak
out on the obviously trumped up nature of the charges are
just as swiftly silenced by the state and arrested with Grandier. Again this is the playing out of a foregone conclusion
as they had previously been outraged by the original exorcism,
and upon being apprised of their positions as baker and inn-
keeper Laubardemont had quipped, "It looks as if we may
soon acquire an interest in the catering trade." Early on it
has been obvious--as it is later made vocal in Grandier's de-

fense speech--that truth in Loudun is only acceptable so long as it does not interfere. Hence, Louis' visit with the bogus "dried blood of our Lord Jesus Christ" and his subsequent mockery of Barre and the exorcisms (Barré: "What sort of trick have you played on us?" Louis: "Oh, Reverend sir, what sort of trick are you playing on us?") become completely acceptable only because, like his Huguenot blackbirds, it is only a game to him and has no bearing on the outcome.

There follows a brief scene in which a spurious test is administered to Grandier--a needle is driven through his tongue in accordance with Sister Jeanne's accusation that if this spot is pricked it will not bleed. Although it certainly appears to do so, Ibert and Adam officially proclaim that it does not, once again stressing the inevitability of Grandier's guilt.

With complete symbolic logic Sister Jeanne, having betrayed her personal Christ figure in Grandier, becomes a Judas figure, going so far as to attempt suicide by hanging. It is a splendidly realized scene as she stands in the rain contemplating the gnarled tree on which she will hang herself, a scene that says a great deal about Russell's complex emotional response to the character. As in the earlier exorcism scene the reactions of the other nuns call into question the easily formed opinion that Jeanne can be construed as a villain in any sense of the word. Even though we have seen no examples of any kind of rapport between her and her charges, their horror at her attempted suicide goes a long way toward suggesting that a true emotional bond does exist. For that matter her act of remorse supports and is consistent with the viewpoint taken earlier in the film that although she is not entirely responsible for her actions, Sister Jeanne clearly recognizes them as an aberration and is terrified by them.

Russell's decision to follow this Judas scene with one in which Grandier utters a prayer that includes the question as to why God has forsaken him further strengthens and enlarges upon the Christ parallel. In that the scene is an objective presentation and not one of Sister Jeanne's interior thoughts or fantasies it places Grandier for the first time in line with a Christ figure for the audience. This is not so much to put Grandier on equal footing with the Deity (for that matter, Russell does not push the Grandier/Christ parallel very far) as it is to secure a foreknowledge of Grandier's subsequent actions. At this point in the film Grandier has achieved spiritual salvation, and like the preordained outcome of his "trial," nothing will alter this fact.

Sister Jeanne, on the other hand, has started something which she cannot stop. Following her botched suicide bid she informs Canon Mignon that she has "wronged an innocent man." This confession, however, does not fit the accepted truth of the situation and so must be discounted. Rejecting Jeanne's confession proves an easy matter for Barré, who merely puts it down to the "devils" speaking through her. (The validity of what these devils say is interesting in that it depends entirely on whether or not it is in keeping with the accepted truth.) Barré's treatment of Jeanne--his implied rape of her as a method of driving out the devils--is not nearly so questionable a move on Russell's part as Joseph Gomez suggests since it serves to solidify the total abuse and perversion of religion in a way that helps smooth over the earlier blunting of this theme due to censorship. Beyond this, Barré's rape of Sister Jeanne makes him symbolically become the sorcerer of his outlandish beliefs. Father Barré has just committed the crime of which Grandier is supposed to be guilty.

Paralleling Barré's defilement of Sister Jeanne, Laubardemont's soldiers ransack and vandalize Father Grandier's house, in itself a symbol, like the city walls, of Grandier's individuality. The scene is structured with great visual wit, albeit wit of a chilling nature: Laubardemont's line "You're going to be tortured" is followed by a shot of soldiers smashing the legs and genitals of one of Grandier's many statues. The scene is also notable as the first example of Grandier's humanization and humility as he confesses his fear of physical torture, even though he believes that it cannot be appreciably different from the pain he has already seen. "Except for its location," Laubardemont warns him, and then offers the consolation, "Hell will hold no surprises for you." There is more than a little irony in the fact that this line is delivered as Laubardemont stands with his back to a shattered window through which the glow of flames can be seen from the street below, visually implying that hell holds no surprises for Laubardemont either.

The trial itself tends to disappoint slightly because of its heavy reliance on dialogue and the fact that it is impossible to generate much suspense since the outcome is all too obvious. Russell is not without cinematic invention, though, and the trial is far removed from the realm of photographed

Finding a Voice 143

stage play--a situation that has plagued every filmmaker who
ever attempted any kind of lengthy courtroom scene. Interestingly, Russell does not use any of the standard dodges
for bringing life into the scene. Comparing his approach to
that of, say, James Whale in The Kiss Before the Mirror
with its ponderously gratuitous three-hundred-sixty-degree
pan around the court, Russell is incredibly restrained in his
presentation. There is camera movement within the scene
to be sure, but none of it is arbitrary. Instead Russell cir-
cumvents the potential for outright boredom by imbuing the
scene with a sense of identity and life into players who are
not central to the proceedings as such. We see Rangier and
Legrand, broken men, obviously forced to side against
Grandier despite their knowledge and feelings, and then there
is a superb bit of characterization in Father Barré, who
reads indifferently throughout (his nonchalance once more indicative of the certain outcome of the trial) and only looks
up when he hears his name spoken as Grandier talks about
the "new" Barré-Laubardemont "truth," "specially manufactured for this occasion." For the most part, however, Russell mainly relies on the intelligent and elegant playing of
his two main actors, Oliver Reed and Dudley Sutton, and in
no instance do they let him down. (Reed's performance in
particular is so good and all encompassing in The Devils
that one resents Vanessa Redgrave's higher billing, and it is
not hard to believe that Reed's billing over Ann-Margret in
Tommy is to make up for this.) One significant change that
Russell has made in adapting the dialogue of Whiting's play
for this scene comes from Russell's omission of the character of D'Armagnac. Despite the prominence of this character both historically and in the Whiting play (D'Armagnac
having been the actual governor of Loudun and a supporter of
Grandier), Russell's decision to eliminate the character has
not, until this scene, been of any great importance. In this
instance, however, the transference of much of D'Armagnac's
defense speech to Grandier himself makes a considerable difference in the strengthening of Grandier's character. On
quite a different level, of course, is the fact that the inclusion of D'Armagnac would have presented a figure of actual
governmental authority in a more flattering light than cur-
rently exists in the film. It is arguable that such an inclusion would have better balanced the film's representation of
government, but it would also have clouded the central allegorical issue of the individual crushed by a government that
has gotten out of control and out of touch with reality.

The final scenes in the film are skillfully constructed

to bring all the various aspects of the film into focus at one time, and as such are largely inseparable, flowing smoothly from one to the other without the sense of counterpoint or cross-cutting of the preceding scenes. The first of these climactic scenes is the barbering episode, where Grandier is made physically as well as emotionally humble as all of his carefully groomed hair, moustache, and even eyebrows are cut off. (Interestingly, this was the cause of a tremendous rift between Russell and Oliver Reed, for while Reed quite accepted the need for the shaved head, he balked at having his eyebrows removed. In the end cooler heads prevailed and Reed's eyebrows were insured against not growing back, but it should perhaps be noted that Reed did not work for Russell again until his cameo appearance in Mahler.) The scene is also notable for the humanization of Laubardemont, who is not merely sufficiently moved by Grandier's situation that he goes out of his way to allow him one last look at himself prior to the barbering, but who is also coming to respect his opponent as a man of power and dignity. The scene overall is linked by the attempted stripping away of Grandier's dignity and the background sounds to the following scenes. As is further explored in those scenes,

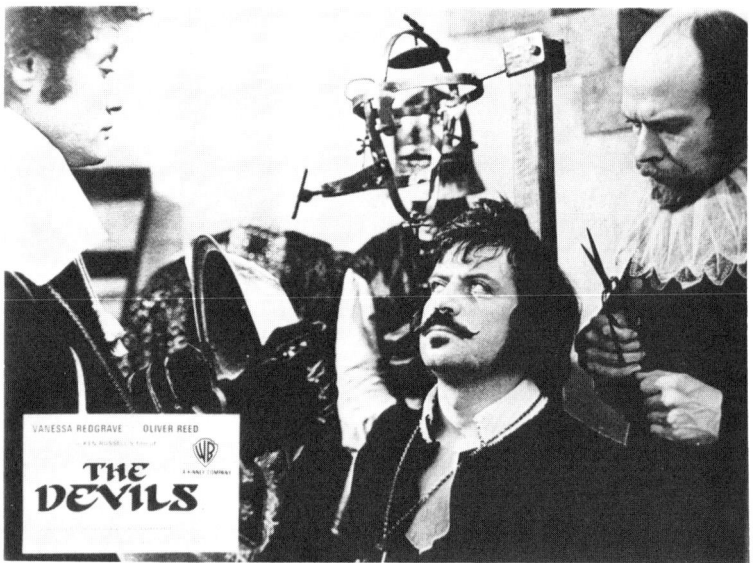

"You have lost." Grandier prepares to suffer the humiliation of having his hair cut off in The Devils. (Warner Bros.)

Grandier becomes increasingly a dignified and even majestic figure as each vestige of his worldliness is removed by his tormentors. While the barbering takes place, the soundtrack carries the sound of a man in the street singing a bawdy song about the events in Loudun, which serves to bring the film's theatricality into focus. The effect of this is not unlike Tchaikovsky's reduction of Nina to an idealized bit of tragic art in his Sixth Symphony toward the close of The Music Lovers. In both instances humanity and human suffering have been dragged down to a level of symbolism without any attendant understanding through that symbolism. In The Music Lovers that symbol is the music; in The Devils it is the bawdy street song, but in the latter film the effect is somewhat weakened by Russell's sharp delineation of the real occurrences and the theatrical. In The Devils theatre is less all pervasive and all-conscious. The characters in The Music Lovers comport themselves as if they were onstage playing out a drama, and it is through the departure from the seemingly preconceived occurrences (e.g., Nina's outburst when Tchaikovsky plays one of his scenes) that serves to give the film much of its dramatic thrust. The Devils is devoid of this tension, and to a great extent it is the price that must be paid for the film's more positive outlook, since Russell has not yet achieved the balance one finds in his more mature works.

Though lacking the dramatic vitality of The Music Lovers' unified style and theme, the theatricality of these final scenes is brilliantly achieved, so much so in fact that the combination of song and barbering prior to Grandier's sentencing (another theatrical event) places Grandier in the position of being an actor being made up for a performance. Viewing the film with this in mind one can see that the sentencing is not only theatrical in itself, but becomes the outline for the remainder of the performance expected of Grandier. It is here that Russell turns the theatrical nature of the situation to his own end, establishing Grandier as a heroic and transcendent figure simply because he does not deliver that expected performance; i.e., he does not go to his death a "penitent man."

The torture applied to him--a scene of such unbelievable power that it is difficult to conceive that the actual sequence of Grandier's legs being crushed amounts to no more than three small groups of hammer blows (the first containing four strikes, the second only one, and the third consisting of two hits) with no graphic visuals at all--fails completely in illiciting a confession of sorcery. Similarly, Laubardemont's rational pleas that a confession will help the Church grow more powerful "until it embraces every human spirit" is to no avail. Indeed it is the very fact that Laubardemont finds it necessary to make such a plea that sets up the basic situation allowing Grandier to realize that Laubardemont, Richelieu, and Barré have in reality "lost" as long as he does not confess. He is morally victorious and in keeping with Russell's general approach to history the implication extends to include a foreknowledge of the future's judgment of his innocence. Again the air of a theatrical presentation hangs over the proceedings as Grandier is "groomed" for his final performance, and this is reinforced by the very fact of the effort to force Grandier to confess, or, in a theatrical sense, to follow the script.

The climactic scene into which the previous scenes flow more than justifies such an elaborate build-up. The journey to Grandier's execution and the execution itself is a rather lengthy scene, but its length is essential for in it Russell brings every aspect of the film into play. As Joseph Gomez has noted the procession retraces the path of the funeral procession for Sainte-Marthe--an effect Russell uses to bring forth Grandier's spiritual growth during the course of the film. As we saw him at the opening he was a proud and vain, if powerful, figure, whereas at the film's climax he has gone beyond that, attaining truly heroic stature. This is underscored by the pause at St. Ursula's where Grandier is supposed to "ask forgiveness of these good women you have wronged." Interestingly--and somewhat prophetically for the first of the film's two epilogue scenes--Sister Jeanne is the first person to, briefly, recognize the inner dignity and strength of the maimed Grandier, as in their single face to face encounter she tells him, "They always spoke of your beauty and now I see it." However, Grandier's response, "Look at this thing I have become and learn the meaning of love," causes her to revert to the Laubardemont-Richelieu script and growl, "Devil ... devil!" Grandier, his legs crushed and useless, is then made to crawl to the place of his execution. Russell is unsparing in his depiction of the brutality of this, and in doing so he enlarges upon Barré's perversion of religion as the exorcist viciously kicks Grandier's bloodied feet while reciting an incantation over the doomed man. Barré's further theatrical trick of spitting in Grandier's face so that Grandier appears to avert his eyes from a cross ("See how he flinches! See how he denies his redeemer!") cements the viewpoint and stresses the image of

Grandier's salvation through suffering in The Devils. (Warner Bros.)

the exorcist as a kind of seventeenth-century carnival barker urging the gathered crowd to enjoy the show. Russell also uses Barré to point up the immense gulf between Grandier even at his worst and the abused religion of Richelieu, where Barré refuses to give Grandier the kiss of peace and instead forces Canon Mignon to administer it. As we have seen earlier Grandier would never have allowed his personal feelings to enter into his functions as a priest in this manner. In a similar vein is the fact that Barré obviously views himself as the star of the show, demanding his audience's full attention even to the extent of subverting the executioner's promise to quickly strangle Grandier prior to the burning by grabbing the torch and setting fire to Grandier ahead of schedule.

With the exceptions of Adam and Ibert--who perform like a very sick Crosby and Hope accidentally kissing each other with this intention clarified by their subsequent "Road"-picture-style "patty cake" antics--and the vengeful Trincant and Phillipe, the townspeople are neither singled out, nor viewed as especially blameworthy even though they behave like exceptionally rowdy theatre patrons. Given the norm as established by the film and the allegorical approach, we find ourselves in no position to condemn the actions of the crowd which are in keeping with the world of The Devils much as our own complacency is to our world.

Grandier's climactic speech through the flames is an appropriately chilling finale for the complex characterization, as he asks only to be forgiven "for defending your city so badly" and cries out to the populace to maintain their walls, i.e., their freedom and individuality. It is hopeless, of course, as the walls will "die" with Grandier, and indeed as soon as his voice stops coming from the flames, Laubardemont steps into the frame, gives a signal, and the walls are dynamited. The scattering of the citizens of Loudun, taken unaware by the explosions, as they try to avoid the flying debris neatly symbolizes the descent of Loudun into chaos with the passing of the voice of reason in Grandier, as well as their blindness to the fact that they were quite literally sitting on a keg of gunpowder.

The two epilogue scenes are designed to explore further the effects of the passing of Grandier. In the first, Laubardemont visits Jeanne in her cell, and aside from letting her (and the audience) in on the fact that Barré has moved on to deal with another case of possession and that Canon

Finding a Voice

Mignon has gone insane because of having destroyed an innocent man, he paints a picture of her future life for her: "Oh, there'll be the occasional tourist to liven things up, but in the end you'll be free to live out the rest of your life in peace ... and oblivion." Russell then gives Jeanne her final measure of humanity as Laubardemont presents her with a rather grisly souvenir of the adventure, one of Grandier's charred leg bones, and her reaction is clearly one of horror for what she has done.

The final scene in the film restates this information in a subtly terrifying manner. As Madeleine passes the executioner throwing Grandier's ashes to the winds, and numbly walks through one of the gaps in the blasted out walls and away from Loudun, Russell pulls his camera to a high angle similar to the angle through which we first saw Grandier, and slowly drains all color from the scene until everything is a deadly washed out grey and black. The death of Grandier, the death of the only individual, has made this world bleak and lifeless. It is with this grim vision that Russell closes his film.

Although it is not quite the work that one might like it to be on a number of counts, The Devils is nonetheless a decided thematic advance for Ken Russell, and in some ways a stylistic advance as well. Unlike its two predecessors, Women in Love and The Music Lovers, The Devils is a compact one hundred and nine minutes. Then, too, with the removal of the excess padding of the earlier films, there is the not inconsiderable bonus of the sparseness of the cinematography, which is in the hands of David Watkin, who seems more in tune with Russell's sense of immediacy. In this film there are none of the artsy flourishes that had marred much of Women in Love and kept threatening to reappear in The Music Lovers. The camera work is every bit as elaborate as in those earlier films, but here it is always an integral part of the film.

To be sure The Devils is not a pleasant film, but that was never its maker's intention. Instead it is an uncomfortable, draining experience--a work of strength and power. Perhaps the greatest assessment of The Devils comes from Russell himself in a small moment from the production film, "Director of Devils," where he is shown viewing the film for the first time with Peter Maxwell Davies' score on the track. At the moment when the walls are dynamited, accompanied by a dissonant outburst of music, there is a shot of the film's creator grimacing and flinching. As a future Russell hero, Henri Gaudier-Brzeska, will put it, offering Russell's own artistic credo, "If it don't give me a lot doing it, how the hell is it going to give anything to anybody else?"

* * *

To overlook The Boy Friend as one of Ken Russell's major works is to ignore not only one of the pure delights of modern filmmaking, but to miss a very important point of Russell's development as a filmmaker. It is not surprising perhaps that Joseph Gomez, who seems to feel that Russell peaked with The Devils, should simply toss off a few lines about the film at the introduction of his chapter on Savage Messiah,[3] but in so doing Gomez limits his own perception of art to the purely "serious." Further, Jack Fisher's rejection of the film's characters as cardboard may have some bearing on Polly and Tony,[4] but such criticism falls disastrously wide of the mark as concerns the subordinate characters. Gene D. Phillips does better by the film in his Russell book, but even so the final impression is that the joys of The Boy Friend are a fringe benefit to Russell's filmography at best. Russell has himself always looked askance at the film, but this, presumably, owes much to the number of unpleasant experiences encountered during the making of the film and MGM's cavalier treatment in cutting the American release print. It is an altogether regrettable situation in that The Boy Friend is a demonstrably better work than such an overrated, albeit serious, film as Women in Love.

On nearly every level The Boy Friend is a remarkable film. In terms of creating a straightforward musical film Russell has proven that he is an endless fountain of creativity, and it is very wrong to consider the film as either a simple homage to or parody of Busby Berkeley. It is no great accomplishment to ape Berkeley's style as A. Edward Sutherland (who had worked with Berkeley on Palmy Days in 1931) demonstrated as early as 1933 in International House. For that matter it is not even especially difficult to transcend Berkeley's technical precision, which was always sketchy to say the least. (In any large Berkeley number someone is invariably out of step, his circles are always lopsided, and in the case of the track-in to the giant close-up of Ginger Rogers in Gold Diggers of 1933 the focus is lost on two occasions.) Russell goes to great lengths to base many of his production numbers on Berkeley originals (he even goes so far as to utilize part of the plot and dialogue from Forty-Second Street),

Finding a Voice   151

but he goes beyond Berkeley in a number of respects. With
the notable exception of "I'm Going Shopping with You" in
Gold Diggers of 1935, Berkeley never made much of an effort to actually integrate his musical set-pieces into the structure of the film. In a strictly literal sense this makes
Berkeley's films as a body come under the heading of films
with music rather than musical films. Russell retains something of this basic structure in that most of the songs in
The Boy Friend (excepting "Any Old Iron," "You Are My
Lucky Star," and "All I Do Is Dream of You") are part of
the stage production of Sandy Wilson's play The Boy Friend.
Russell's major departure from Berkeley is to divide the
stage production from the more fantastic aspects of his musical presentation by the introduction of a fantasy element.
Hence, the elaborate numbers all stem from the imaginations
of different characters within the film, and each of these fantasy elements is kept separate from the next. DeThrill's
fantasies (which roughly correspond to Russell's fantasies)
are distinctly different from Polly's or Max's fantasies.
Resultantly, the DeThrill sequences are showy and Hollywood-
like, while Polly's are more wistful and child-like, and
Max's fantasy is a naive depiction of what he thinks a good
show would look like. On this basis alone The Boy Friend
would deserve inclusion in the pantheon of great film musicals. Rarely, if ever, has such a concentrated effort been
made to link the musical numbers not only to the structure
of the film, but to the characters as well. It is interesting
to note that by creating a mixture of the real presentation of
a musical number with a fantasy presentation, Russell has
fashioned a musical film both in the pure sense and in the
Berkeley set piece sense, and in so doing has established an
almost textbook definition of the two schools of thought. By
relegating the huge set pieces to the realm of individual fantasy he, probably unconsciously, stresses the basic premise
behind the pure musical--that the sudden outburst of a character into song is nothing more or less than the literal depiction of someone walking down the street with a song running through his or her mind.

   Russell goes beyond Berkeley on a purely technical level as well. In effect he has combined Berkeley's flair for
the exotic and penchant for the geometric with the more se-
dately balanced work of Dave Gould, who created the large
ensemble dances for the first two Astaire-Rogers films.
Granted, Gould was capable of flights of fancy that were often the equal of Berkeley (in fact Russell's climactic "Riviera" number is drawn from Gould's concept from Flying Down

to Rio), but Gould was not a fantasist in the sense of Berkeley, nor was his imagination the staple of his peculiar genius. Gould's fantastic aspects were always firmly rooted in reality --the girls in Flying Down to Rio are actually supposed to be on the wings of airplanes flying over Rio de Janeiro. Significantly, the DeThrill fantasies also have a basis in reality, even if that reality is only by virtue of an outgrowth from the real to the fantastic; i.e., the girls on the giant gramophone are drawn from the real gramophone in the stage production, or the soundstage setting for "The Riviera." This, however, is not the major inspiration which Russell draws from Gould's work. Russell has shrewdly allied Berkeley's explosive imagination with Gould's sense of grace, and then imposed his own unique vision on top of this, creating a musical that owes much to the past, while looking toward the future at the same time. The end result is neither Berkeley nor Gould, but rather Berkeley and Gould used in a typically personal Russell manner. This produces a work that succeeds as both homage and a separate piece of art--a factor that has yet to be learned by such diverse creators as Peter Bogdanovich in both What's Up Doc? and At Long Last Love, Mel Brooks in Young Frankenstein and High Anxiety, and Herbert Ross and Neil Simon together with Murder by Death and The Cheap Detective.

The Boy Friend also cannot be lumped together with any of the other nostalgia-oriented works, as it is so clearly superior to anything else on the subject. Bogdanovich may have had an intriguing idea with At Long Last Love in his creation of an almost perfect example of the textbook pure musical form, but among the film's other deficiencies its inability to capture anything of the era it attempted to portray precluded any chance for aesthetic success. It may be argued that Bogdanovich was working with a predominantly non-musical cast, but then so was Russell, since in actuality only Tommy Tune can be classed as a musical performer. Be that as it may, the entire attempt at an evocation of the thirties in Bogdanovich's film was undermined at every turn by a slick 1970's soundtrack. The same may be said for virtually every film musical that has dealt with a particular period--the orchestrations take on the coloring of the time in which the film was made. By virtue of this even films about music (for example, the 1945 biopic of Jerome Kern, Till the Clouds Roll By, and the 1946 The Jolson Story) reproduce nothing of the sound of the era depicted. Russell's film on the other hand does recapture that sound. The importance of the collaboration of Peter Maxwell Davies and Ken Russell

Finding a Voice 153

cannot be overstated in any evaluation of The Boy Friend. Russell inundated Maxwell Davies with recordings of the period so that he could grasp the sort of sound The Boy Friend was to have. Says Russell, "I played him lots of Paul Whiteman, etc., "5 and the closeness of this working arrangement surely pays off in the final track. The sound of the early musicals is deftly captured with all its marvelously unique insistence on a heavy bass line (contributed by a tuba, not an upright bass), a straightforward rhythm section (usually including either a banjo or rhythm guitar), and a battery of various "gimmick" instruments. Later approaches to orchestration may be considerably smoother, producing a richer tone, but in smoothing out the sound, most if not all of the excitement and immediacy is lost also. In the musical track for The Boy Friend Russell and Maxwell Davies restore this with a vengeance.

Admittedly, the American release print of The Boy Friend is something of a bastardization of Russell's original cut, but it is by no means a complete disaster. (That was later accomplished by CBS Television, about whose wholesale butchery of the film there are no words to adequately describe. Gleefully slashing away at about a third of the original, dropping major points of the plot, and stupidly reorganizing the opening of the film, CBS produced an incomprehensible mess that might be charitably likened to those little ten-minute souvenir films from features created for home use.) The American print, which is devoid of fourteen minutes of the original, departs from Russell's concept in a number of areas, but oddly none of the cuts have any bearing on certain aspects of the film being "too British" to travel well as is often put forth. (That is, unless MGM was simply referring to the casting of Barbara Windsor, who is extremely popular in Britain but almost unknown in America, many of whose scenes are among the missing.) Russell's affectionate evocation of the English Music Hall--a factor which permeates much of the backstage scenes--is very much in evidence in either version. A simple comparison of the American print with the post-production continuity script of the British version reveals that the major structural change occurs in the disappearance of a subplot involving the philandering Mr. Peter and the efforts of his wife (who appears not at all in the American version) to catch up with him. This not only dispenses with much of Peter's characterization, but in so doing plays havoc with that of Hortense (the aforementioned Barbara Windsor excisions), whose character becomes somewhat vague in the American print with the removal of her song, "It's So Much Nicer in Nice, " due to the related subplot activities during the number. Oddly, the American print fails to cut one reference to the triangular situation with Peter, Mrs. Peter, and Hortense, resulting in a scene between Hortense and him that no longer makes any sense. Other casualties include the majority of the "Greek Fantasy, " which now looks awkward and truncated, the song "I've Got the You-Don't-Want-to-Play-with-Me Blues, " and bits and pieces casually scissored, to no real purpose, from the beginnings and endings of scenes. Possibly the most curious cutting of all is the editor's indulgence in a bit of "creativity" by splitting up the scene where Max and the company have champagne in the stage box with DeThrill by inserting the scene which originally followed it in the middle. Such a move is not exactly ruinous, but it does indicate the disrespectful treatment of The Boy Friend at the hands of MGM. One assumes that had Russell wanted the scene broken up in this manner he would have done so originally. The fact that the only other cross-cutting of this sort in the film is used to comic effect (so that Percy and Madame Dubonnet appear to have been listening to the call of a "love bird" for an impossibly long time) indicates that it scarcely fits in with the film's overall editing pattern.

Far and away the most shocking aspect to be found in the admittedly not very large volume of criticism on The Boy Friend is the almost total disregard for the complexity of the film, its serious side, the intricate textural patterns within the film, and the almost impossibly well-rounded characterizations. Once again we find ourselves confronted with the problem of attitude concerning the "non-serious" contemporary film. To call The Boy Friend an escapist fantasy is a little like quibbling that Shakespeare's A Midsummer Night's Dream is not serious enough, or calling Chaplin a silent film comic. In strictly Russellian terms it should be remembered that a film does not have to depend on its main character being burned at the stake in order to have a claim on either significance or artistic merit. In analyzing The Boy Friend it can be seen that the film has more than a marginal claim to both.

The shrewdness of Russell's characterizations in the film is immediately apparent in the film's opening shots where we are introduced to Polly singing "I Could Be Happy with You, " while looking at a photograph of Tony displayed in the bar of the Theatre Royal. At once we know that Polly is a dreamer like so many of Russell's protagonists. More-

Finding a Voice

Ken Russell rehearsing Twiggy during a recording session for The Boy Friend. (Courtesy of Ken Russell)

over, we know of her attraction to Tony before we actually see him and without a word spoken about these feelings. Unlike Russell's previous dreamers, however, circumstances always converge to bring Polly back to consciousness and keep her grounded in the real world. In this instance it is the sudden realization that she is late with the drinks and snacks for the stage company that snaps her out of her daydream of Tony. It is just the beginning of a pattern that Russell uses throughout the film, and the pattern is important because it makes Polly's final decision perfectly consistent with what has gone before. Furthermore, this concern--central to most of the characters in the film in one way or another--places The Boy Friend well within the thematic world of Russell's usual concern with the effects of dreams on reality and the gulf that often separates the two. Throughout the remainder of the pre-credit sequence Polly's daydreaming characteristics are constantly brought into focus: she brings Tony an apple, but he has just eaten one (ironically, the apple goes to Alphonse, who is himself hopelessly in love with Polly); she has sent him flowers, but has not the nerve to tell him who sent them; she gazes longingly at a picture of Rudolph Valentino, forgets herself in the dream of romance he represents and whistles in the dressing room with the subsequent outbursts from the others once more bringing her back to reality.

Russell also sketches in the other characters in these scenes to a surprising degree. There is, of course, the aforementioned situation of Alphonse being smitten with Polly. Beyond this Russell provides the beginning of the background on the show's one American performer, Tommy, which also starts the set-up for the film's climactic gag. The character of Maisie as a self-important golddigger is economically established as she responds to Polly's statement that the missing Rita is the star of the show: "Do you really think so?" Finally, there is the establishment of a connection between Maisie and Fay, something which Russell subtly and tastefully touches on throughout the film. (The two women are frequently framed in tight two-shots, in Max's fantasy Fay casually caresses Maisie's leg with her stockinged foot, and it is Fay to whom Maisie looks for reassurance and acceptance when her dreams of Hollywood are shattered at the film's end. This slightly lesbian undertone is never stressed, but it helps to make Fay and Maisie real people with more to them than just their dialogue and musical turns.) Just prior to the credits we are afforded our first glimpse of the Pianist (played with great relish by the film's assistant musical director, Peter Greenwell). Even here the character is brought to life by the simple prop of his ever present cigarette holder and the eternally too long ash that manages to fall down his front or on the keys in nearly every shot in which he is featured.

Following the opening credits we find Polly preparing to clean the stage--her position, later clarified as that of Assistant Stage Manager, seems to be the thankless one of doing anything that needs doing--and the head of the theatre troupe, Max, standing about nervously. The character of Max, especially in the hands of Max Adrian, is one of Russell's most delightfully manic creations, though, sadly, this was to be not only Adrian's last film for Russell, but his last altogether. (The function usually performed by Adrian has since seemingly gone to John Justin: Shaw in Savage Messiah, Count D'Algout in Lisztomania, and Sidney Olcott in Valentino.) Always worried and harassed, yet impressed with his own importance and with boundless energy, still dreaming of that "big break" that must surely come even at this late date in life, Max, too, is a complete character. With his introduction we are brought to the commencement of the play, The Boy Friend, and here, by implication, lie the roots of the dreams of the characters. Here Russell explores the differences, and the similarities, of the characters and situations onstage with the reality lurking in the wings, and the impending return to the mundane and routine following the performance. This is not to say that Russell damns the theatre or dreams or the theatrical experience. In fact he celebrates all these things, and, perhaps by virtue of the type of dreams in The Boy Friend and the fact that the characters can and do survive those dreams and illusions, it is here for the first time that he exposes a true, albeit somewhat amused, love for the foibles and pretensions caused by such dreams. For Russell the Theatre Royal is a magical place and he conveys that magic to us, as we will see shortly.

Appropriately, Russell has placed us up in the gods' gallery for the curtain rise, imparting something of the sense of actually being in the theatre itself. This is one of the most surprising elements in the film, and it is an outgrowth of the same kind of thinking that created the sequence in Song of Summer where a scratchy record so enraptures its listeners that soon only the beauty of the music can be heard. (This finds a direct counterpart later in the film and resurfaces in later films also.) In a very similar manner the tackiness of the settings for the stage play, the stilted posturing of the players, manage to become transformed into something appealing and engaging as Russell draws us ever further into them. At the beginning of the play, however, what is mostly apparent is the very audible squeaking of the rising curtain and the impossibility of Hortense's Cockney attempt at playing a French maid (a sound so horrible that it causes Max to lament, "She's no more French than I am," despite his constant off-stage prompting of "Accent!").

The plot that will allow Polly to live a kind of dream begins developing as the supporting players, Fay, Maisie, Nancy, and Dulcie, make their entrances trading quips with Max about the absence of Rita. Her absence is almost immediately explained by a phone call from the hospital. Rita, in time honored tradition so immortalized in Forty-second Street, has broken her ankle--"Trapped her high heel in the tram line, her foot." ("Ooh, it ain't off?" is Polly's rather gruesome response to this news.) In a wink, Max switches from visions of ruin to the optimistic if dubious pronouncement that Polly should go on in Rita's place on the flimsy pretext--which seems to be news to Polly--that one of the duties of the Assistant Stage Manager is "to understudy everybody's part."

With the plot underway and Polly whisked off to be readied for her debut, Russell introduces two more characters, his alter-ego, DeThrill, and Max's wife, Catherine. DeThrill is rather a study in his striped suit, Panama hat and sunglasses, cigarette holder and cane, though these accoutrements serve to link him to Russell, whose penchant for unconventional garb is well known. (Consider, Gene D. Phillips found Russell on the set of The Boy Friend "inexplicably clad in a sailor suit several sizes too small for him."6) DeThrill's entrance in a gleaming white Auburn Boat-tail Speedster (incongruous for a two-seater it is chauffeur-driven) is a little gem of foreshadowing as three street-buskers who

Maisie, Fay, Polly, and Dulcie in the title number from The Boy Friend on the stage of the Theatre Royal. (Courtesy of Ken Russell)

will later be recruited by Michael ("You did say get anyone, Mr. Max") to beef up the orchestration of Max's song "Never Too Late to Fall in Love" are here serenading DeThrill with that very song as he steps up to the theatre.

Once inside the theatre the chauffeur attends to the ticket buying which turns into a singularly odd encounter with Catherine. (Catherine Wilmer brings more than a touch of the same sort of mental imbalance to the role that she had earlier contributed as Mrs. Crich in Women in Love.) The request for the best seat in the house brings forth the utterly useless response that he could have the "Royal Box" except for the fact "that it's permanently reserved for the Princess Arthur of Connaught." Further inquiry finally leads DeThrill to being given the stage box for one pound ("Must be a small box").

While all this is going on, Alphonse is trying to get Polly ready for her entrance, and in the process Tony comes in to wish her luck. Here Russell immediately reinforces Polly's position as a dreamer, and proves once more that the cliché, properly handled, can be made fresh and effective, as he breaks up the old gag of having Tony remove Polly's spectacles and exclaim, "But you're beautiful!" by tracking in a delirious arc around them as Tony kisses her for luck. "All this in one day--it's too much," sighs Polly as she wafts back into her dream world, from which she is sharply awakened by Alphonse warning that it is time for her entrance.

In the wings Catherine has told Max of her encounter with DeThrill, and once Max verifies "what sort of a 'Thrill' he is," he waxes enthusiastic about being discovered until he realizes that Polly is assaying Rita's part. With consummate tact he decides to stop the show on account of this just as Polly comes into earshot, thereby seriously undermining her already shaky confidence. The prospect of refunding the money, however, has a sobering effect on him and he decides to brazen it out. To boost Polly's confidence he hands her the old Warner Baxter speech from Forty-Second Street-- guaranteed to scare the wits out of anyone about to be thrust onstage--about "The careers and lives of all these boys and girls are depending on you," and culminating in the classic line "You're going out there as a youngster, you've got to come back a star!"

Polly's first few minutes onstage are unreservedly

catastrophic as she blows her lines and answers Maisie's question as to the whereabouts of Rita loud enough for the audience to get an earful. Maisie cruelly upstages Polly and steals from her the letter which has her lines written on it, dropping it on the floor and trapping it under her foot, leaving Polly hopelessly at sea until Dulcie shoves Maisie to one side. Polly, however, does know the songs and once she settles into singing the title tune she improves immensely (despite Max's off-stage cries of "Eyes and teeth! Eyes and teeth!"). She also, quite accidentally, extracts a certain amount of revenge on Maisie as she makes the others look grotesquely out of step by not changing tempo on the chorus. Russell has not thus far really drawn us (or DeThrill) into the show, and so the number is left to Max to envision what it might look like "if only we had money."

Max's fantasy is unlike any other fantasy in the film in both concept and execution, as befits Russell's approach to the personalized fantasy structure of the film. As a piece it is blessed with a nutty lack of logic (Polly, Tony, Tommy, Fay, Maisie, et al. form members of the orchestra as well as perform onstage) and a sense of tackiness, or at best faded brilliance, much like its progenitor. Basically, the sequence is done like an impossible musical review, and the only fantasy in the film that is designed to appear as if it were onstage. It is probably unconscious on Russell's part, but this fact comes across as a little jibe at Berkeley, whose numbers were ostensibly part of a stage show regardless of the fact that the set might be ten stories high and many of the effects necessitated an overhead view in order to be appreciated. Russell does not subvert his own creativity to the character of Max to the extent that the number itself lacks his own signature. On the contrary, there are a number of delights sprinkled throughout the sequence, including, but not limited to, some splendid transitions from bit to bit, e.g., the flying golf ball turning into the stars of the American flag followed by one of the earliest instances of Russell's introduction of a character by having her pop up into the frame; and Tommy's entrance so that he appears to burst through the frame of the previous scene as if it were paper. The entire sequence is aptly summed up by Catherine following the image of Polly as the radiator ornament on a mock-up Rolls Royce, "Polly, the Spirit of Ecstasy? Ridiculous!"

Just as Catherine's remarks drag Max out of the clouds of fantasy, so also do the squeals of the girls onstage perform a similar function for Polly, who has seemingly lost

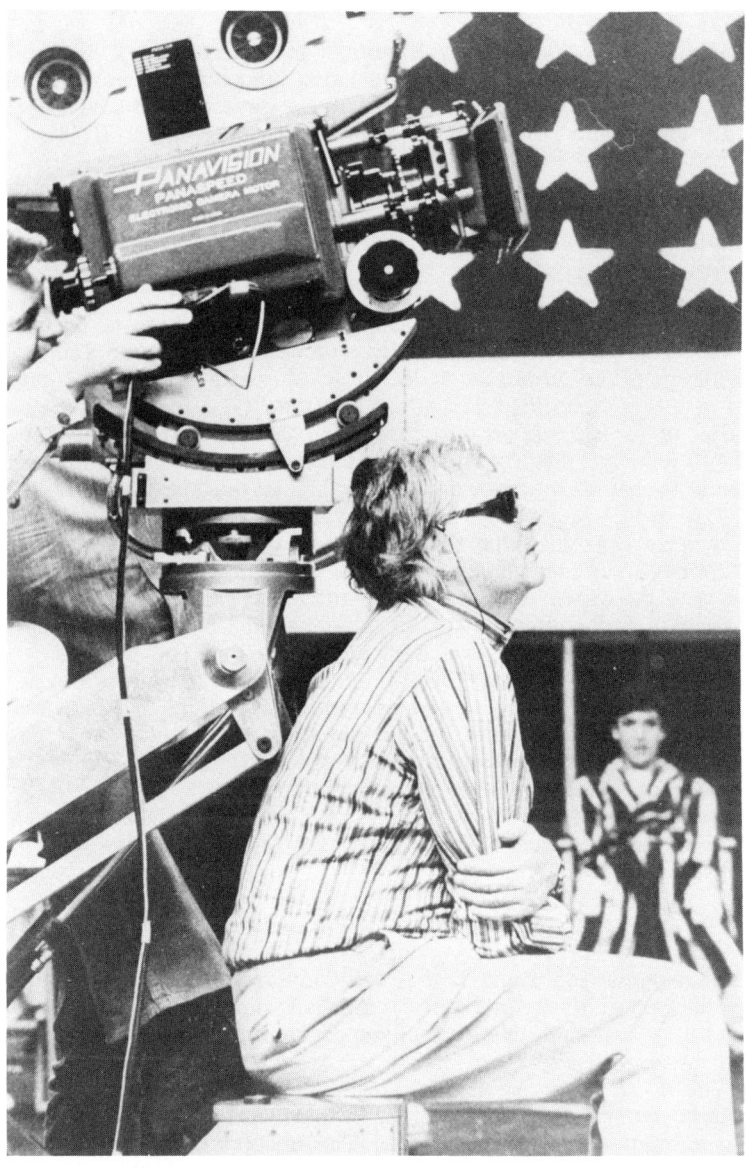

Russell directing Max's fantasy version of the title song for The Boy Friend. Tommy Tune looks on from the background. (Courtesy of Ken Russell)

track of where she is and what she is doing. The reality of her situation is further brought into focus as she tries to run offstage, but is shoved back on by Max with the vague instructions, "Do a Ruby Keeler," until she dances off the other side of the stage only to have Tony thrust her back on again. It is important for the film's development and its inner logic that the dream of being onstage is not Polly's dream. This must be kept in mind if the consistency or irony of the film's conclusion is to be understood and appreciated, and there is, perhaps, no better visualization of it than the image of Polly being shoved onstage from either side.

Polly continues to plow through her role, and in a charming piece of theatricality, as she and Madame Dubonnet walk in place gathering " 'olly 'ocks" while a row of ersatz flowers is squeakily pulled across the stage to give the illusion of movement, she is caught in the lie that her mythical boyfriend has been writing her letters from Paris. Russell's handling of this scene is remarkable in that he opens it in close-shot, imparting to the viewer the feeling that Polly and Madame Dubonnet are really walking through a garden, then reverts to a long-shot so that we see the simple mechanical device by which this illusion is achieved. Russell is too much of a jokester to let the obvious comic opportunity of the situation pass, but one is scarcely prepared for the shambles that is made out of the scene by Michael ambling past behind a cut-out tree and getting turned the wrong way round, Polly overcome by the onion that Alphonse has given her to help her cry and stopping the show cold by running from the stage, or even the marvelous "Oh, what the hell" attitude of Madame Dubonnet, who recognizes disaster when she sees it, and blithely tosses her flowers into the air in happy resignation.

Russell follows this bit of high comic energy with a little scene in which one can recognize the seeds for much of the approach found in his fully matured films. In arguing with Percy (the film's only truly bad tempered character, quite in contrast to his onstage character) Max solves the problem of Polly's cockney accent when Percy complains, "You'll be expecting me to sing 'Any Old Iron' next." Without a pause, Max cries, "Yes!" and Russell cuts abruptly to a brief scene of just that. The brevity of the fantasy and the fact that it cuts through pretense to hit the truth in an economical fashion (Polly's and Percy's backgrounds not being different at all despite what Percy would like to believe) marks the sequence as the direct ancestor of such moments as the "Shadow Fantasy" and the introduction of Max in Mahler, the seduction of Nora by the Doctor in Tommy, etc. It is through this that Max decides to turn Percy's part into that of "a cockney junk dealer--made your fortune in scrap metal after the war. You want to better yourself for Polly, too." Lost in the haze of something like creativity, Max rushes out to do a hasty rewrite, little caring that Percy proclaims, "I won't do it," and pulls off half his fake moustache.

In his search for a pen to write out this inspiration Max finds himself in the girls' dressing room, where he makes the colossal blunder of telling them that DeThrill is in the audience. At first mistaken by Hortense to mean "DeThrill the jellied eel merchant from Cable Street," the idea is quickly put to rights by Nancy. This is one of Russell's cleverest devices, and, interestingly, it is drawn from his own experience. Having taken Twiggy to see an amateur performance of the play, he found himself in a position not unlike the one in which DeThrill finds himself in the film. 7 Certainly Russell has enlarged upon the experience and developed it into the major plot device concerning the supporting players in the film. Much of the ensuing action is built around this knowledge, and Russell's interest lies in depicting the various reactions and approaches of his protagonists when caught up in a dream situation that just might make their fortunes.

The first of the schemers is Maisie, who is also the most destructive. In a beautifully contrived scene between her and Tommy, Russell delineates what turns out to be her efforts to double cross and upstage her partner. The bulk of the scene consists of background information on Tommy's past, but the whole thing is so skillfully played and choreographed--Tommy drifting backwards through bead curtains and out of focus as he explains his amnesia, his impromptu acting out of Eisenstein's Odessa Steps massacre, and the similarly spontaneous looking charade of escaping from an orphanage in the dead of night--that one scarcely realizes that Russell is feeding us plot information. Given Russell's penchant for slightly bizarre detail, it is even possible to overlook the obvious plant of Tommy's demonstration of "The Double Trip Maxie Ford with the Knickerbocker Break," which, within a plot-line so full of interwoven hidden identities and coincidences that it would warm the heart of Shakespeare or Dickens, proves to be very important. Significantly,

Maisie places herself behind the bead curtain to make her request that they take it easy this performance as she has a headache, thereby obscuring her face from Tommy.

    The American print removes the entirety of the dialogue preceding Tommy and Maisie's "Won't You Charleston with Me?" number (along with a number of oddly pointless little scissorings in the previous scene), opting instead to start right in on the number itself. (Like a great many of the later cuts, this tends to obscure the narrative of the play within the film.) Earlier Russell had charmed us with the naive nature of Max's staging, but here he begins to seriously draw the viewer into the play. Unlike the big production numbers to come, "Won't You Charleston with Me?" is intimate in its presentation, never leaving the confines of the stage. Russell's filming of the number is anything but theatrical, however, as he tilts and glides around the stage, setting up a rhythmic editing pattern that increases in its fury when Alphonse apprises Tommy of Maisie's double cross, and climaxes in a thrillingly shot and edited bit where Maisie leaps from the stage, landing hard atop the piano, continuing her dance without missing a step. It is arguable that this is a cheating sequence as no member of the audience could ever view the number as Russell has done, but to take this attitude is to overlook the very real excitement generated by the presentation. In many respects it is reminiscent of the Astaire-Rogers "Can-you-top-this?" dance to "Isn't It a Lovely Day?" in Top Hat, but without losing sight of either the plot (attempting to impress DeThrill) or The Boy Friend's own style.

    Following a brief argument with Percy, who is still balking at playing a Cockney junk dealer, Max has Polly pin the new dialogue to a bunch of flowers so that she and Madame Dubonnet can read their lines onstage. As with the majority of Max's ideas this proves to be less than practical, as Polly and Madame Dubonnet prance around the stage and struggle with the bouquet, contorting themselves into ever more awkward positions to keep the dialogue in view. At this point in the narrative Russell introduces the offstage misunderstanding between Polly and Tony as concerns Tony's relationship with Dulcie. This serves a threefold purpose in

[Opposite:] Graham Armitage, Christopher Gable, Twiggy, Murray Melvin, Brian Murphy, and the cast in the truncated Bacchanal, a casualty of the U.S. print of The Boy Friend. (Courtesy of Ken Russell)

Russell's hands as it relates to a parallel structure with the onstage relationship of Polly and Tony, gently mocks the sort of plot-line one associates with the classic musical films, and also has a direct bearing on Polly's onstage performance. It is only through her very real anguish over this misunderstanding that she succeeds in her role and manages to touch the theatre audience. Chances are that she will never give this sort of performance again, and this is significant in that it makes her final decision a wise one, as well as one that is consistent with her character.

The business with the flowers leads into the sequence that one most regrets is badly truncated in the American print. Not only is it galling to miss the unforgettable spectacle of Max Adrian as Bacchus in this Greek Fantasy, but the cutting of the scene is clumsily accomplished since the entirety is not removed, making the remnants seem patchy and oddly timed. Fortunately, however, the lead in with Russell's marvelous in-joke reference to a sequence in his own Isadora ("Attends, my little Isadoras, today we dance 'Narcissus'") is retained. Russell's original cut had the distinct advantage of characterizing many of the major characters, e.g., the aforementioned Bacchus, Tommy as Mercury, Percy as Zeus, etc. This was beneficial in that it gave the viewer a firm grasp on Polly's perception of the people around her, whereas the American print only details her daydream position as regards Tony. This turns a brilliant idea that enlarged our knowledge of her character into a simple restatement of something we already know.

The scene which follows the Greek Fantasy is mercifully left intact and turns out to be one of the most charmingly funny in the film, even though Russell has chosen to break it into two parts for comic effect. Catherine, now performing her function as a one-woman-band-cum-sound-effects-machine, is the focal point of the scene despite the action onstage. Russell's view of this rather strange lady as she alternates playing violin, bird whistle (which ultimately and unceremoniously spits back in her face), and accordion is wondrously affectionate. Heretofore--and largely afterward --Catherine has appeared so off-centered as to be almost inhuman, but in this one scene she becomes so transfixed by the music she plays and her clever accompaniments to the action onstage that her joy in doing so is transmitted to the audience. There is a great deal of talk about so-called "magical moments" in films, but in this instance it is true, and the sequence remains one of the most engaging things Russell has ever done.

Finding a Voice

In the middle of Catherine's performance in the orchestra pit, Russell cuts away to Polly waiting in the dressing room and her meeting with the thus far mysterious Rita. At first all we see of her is her feet, one of which possesses a most cumbersome looking cast on which she clumps noisily into the room. Russell holds the suspense of our first meeting by cutting away to a reaction shot from Polly, returning to Rita's feet, and only then tilting the camera up to her face. The pay-off is worth the suspense as Rita turns out to be Glenda Jackson in an unbilled guest role. (The casual irony of having Russell's first big star confronting newcomer Twiggy adds another dimension to the film also, in that it brings in the paralleling of a real situation to complement the existing interrelated levels of onstage, offstage, and fantasy.) Once again, Russell falls back on the <u>Forty-second Street</u> material in an affectionately mocking manner, giving Bebe Daniels' old pep talk to Ruby Keeler to Rita, who works it in in the same manner as Max's earlier Warner Baxter dialogue, so that the encouragement seems more potentially damaging than helpful. Little does the egotistical Rita realize that Polly will indeed "go out there and be so great, you'll make me hate you."

Polly's next onstage appearance introduces her stage character to the stage character of Tony in an arch little scene from the original play that Russell progressively opens up until it becomes a positive statement on art and the creative mind. Starting slowly the sequence builds to one of the most complex musical numbers in the film. At first it is only Polly and Tony lip-synching "I Could Be Happy with You" to a gramophone record. Then, at the point where they actually begin to sing, the music on the soundtrack becomes crystal clear and the song has crossed the barrier in the mind from what it really sounds like to what it could sound like. Reality, however, rudely interrupts this when the record becomes stuck, but this pause allows enough space for the DeThrill-Russell imagination to take over, and the image switches to Polly dreamily dancing on a giant gramophone. Tony then appears and the two of them do an Astaire-Rogers styled romantic dance, which Russell photographs from a variety of angles. This dance is followed by a medium close-shot of Polly in a sort of Egyptian art deco headdress, reflected by banks of mirrors on either side of her. Russell zooms back to a fairly long shot revealing a chorus of similarly dressed dancers also on the record, which, in a reversal of the earlier movement, now turns counterclockwise. As the sequence continues to build, Russell cuts back and forth between these clockwise and counterclockwise movements, which combined with his increasingly rapid cutting produces a startlingly vertiginous feeling of pure movement. The real surprise comes with his decision to slow the climax down and recreate the elegance of the fantasy's opening so that the number, like its gramophone motif, becomes circular itself. His final shot is a recreation of Berkeley's "Young and Healthy" number from Forty-second Street, as the camera tracks along the surface of the gramophone record in between the dancers' legs (beautifully, almost luminously lit) and into a tight two-shot on Polly and Tony. With "I Could Be Happy with You" Russell reaches the height of technical virtuosity, and wisely he does not attempt to top it until the film's climactic "Riviera" number, which, even more than this sequence (with its visualization of the growth of a germ of an idea to a full-blown work of art), has as much to do with the creative process as with the film's plot-line.

Alas, it is something of a comedown to return to the slightly wooden dialogue of the play from this stratospheric creation, but Russell manages to keep the situation in check, mirroring our own return to earth with Polly's distress over what she can only perceive as Tony's immediate return to Dulcie once he is offstage. The gap separating Max's show with the fantasy we have just witnessed and that separating-- or seeming to separate--the onstage-offstage Polly-Tony relationship is clearly delineated.

Still reflecting on this wistful mood, Russell keeps the proceedings deliberately low-key for the moment, as Polly sings "You Are My Lucky Star" in the dressing room. Handled very quietly and simply (the entire scene consists of two shots) this is used in direct counterpoint to the flashiness of the previous number. (It is interesting to realize that MGM has gotten more mileage out of this song than anyone has with anything else in a similar vein--save possibly Paramount with "Dream Lover" and "Isn't It Romantic?" or Warner Bros. with Carl W. Stallings' arrangement of "A Cup of Coffee, a Sandwich, and You," used in virtually every one of their cartoons whenever food is shown. Having introduced the song in 1929 in The Broadway Melody, MGM brought it back for Broadway Melody of 1936 (1935) and Singin' in the Rain (1952). With The Boy Friend it travels all the way into the seventies. The later inclusion of "All I Do Is Dream of You" is only slightly less long-lived.) From this wistfulness Russell brings both Polly and the audience back to the reality of the immediate situation by having DeThrill and Maisie (the latter being hell-bent on impressing the great man, though how one attends Brighton College in France as she claims is never made clear) enter and restore the flow from this pause. DeThrill finds Polly charming, but Maisie viciously undermines this attitude at every turn, finally telling him, "She's only an understudy, you know--not a real actress," before dragging him off to a little champagne celebration Max has staged in DeThrill's box.

The episode in DeThrill's box (the sequence split in two in the American print) returns the film to the high gear of the earlier comic sequences. Brilliantly timed, the scene is structured so that everyone is so intent on capturing DeThrill's attention and pleasing him that they all work at cross purposes. A photo in Max's scrapbook which DeThrill mistakes for Max turns out to be Catherine as Hamlet (in her words, "a tragedy"; in Max's, "a travesty"). Maisie interrupts with more "impressive" French, largely consisting of a description of the decor of the Theatre Royal, until Hortense tells her to "shut up." Even that silences her but for a moment. Ultimately, in what appears to be a test of influence, DeThrill smashes his champagne glass on the floor, and everyone except Max ("That champagne cost money!") apes this action.

The brief scene which comes next in the British print and is in the middle of the box scene in the American, is just further reinforcement of Polly's (and our) misunderstanding of the relationship between Tony and Dulcie, as they appear to be ducking into the dressing room for a romantic tryst, believing Polly to be elsewhere.

Russell's handling of the "Sur la Plage" number which follows is similar to that of "Won't You Charleston with Me" in that it contains no visual fantasy, though there is a stroke of soundtrack fantasy, when, fed up with the incessant sound of piano and drums, DeThrill claps his hands over his ears and the track bursts into full orchestration. The number itself is more than slightly reminiscent of King Louis' drag act in The Devils with its smiling painted sun and cardboard cut-out waves. Nonetheless, Russell's construction of the number is sound and exciting, relying for its effects on editing and the inherent charm in the tackiness of the material. There are some really pleasurable surprises in the cutting and choreography--Tommy popping up into the frame in close-shot, made up like a rajah; a pantomime elephant; and the contorted effect of other legs sticking up behind the principals as if they were attached.

Russell continues the pattern of presenting a more or less straight stage number followed by one of the larger fantasy set pieces--i.e., "The Boy Friend" done straight followed by Max's fantasy; "Won't You Charleston with Me" followed by the Greek Fantasy; "Fancy Forgetting" followed by "I Could Be Happy with You"; "Sur la Plage" followed by this number, "A Room in Bloomsbury." ("You Are My Lucky Star" and the later "All I Do Is Dream of You" are exempt as they are unrelated to the stage show.) Sad to say, though, that "A Room in Bloomsbury" is undoubtedly the least successful of Russell's fantasies, though it is possessed of a structural form of more than passing interest, one aspect of which is to be found again in the later and more mature Lisztomania. The ever evolving movement from the stage show to intimate fantasy to the climactic grand scale fantasy is wonderfully conceived. The beauty of the economy of movement from one section to the next is undeniable--onstage Polly and Tony look through the window of a toy house on the crazy golf course, which takes us to Polly and Tony inside the house; from there they leap from the window and in the succeeding shot land in the "Pixieland" setting. The number itself is not entirely without merit, especially in the Bloomsbury attic where Polly and Tony have a nice moment with a series of Astaire-Rogers like thrilling turns, and tumble off the oversized furniture in a manner reminiscent of Astaire's solo in Let's Dance. Given these bits and pieces it is altogether too bad that Russell has fallen into the same trap that ensnared Berkeley in his later work and even marred portions of his mammoth Warner Bros.' productions: a severe case of cuteness. Truth to tell, "A Room in Bloomsbury" outdoes its predecessors in terms of sheer technique (compare the number with its obvious counterparts in the non-Berkeley Carefree and The Band Wagon), but for all that it fails to communicate as part of the fabric of the overall film. The fact that it is too cute--almost nauseatingly so in spots--is less the problem than a symptom of it. All of the other fantasies in the film, indeed all of the numbers, are firmly planted in a time period (roughly 1929 through 1935), and the inclusion of this softed edged, more recent-looking material is jarring. In other instances Russell mixes his inspirations and his own visions and comes up with a satisfying original creation, but he does so within the period and forms a cohesive whole. In "A Room in Bloomsbury" he misfires, and ends up with something that, for all its invention, is neither fish nor fowl. The best moment in the entire sequence belongs to Rita, who, appalled at the audience's applause, turns and in a fit of ill-temper loudly "ssshhh's" them.

Sally Bryant, Moyra Fraser, Caryl Little, and typically paired Georgina Hale and Antonia Ellis surround Bryan Pringle in one of the losses due to MGM's decision to drop the entire tenth reel of The Boy Friend for U.S. consumption. (Courtesy of Ken Russell)

It is here that the American print has its largest gap by the simple expedient of dropping the entirety of the film's tenth reel! Not only does this hamper the characterizations of Hortense and Peter (and in the process make nonsense of the dialogue in another scene), but it also breaks up the pattern of a straight stage presentation followed by one blessed with the DeThrill-Russell imagination. One truly regrets the loss of two songs, one of which expands the characterizations of Percy and Madame Dubonnet (setting up another of the film's parallel structures between stage and reality), and the fleshing out of the character of Alphonse, as well as the furthered Polly-viewer misconception about Dulcie and Tony. The evocation of Berkeley's "My Honey Says, 'Yes! Yes!'" from Palmy Days and "Shuffle Off to Buffalo" from Forty-second Street is gone with the excision of "It's So Much Nicer in Nice," as is Maisie's appearance in that number as Oscar Wilde (furthering the sexual ambiguity of her character). All of this is extremely unfortunate, and in that the entire reel is missing it would seem that this would be the easiest section of the film to restore, and one can only hope that the 16mm distributors will one day see fit to do this much at least, especially as this is the one cut that is actually damaging to the film's structure.

The American print picks up back at the beginning of the eleventh reel, which is very fortunate because in the first scene in this reel Russell sets up a visual pattern in detailing Fay's temptation and downfall under Maisie's influence. In this instance, following Maisie's pronouncement, "Well, we've got to look after ourselves," Russell tracks in to a close-shot of Fay as the advice registers. He repeats this pattern from two-shot to close-shot in the two similar compositions with Fay and Max--the first when she has obviously taken Maisie's advice, and the second when Max fires her for having done so. (DeThrill's smile and wink at her after this last undercuts the harshness of the moment, conveying the idea that it is unlikely that her firing is in any way permanent.)

Maisie's musical number, "Safety in Numbers," is one of the film's most riotous sequences, both in its stage and fantasy presentations. Rife with inspired touches--the offhand destruction of everything she does by Tommy, Alphonse, Michael, and Peter in retribution for her double cross on Tommy; DeThrill's hearty chuckle over her ad-libbed claim that "After all, I'm only seventeen"; DeThrill's growing involvement with the proceedings and the performers as he fantasizes himself into the number--"Safety in Numbers" is completely successful, and this extends to one of Maxwell Davies' best orchestrations, so completely in period even to its mock Jesse Crawford organ part. Some of the effects in the number are extremely simple in their effectiveness, notably the clever lighting making the playing card headdresses appear to turn on and off depending on the manner in which the wearer's head is positioned, and the economy of slipping in and out of the fantasy by direct cuts with no build up. The interpolation of DeThrill into the fantasy at this point is a little masterstroke, as it successfully mirrors his (and our) now total acceptance of the proceedings--the magic of the mind and the theatre have completely broken through the tackiness of the stage show as presented by Mr. Max on the stage of the Theatre Royal.

To further the parallels of the situations found in the film, the following sequence firmly cements the misunder-

Finding a Voice 173

standings about Dulcie and Tony. Just as he and Polly (onstage) are reaching a tender understanding about their feelings, circumstances cause him to answer Dulcie's offstage question, "Have you decided?" with "I love you." Once again reality intrudes and seems to shatter what Polly and the audience would prefer to be true. Russell works this so that it dovetails with Polly's stage misconception of Tony as a thief being pursued by the "rich m'Lord Brockhurst and his wife." It is this paralleled situation that causes Polly to give the heartbreaking performance that is so effective it qualifies as being "so great" that it achieves Rita's request of making her hate Polly, as Rita sits in the audience openly weeping.

As in the earlier occasions of Polly's crises Russell does not let us dwell on them and spoil the overall goodnatured quality of the film, and instead turns to Max's comic antics as he attempts to impress and curry favor with De-Thrill. (It is here that he sends Michael out to get some musicians to accompany his big number in the play--somewhat bigger in the British print.) This is uppermost in the others' minds, too, as Nancy--more or less on the request of De-Thrill--attempts with the dubious help of Hortense ("No ... 'ollywood.... They drop their haitches in France") to learn to speak French. All of this culminates in the most bizarre of Max's scenes with his wife, as he prepares for his number. Catherine, generally giving him a hard time (when apprised that he feels he need dye his hair so the public will recognize him from his lobby photo, she ripostes that the photo is "so yellow with age, you'd have to make up as a Chinaman"), finally extracts a small revenge on Max for referring to her King Charles Spaniel as a dog. Not only has she not "blancoed" Max's spats as she claims, but as she puts one of them on his shoe, it has very obviously been soiled by the dog.

The smallish "All I Do Is Dream of You" number which Polly sings from the catwalk above the deserted stage while watching Tony dance, is similar to the earlier "You Are My Lucky Star" in effect and approach. It is also very probably the finest of the many fine Maxwell Davies arrangements (Russell has already used it as an instrumental on the gramophone in the men's dressing room for the film's opening scenes), possessed of beautifully subtle orchestral coloring and an extremely clever tuba part. The simplicity and wistfulness of the number serves as a pleasant pause before the outcome of Catherine's revenge on Max and Fay's downfall.

Max's "Never Too Late to Fall in Love" number starts out tamely enough as a sketch between Lord Brockhurst and Fay, who is dressed as a nurse, but once she sheds her outfit, revealing a flashy and somewhat daring dress underneath, it is downhill all the way for Max. Unfortunately the American print is somewhat truncated as it removes Max's "latest cinematographic fantasy for the silver screen, entitled 'Beauty and the Bath Chair,'" though the editors were unable to snip the screen for this, now lowering quite incongruously in the background. The number degenerates into a shouting match between Max and Fay as they continue the song after she has climbed from the stage into DeThrill's box. Ultimately, Fay destroys Max, driving him off the stage in shame as she points out, "There's dog's turd all over your spats, sir," much to everyone else's delight.

From this Russell returns to the film's concern with the parallel action of onstage-offstage events in the single longest stretch of the performance presented in the film. Accordingly, this part of the film is also the most deliberately ambiguous as reality and fantasy intermingle and become one (admittedly, this is enhanced in the American print, which removes the transition from reality to fantasy altogether by snipping the opening of Madame Dubonnet's song). Russell begins the scene on an almost hallucinatory note as Percy, Madame Dubonnet, Maisie, Tommy, Dulcie, Alphonse, Fay, Michael, and Nancy do a swirling dance which places them one by one in medium close-shot to deliver their lines (the oddity heightened by their bizarre fancy-dress costumes, especially Tommy's skyscraper outfit and Michael's rabbit suit). This is handled in a dream-like fashion as if it were a continuous monologue. From this Madame Dubonnet comes forth and begins the song for Polly. The first part of the fantasy with Polly seated in a cardboard cutout moon and the rest of the cast surrounding her with their heads only protruding through stars is obviously in reference to Berkeley's climactic "Journey to a Star" number in The Gang's All Here, but Russell's effects do not rely on process work in the manner of Berkeley. It is here far more of a theatrical experience, and it is this change (along with the fact that we quite clearly have Polly singing "that tricky obbligato" of which Rita warned her, thereby anchoring the singing to the stage show) which affords this number so much of its blend of Max's show and the DeThrill-Russell fantasies. Also, at the climax of the number, Polly drops from the cut-out moon into Tony's arms--à la "Room in Bloomsbury"--and this further blurs the distinction. The bulk of the number seems to be drawn from Dave Gould's staging of the daydream version of "You Are My Lucky Star" as it appears in Roy Del Ruth's <u>Broadway Melody of 1936</u>, particularly as concerns Russell's camera prowling through an array of drooping, shimmering strings of beads and streamers which festoon the trees of the set. The entire business is at once simple and effective (again the lighting is of immense help).

  The parallel of the song and situation with Polly's real situation concerning Tony is skillfully worked out so that her actual reconciliation with him--when it turns out that he and Dulcie had been engaged in making her a cake reading, "Happy First Night, I love you, Tony," explaining the suspicious offstage activities--and the reconciliation of the characters onstage occur at the same time. This comes across as an affirmation of the earlier line of Tony's, "Then we're not so different after all," and, indeed, they are not. Similarly, this can be broadened to include the real and the fantastic on a more general level, which Russell suggests may be far more alike than we think.

  It remains for Russell to outdo his previous musical numbers, and this he does in "The Riviera," a fantasy which DeThrill conjures up without the usual lead-in. As previously noted this is based in large measure on Dave Gould's "Flying Down to Rio," but Russell has tied it to the film's situations in such a manner that it becomes the climax of the stage show, a homage to its inspirational source, and DeThrill's last thoughts on the prospect of turning Max's show into a film. DeThrill, fancily garbed in a C. B. DeMille-styled outfit, directs the number on a soundstage, starting with an energetic dance by Tommy and Maisie, which is capped by his finding Nancy still hanging over his shoulder trying to impress him. This leads into the great airplane fantasy (escape from escapism?) at the heart of the sequence. Placing the number on a soundstage in this fashion allows Russell the extra scope to make a statement on the act of creativity and the excitement of it, as DeThrill shouts orders, rides about on a camera boom, and generally seems to be everywhere at once doing everything. Totally stylized, utterly impossible with its geographical displacement and ultimate long track down the top wing of the biplane past many more chorus girls than were there in the earlier shots, "The Riviera" turns its fanciful nature around to strike at a truth by being dramatically sound instead.

  Coming down from this ultimate fantasy we find the

source of DeThrill's vision as a mock-up airplane hauls Polly
and Tony up and offstage while the ensemble sings a reprise
of "I Could Be Happy with You" for the finale of the show.
In so doing he allows a spot for Tommy to do his specialty
of the "Double Trip Maxie Ford with the Knickerbocker Break,'
bringing DeThrill and the audience to a point of extreme interest.
So successful has the performance been that Rita,
in tears, can only hobble dejectedly from the Theatre Royal
along with the other patrons. Backstage everyone is involved
in congratulating Polly on her performance, save for Percy,
who is livid with rage over "ad-libbing, upstaging, a family
row onstage ... cakes and buskers!" and finally concluding
that either Polly or he leave the show. Perhaps it is his
ill-advised reference to Max's buskers, but whatever the
cause it is here that Percy gets his comeuppance as Max
blithely decides to take over the part himself, as he is miscast
as Lord Brockhurst, "far too young."

    Max, too, is soon deflated as he rushes off to settle
things with DeThrill. DeThrill takes a parting shot at Nancy
first. She has studiously managed to learn a sort of French
phrase to which DeThrill responds in German, giving her a
card to give to Polly. Immediately after this he is accosted
by Max, who holds out his hand expecting also to be given a
card. Instead DeThrill gives him a cigar and the decision,
"I think I will make ... Singing in the Rain," and promptly
heads for the exit. Unfortunately, the complexities and well-rounded
approach to these tie-up scenes are blunted in the
American print with the excision of a scene of domesticity
between the Parkhills, Catherine spraying her King Charles
Spaniel with Max's melba spray promising to make the dog
"the most lovely smelling lady in Christendom," and Peter
and Hortense being caught once again by Mrs. Peter. There
is still a good scene in the girls' dressing room remaining,
however, as Maisie rouges her knees and sets off for what
she assumes to be her trip to Hollywood with DeThrill.

    As Maisie is the most objectionable of those persons
attempting to latch on to stardom via the great director it is
only fitting that Russell should make her comedown the most
elaborate. Stepping out of the theatre she calls to DeThrill,
who seems to respond and begins running toward her. Russell
structures ten intercut tracking shots of this action, but
on the last DeThrill dodges Maisie and runs past her to the
theatre exit where Tommy is standing. Mouth agape, Maisie
watches in disbelief as DeThrill demonstrates the "Double
Trip Maxie Ford" for Tommy, and it turns out that DeThrill

is Tommy's long lost father, so it is Tommy and DeThrill who end up in each other's arms and drive off together. In a splendid two-part panning shot (there is a cut in the middle of the shot along the pavement) Russell moves from DeThrill's car pulling out to a close-shot of Maisie, who nervously looks up at the dressing room window to see who has been privy to this embarrassing occurrence. This is followed by a close-shot from Maisie's point of view toward Fay, who is sitting in the window smoking a cigarette. Fay smiles at Maisie, and in a reverse shot Maisie smiles back--an apt metaphor for the resilience we know all the characters will be able to muster despite their various disappointments.

A very upset Nancy throws DeThrill's card into the street as Polly and Tony enter the scene. It is here that Polly must make a decision for, with no little irony since she was not trying to impress DeThrill, the great director wants her to go to Hollywood with him. It is no surprise that, for reasons already made clear along the way, Polly opts instead for a life with Tony at the Theatre Royal. The film then ends with the dejected Alphonse considering taking "the cloth," while Michael tells him, "Like to bet on your first customers?" and Polly and Tony walk down the alleyway to the street in the late afternoon. Russell's evocation of the late afternoon in these scenes is phenomenally good--equal in its own way to the sense of real theatre he has given earlier. At the end of The Boy Friend he captures a feeling, a mood, the aura that we have all felt of re-entering the world after a matinee performance at the theatre or cinema, and it is on this very satisfyingly familiar note that Russell leaves us.

It is, of course, unarguable that The Boy Friend is designed first and foremost as an entertainment--something akin to J. B. Priestley's novel The Good Companions, which, with its Pierrot number and tacky theatrical company, it rather resembles--but, hopefully, the preceding has done something to help set the record straight about the film's being an escapist fantasy and nothing more. In a good many ways The Boy Friend is an unusual work--unusual in that it looks backwards toward the films of its inspiration and Russell's own previous work, and that it looks forward toward the mature Russell films (something that Savage Messiah will also do). There is a distinct feeling of a greater sense of immediacy in The Boy Friend than in anything that comes before it, and Russell's unabashed experimentation in its structure, which extends to the generally unappreciated fact that the film is largely built on real time in that it runs approximately the same length of time that the events would take to happen. It is a work to be reckoned with and cherished for the many levels on which it works, as well as for the sheer delight of it.

* * *

"I need an audience. There's no such thing as an artist who doesn't need an audience. Well, maybe there is, but in that case he's a saint as well as an artist--and a saint first."
--Henri Gaudier-Brzeska
in Savage Messiah

Russell's second--and last--film for Metro-Goldwyn-Mayer was, to some extent at least, designed to recapture part of that audience that Russell had lost after Women in Love, though this may not have been a conscious move on Russell's part. Referred to as Russell's "quiet little film," Savage Messiah did indeed garner, if not more critical acclaim, then less abuse than its immediate predecessors, but owing to a combination of factors, ranging from the lack of a real "box-office" name in the major roles to the fact that it seemed too tame to Russellphiles who had cut their teeth on The Music Lovers and The Devils, it was not a markedly successful film. In the intervening years it has drifted into relative obscurity with only Stephen Farber, who considered it, along with The Music Lovers, to be Russell's best work through Lisztomania, openly championing it. This is altogether unfortunate because not only does Russell use Savage Messiah to make clear many of his personal standpoints on art and artistry, but it is a far more experimental work than its surface has led many to believe, and instead of hearkening back to Song of Summer, Savage Messiah looks boldly ahead to Mahler.

There is something astounding and a little bit sad in the fact that whether or not a Russell film is approached as experimental depends so much on the surface structure of the film: Does it have significant shifts in time? Are there large, fanciful set pieces? etc. Oddly, there are a number of both these elements in Savage Messiah, but they have somehow been overlooked in the rush to proclaim the film's restraint. The point, however, is that neither true experimentation nor true progression is dependent on set pieces and shifts in time frame. They are not, in fact, the elements that particularly make Russell's work unique, though he

Finding a Voice 179

uses them both and he uses them with a very individual brilliance. The greatness of a film does not lie in complexity, for complexity is often mere cleverness disguising a hollow center, note well Lewis Milestone and Brian De Palma. If complexity were all, John Ford's The Informer would be superior to the same director's The Searchers, and this just is not the case.

Another point not in the film's favor as concerns its acceptance as a Russell film is its dialogue-oriented screenplay and its comparative lack of music. Few Russell films are so heavily dependent on dialogue, but it is good, solid dialogue, and Russell's handling of it never once causes Savage Messiah to become a deadly talkathon. Further, though much important information is conveyed through dialogue (including the death of the main character, Henri Gaudier-Brzeska) the film is such that it is almost a mime work with the dialogue taking the place of music. Time and again it is the speed and pitch and volume of the dialogue, combined with the rhythms of accompanying natural sound, which give the film its shape and meaning far more than the words themselves. (This approach was later to prove a godsend when Russell adapted it to mask the deficiencies of the screenplay for Altered States as we shall see.) This also explains the lack of a pronounced musical track on the film. Apart from a bit from Scriabin's Third Symphony, The Divine Poem, and Debussy's "Three Nocturnes, " the music is limited to some highly serviceable, but fairly conventional, original scoring by Michael Garrett, and military band music. What is not generally appreciated here is that even without much music as such on the soundtrack, Savage Messiah with its careful orchestration of the natural sounds of speech and environment is one of Russell's most purely musical films. The reasoning behind this approach to the film becomes apparent once one understands that the film is concerned--to the point of obsession--with the natural.

While one can truly regret that the lack of a drawing power name has hurt the popularity and exposure of Savage Messiah (especially as it is probably the most completely accessible of Russell's works), there can be little quarrel with the performances. The radiant actress Dorothy Tutin in the role of Sophie Brzeska has never been seen to better advantage on the screen. Her performance is so spellbinding that it prompted even such a devout Russell hater as John Simon to praise it while damning the film. [8] Hers is not the sole great performance in the film, however, as there are fine characterizations by Helen Mirren, Lindsay Kemp, John Justin, Michael Gough, Otto Diamant, Eleanor Fazan, and Peter Vaughan. The real surprise though is the virtually unknown Scott Antony, who not only fills the bill as far as Russell's concept of finding an actor who looks physically imposing enough to wield a hammer and chisel with believability, but who also comports himself beautifully in an exceedingly difficult role. Under Russell's tutelage Antony manages to walk a very thin line between complex genius and ill-mannered oaf, and to cope amazingly well with Gaudier's character--one moment the brash young artist, self-assured and possessed of a divine spirit and knowledge beyond his years, and the next moment a slightly terrified young man, lonely, unsure, little more than the boy of his chronological years.

In order to fully understand and appreciate Savage Messiah it is necessary to comprehend the background of Russell's desire to make the film in the first place. Having read H. S. Ede's book at a crucial and not too pleasant time in his own life, Russell drew on the work for his own courage and inspiration, so that when the opportunity to make a film of the book presented itself, Russell jumped at the chance feeling it to be the perfect vessel to expound many of his own views on art, and to give the same kind of courage and inspiration to others that he had received years earlier. Working with the poet Christopher Logue (who had played Richelieu in The Devils), Russell managed to turn Ede's largely non-narrative biography into a tenable concept, and then set out to make the film for the smallest amount of money possible--in part because much of the film's $750,000 was Russell's own and also because the studio was less likely to monkey with a film costing so little after the fact, which would preclude much chance of another traumatic experience like The Boy Friend.[9]

Savage Messiah marks Russell's first association with Lee International Studios, a facility which Russell has termed "a derelict biscuit factory on the banks of a stagnant canal,"[10] and which Joseph Gomez later said, "looked more like a blitzed-out factory"[11] than a film studio. Despite this seemingly uninviting atmosphere, Lee was to become the home of several of Russell's best films. Similarly this film reintroduced BBC colleague Dick Bush back to the fold as director of photography. Bush firmly establishes himself as the quintessential Russell cinematographer with Savage Messiah, and subsequently reinforced this position with Mahler, Tommy,

Finding a Voice 181

and the two Clouds of Glory films. All in all the Savage
Messiah company appears to have been a most happy family,
and the harmony of this, as well as the openheartedness of
Russell's attempt with this film, shows in the finished prod-
uct--his most unreservedly optimistic up to that time.

From the film's very first image the concern with the
natural becomes apparent. With only the sound of pen scratch-
ing against paper we see a close-up of a skeletal hand being
sketched, zooming back from this the film's title and subtitle
("The story of a young French art student and the lonely
Polish woman he met in Paris just before the First World
War") appear sequentially superimposed on the left of the
screen. Moving to a longer shot we see Henri seated at a
table in the library sketching this from his own hand, even
though a book with an anatomical reproduction lies open on
the other side of him. The natural sound and Henri's choice
of a real hand over the textbook rendering places the film itself in the mold of being drawn from life. The arrival of
Sophie interjects a new note into the film as she immediately
becomes involved in an argument over "her" seat at the table.
Finally ousting the interloper from her seat (which happens
to be next to Henri) she takes her place and methodically
deposits all the paraphernalia she appears to deem necessary
for her task, writing a novel ponderously entitled, Truth: A
Novel of the Spirit, on the table. No sooner has this curiously aggressive woman begun to write than Henri attracts
her attention with a folded paper bird. Sophie smiles at him
and he gives it to her, then ingenuously states that he is
lonely and wonders if she is. Obviously surprised by this
openness Sophie tells him, "Of course, I am." The delicacy
of this all important scene is astonishing. It is economical
to the extent of being spare, yet there is nothing rushed
about it, and every move of both characters is logically
prompted by the other. Henri is at first attracted by Sophie's
spunk in dealing with the young man occupying her chair,
then amused by her preparations for writing and by the por-
tentousness of her novel itself, so, in turn, he amuses her
with his paper bird. Sophie's pleasant smile answers this
move, prompting his declaration of loneliness, the directness
of which causes her response.

Even so, both are still something of an unknown quan-
tity to each other, and to the viewer, so that Henri's outbursts about art culminating in his public speech atop the
elaborate public fountain once they are outside the library
comes as a surprise. In some ways it is reminiscent of

Scott Antony as Henri Gaudier-Brzeska espouses his views on art in a moment of high-spirited spontaneity in Savage Messiah. (Courtesy of Ken Russell)

Birkin's outburst at the war memorial service in Women in Love, but with far more point. Birkin likes to believe that he is somehow different from other men. Henri Gaudier is different. His sudden need to clamber up on the fountain and lecture any and all on the immorality of art and its potential for corrupting youth and then, in something of an about-face, loudly proclaim an artistic credo is a purely spontaneous, compulsive act (even if it is partly to impress and embarrass Sophie). The sequence also establishes the film's rejection theme, ending as it does with Henri on the run from the police. Throughout the film Henri--with or without Sophie--is thrown or chased out of no fewer than five separate places, including jail. That both he and Sophie are rejected by society is implicit in their mutual loneliness, but it is here that we find this openly voiced for the first time. Before making his escape, however, Henri calls to Sophie to meet him at the library on the following day, and in a signifi-

Finding a Voice

cant move, linking both Sophie and art to a romantic impulse, he kisses the statue which shares the frame with him. Instead of following him as he leaves, Russell moves his camera to center the statue in close-shot and by the emphasis of this move foreshadows the film's ending: art remains after the artist.

In the following scene it is obvious that, despite her protestations about not liking men, etc., Sophie is drawn to Henri so much that work has become impossible. We see her sitting at her place in the library with everything arranged just so, but instead of writing she merely stares blankly into space. At least that is until Henri arrives, noisily slamming two large books down on the table. Typically, Sophie tries to appear busy, and Henri sets up a disturbance, telling her his name and proposing marriage. When she rejects his offer of marriage, Henri suggest that they live together. Trying to put him off Sophie proclaims that she sleeps "with everyone." "Good," Henri counters, "I'm part of everyone." There is scarcely anything Sophie can say that Henri cannot refute, or at least find a suitable remark for. On a first viewing the style of the courtship may seem odd for a time, but it soon becomes clear that Sophie is not just willfully argumentative and that Henri only uses his brashness to cover his insecurity.

Of all Russell's films <u>Savage Messiah</u> is the most preoccupied with the use of the tracking shot. In the exterior shots in particular Russell's camera is very rarely still as it follows Henri and Sophie about. This is obviously a move on Russell's part to keep a feeling of movement in a film that could easily have bogged down into incessant talking. The effect, however, goes beyond this to convey a sense of restlessness in the characters themselves and to give a far better feeling of place than stationary shots would have done. The market scene which follows their second encounter in the library is a perfect example of the intelligent use of the tracking shot in <u>Savage Messiah</u>. In following the pair of them as they progress from vegetable vendor to vegetable vendor, dodging in and out to retrieve vegetables that have been discarded as worthless, Russell conveys something of the feeling of actually walking through such a market. Similarly it affords a subtle approach to the visual metaphor at the core of the scene. While Sophie haggles with a vendor over the price of a leek, Henri nonchalantly pockets a couple of carrots from the other side of the vegetable stand. The indication is clearly that Henri and Sophie, despite their seeming ideological gaps, both benefit by the other's presence against a hostile world. Had Russell broken the shot down into a conventional series of long, medium, and close-shots, the spontaneity would be lost, and what now appears to be an act of resourcefulness on Henri's part would come across as calculated thievery. Here, too, the tracking shot--as opposed to the swirl of various broken up tracking shots in the sequence outside the library in the park--becomes a progressively tightened two-shot, until late in the scene when Henri confesses to Sophie, "I don't want to be other than I am; it's lucky to be what I am," but qualifies this with the fear of not being able to accomplish what he wants on his own, there is very little of the screen that is not filled with them. In effect, together they overcome their unfriendly surroundings.

This line of visual logic holds throughout the following scene where Sophie takes Henri home with her as a "simple act of artistic companionship." The scene begins with the pair of them included in the same frame, but as they go upstairs and Sophie becomes more and more abusive in her arguing with Henri, she moves forward and we follow her, momentarily losing Henri as she claims to know his "sort." Once they reach the door to her room, Russell introduces a set-up of three close-ups which serve to isolate the characters from each other. First there is a big close-up of Henri delivering his coup de grace line to her, "And you're old!" This is followed by a similar close-up of Sophie's half hurt, half enraged reaction, and a final close-shot of Henri as the door is slammed in his face. The breathless nature of the editing adds immeasurably to the impact of the scene's sense of separation, conveying the idea that Henri realizes he has gone too far the moment the words are out of his mouth, and that Sophie is reacting as much in surprise that Henri would say this as much as in anger that he has said it. Finally, there is the immense sense of isolation in the final close-shot of Henri, which is just off-center enough to make the left side of the frame (which, as Joseph Gomez has noted, comes to be associated with Sophie[12]) seem unbelievably empty.

Despite this the next day finds Sophie sitting by herself in the library, forlornly waiting for Henri, who does not appear. Remembering that he claims to work for the Lartigue Art Gallery she goes there to look for him. Russell handles the sequence with great good humor, as Sophie, for the first time, in an attempt to buffalo the gallery guard, claims to be Henri's sister. (Soon this is the position in which she feels herself to be.) Directed to the trade entrance, she goes to the side of the building and climbs up on a horse drawn wagon to look through a window. In a satirical point of view shot Russell pans along a row of blue-smocked artists all reproducing the same painting in various stages of completion before lighting on Henri at the end of the row. Sophie's cry, "My God! A forger!" attracts Henri's attention, but unfortunately also causes the horse to bolt, pulling the wagon from beneath her. As Henri rushes to her aid, Russell abruptly switches the scene to Sophie's room where she has finally taken him.

The scene between the two of them is one of the best known in Savage Messiah, and intriguingly it is a foreshadowing of the only slightly more famous "torso" scene later in the film. In both instances the scenes are largely monologues, this one belonging to Sophie and the next to Henri. Both are constructed around an almost stream-of-consciousness outpouring of emotion--Sophie's life story and Henri's artistic philosophy--rattled off while the speaker works at something else: Sophie chopping vegetables, Henri sculpting the torso. The scene begins innocently enough with Sophie commenting that she is "entertaining a criminal," and Henri responding that a good copy is better than a bad original. Perhaps the most amazing element of the early portions of this scene is the lengths to which Russell and Logue have gone to make Henri and Sophie three-dimensional characters, especially when, given the film's intent as a statement on the creative process, the characters might well have fallen by the wayside. Quite the contrary, the script, the acting, and the direction all combine to interweave the important points about creativity with unbelievably realistic, almost slice-of-life, actions and words keeping the specter of the soapbox at bay. In this instance there is much by-play with Sophie's concern over making "a mess" by sharpening a drawing pencil, the first indication of her addiction to peanuts (never stressed, this charmingly realistic quality runs throughout the film, in fact nearly every shot of Sophie in bed has her surrounded by peanut shells), Henri's sketching, and, of course, Sophie's soup preparations. The odd thing about the criticism on this scene is that it all centers around the idea that Sophie simply spews forth her life's history, when there is far more to it than that. In the first place Sophie's life story is not a recitation of events so much as of feelings. The facts about her life are interspersed with almost incoherent outbursts and observations which seem to jump around in time so that at one moment she appears to be telling a story of keeping a lustful

employer away from her ("I know what you've got at the top of your legs, I'm the biggest whore in the Latin Quarter"), and then suddenly shifting ground so that this might also apply to Henri as she tells him that she has started more novels than all the drawings he might ever do in his life. This is a very significant development of Russell's storytelling technique as concerns historical personages, for though Russell's portrait of Sophie hints at incipient madness, he does not follow it to its end. In Savage Messiah, and to an even greater extent in Mahler, Lisztomania, and Clouds of Glory, he works on the assumption that the viewer either brings some previous knowledge to the film about its subject, or that the viewer will be moved by the film to seek out this knowledge after the fact. (It should be remembered, however, that Russell never makes this a prerequisite for comprehension of the film's narrative.) Of course, Sophie's actual descent into madness, which followed Henri's death, has no bearing on her relationship with him as such, and it is that relationship that forms the center of Savage Messiah. Further, her story by virtue of its emotional sincerity is the first thing she has said to which Henri has no answer. Instead of being prepared with a witty comeback, the best he can do is tell her that the cabbage is burning and continue his drawing of her until his pencil breaks. To see Henri thus emotionally moved is the first indication the viewer has been given of the depth of his attraction to Sophie. Russell and Logue then give us a scene that throws the same kind of illumination on Sophie.

Their trip to visit Henri's "real" (as opposed to his "natural") mother, the Louvre, has much to say about Russell's own beliefs in the functionality of art. For Russell art, like history, is a wonderful living thing with a point and a purpose and nowhere is this more clearly illustrated than in this very scene. Once again, the sequence makes good use of some very fluid tracking shots, both on the street prior to the museum visit and in the building itself. The scene hinges on the most ridiculous of small details, museum guards upset over Henri's shirttail hanging out, and from there snowballs into something of a seriocomic free-for-all. The tone of the museum is set at once as we find well-dressed spectators frozen into rapt attention over their guide books. (Sophie very aptly refers to them as "wax-

[Opposite:] Russell directing Scott Antony for the forging scene in Savage Messiah. (Courtesy of Ken Russell)

works.") Russell's camera glides past this image with a frightfully dim looking guard who proceeds to try to tell Henri about his shirt. Henri, however, assures him that this is perfectly all right as "most of the people in here are naked." If this were not bad enough, Sophie decides to make a statement on a painting of The Rape of the Sabine Women, Henri helps out no end by pointing that one of the men in the painting has "more hanging out than his shirt." The situation has now become bad enough that it alerts more museum guards, the main one of whom (in a delicious cameo by Peter Vaughan) can fully sympathize with Henri's desire to doff his hat to the Mona Lisa, as this is something he himself does "at least once a day, but then, sir, I am properly dressed." Sensing disaster, Sophie makes the mistake of attempting to tuck in Henri's shirt which only earns her his loud exclamation, "Madame, will you take your hands out of my trousers!" At this point Henri spots the display of a giant Easter Island primitive head and runs toward it screaming, "My God!" and addressing it as "Brother," telling anyone in earshot, "This is where it all started." The attendants are marvelously unconcerned about whether or not Henri's response to the head has any validity, and are only worried about the volume of his voice which "might disturb the taxpayers enjoying the benefits of cultural democracy." Henri disappears behind the head, and in an almost magical bit of business the guards circle it, certain that they have him trapped, but when they pounce on him, it is Sophie whom they find. (Again the implication of the two of them "against" society being more viable than either one alone.) Henri has instead clambered to the top of the head, which becomes a soapbox from which he can address the people. In a moment of inspired lunacy (which says much about the limitations of museum mentality and their burning desire for decorum at all costs) the main attendant is wheeled toward Henri on a huge platform ladder, offering very standard rhetoric on the exhibit being stone "and very valuable stone, and if we allow one person to touch it, then everyone will be wanting to touch it." In the meantime Henri has begun lecturing on the function of art--"Art is alive. Enjoy it. Laugh at it. Love it or hate it, but don't worship it. You're not in church!"--and then, as he begins showering a delighted public with his drawings, he continues, "Wipe your arses with it! Hang it on your walls! But use it!" By this time the museum guards have gotten ahold of him, but really they are too late since both Henri and Russell have made their point. Henri is being attacked for his lack of the proper respect for art and propriety (externalized by his shirttail, his loud talking, and overly enthusiastic responses) in exactly the same way Russell had been attacked for his similar transgressions through <u>The Music Lovers</u> and <u>The Devils</u>. In so doing, however, sight has not been lost of the characters of the film for it is through this outburst that Sophie looks at one of Henri's drawings for the first time in the film. It is one of the drawings Henri has thrown from the top of the statue, and she stands, silent and transfixed, staring at it in the midst of the chaos around her. Here she has discovered, through Henri's speech and his drawing, the same depth of soul that Henri found through her outburst while chopping vegetables.

Of course their reward for this display is to be tossed into the street into a passing funeral procession (a particularly vicious barb at the museum). Hurling abuse at the guard, casting doubt on his parentage, Henri gathers up his belongings and moves out of the street, vowing never to set foot in the museum again, "Let them keep it pure and air-conditioned for the American tourists." "Boy, your real mother turned out a real bitch," Sophie comments, and Henri decides that they should see if his "natural" mother might treat them better. Despite Sophie's protestations that she wants to go home, he drags her after him telling her, "We have no home."

Russell opens their briefly idyllic visit to the country on a close-shot of some quacking ducks in a stream. Henri is watching them, and his contented expression again points up his child-like simplicity and his obsession with the natural. His reverie is abruptly shattered, however, as his mother calls out to him, and he has to run to catch up with their carriage. From the onset it is apparent that Henri's parents neither understand nor approve of this relationship. His father maintains that Sophie "looks like a widow," and his mother has the unhappy knack for turning the simplest comment Sophie might make into a personal insult. There is even some implicit name-calling on Madame Gaudier's part as she tells Sophie that there is no room for her at the house, but they have fixed up the "old dairy" for her. (Ironically it turns out that this used to be Henri's room, which gives her insistence on calling it the "old dairy" added nastiness.)

There is a haunting little scene of Sophie prowling around Henri's old room, carrying a lamp, and inspecting the things he collected as a child: butterflies, bird eggs, animal skulls, a carving of a duck, and other things either from or created from nature. The best single part of the country sequences is certainly the beautifully naturalistic scene by the duck pond which follows. Designed with an eye toward the choreographic and set to an excerpt from Scriabin's "The Divine Poem," the scene is really little more than Henri sketching while Sophie writes, but Russell's handling of the action transcends this. According to Joseph Gomez this lovely scene is an on-the-spot invention of Russell's, 13 and indeed the mark of spontaneous inspiration is on it. At the beginning Henri is sketching ducks (like those which open the overall country scenes) and Sophie looks on. Heightening the sense of a real occurrence just happening naturally before our eyes, a large bumblebee wafts lazily into the frame. From this point Sophie begins to write and Henri turns his attention from sketching the ducks to sketching Sophie. She then rests blissfully against a tree. Henri moves to her and delicately strokes her face, outlining her brow, her cheekbones, her lips with his fingertips as if she herself might be a work of art he was creating. Sophie's hand is drawn up to his, and she takes his hand and presses it to her lips. Henri then draws her hand to his face and kisses it (a strand of saliva clinging to it as she pulls it back adding to the scene's intense naturalism). Russell's camera moves with the hands outstretched between them in a touching image of their spiritual communion.

Underscoring the inherent transcendence of the spirit glimpsed in this last image Russell dissolves from it to Henri's father's coarse working hands manipulating a brace and bit. There is an awkward moment of disorientation as the camera moves back from this and our eyes naturally travel toward two figures moving along in the background so that Henri and Sophie's entrance in medium shot on the right of the screen is unnecessarily jarring. Russell pans with them past the disapproving stare of M. Gaudier. After Henri and Sophie, having reached a spiritual union, decide to "plight their troth" to one another, we stop following them and hold back at a respectful distance, unlike the staring M. Gaudier and Mme. Gaudier, who is peering out a window. In plighting their troth, they give each other "something that will last forever." This something turns out to be their names, and it is thus that they become Henri and Sophie Gaudier-Brzeska.

Typically, this happiness is short-lived, but it nonetheless is a move that gives Sophie the courage to be more open with Henri about herself. Things that were only implied

Finding a Voice   191

in her earlier monologue now become clear as she tells Henri of the difficulty in finding love in her life to the point where one "settles for something less." She confesses that she did not come to Paris to find a "creative atmosphere" in which to finish her book as she had originally claimed, but rather to kill herself--something she could not bring herself to do for fear of the "worms and the dark." For the moment they are at peace with one another as Henri tells her that she has found her lover, but their celebratory hug on having defeated each other's loneliness is shattered by the arrival of the mayor and some gendarmes. Even their comradely embrace is misconstrued by the intruders as proof of the allegations they are bringing with them. The mayor proceeds to read a letter he has received ("'Honoured sir'--that's me") in which Sophie is said to be utilizing the dairy "for the improper reception of men," and demands that she be removed not only from it, but from the district. The mayor then claims that the signature is illegible, though from Mme. Gaudier's lack of surprise and her subsequent plea that Henri stay with them, there is little doubt as to its origin. Not at all surprised by this kind of treatment, Sophie exclaims, "Right! Form a queue ... outside ... youngest first!" Henri, on the other hand, is so outraged that he pushes the group out the door in a body with the aid of a nearby storage rack. Obviously, there is no recourse as Sophie has not been accused but convicted by the letter.

Russell cuts straight to the two of them setting off down a long, twisting road with a few possessions in a wheelbarrow. The sky is grim and forbidding and the road looks impossibly long and difficult. Henri, however, is only enthusiastic as a crack of thunder causes him to look heavenward as if the noise were a blessing--"Greetings, Father, and help us to find a cheap room in London." His enthusiasm is infectious and the pair of them start off down the road, laughing, accompanied by a jaunty, hopeful tune.

London does not look especially promising, though, in the first two glimpses we get of it. Henri has found some sort of temporary employment working a pneumatic drill, and Sophie has been reduced to attempting to beg with the aid of a bundle wrapped up to resemble a baby. (This works fairly well until a policeman has a look at the "baby," and "confiscates" her earnings.) Henri's job on the other hand is not without its rewards, as Russell zooms back to a high angle shot and we see he is drilling out the nipple of a nude woman he has sketched on the pavement he and the work crew are demolishing, the drill having become a surrogate penis. Upon completion he raises his arms like a music hall artiste receiving the applause of his fellow workers and a group that have gathered to watch. Their joyous response to the healthy vulgarity of his performance is similar to the reception of the crowd in the museum who happily clamored for the drawings he was throwing around. There are similar appreciative moments in later scenes as in the scattered applause that greets his rude song at the Vortex and the smiling soldiers who surround him in the war snapshot. This has been largely overlooked or ignored in dealing with the film and Russell's depiction of his protagonist against society. These scenes attest to a basic belief that it is the authority figures (here the politicians, bureaucrats, and the like) and the elitist groups (later in the film represented by Shaw and his coterie of "in" people) who thwart art--who attempt to stamp out the unorthodox or the outsider so that work that might very well please or help others never has the chance to do so. After all the public at large cannot very well be expected to understand or appreciate that to which they have not been exposed. This is very much the case with a great deal of Russell's work, which has been so distorted and misrepresented by the critical powers that be in reviews (which for all their hell-fire rhetoric frequently come down to nothing more, in terms of justification, than "I don't like it") with the stamp of authority that comes more from exposure and familiarity than from intrinsic merit. The trick, Russell suggests, is not to doubt your own worth--not to let the so-called intelligentsia kill your own inner divinity--and this is what much of <u>Savage Messiah</u> in particular is about.

The Gaudier-Brzeskas have, however, found that cheap room in London, a partially subterranean dwelling which combines the worst qualities of the factory, the prison cell, and the sewer, inadequately summed up later by Gosh Boyle with the comment, "God! What a barn." It is also about as noisy as a factory with trains roaring past just outside, which is particularly unpleasant for Sophie. (We already know from her conversation with Mme. Gaudier that she is terrified of trains.) Russell brilliantly conveys the feeling of claustrophobic entrapment that Sophie feels in a single shot, where the camera tracks in on her, pressing down on her as if it were a train when one passes outside. Sophie can only huddle on the bed and try to block out the horrible racket. It is in this state that Henri finds her when he returns and his remarks about her inability to write because of the noise and the squalor (reminiscent of his earlier statement, "You have

Finding a Voice   193

to create your own atmosphere") are less cruel than indicative of the creative gap between them. That Sophie has largely rejected her own artistic inclinations was implied in a previous scene where she had told Henri that he would "do work for everyone," and Henri had countered with a similar remark about her novels, which Sophie very nearly dismisses then and there. For Russell, Sophie is one of the many who had not really the stamina to keep her own divine spark from going out, and she now sees Henri as the outlet for her creative desire. Russell's films, both before and after Savage Messiah (though more so after), abound with this line of thought: persons outside the artist who possess no great artistic gift themselves, but serve as a catalyst for the artist. This is most pronounced here and in Mahler and William and Dorothy, and finds its reinforcement in its absence for Russell's more troubled heroes in The Music Lovers and Rime of the Ancient Mariner. For that matter the thematic reasoning extends to Russell protagonists other than artists, notably in the relationship of Grandier and Madeleine in The Devils (which also contains the negation of the relationship in Sister Jeanne), Tommy Walker and his father in Tommy, and Eddie and Emily Jessup in Altered States. Lisztomania contains something of the artist-catalyst relationship in the early days of Liszt-Marie D'Algout combination and points up an unwholesome underside in a view of such a relationship put to evil ends in the Wagner-Cosima marriage. One also finds the lack of the relationship as far back as Isadora and as recently as Valentino. The most obvious of the earlier artist-catalyst situations is in Song of Summer, where the composer Delius feeds off those around him, Eric Fenby, Percy Grainger, and his wife, Jelka. Perhaps Savage Messiah, however, is the clearest and cleanest depiction of such a relationship for Henri neither feeds off Sophie, nor does he stifle her, in the manner of Delius and, to a lesser extent, Mahler. Also he does not betray her as William betrays Dorothy by marrying. (Oddly we find Henri's cry that fame "will make no difference" in his love for Sophie echoed exactly in William and Dorothy on the subject of William's impending marriage.) Nor are there the unwholesome undercurrents of forbidden love that one finds in The Devils and William and Dorothy.

In order to support the pair of them Henri takes a job translating letters for a Mr. Saltzman, an elderly German who, unlike most, is remarkably sympathetic to Henri and his art ("Mrs. Saltzman thanks you for the drawing. It is framed already and hanging in the drawing room"). It is he who arranges Henri's meeting with Mr. Corky, an art dealer. (Henri's job translating letters, like an earlier offhand remark to Sophie that he will learn Polish in order to read her novel, is a touch of authenticity, based on the historical Henri's felicitous knack for picking up a new language in a matter of weeks.) Apart from the Gaudier-Brzeskas, Angus Corky is the film's only major sympathetic character, a slightly fey little Scotsman who acts as a calmly appreciative counterpart to Henri's bumptious enthusiasm. Actually, Corky puts up with a good deal of abuse at Henri's hands (though it is good-natured abuse) including the insistence on calling him Porky instead of Corky. (This, by the way, is utilized consistently and coherently throughout the film and not in the confused manner Joseph Gomez implies when he states that Corky is "sometimes" called Porky. 14)

Angus Corky is one of the few figures of fun found in Ken Russell's works who is also consistently sympathetic. Nor does Russell leave him as a mere bit of comic relief. The character is much more fleshed out than that. Corky may be incredibly affected and mousey, but there is never any question of either his intelligence or his genuine appreciation of Henri's works. The first encounter between them is charmingly played and written, and it contains great beauty in the simplicity of its natural lighting and the economy of Russell's overall approach. Broken down into a simple series of alternate close-shots, a medium establishing shot, and a quite startling medium long-shot played in silhouette, the scene where Corky looks at Henri's drawings for the first time romanticizes art without deifying it. The scene is also designed to give weight to Henri's position as an innocent despite his brashness in that he mistakes Corky's offer of five pounds for one of the drawings to be an offer of five pounds for the lot--"You mean five pounds each? You're an idiot!"

Russell follows this with one of his most purely comical scenes in which Corky has to come to terms with the dismal quality of the Gaudier-Brzeskas' food and the full-blooded, eccentric approach to life of his new friends. As Joseph Gomez has noted the scene has a very solid basis in real life, 15 but this is not what matters, nor is it what makes the scene funny. The success of the scene lies in its skillful playing and Russell's subtly dynamic visual approach. (In some respects one might feel that Russell's more relaxed camera in Savage Messiah is due to the boundless energy of his protagonists, although for those who take

Finding a Voice 195

the trouble to familiarize themselves with the film's visual pattern it becomes apparent that much of the relaxed attitude of the work is an illusion.) After arguing with Sophie about a pair of earrings he has wasted "good money on" being for him and not her, Henri decides to pierce his own ears so that he might wear them. The great physical energy of the scene is conveyed almost entirely through its editing, which Russell purposefully builds to a pitch. First Henri leaps from his seat at the table and runs into the studio section of the room. This is done in long shot. Russell then cuts to a fairly tight medium close-shot as Henri raises his intended tools, a hammer and chisel. This is followed by a similarly tight shot on Sophie's horrified reaction. Russell reverts to the long shot as Sophie chases him about the room in an attempt to stop him ("They'll think you're a pansy!"). During all this there is an intercut to a medium close-shot of Corky spitting a rancid vegetable back into his spoon. At length--again shot from some distance--Henri traps Sophie with the bed and proceeds to "pierce" his ear. In a blinding flurry of quick cuts--the hammer raised, Sophie pleading for Henri to stop, the hammer coming down, Henri upsetting the dinner table, Corky and his chair falling over backwards, Sophie embracing and comforting Henri only to discover he has done nothing--Russell brings the sequence to a head. He does not end the sequence on this note, however, and gradually leads out by returning to the more distanced medium and medium long-shot approach as Sophie and Henry tussle on the floor in the midst of the spilled soup, and Corky makes his exit expressing the hope that they will dine with him soon. The sequence is a minor masterpiece of dynamic story-telling through basically rudimentary editing techniques, applied in precise and refreshing ways.

In an almost direct counterpoint to the previous scene's earthy comedy, Russell's next scene is a transitional one of more than usual power, conveying something of the act of creativity and the almost mystical release of the spirit through it. In order to present this more spiritual thrust, Russell has designed the sequence around a series of gliding zoom shots instead of abrupt cuts, and accompanied it with the "Sirenes" section of Debussy's Three Nocturnes. Though it may be completely intuitive on Russell's part, his utilization of excerpts from all three of the Debussy Nocturnes would appear to serve a consciously thematic pattern in application. He places the works in reverse order, beginning here with the climactic piece, which is indicative of Henri's compulsive drive toward art as if art were the "Siren" of the title. His later applications--the "Fetes" or "Festival" section at a celebratory moment, and the "Nuages" ("Clouds") following Henri's physical, though by no means spiritual, death and thereby imparting a heavenly atmosphere of the soul released--are similarly well-judged, precluding much chance of mere coincidence, though not ruling out a subconscious judgment.

The sequence opens with a shot of a tiger pacing in its cage, followed by a zoom-in on Henri sketching the tiger. This action is interspersed with a slow zoom-in on Sophie backed by a placid lion in a cage behind her. The symbolism of the imagery is perfectly suited with Henri quick and restless like his subject, and Sophie calm and watchful like the lion in the background. One quick cut in particular from the tiger to Henri gives the artist a cat-like bearing. Russell underscores the force of Henri's obsession with the image of the tiger as he has drawn him by having one shot of the tiger moving forward printed three successive times. From this he moves in a time-shift to Henri sketching the five-bob prostitute we saw him hire earlier, but did not see anything other than the three resulting drawings done from the encounter. Once again the scene is largely done in gliding zooms--the prostitute obviously delighted with the fact that Henri finds her aging body worth sketching, the point being that where others see only a caged tiger and a worn-out whore Henri can discern a beauty within and, more importantly, can make us see that essential beauty through his translation of it onto paper.

Russell moves from this scene to Henri's first encounter with Corky's "friends," and in so doing utilizes a reversal of one of his favorite devices. Where in early instances, notably in Song of Summer and The Boy Friend, the tinny sound of a gramophone is overcome by full-range modern recording as the idea of the music breaks through the limitations of the actual sound, Russell here goes from the full-bodied sound to the sound of a tinny gramophone playing the same piece of music as a harbinger of the base approach Shaw's Vorticist group has toward art. In a splendid and quite unorthodox approach to the introduction of a scene, Russell's camera prowls in an intricately choreographic manner from one close-shot to the next--from Henri to the wild-haired Kate to Sophie to Shaw to the superbly enigmatic Mavis Coldstream--as each speaks on what the music means to them. Typically, Henri's is the deepest analysis and Sophie's the kindest, whereas the others are off on curious tangents

of their own. For Kate "it reeks of sex," and, in response
to Sophie's "I see light," Shaw snidely comments that "One
never sees anything else with an impressionist," while Mavis
wanders past espousing that she "thought it was a ballet
about homosexuality." At this Russell cuts to what would
normally be considered an establishing shot of the whole
group of people seated around Corky's apartment. Much to
everyone's horror, Henri replies to Kate's inquiry as to
whether or not he associates impressionism with homosexuality that "it's a lot of cock." Corky attempts to save the
situation by announcing that supper is ready, but the basic
incompatibility of Henri and Sophie with this pretentiously
trendy group precludes any chance of lasting success.

    It is easy to understand where Joseph Gomez drew
his analogy that the following "dinner table sequence" owes
something to the "fig eating scene" in Women in Love, 16
but difficult to think of the scene as being actually derivative. This is largely due to the fact that unlike anyone in
Women in Love--especially Birkin--Henri and Sophie are
genuinely spontaneous characters. Where Birkin says something with the calculated idea of shocking, Henri and Sophie
say and do shocking things simply because that happens to
be what occurs to them. Further, if the dinner sequence is
derivative of this scene, it is derivative in the best sense,
for this plays much more smoothly and Russell has become
much more adept at handling groups of people in the intervening three years. The smooth flow of the scene is at once
apparent as Russell moves with Kate's head in close-shot as
she accepts a mussel from the Tom Buff character and moves
in on Shaw in an unbroken sweep to ask if he has read something. One feels that the subsequent answer from Shaw tells
as much as needs be known about his character as he disdainfully notes that he has not read the work in question, but
has read the reviews, which he appears to feel is much the
same thing. Sophie's comment that she does not read reviews finds momentary backing from Kate and Tom, but her
alliance with them is of very short duration, and soon things
are even worse than they were before supper, when, in response to an argument about differentiating between "the news
and the views," Henri blurts out that he does not differentiate, but rather, "I wipe my arse with both." Sophie then,
in response to Henri's joke that she sings and Shaw's question as to whether she knows Polish folk melodies, sings a
kind of Slavic mishmash "entitled 'Melancholy Mazurka,'
translated from the Polish by Sophie Gaudier-Brzeska," a
wildly incoherent song detailing the antics of "Two fleas living

in a rhubarb tree," with a chorus largely consisting of laughing and clapping. The overall response is one of disbelief and horror at the appalling spectacle, though Corky again tries to smooth things over by applauding at the song's climax and is unenthusiastically joined by Mavis. Even though Russell's reaction shots during the song are humorous, this little comedic gem belongs almost entirely to Dorothy Tutin, who energetically throws herself into the part, completely giving herself over to the song and just as completely stopping dead when the seemingly interminable composition finally does reach its end. By now we are not in the least surprised by Sophie's denunciation of the group as the "offspring of chimpanzees," nor by her charmingly approving wink at Shaw when he expresses the thought that he liked the song, "but I don't think I like you." (This, by the way, is the same response she gives to the museum guards when they pounce on her instead of Henri in the Louvre scene, placing Shaw on more or less the same level.) Somehow something approximating order is restored to the extent that Henri boasts himself into a corner by inviting Shaw to see a nonexistent statue and securing a promise that Shaw will come the following morning at nine. As they leave, Sophie comments that Henri has "done it this time."

Henri, however, has no doubt that he can fashion such a statue as he has described to Shaw by that hour, and he and Sophie rout Corky out of bed to help. The three of them set out to explore a graveyard in search of a suitable stone for the project. For such an obviously bizarre sequence Russell is surprisingly restrained, content to let his camera make us a part of the nocturnal foray into the graveyard, creeping along with the trio in what is probably the longest single take in a Russell film up to that time. Despite the pleas of both Sophie and Corky, Henri will not be rushed in choosing a "proper stone," pointing out that "Michelangelo used to spend six months in his favorite quarry before picking a stone." Sophie reminds Henri that he loathes Michelangelo, or so he had told her in their first encounter. Henri, however, has been maturing all the while and mutters, "I'll have to admit he's getting better--getting better all the time." This echo of a popular Beatles song in Henri's dialogue is not mere willfulness on the part of Logue and Russell, as it, like the dinner table scene's reverse F. D. R. impersonation, "I love war," is indicative of the more allegorical side of the film--an aspect which is becoming more and more explored as the film progresses. It is, of course, typical of Russell's approach to history that the well-applied

Finding a Voice

anachronism is brought into play in order not necessarily to make things seem more relevant to our time per se, but to make them more accessible to the modern mind. Unfortunately, even Russell's most ardent defenders have pretty thoroughly managed to overlook the allegorical implications of <u>Savage Messiah</u>, perhaps because Russell's approach here is <u>a bit too subtle</u>. Even here this is not dwelled upon as immediately afterwards Sophie finds the perfect stone for the project and we become easily distracted by the humorous job of removing the heavy stone and Logue's cleverly rhymed dialogue.

The switch to the Gaudier-Brzeskas' room moves the film from the cool blue of the cemetery at night to the fiery warm of oil-lamp lit interior in a way that increases the idea of the creative fire of the sculptor. (It is little wonder that one of the more recent books published about Gaudier-Brzeska and his work is entitled <u>Burning to Speak</u>.) This is the beginning of the film's most <u>famous set piece</u>, the so-called "torso" scene, which as we have previously noted has a direct bearing on Sophie's earlier monologue. As a preliminary to the actual sculpting Russell provides us with a wonderfully conceived bit where Henri and Corky saw the marble to the correct size. Logue's dialogue manages the not inconsiderable feat of giving us all the background information--Corky's firm belief that Shaw will not actually come and a time frame so that we know Henri has only six hours in which to do the statue--without seeming to do so. After this Russell telescopes time to the point where the marble is in position for carving and Henri is just finishing his outline drawing on it for the finished product. The screenplay lulls the viewer into a good humor by virtue of a slightly ridiculous anecdote which Henri tells about a little bird having its head bitten off by a fox because, having been saved by a kind man from freezing to death by having been plopped into the middle of a newly "laid cow puddle," the little bird gives his location away by chirping. The upshot of this is Henri's moral that "It's not always your enemies who drop you in the shit, and not always your friends who get you out, but once you're in it, keep your mouth shut." The screenplay's point in the story is something quite different, however, as it places the viewer in a comfortably receptive condition-- just the right mood for Russell's philosophic discourse on art and the artist, which is the centerpiece of <u>Savage Messiah</u>. Stylistically, there may be a certain similarity to <u>Gulley Jimson</u>'s story of his artistic conversion at having seen a reproduction of a painting by Matisse that everyone

else laughs at, which is found in both the novel and Ronald
Neame's film of Joyce Carey's The Horse's Mouth, but thematically, Henri's discourse is purest Russell. It is a long
speech, broken into three parts as the statue takes on more
form with each section, but it never seems unnatural. Quite
the contrary, the speech, like Sophie's earlier one, is a subconscious flow of words and thoughts, serving the utilitarian
purpose of helping Henri keep awake for the duration of his
arduous task. The themes explored throughout the discourse
--the need of the artist for the spectator, the distrust of the
artist who "surrounds his work with a lot of hocus-pocus"--
are all as germane to Russell and his film as to GaudierBrzeska and his sculptures. Even the statement on allowing
"the stone to lead you in," following the curious self-life of
the medium through which the artist is working, is much the
same as Russell's own spontaneity and flexibility at the time
of actually filming. Russell, like Gaudier, knows the impossibility of trying to follow a preconceived plan too closely.
In Gaudier's case perhaps the grain of the stone may not allow exactly the pattern originally invented; in Russell's case
he may have misremembered the exact layout of a location
during his preplanning and have to rethink the design on the
spot to match the reality. There is one rather curious reference to Yeats's poem to Maud Gonne, "When You Are Old
and Grey and Full of Sleep," in Henri's advice to Corky
that he buy up some Cezannes to "keep us all in luxury when
we're old and grey and sick of sleep." Since Yeats's poem
is a reminder to Maud Gonne that despite the unconsummated
nature of his love for her, he has loved her more deeply
and spiritually than any of her actual lovers, its inclusion
here is particularly apropos of the Henri-Sophie relationship.
The main thrust of the scene, however, is surely the idea
of the artist needing an audience. This is partly apparent
in Henri's insistence on having the exhausted Corky remain
awake so that he can talk to someone, though the monologue
itself imparts most of the information, culminating in the
thought, "if there isn't someone there to look at it--Zut! as
my divine sister would say. There's nothing, just a lump of
stone. Put St. Paul's Cathedral in a cardboard box, and
what have you got? A heavy box." To quite a large extent
this is by way of being an explanation of Russell's attempt to
reach a greater audience through this very film.

Despite the scene's heavy use of dialogue--something
rather unusual for Russell who generally prefers to make his
points on a more visual level--it is by no means devoid of
cinematic interest. Russell's camera prowls around the

statue while Henri works (at one point, unfortunately, catching a quick glimpse of the studio lighting source, though this is only apparent when screening the film in a 16mm copy as a modern-day theatre screen invariably crops the top and bottom of any film shot "flat" in the Academy ratio), rarely resting in one place. This not only breaks up the potential tedium of a lengthy monologue, but imparts a real sense of the formation of a sculpture out of a piece of stone. As the camera glides around and up and down Henri's statue we are able to see the sense in his work, to get a genuine feeling for the stone itself. Then, too, there is Dick Bush's extraordinary lighting--dark and yet warm--which picks up the glow in Henri's protective goggles and the glint of his hammer, giving the artist a truly mystical appearance like some mythological figure forging something real, something living.

For anyone who has ever been carried away with the act of creation to the point where time loses all meaning and something within drives one onward toward the completion against any physical common sense, the final moment where Henri holds his head under the tap after completing the statue has the ring of truth. Physically exhausted, there is nonetheless an almost uncontainable sense of real accomplishment, completely banishing the reality of the everyday commonplace. As Henri shouts to the commuter train bearing its passengers into the ostensibly real work-a-day world, "Ah! You've never done an honest day's work in your life!" the feeling is genuine. The creation of the torso--the act of its creation--has become somehow more real than anything.

Henri's elation is short-lived as always when it proves correct that Shaw is not coming to look at the torso as Corky had warned. The scene of the messenger boy bringing Henri an apologetic telegram from Shaw is a perfect example of Russell's attention to detail in what, in lesser hands, would be a mere throwaway scene. Russell has an almost von Stroheim obsession with background detail, as evidenced here, in the final shot of The Boy Friend, in nearly all the train sequences in Mahler, in the studio scenes in Valentino, and in every one of his numerous crowd scenes. In this instance Russell is not content to merely record the interaction between Gaudier and the messenger boy, though it is quite good in itself as Gaudier moves from joking high spirits to deflation at the news and finally to anger over Shaw's attitude. Instead the overall scene brims with the atmosphere of the surroundings. Shot in simple reverse angles on Henri and the messenger boy, both backgrounds are filled with the occurrences of a great city in the early morning. Behind Henri two laborers load sacks of coal, while to the rear of the messenger boy we see people on their way to work in the start of the day. The attention to detail would be astonishing in itself, but it also serves to establish the "real" outside world taking over from the world which Henri had built for himself during the night.

In a straight cut to the statue being wheeled along in the same wheelbarrow that had earlier served to cart the purloined stone from the graveyard Russell switches from the mood of defeat and incipient anger to one of sheer defiance. Cutting to a longer shot we pan with Henri pushing the wheelbarrow along in a very determined manner until he reaches Shaw's Art Gallery. Russell wheels his camera up to the plate glass window as Shaw's girlfriend waves at Henri, and Shaw turns his attention from a customer to the activities in the street. His disgust quickly turns to terror as it becomes obvious that Henri intends to throw the torso through the window. This is exactly what Henri does do, shouting, "Nine!" (the appointed hour for Shaw's visit), and spitting contemptuously.

In a wonderful reversal of what we expect, Russell cuts to Henri struggling with two jailers, but it turns out they are trying to force him out of a jail cell, not into one. "I'm a hooligan! I don't deserve my liberty! Let me into this cell immediately!" Henri cries as they try to extricate him from the premises. Sophie and Corky hurriedly try to explain that Shaw has dropped the charges and that Corky has paid for the window as a down payment on the statue. Henri will have none of it, however, because "If I get off it means I didn't do anything. I'm glad I did it." Once again Russell's attention to detail is seen to good advantage, and he milks the comic possibilities of the scene for their full worth by simply adding a great deal of unstressed visual business for his players--Henri struggling with his jailers being dragged past a well-dressed woman talking with the desk sergeant; Sophie and Corky attempting to help usher him out the door; a bemused prisoner watching from behind bars in the background; Sophie getting her umbrella handle caught on the telephone cord, etc. Restating that this is essentially the same kind of rejection that Henri received at the Louvre, he utilizes the same high angle long-shot approach to their exit into the street. It is also worth noting that this scene finds an antecedent in the film version of <u>The Horse's Mouth,</u> which begins with a prison that is only too glad to be able to release that film's artist, Gulley Jimson.

The next scene represents a complete departure in mood and approach as Russell pans up from a pile of peanut shells to Sophie and Corky sitting in the space in front of the studio and talking. Sophie has decided to accept a post as a governess (a function she has served at other odd points in her life) partly because they need the money, and partly because she feels she must have her life to herself "for a few months."

That Sophie is a balancing and calming influence on Henri becomes immediately and forcefully apparent as soon as Corky and Henri pack her off in a taxi. "Never mind, I too love solitude," Henri calls after her, and then rushes up to Corky crying, "Free! Come on, Corky, let's go and find some women!" As they walk along Corky suggests that they might visit Mavis Coldstream, but Henri is in search of something quite different--"big, fleshy, breasty women." Almost by magic such a woman appears before them on the sidewalk asking Henri for a light. Her cigarette, however, is no cigarette, but the fuse of a firebomb which, once lit, she hurls at a nearby mailbox crying, "Votes for Women!" Corky is appalled, but Henri is fascinated, taking Corky's hat around for donations (as he has suggested Sophie should have done during his speech in the park), and taking up the defense that "anyone who provides a little public warmth on a cold night can't be all bad," while rallying to her cause. This is the heated introduction to Savage Messiah's most outrageous female character, Gosh Boyle, who will more than live up to the destructive and volatile implications of her first appearance. When the police arrive and Gosh takes flight, Henri pulls Corky after him in pursuit--"After her, Porky. She's our man!"

The chase leads them to the Vortex, which Corky describes with some awe as "Shaw's new nightclub." Gosh gets in immediately, but Henri and Corky are detained at the door. Russell cuts directly to the inside of the nightclub with a close-up of a pair of very rouged lips sticking through a cutout in a painting asking, "Why give a vote to a woman?" The camera zooms back revealing the overall canvas of a reclining nude, at which point Russell cuts to a looming close-shot of Shaw mouthing the words being spoken by the lips behind the painting, leaving little doubt that the Vortex is just another means for Shaw to control art, artists, and current trends. The set itself is a masterpiece of design by Derek Jarman. Done in a deliberately anachronistic style in harsh reds, blues, and yellows, the falseness and fraudulence of Shaw's manufactured world stands out in sharp relief from the otherwise natural pallet of Savage Messiah. Russell's use of the anachronism here is particularly praiseworthy since the setting and even the odd make-up used on one eye of Shaw's girlfriend draw a direct parallel to the worst of not only contemporary artistic cliques, but are sufficiently stylized so as to suggest a criticism of this sort of society yet to come. It is really of no particular time and so it is relevant to any time. (It might be interesting to note that the red-blue-yellow color scheme found here is repeated by Russell in the three monochromatic images that Tommy Walker, Russell's victim and hero of the modern age, perceives in the mirror in Tommy.)

At the end of the painting's "speech," Gosh appears onstage and slashes the canvas, turning afterwards to the audience and exclaiming that "Old masters exploit young mistresses!" By now Henri and Corky have gained admittance to the club and make their way to Shaw's table, where Henri immediately usurps Shaw's seat, helps himself time and again to champagne, and even takes the cigarette right out of Tom Buff's mouth, enthusiastically responding to Gosh's hideous "Votes for Women" song--something which through a combina-

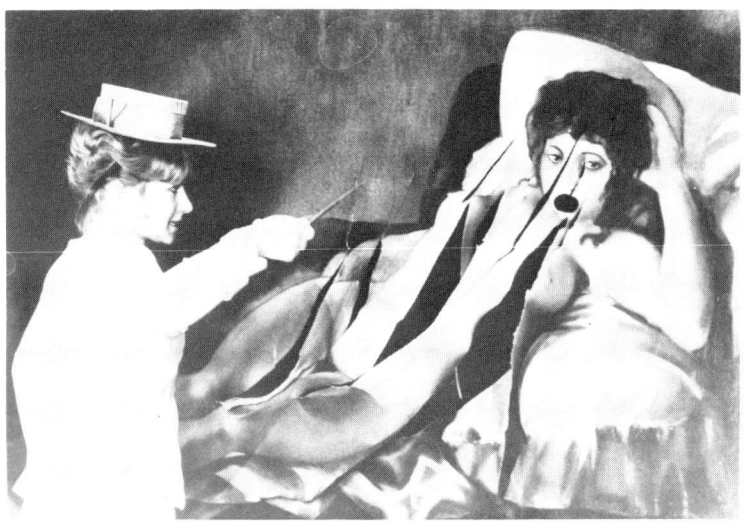

"Old Masters exploit young mistresses!" Gosh Boyle attacks a piece of academic art at Shaw's nightclub, The Vortex, in Savage Messiah. (Courtesy of Ken Russell)

Finding a Voice

tion of its own insipidity and Gosh's voice makes Sophie's "Melancholy Mazurka" seem like a masterpiece. Not surprisingly Henri's high spirits and good natured vulgarity do not sit well with Shaw's group, but then Henri is pretty much openly hostile toward them by now as indicated by his groan of "Oh, no," when Shaw walks onstage. Shaw makes the mistake of remarking on Henri's conduct so that when he delivers a weak joke about having hoped to follow Gosh's "act" with "a quick sketch by Pablo Picasso, however, this being Monday, he's having his drawing lesson," the irrepressible Henri leapfrogs off the table over Shaw, announcing, "You're lucky, I'm here to replace him." Wishing to preserve what little decorum is left Shaw assumes an attitude of watchful exasperation, while Henri takes over the stage, declaring himself, "the new genius of the planet earth" and launching into a rude ditty he calls, "Concrete." In a quick close two shot he kisses Gosh and advises her to take her clothes off "or we're sunk," and begins the tale of his "concrete Venus with the all-electric crotch," complete with gestures. Shaw soon has had enough of this and has them forcibly removed from the stage and the Vortex with Henri extolling the virtues of free expression. Once on the sidewalk Henri is incensed because he remembers "a much dirtier song," but Gosh dissuades him from attempting to go back in by promising "something much better we could do." Henri jumps to the obvious conclusion that this statement has romantic intent, but Gosh's desire is to "blow up the Royal Academy of Art." The attendants from the club toss the rest of Gaudier's belongings into the street (à la the museum guards throwing his shoes, hat, and portfolio after him), tell them not to come back, and close the door plunging them into the darkness of the night. Russell tactfully opts to end the scene here.

In a reversal of the Vortex scene Russell cuts to Sophie at a train station reading a letter from Henri in which he plans to meet her at Portland for a brief holiday. The cheeriness of the open air platform stands out from the confines of Shaw's club, as does Sophie's relaxed contentment. Her attitude is soon altered, however, for the train on which Henri should arrive pulls into the station and pulls out with no sign of him. A train pulling out on the far track moves out of view and reveals Henri, flowers in hand, waving and calling to her. "I got an earlier train and it didn't stop, so I had to come back," he shouts, running across the tracks to meet her. Halfway across he trips, dropping his hat and the flowers. Sophie is at first amused, and then terrified as

she spots an oncoming train, but Henri is so concerned with
gathering up the flowers that he very nearly does not notice
the train. Russell plays the scene for all the suspense it is
worth, panning from Henri to Sophie to the train, and then
intercutting as the tension builds. He even goes so far as
to have Henri slip and fall a second time just as he is about
to get out of the path. Only then does Henri barely miss
the train, which plows directly toward the camera. Russell
quickly cuts to a side view as Henri emerges as if by magic
into the frame with his somewhat bedraggled flowers, or at
least as many of them as he could save. Certainly the scene
is a symbolic one, illustrating what Stephen Farber sees as
Russell's concern over the beautiful "seized from the jaws of
death"[17] (an idea that can as easily be applied to Henri himself as to the flowers), and it is clearly a visualization of
Henri's compulsion for beauty--real beauty--no matter what
the cost. Another aspect of the scene, though, is the dazzling
series of emotions through which Sophie is put in a matter of
a minute or two at most. Her rapid fire journey from content anticipation to severe disappointment to elation to amusement to stark terror to relief is <u>Savage Messiah</u>'s most profound statement on the strain through which her relationship
with Henri puts her. It is the reverse of the calming influence that she has on him, and as such the scene can be seen
to mirror Henri's illusory elation at being temporarily free
from her influence, as well as providing a clear point of understanding as to why she might want to be away from him
for a time.

Thus far in the narrative Russell has pretty well left
the subject of the differences in the ages of his two protagonists to Sophie's dialogue and to the implicit differences in
their respective levels of maturity which are scattered throughout the film. He now chooses to address the situation openly and not surprisingly visually. Following a brief scene in
which Sophie attempts to find them a room "in which I can
also stew some herring for my brother," Russell stages a
most poignant statement about youth and age. Fed up with
the fact that no one is disposed toward renting them a room
(whether through disbelief in the brother-sister relationship
or simply because no one is too keen on having Sophie stew
herring), Henri decides that they have "wasted enough time
already" and heads off to see the ocean. In a tracking shot
down a depressing, muddy lane Russell keeps his camera
just ahead of Henri with Sophie struggling along in the background, trying to keep up and carry her burden of flowers
and herring. She is understandably concerned about their

Finding a Voice

The most obvious example of the difference in the ages of Henri and Sophie, as he carries her to the sea in <u>Savage Messiah</u>. (Courtesy of Ken Russell)

accommodations and Henri's lack of concern and consideration. Ultimately she drops her basket and throws Henri's flowers in the mud, calling him a bastard. Henri turns to look at her, then goes back and picks her up, carrying her the rest of the way. This, perhaps, is the ultimate justification of Sophie's great need for this relationship. Her mood quickly shifts to high good spirits and two of them set off for the sea.

In a telling abrupt cut, Russell moves from the confines of the dreary lane to the rocky shore leading to the sea--the rough-hewn natural surroundings at once overwhelming and freeing his characters. After telling Sophie about an exhibition that Corky is going to give him, and for which he wants her to write the catalogue notes, Henri spots something that excites him. Russell starts building the excitement even before we see what Henri has seen by bringing up the "Fetes" section of Debussy's Nocturnes on the soundtrack and then cutting to a long shot of Henri climbing atop a mountainous pile of stones cut from the rocky shore. Russell's handling of the scene is remarkable in that, through two simple tricks and his own mystical approach to mountains (or in this case a surrogate mountain), he manages to communicate Henri's excitement to the viewer. The buildup of our expectations by the music and the time compressing cut to the long shot in which Henri is much further up the mountain of stones than real time would allow, gives the scene a magical quality, as does the larger-than-life response of the artist to his medium. Proclaiming this to be enough stone "to last at least a fortnight," Henri flings off his shoes in order to better "connect" with the stones, and capers along the top of the pile, caressing individual stones. His exultant pantheistic cry to his "Great Father Sun" to "Gaze down on your children in their delight" not only punctuates the scene, but ties it to his earlier response to a crack of thunder, and his final letter from the war, as well as presaging such scenes as the implicit salvation at the end of Tommy.

As usual, the celebratory mood is transitory at best and Russell is not lost for a visual metaphor in conveying the loss of this mood. Coming down from the rocks Henri announces that a ramshackle hut shall be their new home and Sophie happily joins him there. "It is beautiful," comments Sophie, "And it's quiet." As she enters the structure, Russell tracks around the hut to its side, a large portion of which is open to the elements. Inside, Henri reaffirms his love for her and Sophie yields to his emotions. So confining

Finding a Voice

is the space inside the hut that we are not allowed entry at all and assume the uncomfortable position of being voyeurs, peeping in either through the large hole in the wall or through the front door. The interior is dark and it cuts off our view of the outside world, just as it cuts off Henri and Sophie. Suddenly, she comes "to her senses" and stops dead Henri's attempts at love-making, quickly leaving the hut. When we next see the outside world, it is no longer the bright, sunny world we saw prior to going into the hut, but a darkening and rather forbidding one as the sun is going down, presenting the "dark side of things" of which Henri had accused Sophie of always seeing. Reality has intruded upon them--it is getting dark, they have no place to sleep, and their insecurities have resurfaced. The two are even physically changed. Instead of dancing with joy, Sophie has become enmeshed in finding her bag. Instead of extolling the joys of nature and art, Henri hobbles along slowly, now leaning against a rock rather than climbing atop it in order to put his shoes back on.

Russell cuts to Henri sketching a nude, which turns out to be a representation of Gosh Boyle, who, in a scene which was picked up rather tactlessly and tastelessly for the British advertising campaign for the film, parades around her father's house stark naked. The ad campaign, quoting from popular press reviews, happily touted that Russell "reveals Miss Helen Mirren full-frontal in a scene longer than the normal glimpse." Although this is an indisputable fact, it makes the scene out to be erotic--something that it quite clearly is not, nor was it intended to be. Russell is not out for a quick sexual charge here (though denying his interest in sexuality in his films would be just about as futile as trying to assert that they were shot in black and white, and we just perceive them to be in color). In this case there is nothing even remotely sensual about the proceedings. The previous fully-clothed scene between Henri and Sophie is far more sensual. Henri is completely apathetic about Gosh's nakedness--her body is merely the raw material for the sketch he is doing. This is in contrast to Gosh herself who is not involved in art or much of anything else except herself. She has become completely bored with her part in the suffrage movement and is only toying with the idea of art as a potential replacement. Her dialogue during the scene is not dissimilar in design to either Sophie's or Henri's two set piece monologues, but the difference is in content, which is utter rubbish, as she jumps around inanely from her newfound interest in sculpture to the number of poets she has slept with to her desire to "leave something behind me which was never there before" (a sentiment to which Henri advises her that the "lavatory's outside"), to her astrologer's belief that "Virgos are subject to 'Cosmic Boredom,'" to a desire to dance naked at Henri's exhibition, to babbling about whether or not animals have souls. Russell shrewdly connects this last to the introduction of her father, Major Boyle, who thinks his horse is "almost human." It is Major Boyle whom Henri has come to sculpt. As an indication of the position in which the Major holds his horse, he rides it into the house, slowly circling Henri like a mounted vulture. "Would you like me to keep still?" he asks. Henri promises that this is not necessary and he will sculpt Major Boyle just as he is, "horse shit and all." Nonetheless, the Major is skeptical about art and artists and artistic insight. He wants a piece "recognizable to the naked eye of a well-trained fighting man at the distance of forty paces." At least that is until he is apprised of the fact that Henri charges by the cubic foot, at which time he opts for a bust. Russell conveys the sudden change by the simple expedient of stopping the camera, removing the horse, and placing the Major in a chair, in a manner reminiscent of the old Méliès' trick films. The application of this simple approach here is particularly apt as it underlines the magical aspect of art and points in the general direction of immediacy through simple effects that Russell's work is taking in <u>Savage Messiah</u> and even more in his next films.

It is here that the subject of impending war resurfaces, and it is the mood of the coming war and the war itself which is now moving to the forefront of the film. The basic obscenity of war in general and of World War I in particular is pretty well summed up by Major Boyle's offhand response to Henri's question about when the war will start--"Middle of August would be a good time." In retrospect of the entire film as a piece, the Major's subsequent inquiry as to whether or not Henri would die for his country is shatteringly ironic. The introduction of Major Boyle as a pompous ass is not limited to the reintroduction of the war, for while it by no means makes Gosh into a sympathetic character, it does explain her character to some extent.

Gosh's character is further delineated in the next scene where she cannot comprehend Henri finding a kind of beauty in sketching a sick beggar when he "could have naked me instead." Further, her interest in art is already being undermined as her attention is quickly drawn to a street riot in which rabble rousers have been exhorting the "workers of the world" to "unite." That Henri is on the verge of completely jettisoning Gosh because of her innate shallowness is apparent in his contemptuous command that she go brew tea when he notices her interest in the riot. This all by the way of being a buildup to a confrontation between Sophie and Gosh.

Sophie has returned from her tenure as governess and is diligently cleaning the studio apartment when Gosh enters. In a deft touch Gosh mistakes Sophie for a servant, and Sophie mistakes Gosh for a potential customer. Sophie takes Gosh's high-handed abuse and affected desire for Indian tea "with a dash of China" while laboring under this misapprehension. As soon as she discovers who Gosh is, however, her mood changes and she becomes openly hostile, deliberately splashing her wash water on Gosh's skirt. With the entrance of Henri the situation quickly degenerates into a free-for-all as the two women trade insults and Sophie sets up a folding screen around the bed so that Henri and Gosh can carry on without being disturbed by her presence. Sophie sets about scrubbing the floor and singing her "Two Fleas" at the top of her voice, while Gosh, astride Henri, berates her and her influence on Henri at a similar volume. The occurrence is the final nail in Gosh's coffin for Henri, who makes mock of her attempts at undressing him throughout and lewdly apes the acts of a passion he obviously does not feel. Finally, Gosh has enough and makes a hurried exit. For a brief moment Sophie is terror-stricken that she has gone too far, but Henri's happy response that she has not changed banishes this and the two are soon in each other's arms, Henri joyously swinging Sophie around as a train thunders past. The full-throated vulgarity of the scene is by no means arbitrary as it combines the elements of the two previous scenes in one scene and in so doing crystallizes the point about Henri's truly faithful love for Sophie. Gosh is unabashed about parading around in front of him nude and is more than willing to make love to him, but this is not what Henri wants. She may be nearer his own age; she may be more conventionally attractive; but it is Sophie whom Henri loves. Significantly, his sketch of Gosh was of a body with an unidentifiable head; the various sketches he does of Sophie throughout the film may be stylized, but are always recognizable as Sophie. Much like Russell, Henri insists on representing the truth from his own viewpoint. Therefore, Sophie is a real person like her character, whereas Gosh is just a body without a real head. She is not real at all, but an affected confection--even the five-shilling prostitute comes off better because of her reality.

The thundering train noises which occur at the end of the scene lead readily into the next scene, a confrontation between Henri and Sophie in which she has decided to move to a new room because of the unbearable noise of the studio. It is obvious, too, that the encounter with Gosh has had an effect on her as she is once again insecure about her relationship with Henri, withdrawing her promise to marry him if he still wants her after the exhibition and substituting a compromised "we'll see." Russell brilliantly imparts the emotional strain of the separation on Sophie in his editing of the scene, which makes every blow of the hammer with which Henri is packing pieces for the exhibit seem to be a direct blow to Sophie by intercutting close-shots of the hammer blows with close-shots of Sophie's agonized face when the argument reaches its peak. Russell uses a long shot as she walks up the steps to leave, moving in to a fairly close medium shot as he briefly repeats the editing pattern with the hammer blows just before she walks out the door. It is the last time we see Sophie in the studio, and Russell reverses the layout of the shots for his film's ending.

That the war is encroaching more and more is economically conveyed in the next shot when through the bars which separate the foreground of the studio from the outside world we see a military band march by, playing "It's a Long Way to Tipperary." In an unusual bit of time compression, Henri looks up from the statue on which he is working, so that the reverse shot appears to be what he was looking at, but even though the music on the track is the same it is now night and in the pull-back from more crowds and military goings-on we see Henri much further along with the statue. The statue portends impending disaster for those familiar with Gaudier-Brzeska's work, for it is his "Birds Erect," his last major work, and, one might note, one of his most advanced. While he is at work on this, Gosh arrives in her "dazzling new war outfit" with a handbag of her own design to take to the front. The war has become her new "cause," and as she puffs on a cigar she wants to know when Henri is going. (Cigars and cigarettes take on a symbolic life in Savage Messiah, suggesting the unwholesome affectations of Gosh's cigar and Shaw's Black Russian cigarettes as opposed to Henri's either hand-rolled or purloined ones.) Despite the fact that the air is charged with the excitement of the war (the constant sound of the marching bands and the incessant parade of soldiers and cannons) Henri does not quite grasp where she expects him to be going. Truly her father's child she cannot comprehend that Henri should not be consumed with a desire to go to war. "I'm staying here with these birds," he tells her. "Where on earth would I ever see a bird like that?" Gosh asks, unable to fathom the statue. As if in mute answer to her disbelief in the reality of the work, a large chunk of powdered stone lands on her shoulder like a bird dropping. Thoroughly disgusted with Henri's lack of patriotism, Gosh leaves him to his work.

Cutting directly to Henri at work on another statue, we see that even Corky has been affected by the war hysteria. When Henri asks him to christen the new work, Corky suggests, "Trench Mortar Firing a Grenade." No, Henri tells him, "Bird Swallowing a Fish." Corky illustrates that other artists have joined up to fight--or, more correctly, to get commissions as "war artists"--and that Henri might as well do the same. Henri, however, has other ideas about the importance of what he is doing, and this is expressed in the next scene.

Seated atop a huge stone on which he has sketched a maternity figure, Henri chips away at his seemingly insurmountable task of reducing this great stone to the statue he wants, while he argues with Sophie. She calls him a parasite, an idea to which Henri takes exception because he feels he puts "something back into the pot." Sophie, however, tells him that all he does is "amuse the educated," which we know is not the case from the overall anti-elitist tone of the film. She too leaves him at his work as he proclaims to himself, "I don't care what they say, I am responsible. Things are beautiful and that helps." His belief, though, is soon shaken as a news vendor cries out about the destruction of Rheims Cathedral. As Henri reaches through the bars of the courtyard to get a paper, the sound of military music rises on the track and remains there as he sits down to consider the situation. The war and the atmosphere of war have finally affected Henri.

He tries to go to Sophie that night and "make an honest woman" of her before going away to the war, but Sophie does not, at first, believe him and sends him off. Suddenly she wonders if he might have been seious and rushes to the window to call him back, but by the time she reaches it there is no one there, only the sound of Henri's footsteps retreating into the night.

There follows a short scene accomplished in one long take as the camera slowly zooms in on Sophie seated on a

Henri working on the piece "Bird Swallowing a Fish," which Corky misconstrues as "Trench Mortar Firing a Grenade" in <u>Savage Messiah</u>. (Courtesy of Ken Russell)

The snapshot sent back from the front shows Henri's realization on a rifle butt of the Madonna and Child he was starting in stone in London in Savage Messiah. (Courtesy of Ken Russell)

bench in front of the tiger cage at the zoo as she writes a letter to Henri in which she tells him of her misunderstanding of the sincerity of what he called up to her from the street. Further, she reaffirms her love for him and promises to marry him after the exhibition "as I said."

From the simplicity of this scene Russell shifts to a close-shot on the whirling legs of dancers at Shaw's nightclub. In a focus shift he brings Corky's hands, holding a letter from Henri, into view. Corky reads aloud from this to Shaw and Tom Buff, who view the whole thing with cool contempt. As Corky reads of Henri's having fashioned "a small maternity statue from the butt end of a German rifle," Shaw can only comment that such a piece would be a "salable item." Corky's reading and the reactions of Shaw and Buff are intercut with the actions of the dancers, giving the scene and Shaw and Buff a greater sense of frivolity in the face of something serious. The quick cuts to the dancers even mock the war as their hands are sometimes poised in a saluting fashion. Corky concludes the letter: "Every night we go out and kill Germans. I have killed at least four Germans myself. When the big shells go off, it sounds like thunder, and I say 'Father.'" "Whoever wrote that," responds Buff, "should be shot." Corky simply looks up at him and says, "He was, last Thursday." Significantly, the three of them have been bathed in red light up to this point, but on Corky's delivery of the final line he is shown in natural light, reflective of the difference of his position.

The Debussy "Nuages" from the Nocturnes floods the soundtrack as Russell cuts to a close-shot of the grief-stricken Sophie crying. Russell's handling of these final moments in Savage Messiah is much bolder than anything written about the film would suggest. In the first place, his reticence about showing the war is far more terrible than anything he might have shown us. It is also extremely logical as we have remained in the safety of London with the others. Instead of seeing Henri die, we learn about it secondhand. We have had no time to get used to the idea and the vibrant artist of Savage Messiah is just cruelly plucked from us. Beyond this the rather lengthy sequence of the exhibition is daringly placed very late in the film after the action is over. It is also something of a time-shift as one assumes that this is the Memorial Exhibition of 1918, though Russell is not committed to this point as a historical fact. (Among other things he shows us works that were not included in that showing.)

Beautifully lit and photographed the camera takes in the works of Gaudier-Brzeska. We see his "Portrait of Horace Brodsky," his "Wrestlers," his "Workman Fallen from a Scaffold," his "Crouching Fawn," etc., and, of course, "Bird Swallowing a Fish" and "Birds Erect." Russell has a great advantage over the usual textbook illustrations of the works as he can give a greater sense of the three-dimensional aspect of the pieces by placing them on revolving platforms, and by panning over them, his camera caressing the various forms. We have the advantage of feeling that we knew the artist at this point, too, and the statues strike us with a potent force that might not otherwise exist on the same level. The onlookers at the gallery in their own way reflect Henri's outlook on art as espoused from the primitive head--some admire, some laugh, and some are baffled.

Russell is very careful that we not forget the human element of the film, and he keeps us from doing this by simply intercutting shots of the grieving Sophie every so often. It would be wrong to suggest, however, that this is a "downbeat" move, pure and simple, because the suggested eternity of the works of art themselves and the idea of a released spirit in the music are evocative of a life beyond our worldly grasp. The scene climaxes on a snapshot of Henri surrounded by smiling soldiers as he holds up the maternity statue of which he wrote. Russell closes on this note--"Things are beautiful and that helps," Henri has said earlier, and like his saving the flowers from the oncoming train, he has here fashioned beauty from the horrors of war, and from the expressions on his fellow soldiers' faces it is unarguable that such things do indeed help.

Russell cuts from this to the unfinished sculpture in front of the studio, and we recognize it as the same carved on the rifle butt. As the "Nuages" fades on the soundtrack, the camera pans over to Sophie looking at the great lump of stone that would have been a statue, and the sound of a marching military band comes up on the track. Russell cuts to an extreme long shot of Sophie standing by the stone, as a victory parade moves across the background. She slowly walks back into the studio as the camera zooms in slowly on the stone. When it fills the frame Russell superimposes the words, "Henri Gaudier-Brzeska, killed in action at 1:00 p.m., Fifth June, 1915 at Neuville St. Vaast, France, aged twenty-three," so that the stone which should have become a sculpture becomes a tombstone in a bitter reversal of the earlier tombstone which became a statue. That the work survives, that the spirit of Henri survives his physical death is inherent in the recurrence of the jaunty, hopeful theme that marked the couple's journey to London over the film's closing credits.

It should be noted that Russell's depiction of Henri's attitude about the war is his major historical departure in Savage Messiah, for the historical Henri had far fewer reservations about the war than Russell's Henri. Nonetheless, it serves a function within the film that can only be appreciated with historical hindsight. Russell, after all, knows what most people know, what most historians are agreed upon, but which Henri would not have known. Namely, World War I was one of the most singularly pointless, avoidable, and downright stupid confrontations of all time. That Russell should feel compelled to use Savage Messiah to put forth his own response to the shocking waste of the war is perfectly understandable and certainly in keeping with his approach to history. Then, too, it should be remembered that Savage Messiah's anti-war theme is bound to be affected by the time in which it was made as well, so the allegorical Viet Nam implications are hard to ignore. Russell's approach to the war, however, has curiously far-reaching overtones which are, no doubt, partly drawn from the World War I veterans' depression status as "forgotten men," but which seem oddly more applicable to the Viet Nam era, and that is in the responses of Shaw and Buff at the Vortex throughout Corky's reading of the letter. Even though Henri's abstract sentiments about killing and the war and the shells sounding like thunder may be hard for us to comprehend, we might bear in mind that he is at the front for the specific purpose of killing Germans. What right, therefore, do Shaw and Buff or we have to criticize him for doing just this? There is an unsettling and unpleasant similarity in this to the reaction many of those returning from Viet Nam have felt. Russell offers us no easy answers. Savage Messiah is no easy film.

In many respects Savage Messiah is the best film Russell had made at the time of its release. Russell's greater freedom through a deceptive simplicity makes many of its subtle experimentations seem far more trenchant today than those of The Music Lovers or The Devils. Unlike those films Savage Messiah carries little dead weight in its total dismissal of cleverly artificial scene-changing devices and the like. Story and point are starting here to take greater precedence, as are the more smoothly interpolated allegorical and commentary moves that one finds here and in The Boy Friend. Russell's reliance on the straight cut becomes even more pronounced in his next films, where the dissolve which had been window dressing in some of the earlier works, takes on a significance of its own. By the time of Clouds of Glory, when Russell reintroduced the dissolve as a transitional device, he did so with conscious intent of its own design.

No matter what one may think about Savage Messiah in the end there is no way around the fact that its unexciting box-office performance had an adverse effect on Russell's career. The director worked on a number of projects, but could sell none, including The Angels, which in part finally became the cornerstone of much of Tommy. It would, however, be over a year before he would release another film, but that wait proved well worth the time since Ken Russell was right on the verge of his greatest works.

NOTES

1. Crist, Judith. Review of The Devils. New York, 4 (July 26, 1971): 51.
2. Huxley, Aldous. The Devils of Loudun. New York: Harper & Row, 1965, p. 25.
3. Gomez, Joseph. Ken Russell: The Adaptor as Creator. London: Frederick Muller, 1976, pp. 165-166.
4. Fisher, Jack. "Three Paintings of Sex: The Films of Ken Russell," Film Journal, 2 (September 1972): 32-43.
5. Personal Correspondence with Ken Russell, November 1982.
6. Phillips, Gene D. Ken Russell. Boston: Twayne, 1979, p. 152.
7. Cited in Phillips, Gene D. Ken Russell, pp. 152-153.
8. Simon, John. Review of Savage Messiah. New Leader, 55 (February 7, 1972): 14.
9. Phillips, Gene D. Ken Russell. Boston: Twayne, 1979, p. 113.
10. Cited in Phillips, Gene D. Ken Russell, p. 113.
11. Gomez, Joseph. "Russell's Methods of Adaptation: Savage Messiah and Tommy," Ken Russell, ed. Thomas R. Atkins. New York: Simon & Schuster, 1976, pp. 83-84.
12. Gomez, Joseph. Ken Russell: The Adaptor as Creator. London: Frederick Muller, 1976, pp. 177-178.
13. Ibid., p. 179.
14. Ibid., p. 173.
15. Ibid., p. 174.
16. Ibid., p. 180.
17. Farber, Stephen. "Russellmania," Film Comment, 11:6 (Nov.-Dec. 1975): 41.

CHAPTER 8

THE MATURE FILMS

"Mahler," "Tommy," and "Lisztomania"

> "In conceiving the work I was never concerned with a detailed description of an event, but at most with that of a feeling."
> --Gustav Mahler[1]

The statement above from Gustav Mahler might well be a statement from Ken Russell concerning any of his films, but it has a singular significance when applied to his film on Mahler. In Mahler, as in the later Lisztomania, the viewer hoping for a string of textbook facts is bound to come away from the film with the impression that little, if indeed anything, has been learned. Mahler is not a history lesson (neither for that matter had any of Russell's previous biographies been), nor is it, as Russell once attested, '[s]ome of the things I think about when I listen to Mahler's music."[2] It does not neatly fit into the category that Gene D. Phillips would place it as a thematic companion piece to The Music Lovers. As a history lesson it is decidedly short on facts, though the facts it contains are essentially accurate. Russell's statement on the film is indisputable so far as it goes, but it simply does not go far enough. And Gene Phillips' categorization of Mahler as occupying a similar position to Tchaikovsky in Russell's estimate of him as a human being is at odds with the evidence presented on the screen. Mahler is, however, a film about Gustav Mahler and his music, the end effect of which is designed to give the viewer a sense or feeling of having actually known Mahler and what sort of a person he was and why--an effect that could not have been achieved by more traditional methods. On another level Mahler is a film about relationships, a film about responsibilities, a film about film, and, in a number of respects, a film about Ken Russell.

220

Despite his qualifications about the proximity of his birth date and that of the composer (Russell's being July third and Mahler's July seventh), Russell obviously meant something more when he said, "In many respects it's a film about me."[3] Even considering such things as the cryptic autobiographical rumblings that run through the films of Josef von Sternberg, or even the all-out egotistical wallow of Bob Fosse's All That Jazz, Mahler is probably the single best example of a filmmaker revealing his own life on the screen.

Quite apart from the similarities of their birth dates, there are a number of striking parallels between Russell and Mahler: the intense love of nature, the all-consuming passion for their respective arts, the hostility with which their work has been greeted by much of the critical populace, the conversion of both men to Catholicism, and the not inconsiderable parallel of the Gustav and Alma Mahler relationship with that of Ken and Shirley Russell. In light of the relatively recent statements which Russell has made concerning his marriage and the reasons for its dissolution,[4] the situation as presented in Mahler takes on added significance. Mahler's fears and worryings about Alma's fidelity to him are of a particularly abstract nature and are presented as such to the viewer. He and the viewer can both put a name to her possible lover, but none of the evidence on the screen proves Alma guilty of any wrongdoing. On the contrary, the affair between Gustav and Anna von Mildenberg is much more overt, which places the characters in the film in roughly the same position as that in the Russell marriage as put forth by Russell. In making neither Max nor Anna even remotely likable characters Russell is telling us something about the situation on a broader level, and in putting forth some very fair reasons behind Gustav's and Alma's actions he brings this point home. Alma's possible indiscretion is quite simply based on the fact that she feels Mahler loves his music more than her. Only slightly more oblique, and growing out of Alma's feelings, is Mahler's attraction to Anna von Mildenberg, who is everything Alma is not. Most particularly she does what Alma cannot do--worship Mahler's music and thereby feed his ego. Just how much of this parallel is intentional and how much is intuitive on Russell's part is impossible to say. Happily, in the case of Mahler, all of this arises very naturally from the story at hand and is not in the least self-indulgent. In painting his portrait of Gustav Mahler, Russell has not added anything that does not belong. The fact that it tells us so much about the filmmaker is purely a bonus, though it undoubtedly enters into the reason that Russell is so well able to depict the marital situation and it underlying causes.

Mahler is a unique film in many areas. Ludicrously underfinanced at £160,000 (roughly half the cost of a single episode of The Incredible Hulk), it affords the rare chance to see an established filmmaker working almost completely without a net, and in making the film Russell has actually turned this to his advantage. Joseph Gomez has said that to some extent Mahler is Russell's most experimental film[5] and in a purely technical sense this is true. It is almost impossible to conceive of a film more suffused with the splendor of natural lighting and shimmeringly natural exteriors. Pictorially Mahler is the high-water mark in Russell's association with cinematographer Dick Bush. The brilliant use of wide-angle lenses in the train compartments, the flickering of light as the train passes through deep woods, the breathtaking shots where we can see through the train windows on both sides of the carriage at once, all these linger in the memory far more than the most carefully controlled studio interior. Filmed on a real moving train with nearly all of the lighting coming strictly from natural sources and with no process work whatsoever,[6] the framing sections of Mahler are a technical wonder.

Structurally, too, Mahler is a complete departure from the earlier films. On one level it consists of a framing story and flashbacks, but this is a most elemental reading of the work and does not do it justice. Mahler's framing story is, in itself, partly real, partly metaphorical, as are the flashbacks. The flashbacks and fantasies are so finely interwoven into the narrative with the framing story that all parts intermingle and fuse into one unified whole of an astonishingly layered atmosphere.

The breakthroughs represented by Mahler are not entirely surprising as it is the first of Russell's films to be made from a screenplay written by him that is not based on a single work. Prior to Mahler the closest Russell had come to a completely original screenplay was the framing story for The Boy Friend. An original screenplay, and the freedom of it, and the good working relationship Russell found with producers David Puttnam and Sandy Lieberson are evident throughout the film. Russell's camera and his imagination soar as never before in Mahler, as he explores hitherto untouched ground.

The Mature Films

Musically speaking Mahler is also an advancement over his previous films, due in no small part to the composer's relatively limited output. In The Music Lovers, for example, it had been necessary to represent a fairly small cross-section of Tchaikovsky's music because of the sheer size of his output. In Mahler Russell is able to present generous excerpts from Mahler's First, Third, Sixth, and Seventh symphonies, and smaller, yet representative, portions of the Second, Fourth, Fifth, Ninth, and the unfinished Tenth Symphony, along with two of the Kindertotenlieder (Songs on the Death of Children). Then, too, Russell's approach and attitude toward Mahler's music is quite different from what it was toward Tchaikovsky. (Russell intimates as much in his statements that while filming The Music Lovers he grew tired of the music, but that with Mahler he found he could listen to the music over and over with no loss of appreciation. 7) The approaches themselves bear this out, for although much of the music in The Music Lovers is used for a satiric thrust at the composer and his dreams, this is never the case in Mahler. Any criticism that Russell may have to make about Mahler has nothing to do with his artistry.

Similarly here Russell is interested in the thoughts behind Mahler's music, in his influences--conscious or otherwise--in the actual process of the creation of the music, which is in no way like his approach to Tchaikovsky. (There are, however, glimmerings of this attitude in Song of Summer, especially the beautiful little sequence where Percy Grainger and Jelka carry Delius to the mountaintop, but there Russell is just as concerned with the abusive physical demands made on his friends by Delius, and with those friends' sacrifices, as he is with delving into the music.)

To fully appreciate Russell's achievement in Mahler it is necessary to examine the entire fabric of the film, because on the outer surface Mahler seems a relatively placid work, even idyllic, but underneath that surface lies a work of such maturity and daring that The Music Lovers, The Devils, and Savage Messiah pale in comparison.

Mahler opens on an idyllic note to be sure, but this is soon shattered as the lakeside hut we are watching inexplicably bursts into flame to a blast of music from the first movement of the Tenth Symphony. The camera then slowly zooms in on the burning hut, as flames fill the screen, Russell cuts to a quick shot of Mahler being burned alive and the title, "MAHLER," comes up on the screen. This is followed by a shot of Anna von Mildenberg reaching out as if to caress the flames and Putzi (one of Mahler's two children) glimpsed through the fire. As arbitrary as these images seem, there is a definite thematic and symbolic reasoning behind them, and an acute sense of drama not always appreciated to the fullest. (In terms of drama one need only cite the fact that Russell does not--as is generally supposed--begin zooming his camera until the hut has burst into flames, thereby making it impossible on subsequent viewings to ever be completely ready for the explosion of flame. Had Russell begun his zoom earlier the viewer could easily pick the point in the movement when this would occur.) Gene D. Phillips is partially correct when he asserts that the fire is indicative of the creative fire that burns within the hut, 8 but it is more the creative fire that burns within the composer himself--the fire that is destroying him. More, it is dangerous to those around him. The children seen in a visualization of Alma's later remark, "You'd rather sacrifice all of us than lose one note of your wretched music," foretelling of Putzi's death is indicative of this. It is only Anna von Mildenberg, the woman who will be seen to worship the composer and not the man, who is not only unharmed by the flames of this creative obsession, but actually seems to welcome them. (In this respect she can be seen to have a relationship to Tchaikovsky's Madame von Meck, and her later vulture-like appearance on the prow of an approaching boat underscores this parallel.) On yet another level, the destruction of the hut is the destruction of innocence--the death of happy days spent in Toblach, a death once again caused by the creative obsession. On a musical level, Russell has conjured up visions of death by his very choice of a piece of music from the very end of the last thing Mahler completed, and his placement is equally good in terms of achieving something of the effect of the entire movement in a brief excerpt as it presents much the same jolt in the film that it does in the movement. This music, or part of it, will recur twice in the film, and on both occasions is also associated with death. With this in mind it is only possible to view this scene as being more concerned with death and destruction than with any sort of creative fire on a positive level.

Continuing for the moment in a metaphorical vein, Russell cuts to a rocky shore and a selection from the early part of the first movement of the Third Symphony comes on the track. A woman (Alma as it turns out) sheated in a cocoon struggles vainly to break forth and, failing this, crawls over the rocks to caress one rock in the shape of Mahler's head. Much like the splendidly designed opening of The Music Lovers this scene appears not only arbitrary but slightly incomprehensible on first glance. Unlike the earlier sequence, however, the dialogue in the following scene makes clear the actions of the Chrysalis sequence. Even without a grasp on the underlying meaning, the sequence is stunningly conceived in its delicately sparse movement of camera and rhythmic action. Musically the choice of this movement of this symphony finds a symbolic position in the film, and the symbolism comes very naturally from the composer himself. Mahler originally titled this movement, "Pan Awakens; Summer Marches In," and the opening section depicts the struggle of the forces of summer (life) against the opposing winter. In the film this is visualized as Alma's struggle within the chrysalis, with Mahler as the rock representing the force that is holding her back. Within the music as utilized in the scene Alma's movements can clearly be seen as a direct outgrowth of Mahler's music--her one moment of triumph as she bursts from the outer sack corresponding with the call of the horns, identified by Egon Gartenberg in his study on Mahler's music as "the surge of life."[9] When watching a sequence such as this, so obviously designed to the music, John Simon's criticism that Russell has cut the music to fit the film rather than the other way around makes little sense.[10] At no point in the film does Russell tamper with the internal structure of an excerpt as this implies, and this scene is a good case in point. (Truth to tell, Simon runs his attack on the film aground when he attempts to cross over into musical criticism. His unwarranted derision of conductor Bernard Haitink--who is seemingly guilty by association--betrays his ignorance of Haitink's standing in the musical world as, among other things, one of the foremost Mahler interpreters of our time.)

At this point in the film Russell introduces the framing story as Mahler, sitting in a train carriage is awakened by a piercing train whistle. The ensuing dialogue with Alma explains the previous scene--"I dreamed. I imagined. The first movement of the third symphony kept going through my head.... You were part of the dream, too. You were a living creature struggling to be born." Alma's bitter retort, "At last! You've noticed," lets us know that not only is this a long-standing difficulty between them, but that much of the film will be concerned with this aspect of the relationship. Having thus established a tension between his two main characters, Russell is ready to develop his film to its full potential.

When Alma leaves the train, Mahler gazes from the window at a young boy swinging on the station posts in a dreamy evocation of the fourth movement of the Fifth Symphony. This little piece of film is designed to call to mind Luchino Visconti's ersatz Mahler film, Death in Venice (as is the man sitting on a bench coyly watching the action, who is made to resemble Dirk Bogarde in that film), but it is not the simple in-joke that Joseph Gomez takes it to be.[11] In calling the Visconti film to mind Russell is at once stressing the aura of impending death which hangs over the film, refuting Visconti's reading of Death in Venice as a biography of Gustav Mahler, and creating a scene that stands apart from Visconti as totally charming and far more unforced than its parent scene in Death in Venice.

Mahler's reverie is interrupted, however, as he is quickly besieged by a reporter, "Siegfried Krenek, Journalist, Toblach News." Unimportant though the encounter seems, it is a good example of the economy Russell has employed in Mahler in the conveyance of facts to the viewer. Within a very brief space of time we are made aware of the period of time being covered; are given an idea of the state of Mahler's health and certainly his nerves; and allowed some insights into his personality (Krenek: "Which do you prefer, composing or conducting?" Mahler: "I conduct to live. I live to compose.") which, when combined with Mahler's reference to himself ("I certainly drove one musician too hard") sheds further light on the obsessive nature of his creativity. Similarly, this is the first indication within the film of the parallel between Russell and Mahler. When Mahler says that he returned to Austria in order to find "someplace near Vienna where the grape grows and the sun is warm, and I can breathe again," Krenek immediately counters with, "Congestion of the lungs. So it was ill health." To this interpretation Mahler, in a voice weary with the familiarity of it all, responds, "Why is everyone so literal these days? I was speaking metaphorically." And indeed one finds the origin of this statement in an interview Russell had with Gordon Gow.[12] At the same time it is a statement that could very well have come from Mahler (consider the quote at the beginning of this chapter), and no distortion is necessary for Russell to utilize the response in this text.

Krenek's withdrawal, in which he completely ignores Alma, sparks the film's next fantasy, which presents Alma as a literal version of Mahler's shadow. The music in this instance comes again from the first movement of the Third

Symphony, recalling Alma's struggle for an existence of her own outside of her famous husband. Russell brings the point home forcefully as she is juggled about and ignored by people clustering around the famous composer, capped by a superb coup of geographical disorientation as Alma is suddenly and joltingly seen completely disassociated from Mahler on the floor below. Russell zooms in on her as she looks up accusingly, and the horns of the "surge of life" sound on the track. From this he abruptly cuts back to reality and a bitter close-shot of Alma as the horns cry out again and she tells Mahler, "I might as well be your shadow for all the notice anyone takes of me."

Fantasy sequences are indeed part of the overall Russell approach to filmmaking and are not unique to this film, but the use of the sequences in Mahler and subsequent works is different than that in The Music Lovers or The Devils. In those earlier works the fantasies are designed not only to make a point, but to advance the plot or to provide a characterization. In this manner it can be seen that Russell's approach to fantasy in Mahler is more commentary and that the closest forerunner to this approach is the brief "Any Old Iron" number in The Boy Friend. (In fact, all the fantasies in The Boy Friend are more closely related to Mahler and the later films than they are to the earlier works.) In Mahler there is always a basic viewpoint to the fantasy, which is in itself less a fantasy than an attempt to capture the feeling of the character experiencing the fantasy. This is why there is invariably a lead-in to the fantasies in the film, just as they are always referred to in the dialogue after the fact. Then, too, the fantasies in this film like those in The Boy Friend belong to relatively normal characters. As such they are on quite a different level than those of Tchaikovsky or Nina or Sister Jeanne. Russell presents them differently, also. There are no tricky transitional devices separating the fantasy from the film so that it becomes in Mahler more of a part of the flow of the film. This rejection of cinematic artifice for its own sake has been nurturing in Russell's work since The Boy Friend and is certainly evident in Savage Messiah, but Mahler is the first completely serious film utilizing large stretches of fantasy to ascribe to this more austere approach. In Mahler, where the fantasies are an actual part of the flow of the film, the result is a film made up of pieces so tightly interconnected that the effect is that of an unbroken narrative.

Further argument with Alma results in Mahler being

The Mature Films   229

left to himself in the compartment, where in one of the
film's richest sequences, he remembers the earlier happier
days of marriage. Unlike the pastoral fantasy in The Music
Lovers, or even the more closely related Chaplin "Liebestraum" fantasy in Lisztomania, this section of Mahler is
able to combine the facets of man and artist in one sequence.
As in The Music Lovers the tone of the sequence is slightly
satirical, but here the satire is very gentle and almost loving. Mahler's demands on Alma--to silence the countryside
noises ("The crows are the worst offenders and if you can
dispose of any unhatched generations while you're about it,
you'll save yourself a lot of future work")--may seem unreasonable, but Russell finds a sweetness in them that would
have been unthinkable with Tchaikovsky. Also, this is helped
by virtue of the fact that the bulk of the sequence deals with
the act of creation (in a visual equivalent of the dialogue
oriented "torso" sequence in Savage Messiah) as much as
with Mahler's unreasonable attitude toward his wife. The
creation segment of the memory (it can scarcely be called
a fantasy even though it is highly stylized) is a double-edged
sword celebrating and poking fun at Mahler in the same
breath because despite his pleas for silence, every sound
that Alma stills finds its way into Mahler's music. Russell's structure of the sequence is quite broad musically
speaking, and yet the music, coming from four different
symphonies, is always used in an appropriate manner.

   The sequence begins as Alma quiets the baby with a
rattle, which finds its counterpoint in an excerpt from the
beginning of the first movement of the Mahler Fourth Symphony. The choice is well judged in consideration of this
symphony within the Mahler canon--in 1902 the music critic
Max Kalbeck had said, "What touches us most in Mahler's
symphony is the feeling which emanates from the work. The
longing for simplicity--'Unless you become children you will
not enter God's realm.' Mahler's G Major symphony is a
work for children and those who will become children."[13]
Such a work certainly belongs in a sequence dealing with
this more innocent time in Mahler's life. Having thus expressed the simplicity of Mahler, Russell next plunges directly into Mahler at his most mystical and complex. As
Alma quiets the cows on the hillside by removing their bells,

[Opposite:] Alma Mahler on the banks of Derwentwater (one
of Russell's favorite locations) removes the baby from her
husband's earshot in the "creation" sequence of Mahler.
(Courtesy of Ken Russell)

Mahler's mind, to an excerpt from the first movement of
the Sixth Symphony, projects itself out of the hut across the
water of the lake, flying into the snowcapped mountains,
where in a bold move, Russell cuts to a pull-back shot of
the earth viewed from outer space as it revolves. This last
image then dissolves into Mahler's head. It is a startling
moment, all the more so because of its presentation of an
internal experience in an otherwise externalized series of
events. The utilization of the Sixth Symphony in this instance (though partly due to the composer's orchestration
which calls for cow bells) is the first indication of the peculiar significance of this work in the relationship of Gustav
and Alma. From it Russell turns back to Mahler's simpler
nature with a church bell inspiring the climax of the fifth
movement of the Third Symphony. (In itself this evocation
of the Third Symphony is a note of dissent, recalling as it
does the Chrysalis and Shadow fantasies, which illustrate
Alma's dissatisfaction with her life.) A piping shepherd then
finds his way into the first movement of the Fourth Symphony
with which the sequence had opened, restating the tone of
idyllic simplicity. The final and most lengthy episode, while
still concerned with Mahler's unconscious influences, is perhaps the finest statement Russell has ever made on the wonder of creation. Alma, having bribed a local band into silence with a round of beer, directs a silent dance for the
patrons of a beer garden, which Russell intercuts with Mahler circling the floor of his hut conducting, in his mind, the
second movement of the First Symphony. Despite the fact
that this movement leans heavily on the exact type of music
Alma has silenced--the Austrian peasant dance or Landler--
the final impression is that of the moment in creating any
work of art where everything comes together in the mind and
the artist knows exactly what the final product has to be like.

The memory does not end at this point, however,
which is important to the density of the film's structure,
since there is no smooth way of passing from the Creation
section directly back into the framing story. Instead Russell
chooses to further detail the Gustav-Alma relationship. Upon
returning from her mission of silence, Alma is greeted by
Gustav in bathing costume running out the door of the hut,
chiding her for not having "scared the crows off," and diving
into the lake. Russell's decision to accompany Gustav's
swim with an excerpt from the final movement of the Second,
or Resurrection, symphony, combined with the establishment
of a visual motif--Gustav floating on the water staring into
the clouds--to which he will return, heralds the change from

Mahler the work obsessed creator to Gustav the man. (This is also consistent with Russell's symbolic view of water as a means of purification.) Emerging from the lake, Gustav engages in some playful fighting with Alma, who has dressed up a scarecrow to resemble him, and, as the play turns to softer emotions, Russell introduces the second subject of the first movement of the Sixth Symphony for the first time. Having thus reestablished the more personal aspect of the framing story, Russell can effortlessly return to it by simply cutting to Gustav still sitting in the position in which we last saw him in the train, the excerpt from the Sixth Symphony still on the track as the bittersweet memories wash over him. Then to reinforce the gap which has developed between Gustav and Alma, Russell cuts to Alma standing alone in the train corridor, facing the opposite direction. Their geographical positions not only physically separate them, but also place them on a more symbolic level of separation--Mahler, his back to the engine, is looking backwards, figuratively and literally, while Alma appears to be looking forward.

The film's next major sequence occurs as the train pulls into a station where the populace have gathered to honor Mahler. As the sound of the band on the platform drifts into the compartment, Mahler starts laughing, "Christ! Why do they always homor me with the sound I detest most? A brass bloody band." Alma reminds him that this is because "[you] wrote so many of them into your symphonies," and further concludes that "they'll be bound to want a speech." Mahler tells her to make the speech for him and heads for the safety of the lavatory. When pressed for information as to what she should tell the reception committee, Gustav suggests, "Tell them their music gives me the shits." The dialogue here may seem slightly anachronistic, but the point is clearly made by the bantering nature of the delivery and the smiles the pair exchange at his suggestion that there is still a bond between them. They have drifted apart to be sure, but there is something there nonetheless, and this is essential to the film.

Once inside the lavatory, the brass band transports Mahler back to his childhood, and Russell's interpretation of the childhood in terms of two short stories by Isaac Babel, "The Story of My Dovecot" and "Awakening," has prompted much criticism. This criticism ranges from John Simon's cry of "plagiarism"[14] to Hollis Alpert's denunciation of the scenes as so anti-Semitic that they "might have been written by Dr. Goebbels."[15] (Alpert was apparently unfamiliar with the source.) To some extent, Russell's position is indefensible, but only because the film fails to credit Babel's stories. This would appear to be an oversight, when one considers the number of contributions the film does credit--Paul Dufficey's oil painting, Janet Deuters' design of the chrysalis sequence, William Blake's words for "Alma's Song," etc. At the same time it seems extremely improbable that Russell would have believed that the Babel material would go unrecognized, and the simple fact that he has never made a secret of its inclusion tends to support the view that the lack of credit to Babel is accidental. The question of authorship to one side, it is undeniable that the Babel stories serve Russell's purpose quite well, though whether or not they suit better than anything Russell might have written, as the filmmaker claims, is open to question. Nonetheless, Russell's adaptation of the stories to strictly Mahlerian terms is skillfully done and the changes in Babel's stories are quite to the point.

Actually, there is very little of "The Story of My Dovecot" in Mahler, and the bulk of the childhood scenes are a remarkably homogenous blend of "Awakening" with aspects of Mahler's life and the visual-aural pattern of the overall film. The Jewish humor with which the dinner table scenes are imbued (and to which Alpert so strenuously objected) is drawn directly from the Babel story, save for a Russell in-joke reference to his agent at that time, Robert Littman, and some obviously good-natured foolishness concerning what Liszt, Rubinstein, and Moscheles make by the hour. (This in itself finds its origin in Babel, where the desire is to be a virtuoso violinist and similar comparisons are made to Jascha Heifetz and Mischa Elman.) At no time does Russell make the Mahler material subservient to the demands of "Awakening." The character of Old Nick, who introduces young Gustav to nature, is firmly planted into the overall film, if only through his playing "Ach du Lieber Augustin" and "Frère Jacques" on the concertina. The first melody has a particular significance to Mahler, as he confessed to Sigmund Freud in his solitary visit to the man. It was the melody that invariably reared up in his head just at the moment when Mahler would feel he was on the threshold of achieving his dream of "the music of the spheres."[16] The second is more germane to the film since "Frère Jacques" forms the basis for the third movement of the First Symphony, which is used for the Funeral fantasy later in the film. (Old Nick reappears in this later sequence--a fact which seems to puzzle Joseph Gomez, but which is consistent with his ostensible inspiration of the composition.) Further unifying the childhood sequences with the overall film, Russell repeats the visual motif of staring into the clouds from the idyll scene (again there is the rebirth idea here as this comes after Gustav has nearly drowned); the use of the first movement of the Fourth Symphony as the basis for young Gustav's "Kitten Serenade" is a felicitous choice as well. Perhaps the single most telling example of Russell's absorption of the material for his own purpose occurs at the moment Gustav's father finds out that the boy has not been attending his piano lessons. Gustav's flight to the bathroom has already been established by the adult Mahler's similar retreat to the train lavatory in an effort to avoid a different sort of unpleasant encounter, and Russell's intercutting of the memory with the present serves to enforce this parallel. Also of significance is the change from Grandmother to Mother as the speaker of the line, "All we lack in this house is blood--I have no wish to see blood in this house." Combining this alteration with the visual impact of having Gustav's mother then lower her hands from her face, revealing the blood from where her husband has struck her, brings home the historical position of Mahler's parents. Russell has previously hinted at this in the sequence, making it quite apparent that Gustav's mother is more than a little afraid of her husband. By all accounts this is historically accurate as Mahler's mother was seemingly a shy, gentle, even somewhat cultured woman, who had been married off to Bernhard Mahler, who was exactly the opposite.

The scenes which follow of young Gustav in the forest at night are drawn from "Awakening," but only for their basis. In an exceptionally smooth blending of an excerpt from the first movement of one of the composer's less popular works, the Seventh Symphony (Song of the Night), leading into the climax of the third movement from the Third Symphony, Russell has built his wordless scene. Curiously, he does not utilize the actual Nachtmusik of the Seventh Symphony, but considering the exquisite delicacy of the first night scenes --Gustav skipping stones on the lake, the inserts of the forest animals, the lovely moment when the moon comes from behind the clouds--it is difficult to quarrel with his choice of the music. The transition to the Third Symphony comes with the arrival of the white horse and is significant of Gustav's attempts to become in tune with nature--in fact, the movement excerpted is subtitled, "What the Animals in the Forest Tell Me." The sudden appearance of the rearing horse is startling (strangely, more so upon subsequent viewings) and although Gustav's mounting the horse and riding off may be, as Joseph Gomez suggests, somewhat derivative of Elgar,[17] it is nonetheless riveting, and an apt symbol of Mahler's being at one with nature. Russell's editing pattern in this case is actually more reminiscent--with its alternating shots of horse's hooves and head and its building rhythm--of Mamoulian's editing of the chase in Love Me Tonight than it is of Elgar.

Mahler's memories of childhood are here interrupted by the arrival of an exotic black man in a turban wishing to use the facilities. Upon returning to his compartment with the unpleasant surprise of finding a character called Max in residence. (Max is a Chiluvsky-like character symbolizing all of Alma's extramarital admirers, real or imagined.) Russell underscores the threat Max represents in Mahler's mind by accompanying him with an excerpt from the first movement of the Third Symphony (later superseded by an extract from the first movement of the Fifth in another seamless joining of two excerpts part way through the sequence), tying him with Alma's struggle for a life and identity of her own. This is reinforced in a very unsettling fantasy in which Max throws leaflets from the moving train, one of which lands at Mahler's feet. (Mahler is now standing by the edge of a forest through which the train passes.) He reads the note, becomes angry, and thrusts it at Alma when she walks up, ordering her to read it. Alma already has one of the notes, however, and knows its message by heart--"Dearest Alma, I love you. Max." She promptly folds her copy, places it in the front of her dress, turns heel and leaves Mahler standing alone. The scene is extremely disconcerting, partly due to the abruptness of its interjection and the sense of physical alienation it arouses in placing Gustav and Alma on the train and in the landscape at the same time, making the boundaries of memory, fantasy, and fact nonexistent. Its real power, though, comes as much from the coolly formal order of events (Alma's offhand attitude, the neatly planted and trimmed row of trees she walks through, etc.) and Russell's detached approach to it, which is all the more effective in that it is the only fantasy in the film not designed so that dialogue leads up to and away from it.

The dialogue exchange between Gustav and Max that follows the fantasy is one of the most completely successful dialogue scenes in any Russell film. Like the film itself, Russell's dialogue is, in this instance, a richly detailed tapestry, inextricably linked to the historical Mahler and to

The Mature Films   235

the film itself. The exchange concerning Mahler's religion--
"I forgot, you're not a Jew are you, now that you're famous.
What religion are you?" and Mahler's reply, "I'm ... a composer"--foreshadows the section of the film detailing Mahler's
conversion to Catholicism, which is a number of scenes away.
Similarly the barbed dialogue about the idea that "no great
composer of symphonies ever gets past nine" is peculiarly
appropriate to the historical Mahler. In the film Mahler
bluffs Max by telling him that he is not superstitious, but in
reality Mahler was so terrified of dying after his ninth symphony that he avoided composing it by instead composing the
symphonic song cycle Das Lied von der Erde (The Song of
the Earth). This dialogue is also in keeping with the film's
feeling of impending and inevitable death. Much in the manner of the musical reference to "Frère Jacques" and "Ach
du Lieber Augustin, " and the later intercut of Mahler running
along the beach after the doctor has warned him against
physical exertion, the meaning to its fullest extent is not
abundantly clear to the viewer with no knowledge of the composer.

   After ordering Max to leave, Mahler is presented with
the news that Alma has succeeded in finding them a less
noisy compartment as Gustav had earlier requested, but his
encounter with Max has provoked a fit of childishness and he
refuses the offer to trade for another compartment. He is
too late in his decision to forestall the arrival of the African
Princess who agreed to the trade. Her initial words, "I understand you're searching for tranquillity, Dr. Mahler, "
make Gustav feel that she is possibly a kindred spirit. Her
subsequent remarks, ending with "It's a pleasure to meet
someone who really knows what it's all about, " indicates this
even more clearly. Mahler's response, though, "The music
of the spheres, you mean" is greeted with a reply that completely shatters his notions: "No, I mean death. " In a
boldly direct reversal of the stylized sound principles developed by Rouben Mamoulian in Love Me Tonight, where the
sound of a vase crashing becomes an explosion, Russell increases the impact by placing three full seconds of silence
on the track. The effect is chilling, almost terrifying--the
silence of the grave. Completely unaware of her blunder,
the Princess happily continues her dissertation on the subject
of death, triggering his own memories of explaining God,
death, heaven, and hell to his children.

   The layered construction of this sequence is remarkable. Walking back from his composing hut, Mahler comes

upon his children, Putzi and Glucki, looking through a book of Gustav Dore's religious engravings, and one of them asks, "Who's that man flying through the air?" Mahler looks at the book, and Russell inserts a section of panning over the drawings and zooming in on details, accompanied by an excerpt from the final movement of the Second Symphony. The effect is stunning. The pictures gain a remarkable feel of depth and are perfectly suited to the implications of the music. It is reminiscent of the presentation of the Gaudier-Brzeska sculptures at the end of Savage Messiah. At the conclusion of this, the child repeats her question. (In the same way that the lead-in to the memory--"Yes, even death the joker, death the lover"--will be repeated by the Princess on returning to the framing story.) The actual dissertation on the nature of God is very much in the mold of Russell's personal Catholicism and mysticism, but is nonetheless consistent with Mahler. The same is true of the second discussion with the children about heaven and hell, which is similarly tied to Dore's drawings and matched to the fiery opening of the fourth movement from Mahler's First Symphony. (Typically, Russell will build on the ideas put forth in this scene and develop them into a more mystical visual presentation in his next film, Tommy, with its implications of a universal salvation.) Russell's handling of these discussions and the framing story with the Princess serve to point up, like Mahler's claims that he is not superstitious, the very real fear of impending death. The children delightedly chant that in order to see God, "We're going to die, die, die, die, die," which returns us to the Princess and her repeated line about death. Death constantly looms before Mahler in the film, and no amount of bluff or intellectualization on his part can help.

The return to the framing story prompts a dialogue between Mahler and the Princess which recalls Mahler's outburst at Max--"I'm sick of being told how my music speaks to people"--when the Princess insists that "your latest symphony, the Ninth, is all about death." Despite the fact that she has the composer's word that this is not entirely so, she is adamant because she read "about it in the New York Times," a source which is obviously more unimpeachable than the work's creator. (It is impossible to escape the idea that all of this reflects the manner in which Russell's films and intentions have been misread, ignored, distorted, or pummeled by uncomprehending critics.) Still Mahler informs her that "instead of death, you should read 'farewell'-- the symphony is a farewell to love," and in so doing reintegrates the Gustav-Alma relationship into the narrative. To a very final sounding excerpt from the first movement of the Ninth Symphony, Mahler thanks the Princess and departs.

On a first viewing it may seem that the emphasis on death is a bit heavy at this point in the film. Certainly it has caused the film to swerve from the central relationship theme, but it is part of the film's overall design. The death imagery that has thus far occurred is a buildup to the first of Mahler's two major fantasy set pieces. Having apparently decided that changing compartments is preferable to the Princess' New York Times inspired ideas, Mahler heads for the new compartment. Once there he quickly reverts to the childishness he previously displayed, acting out a charade of looking under the seats on the chance of discovering "any more of your lovers about." He then insists on pulling a suitcase down from the luggage rack, countering Alma's protests with, "I'm not dead yet. You'd all like to see the back of me--you, Max, Kokoschka." His foolishness, however, causes a sudden pain in his chest, and he sinks to the floor, crying, "Beethoven!" while the blast from the Tenth Symphony heard at the film's opening sounds on the track. (The "Beethoven!" outcry is simply a Russellian in-joke based on Mahler's actual last word, "Mozart."[18])

In a sequence inspired in part by Carl Theodore Dreyer's Vampyr, Russell details Mahler's fantasy funeral. Outwardly this seems one of the strangest occurrences in the film, but it has a basis in fact, has been well-integrated into the film's fabric by the preceding events, and is one of the clearest examples of Russell's personal view of history. In reality, Mahler did once suffer a mild form of mental breakdown in his dressing room before a performance. The flowers of well-wishers appeared to him to be for his funeral, and until they were removed he could not be convinced that he was not dead. (Russell refers to this directly in a later patch of dialogue when Alma tells him that the children on the train station platform want to give him their bouquets, and Mahler calls them "wreaths.") Such an idea is psychologically sound as well since Mahler was more than a little morbid. (Consider the fact that most of his symphonies contain a funeral march.) The very strong emphasis on death in the two preceding scenes leads into the funeral fantasy, and even the film's opening foreshadows the cremation of the fantasy with its burning hut linked musically to Mahler's attack in the train carriage, and the shot of Mahler, just prior to the credit title, being consumed by flames. Controversial though the mere fantasy element of the scene has been, it is Russell's vision of history that has caused the greatest criticism, and this is also true of the later Conversion fantasy. Both Joseph Gomez and Gene Phillips quibble with Russell's basic premise that if one takes a 1911 Austrian soldier in a black mourning uniform and projects him into the future, the end result is a Nazi S. S. officer.[19] Russell's phrasing of this idea may be a little fanciful, but the idea itself is consistent with Russell's attitude of historical responsibility. The S. S. officers carrying the living Mahler off to be cremated is nothing more than a development of the same idea presented as far back as The Music Lovers, where Nina is pictured in the insane asylum during Tchaikovsky's lifetime. Historically it is inaccurate, as are the S. S. men here, but since Tchaikovsky is shown to be partly responsible for Nina's state, Russell's shuffling of time becomes dramatically and symbolically valid. By the same token Max's sneering remarks about Mahler's Jewishness, and the overall anti-Semitism faced by the composer in the film, serve to make this broader allegory work on a similar level. This is not to indicate that Russell has lost sight of the overriding theme of his film in using allegory. Anti-Semitism in its most vicious and readily identifiable form is Nazism. Too much is read into Russell's Nazi images that is just not there. For Russell the use of the Nazi is mostly an effective cinematic shorthand designed to convey the prevalent anti-Semitism of Mahler's time to the modern viewer. (We know, after all, what this brand of anti-Semitism led to.) The Nazi imagery in this case is secondary to the death and betrayal themes, but Russell is not concerned in Mahler with creating a series of peaks in a flat framing story landscape and is not viewing the funeral as an actual culmination. Part of the remarkable density of Mahler comes from the flow of one idea, one image, one scene into another so that everything is interlocked. Krenek, the journalist, hinted at anti-Semitism; Max implied it; the childhood sequences touched on it; the Nazi pall-bearers become its concrete symbol and are leading the film's development toward the later Hugo Wolfe and "Conversion" scenes. The amazing thing about the fantasy sequence is that, despite a proliferation of ideas, there is nothing arbitrary in it. Every aspect of the scene is a visualization of some other part of the film--the brass band for which the funeral procession has to stop is an outgrowth of the band on the station platform; Alma's lewd dance on the coffin and her striptease are both drawn from the film, an acting out of Mahler's line, "You always wanted fame. Well it looks as if you'll have to settle for notoriety"; her mock love-making with the gramophone is a foretelling of her later confession that she felt Mahler loved his music more than her. Even the music itself, the third movement of the First Symphony, finds its counterpart elsewhere in the film, as already noted, with Old Nick's rendition of its parent theme in the childhood scenes. This music and the presence of Old Nick within the scene suggest that Russell does not want us to view Mahler as a victim, except, perhaps, of his own mind. The music is his creation. His fantasy is born of his fear of death and his fascination with it. Alma's actions are his fabrications, based to a large extent on his guilt in repressing and ignoring her. His compulsive work habits and his obsession with his art having left him no time for others, leaves him no mourners to grieve over his passing. For Russell, Mahler has done all this to himself, and with the funeral he begins to realize this. Significantly, after this sequence, Mahler actually begins to set things right.

The return of the framing story finds Mahler being comforted by Alma after his attack. Russell's placement of the characters--Mahler lying with his head in Alma's lap--works on two levels at once, stressing the child-like nature of his character, while also indicating the beginning of the characters' reconciliation. The fact that Mahler is here child-like should not be confused with his earlier petulant childishness. For Russell, and for Mahler, childhood is innocence, and in assuming this role Mahler takes the first step in reclaiming that innocence. As Mahler tells Alma of his dream--"I was dead and yet alive. You and Max were mocking me"--Russell leads into the film's most structurally complicated section. Thematically, the scenes which follow serve to balance things out between the characters, as Alma's experiences at Gustav's hands all relate to experiences of his own making.

Russell begins the central Alma memory with Ann von Mildenberg (Gustav's "busty opera star") singing "Alma's Song," one of the compositions Alma had been trying to get Gustav to assess in the Pastoral-Creation sequence. It is a simple work, using William Blake's "Song (How Sweet I Roamed)" for its words. Blake's words are well applied to the Gustav-Alma relationship, i.e. "He caught me in his silken net, and locks me in his golden cage," and "... mocks my loss of liberty." Upon completion of the song Gustav and Anna do indeed make mock of Alma's composition, though not with any direct viciousness on Gustav's part. Gustav's actions are not borne of malice, but he is too pre-

occupied with his own work, and with impressing Anna, to pay much attention to either Alma or her song. Instead, he launches into a ridiculous critical duel with Anna concerning the derivative nature of this composer as relates to that composer, culminating in a remark about Tchaikovsky, prompting Gustav's in-joke response, "Ach! For Music Lovers everywhere!" Gustav's attitude toward Alma's aspirations as a composer is largely a protective one. He does not want her to be hurt by rejection and critical abuse. This thought prompts his memory of someone he knew who did get hurt in this manner.

The sudden departure from Alma's memory into Gustav's memory of Hugo Wolfe (in essence a flashback within a flashback) may seem to foreshadow the narrative slip of placing June Mathis' fantasy within Natasha Rambova's memory in Valentino, but in Mahler the effect is to strengthen the bond between Gustav and Alma. By placing Gustav's memory within Alma's, Russell not only explains to the audience the reason Gustav feels as he does, but implies that Alma either is or should be aware of this reasoning as well.

The memory begins with an excerpt from the third movement of Mahler's quirky Seventh Symphony, as Gustav and his sister, Justine, are presented to a man identified as Emperor Franz Josef. The "Emperor" immediately begins questioning Gustav about his application for the post as conductor of the Vienna State Opera and mistakes Justine for Gustav's wife. Having more or less satisfied himself with Gustav's technical competence, the "Emperor" then wants a display of his "social qualifications," specifically a sample of his ability to waltz. Gustav and Justine follow his command, dancing to the eerie waltz of the third movement. The sequence is unsettling for much the same reason that the earlier scene of Gustav and Alma with Max's love letters had been--the calm, off-hand nature of the presentation. Something is quite obviously wrong here, but the Emperor's placid nature, the ready acceptance of his command by Gustav and Justine, and the formal gardens through which they move, give the scene a very ordered feeling, serving to heighten the unnatural quality of the proceedings. The dance over, the Emperor decides he wants to know more about Gustav's qualifications. Gustav tells him of a series of German mu-

[Opposite:] Alma listens while Gustav plays and Anna von Mildenberg sings "Alma's Song" in Mahler. (Courtesy of Ken Russell)

sic he had presented, "where I performed, with some success, the works of Richard Wagner." The Emperor expresses his dismay over this, orders Gustav to drop his trousers, inspects him, and confirms his suspicions--"As I thought, a Jew." Regretfully, he informs Gustav that, owing to the influence of Cosima Wagner ("... an even greater anti-Semite than her late, lamented husband"), his Jewishness precludes any possibility of attaining the post he desires. "It's a pity, too," the Emperor continues, "You dance divinely." During the last part of his conversation-- on the line, "My hands are tied"--the Emperor has crossed his arms in front of himself in a straitjacked fashion, and he ultimately falls backward from the pool edge of the fountain on which he is sitting into the pond behind him to take his "therapeutic waters." Asylum guards rush out and pull him from the fountain, while a doctor advises Gustav to take Justine away since "Herr Wolfe is likely to become violent and abusive."

Several critics have objected to this scene. Stephen Farber goes so far as to purport that it has all the earmarks of a scene from a "cheesey student film,"[20] while others have simply opined that it is historically inaccurate. (Russell's belief that Hugo Wolfe went mad from critical neglect and abuse is not the generally accepted view [syphilis], but it is by no means unique to Russell.) One cannot help but feel that the major reason for the objections to this scene lies more with the feeling of having been led up the garden path, and critics do not, as a body, much like being taken in by a filmmaker. In all fairness, however, it should be noted that Russell has not cheated. The music, the design, the dialogue, the structure, and the basic situation all serve to indicate that things are not what they seem on the surface, a fact that makes Farber's criticism of the scene more than a little untenable. (Farber is one of the very few critics who has championed the Conversion sequence, and it does not make good sense to accept that sequence and reject this one. At the same time Farber's overview of Mahler as a "grab-bag of flashbacks"[21] indicates that he has not digested the film's structure in the first place.)

The brief scene which follows, where Gustav visits Hugo in his cell (typically, the immersion in water has returned Hugo to himself to some extent) is largely notable as it fits into the overall scheme as an introduction to the idea of duty and responsibility. In the discussion with Hugo's doctor, Gustav worries about the effect of his getting the post of Court Conductor on Hugo. "Would that stop you from taking it?" the doctor asks, and further comments, "We all have our responsibilities. Mine is to Hugo. Yours is to your family." In this Russell sets the stage for the themes of the scenes which directly precede the Conversion sequence.

Returning from the Hugo Wolfe scenes to Alma's memory, we find Gustav reiterating that he does not want to see Alma hurt, "leave composing to those too stupid to do anything else." Having thus dismissed her musical ambitions he settles into rehearsing Wagner's "Liebestod" with Anna, sending Alma off to put the children to bed. In the scenes which follow of Alma burying her songs in a pencil-box, while the orchestral version of the "Liebestod" throbs on the soundtrack, there has been a critical tendency to side completely with Alma's situation, and this does not appear to be Russell's intention. The scene is beautifully moving, but if we take the various aspects and see how they interrelate, we find there is considerably more here than "Heartless-Gustav-stomps-on-Alma's-compositional-aspirations." There is an ambiguity in Russell's position. He is undeniably touched by Alma's pain, but he is not uncritical of her attitude. The aspect of the child's pencil-box and the striking similarity between her journey into the woods at night and young Gustav's nocturnal foray cuts two ways. On the one hand it is evocative of the idea that her aspirations have been killed in their early stages; on the other it makes her actions appear slightly childish. Then there is the case of the "Liebestod" on the soundtrack. Russell's Wagner sentiments to one side (though they certainly have a bearing on the situation since the "Liebestod" here, like Professor's Sladky's Wagner bust-cum-piggy-bank, and Hugo's Wagner statements, helps connect the film with the upcoming Conversion), his attitude on Romanticism as a kind of death wish would seem to eliminate his use of the one composition--the "Liebestod" or "Love Death"--which so clearly states this idea of desirable death at face value. By virtue of the music alone, Alma is clearly dramatizing herself in a very theatrical manner, reminiscent in every respect of Isadora's specious suicide attempt in Isadora, which also utilized the "Liebestod."

Returning from the flashback, Gustav tells Alma more about his funeral nightmare, "I wanted to live so very much, but you didn't take any notice," again equating this fantasy with the guilt of his inability to perceive Alma's needs. The framing scene in this instance is very brief, merely a bridge to the memory leading to the Conversion. To this end Gustav insists that Alma must decide between Max and him before the train reaches Max's station, but that the decision must be "made out of love, not duty." The idea of sacrificing love to duty, or to an idea of duty, prompts the memory of his decision to convert to Catholicism.

The sequence which leads to the actual Conversion, and the Conversion itself, is not really a separate memory from the interior one (the Hugo Wolfe section) of Alma's flashback. Indeed, the family scene preceding the Conversion fantasy fits into chronological order with the visit to Hugo. A great deal has been made over the supposedly inappropriate nature of the scenes dealing with Mahler's change of religion. The most common complaint is that the Conversion fantasy is at odds with the bulk of the film, but if the overall design of Russell's structure is analyzed it becomes clear that not only does the sequence fit into the framework, but that he has been building up to it for some considerable time. If there is a particular flaw in the inclusion of the scene it is simply that the understanding--on any but a superficial level--of the Conversion perhaps rests too strongly on a knowledge of the filmmaker and his films. Unlike the inclusion of the jail scene in <u>Valentino,</u> this scene is not the willful insertion of a Russellian element just to have one--it develops from the narrative and the feelings of the filmmaker. Historically, we know that Gustav Mahler did convert to the Catholic faith, and despite whitewashing claims that this was of no great significance to Mahler as he was always more mystical than Jewish in outlook, the primary reason for the conversion was undeniably to further his professional career. With this in mind it seems incredible that anyone could believe that a subjective and personal creator like Russell, who converted to Catholicism out of genuine spiritual need, would react other than he has to Mahler's conversion. If we are going to grant Russell's right to a personal interpretation as a filmmaker, then it must extend to this sequence fully as much as to the "1812 Fantasy," Sister Jeanne's crucifixion fantasy, etc.

Russell's buildup to the Conversion is shrewdly conceived and executed, starting slowly and then gradually progressing as nominal realism becomes more and more off-center until it erupts into the total stylization of the fantasy. Gustav lies on a bed, reading a newspaper and smoking a cigar, while his brother, Otto (referred to and introduced in the Hugo Wolfe section), plays a rather monotonous composition called "Sunset" on the piano. Gustav's inquiry as to the title and his subsequent pronouncement of the piece as "interesting," starts a family squabble when Justine chimes in, "Interesting's easy; Beautiful is hard." Suddenly we find outselves, as Gustav himself does, in a variation on the Babel inspired dinner sequences. Only now it is Gustav who is in the position originally occupied by his father, and though he handles that position with more compassion, he has nonetheless become like his father. His ultimate decision to convert to Catholicism is Gustav's own version of the get-rich-quick panacea of his father's notion of turning his son into an instant child prodigy. (Russell underscores this viewpoint immediately after the Conversion fantasy by hearkening back to Gustav's mother's image of her son playing at Buckingham Palace in Gustav's dialogue with Justine.) As the scene builds, Otto takes on the characteristics of Chico Marx in his piano playing and cloth hat, while Gustav with his cigar and straw-boater like hat becomes Groucho. With his decision to convert (delivered Groucho style with a flick of the cigar and a knowing look at the camera), Justine utters a cry of horror, and Russell quickly cuts to a third Mahler brother, Alois, made up like Harpo and wildly honking a taxi horn, heralding the start of the Conversion sequence while simultaneously stressing the ludicrous nature of Gustav's position.

Presented as a kind of silent film (complete with title cards) within the film, "Mahler's Conversion to Catholicism," is the most universally disliked scene--as concerns Russell's supporters--in any Russell film, but, as previously noted, this is mostly due to misunderstanding. To say that it would not be out of place in Dance of the Seven Veils, or that it is a harbinger of the sort of thing from which Lisztomania will be formed, is to miss the point. It is undeniable that the sequence, even though skillfully worked in, is harsher than the rest of the film taken as a whole, but it is Russell's desire to be harsh in this case. Asking for the sequence to be more at one with the overall film is very much the same as asking Russell to either admire and accept everything about Mahler, or to dislike and reject everything. On the same level, Russell's utilization of the silent film format and his depiction of Mahler doing impersonations of Stan Laurel and Al Jolson, are, like the lead-in sequence, geared to reinforce the absurdity of the conversion itself. Moreover, they serve to parody the idea of an actual transformation--Gustav is no more Laurel or Jolson than he is a good Catholic.

Robert Powell as Mahler offers up his Jewish faith to Antonia Ellis as Cosima Wagner in the silent film fantasy "Mahler's Conversion to Catholicism" in Mahler. (Courtesy of Ken Russell)

It is all role playing, and the role is that of a character in a farce. As Russell points out, Mahler is not actually converting to Catholicism, but to a Wagnerian variation on it--a mockery--and that is what he has chosen to depict. The Conversion is a hollow parade of carnival style events (something of a literal visualization of Grandier's line in The Devils, "You have turned the House of God into a circus, and its servants into clowns"). Further the circus aspect of the conversion is not very far afield from many uninformed and ill-conceived notions of such a conversion. It is very much in the mold of Cordelia Flyte's intentional fabrications to a convert--with stories of monkeys in the Vatican and a request box for the damnation of souls--in Evelyn Waugh's Brideshead Revisited. The concept of the fantasy as a silent film is a particularly clever bit of symbolism itself. Mahler's Jewishness enforces on him a (musical) silence that upon the completion of the ceremony erupts (via the title, "Then came the Talkies!") into sound as Gustav and Cosima Wagner sing a prody of Wagner's "Ride of the Valkyries": "You're no longer a Jew-boy. Now you're a goy," etc.

The lead-out from the Conversion fantasy is, in its own way, just as jarring as the fantasy itself, but in this case it is the transition from the absurd to the serious that shocks, bringing the viewer back from the comedy of the Conversion to the earnestness of the central story. Upon completing his transformation from Jew to Catholic, Gustav sets out in high spirits to celebrate his good fortune and new found acceptance, taking home a magnum of champagne "to be baptized into the house of Mammon." Once he and Justine arrive home, however, they find that Otto has killed himself, leaving the note, "One less mouth for you to feed," making Gustav's conversion even more hollow than it first seemed. Otto's suicide (accompanied by the same excerpt from the Tenth Symphony used with the hut bursting into flame and Gustav's seizure) also returns the film to the idea of impending death, which confronts Mahler at every turn.

In the framing story, Gustav reasserts his viewpoint that Alma must decide between Max and himself, and that her decision must be based on her feelings. As the train pulls into the next station where a doctor is waiting to examine Mahler, death appears again in the aforementioned equation of the children's flowers with funeral wreaths. The arrival of the doctor and his question, "When did you suffer your first attack?" combines with the image of the children and flowers to conjure up the memory of the death of Gustav's daughter, which shortly preceded that first attack.

The sequence detailing her death and the relation of it to the Kindertotenlieder is, like the Conversion framed into the narrative by inner framing scenes, but the central portion of this memory cannot be called a fantasy. The very fact that so little has been discussed about this segment of the film is indicative of much of the misconception about Mahler on the whole. This is not entirely incomprehensible as Russell's placement of such a key element in the film at such a late point in the narrative is unorthodox, to say the

The Kindertotenlieder segment in Mahler. (Courtesy of Ken Russell)

least. It should be noted, though, that much in the same manner that other sequences in the film are inherent in the material already presented prior to their actual occurrences, so too is this. With this in mind the importance of the film's opening scene returns to the forefront. It is the statement of an overview of the film's theme of Mahler's obsessive compulsion to create--a destructive compulsion in that it can blind him to everything else, destructive to those around him and to himself. The connection of the film's death imagery with the innocence of childhood played out in this sequence crystallizes the theme of Mahler's fall from grace by the loss of his own innocence. In fact he attempts to allay Alma's fears that "Songs on the Deaths of Children" is not tempting fate with the idea that "There are many forms of death. Those songs are on the death of innocence." Alma, however, views death as death and wants no part of it. In tossing the music onto the waters of the lake behind her, she accomplishes nothing. It is just whistling in the dark, like Gustav's attempts at escaping death by ignoring it. In one of the film's most telling compositions, Russell shows the reflection of the music on the water with Gustav in the background behind the window which separates him from Alma as he tells her, "They're still there."

The central portion of the flashback concerning the death of Putzi is structured to an unorthodox translation of the sixth and final of the songs, "In Stormy Weather." The translation of the song, like the sequence itself, is thematically and dramatically correct despite any juggling of dates, occurrences, or words. In many respects this is the most carefully constructed scene in the film, delivering an encapsulated version of Gustav's loss of innocence through his neglect of wife and family, both through the obsession of creativity and his dalliance with a woman who does not question that obsession, but welcomes and is attracted to it. Anna von Mildenberg's reappearance, standing on the prow of the approaching boat and garbed in black, makes her a grim threat of death, and in occupying Gustav's time and thoughts this is what she becomes. (It is arguable that Gustav's neglect had no direct bearing on Putzi's death--it almost certainly could not have--but that is not the point. Russell is concerned with the feelings Putzi's death engendered in both Gustav and Alma in driving them further apart. The scene is a realization of Alma's fear and Gustav's subsequent feelings of guilt.)

The sequence is also notable for the heartbreakingly

matter-of-fact presentation of the actual death of the child, achieved with remarkable economy. Very simply Russell shows Putzi sitting up in bed, crying, "Mummy!" and cuts directly to a shot of her tiny coffin lying atop the piano. There is no heavy-handed death agony, no breast-beating melodrama (compare the restraint here with Visconti's approach to the same material in Death in Venice), and the emotional impact is all the greater for the lack of it. The avoidance of such a scene keeps Gustav distanced from his child (as does the cry for "Mummy"), and the mute eloquence of the coffin on the piano carries the poignancy of the thought that Putzi has been sacrificed to Mahler's music.

The flashback closes on a similarly simple and restrained note. Gustav sits at his piano, quietly playing the third of the songs in the cycle, while mentally reciting the words: "When your dear mother comes through the door, not on her face does my first glance fall, but on the spot at her side where you should be." This is acted out in silence as Alma enters, crosses to the piano and takes Gustav's lamp, leaving him alone in the dark--a visual equivalent of the words to the song and of the silence on the track in his earlier encounter with the African Princess. On this silent note of hopelessness, Russell closes the flashback portion of his narrative.

In the return to the framing story, Gustav and the doctor discuss the coincidental nature of Putzi's death and "those morbid songs of yours." The doctor, though, can find nothing very much amiss with Gustav other than "a slight throat infection," and assures him that if he will take care of himself all will be fine. There is more than a touch of irony in the fact that Gustav should receive the news he most wants to hear from a man to whom his artistry means nothing. (The doctor professes to be tone deaf.) Nonetheless, the doctor's verdict carries enough weight that Gustav begins to live again. No longer afraid of the "funeral" flowers, he happily accepts the bouquets from the children outside the train and signs a few hurried autographs as they pull out of the station. The action (from left to right) is counterpointed by Russell's insertion of the reverse action of Mahler running through the woods accompanied by the third movement of the Fifth Symphony. The intercutting delivers two thoughts at the same time since it symbolizes the feeling of freedom Gustav is experiencing in the ostensible dismissal of his fear of death, while the train continues moving inexorably toward that death. The use of the Fifth Symphony here also recalls Max and the latter section of his fantasy sequence, and the peculiarly unresolved nature of the ending of the excerpt reminds us of the similarly unresolved triangle situation.

The reconciliation of Gustav and Alma which follows is in itself a measure of that freedom Gustav is experiencing. True to the pattern of the film, Gustav will turn out to be right in thinking himself to be a terminally ill man, but the fact is that in trying to find the meaning of his life--in facing his shortcomings and failings, and in facing death, he has reclaimed himself. On its most mystical level the train journey is akin to the mystic's "Dark Night of the Soul," and its outcome, reflective of the film's earlier moment of supreme tenderness in the idyllic flashback, is the regeneration of the spirit, reclaiming innocence. Gustav's creative ability is not in question. It is part of the inner divinity of mankind, but his perception that Alma is a part of that creativity, that she is something beyond "mistress, music-copyist, or your whore," is the element that allows Gustav to become innocent once again. It is extremely significant that Russell's character here, for the first time, is allowed to perceive his failings and dependencies before it is altogether too late.

The actual ending of the film, which Russell claims was designed in its bittersweet tone to "out Hollywood Hollywood,"[22] is still something quite removed from the shattered hopes climaxing The Music Lovers, The Devils, or even Savage Messiah. The final moments, particularly the telephone conversation of Dr. Roth which lets the audience in on the fact that Gustav is indeed dying, do have a satirical side (in the casting of Hollywood veteran George Colouris as Dr. Roth, for example), but the lingering impression is of Alma and Gustav walking along holding hands, like the renewed innocents they have become, and the final freeze frame of Gustav's smiling face on his line, "You can go home, Doctor. We're going to live forever." Of course, Gustav will shortly be dead, but that death will be coming for quite a different man than the waspish neurotic we first saw in the train carriage complaining about drafts and being over the wheels.

"The best film I have made about an artist"[23] is how Russell summed up Mahler, and in a strictly literal sense he is right. It is certainly a more balanced view of Mahler than The Music Lovers had been of Tchaikovsky. In Mahler

Russell has achieved a perfect blend of artist and man, and though it is completely arguable that this is the result of the subject matter, that in no way accounts for the same blend and balance in the films which follow. Russell's outlook on his protagonists is becoming increasingly compassionate. The key to this development, which is already beginning in The Devils, The Boy Friend, and Savage Messiah, lies with Russell himself, and his abortive attempts with a screenplay called Music, Music, Music. In his correspondence with Gene D. Phillips, Russell noted that he had fought the screenplay and lost, because it was continually too down-beat and depressing. It mattered not what composer he was dealing with (the film was to contain an encapsulated history of music) the result was always the same: selling-out, compromise, etc., and as his desire was for a more "personal and optimistic"[24] film, he tabled the project. It was this attitude as much as anything that produced Mahler and helped foster the films which follow it. Mahler marks a turning point in Russell's filmography and its importance cannot be overstated.

It is extremely unfortunate that Mahler has never been granted a major release in the United States, so that for anyone outside of major cities and art house cinemas the film remains obscure. The showing of it on the Public Broadcasting System was no great help, either, as it was a bastardization of Russell's original. For reasons never fully explained, PBS opted to censor both the Funeral fantasy and the Conversion fantasy (shockingly without any warning that the film had been edited). Although this did not render the film incomprehensible as has been claimed--PBS was undoubtedly thankful that the dialogue following the Funeral scene described the occurrence in sufficient detail to help smooth over its removal--it was decidedly injurious to the film's dense textural structure. (The cutting of the central fantasy dealing with Mahler's conversion in particular was damaging as the snowballing lunacy of its lead-in scene no longer leads anywhere and just looks foolish.) The most galling aspect of the PBS version of Mahler is the inescapable feeling that had the film been made for television in the first place and appeared on Masterpiece Theatre or Great Performances it would have survived intact--the nudity in the Funeral fantasy amounts to no more than that in Brideshead Revisited, and is not much more than appeared in Russell's own Isadora. The reasoning behind the scissoring of the Conversion is vaguer still, and PBS Vice President Eric Sass' claim that "the symbolism worked well in the theatre, but we had to think of our viewers,"[25] neither makes the situation any clearer, nor does it speak well of Public Television's opinion of its viewers. Further, Sass' espousal that the cuts were made "with Russell's permission"[26] is a statement that Russell vehemently denies and adds, "It was done over my head."[27]

During the editing stages of Mahler, Russell commenced work on his next film, Tommy, a work that would further the idea of his "personal and optimistic" filmmaking, and, in direct counterpoint to the obscurity of Mahler, would prove to be one of his best known and most popular creations. On the surface it might seem that no film could be more unlike Mahler than an adaptation of a rock opera, but as we shall see, the two films are strongly connected. Mahler is only the beginning of a creative outburst that would produce two more films, which, taken as a group of three, represent Russell at his purest and most undiluted. In terms of personal vision and maturity, Ken Russell had arrived.

* * *

Had Ken Russell never made anything other than this monumental work he would still deserve a place in film history. This may, on the surface, appear an odd evaluation, for certainly Tommy is drawn from the most unlikely source, and the most unpromising. Indeed, the marriage of Russell and rock music raised more than a few eyebrows (except for those detractors who felt that Russell had finally descended to his proper level). And if one was familiar with the 1969 album, a rather poorly produced, dramatically neuter concept album and scarcely the "rock opera" it was touted to be, the prospects looked positively grim. To have immediately written off the film as a bad job, however, and quite a few did so, was to forget that Russell had already made at least two films from dubious sources in adapting The Music Lovers from Catherine Drinker Bowen and Barbara von Meck's madly florid Beloved Friend, and turning H. S. Ede's basically non-narrative Savage Messiah into a viable story. Further, such a dismissal failed to take into account the not inconsiderable development of composer Pete Townshend in the intervening years, or, for that matter, to fully assess the theme buried within the 1969 album. Russell, on the other hand, grasped that theme at once, recognizing that Tommy was so central to his personal thematic overview that he almost might have written it himself. Of course, the possibility of developing a film entirely through music, mime, visual unity, and choreography was a bonus that had an instant appeal for a filmmaker who is, self-admittedly, uncomfortable with dialogue. So Russell, despite the occasional "purist" outcry that he had "sold-out" to commercialism, began to transform Townshend's concept album into an almost completely original work--as much Russell as Townshend, but with no distortion of the composer's intentions.

Actually, in accusing Russell of selling out to commercialism the "purist" was working on the false assumption that Russell was previously not a commercial filmmaker--an idea that conjures up the bizarre vision of Russell securing financial backing for his earlier works by assuring his investors that they will lose money. Ironically, Townshend's collaboration with Russell was viewed with an equally jaundiced eye by supporters of the original album, who believed adapting it to the screen at all--much less allowing Ken Russell to adapt it--was tantamount to sacrilege, and that Townshend had "sold out" to Russell! Certainly Russell had an effect on Townshend, particularly concerning the application of dramatic development in both musical and narrative terms. That Russell actively participated in the film's musical development is evident in his unpublished 1973 screenplay for Tommy, which contains very explicit instructions about the music, but one need only listen to Townshend's concurrently produced album, Quadrophenia, on which Russell did not participate except perhaps as an influence (though he was present during some of the recording), to realize that the soundtrack of Tommy is representative of Townshend's musical growth at that time. Both purist viewpoints are similarly wrongheaded in that neither bothers to take into account the need for growth and change in the artistic vision of their respective heroes. As far as the film's commercial prospects are concerned, Russell remarked at the time that the fact that it was a rock opera would help enormously because "people will come to see it,"[28] an idea completely in keeping with his stance on the need of the artist for an audience as put forth in Savage Messiah. Much like Gaudier-Brzeska in that film, Russell was not putting his "St. Paul's Cathedral in a cardboard box," and winding up with "a heavy box," in making his film of Tommy. Quite the reverse happened as it turned out--Tommy was seen by more filmgoers than any of his previous films, exposing his unique talents in a manner undreamed of with his less commercial projects.

Thematically, stylistically, and structurally Tommy is the centerpiece of the trilogy begun with Mahler, even

The Mature Films   255

though the film may at first seem only slightly related to the
first film. Even though it is an impossible and useless
game to attempt to reach any valid conclusion about the superiority of any single film of the Mahler-Tommy-Lisztomania
set, Tommy is undoubtedly the most cohesive of the group.
As an overall work it is perhaps too broad in concept to attain the warmth of Mahler, and its structure is less radical
than Lisztomania or Mahler. (This second comparison is
slightly deceptive in the case of Lisztomania since it actually
moves in a stylistic-thematic straight line; it just appears
not to because it follows no rules but its own.) The structure of Tommy is a more radical version of the structure of
Mahler in that it also utilizes the heavily layered texture of
the former film while jettisoning the skeletal framework. To
some extent this is simply due to the nature of the storyline itself, which allows Russell free reign to create scenes
that, in another context, might appear arbitrarily injected,
but here add to the film's density and richness. In place of
a more traditional form of narrative, Russell has imposed
a circular structure on the film. This is not only circular
in the sense that John Ford's The Searchers is circular in
that it ends as it begins, though this is also true. The circular structure in Tommy is much more controlled. As the
film opens we see the sun going down in front of Captain
Walker, and at the conclusion we see it rise on his son,
Tommy. This much is readily apparent, but in Russell's
hands the structural implications are taken much farther.
From the opening shot to the shot of a burning automobile in
the London Blitz, there are seven shots. Similarly, there
is a mirror image of this in the seven shots which comprise
the film's climax, from the burning holiday camp to the shot
of Tommy reaching out to the rising sun. Moreover, Russell has structured the film so that it reaches a stylistic
and technical high point at the midway mark in the narrative
with the "Pinball Wizard" sequence containing just under one
hundred and fifty separate edits, or nearly twice as many as
the next most editorially complex sequence. This seems to
have been a purely intuitive move on Russell's part as he says
that this was "not planned at all--at least consciously."[29]
Naturally, this sort of technical achievement by itself would
be on the level of constructing the Taj Mahal out of sugar
cubes, but in that it gives Tommy a unique balance, allowing
the film to proceed from stateliness into carefully controlled
hysteria and back to stateliness in a smoothly logical manner, it is something else again. Perhaps of even greater
significance is that the spherical structure of the film has a
direct thematic link with the finished product, as the spherical

shape, symbolic of the sun, is continuously represented throughout the film in ball-bearing bomb loads, pinballs, round mirrors, gigantic pinball-like harbor floats, and even in the circular blind goggles, corks, and earplugs that Tommy's disciples are forced to buy and wear. Brilliantly integrated into the film, Russell's circular construction of Tommy is one of the great marvels of filmmaking.

Since Russell is a filmmaker who has continually grown and evolved as his work has progressed, it is scarcely surprising that the seeds for the circular images are in evidence as early as Song of Summer. In fact the mountain-top opening and closing of Tommy might well have been inspired by Delius' journey up the mountain to see the sun one last time before going completely blind. (There is certainly a vague similarity to the mountain imagery in Dante's Inferno.) Nor is it unexpected that the loss of sight and life are symbolized by the black-centered poppy crosses and black goggles, which are reminiscent of the eclipse of the sun depicted beneath the credits of Song of Summer, and to which Russell will again refer in Lisztomania and Altered States. Whatever the source, the opening image of Tommy is a rarity in its boldness and quickly establishes the style of the film as being concerned with dramatic validity over any sort of conventional realism. When the sun sets at the opening it is still daylight. Likewise, at the end of the film it is light prior to the sunrise, but in neither case does the viewer question Russell's judgment because it is dramatically correct.

The entirety of the film's prologue is blissfully economical visual storytelling. The first shot establishing Captain Walker's impending doom is brought into realization by the final shot in which he is seen going down in his Wellington bomber. In between these shots Russell smoothly etches the tenderness and genuine goodness of the relationship between Captain Walker and his wife, Nora. The husband-wife relation is handled in a clearly idealized and wholesome manner as a series of small tableaux--the couple atop the mountain planning their itinerary for the day, making love in a mountain pool, lying under a flowering tree, silently dancing in a large empty room--in a way so that Russell achieves a fine balance of healthiness in his characters. So well drawn are these vignettes that the characters never become cardboard, nor does their wholesomeness become antiseptic. More, they attain a large measure of our sympathy in a very short time. So strong is this sympathetic attitude that their separation at the railway station, in a beautifully realized series of strikingly simple and ghostly shots, is genuinely moving, as is the seemingly mystical connection between husband and wife after the separation. It is essential to the film that this sympathy be achieved in a brief space of time, due not only to the complexity of the Russellian sin-guilt-redemption theme as applies to Nora's character so that the viewer never totally loses sympathy with her, but also because of the brevity of the physical presence of Captain Walker. For Tommy to work, his spiritual presence must be felt throughout the film's length, and the accomplishment of this aspect is, in itself, a small monument to the collaboration of Russell and that brilliant actor, Robert Powell.

The unusual economy of Russell's actual physical structure of the film is immediately apparent. With the single exception of a combined utilization of the transitional device of throwing one image out of focus and matching it to a similarly out of focus image and a brief dissolve (an effect that Russell and Dick Bush were later to elevate to a level of high art in Rime of the Ancient Mariner), all the various tableaux are simply butted up against one another, giving Tommy a sense of immediacy--even urgency--that would have been unlikely had they been linked with dissolves, fades, or optical wipes. The overall film is constructed in this fashion. There is one split-second black-out, no wipes, and all the dissolves in Tommy are used symbolically, almost as special effects, within the body of some individual sequences, but never to join one sequence with the next. In this respect Tommy is Russell's most Cocteau-like creation. At the time of its release one critic remarked that it was the film "Cocteau would have made had he liked rock," a statement in all likelihood on the abundance of mirrors and the mirror as a mystical object in the film, which automatically calls Orpheus to mind. The major similarity to Cocteau, however, lies in the refreshing and very elemental use of special effects that do not call for a bloated budget and two hundred technicians. Cocteau's Orpheus, like Russell's Tommy, is a mystical tale told within a modern format, using basic slow-motion, rear-screen projection, film printed backwards, and dissolves in a mystical fashion. In both cases the effects are essential to the film, but unlike the typical special effects extravaganza, the simplicity of the approach never bogs the viewer down in the game of wondering how the effect was achieved. As a result both films emerge as brilliant symbolic narratives, dazzling the viewers without distancing them.

With the ostensible death of Captain Walker the prologue ends, and Russell shifts to Nora's job in a defense plant, where we see her loading ball bearings into artillery shells. It is here that the telegram announcing the fact that her husband is missing is delivered, and also where Russell introduces the first instance of the human voice into the film via Pete Townshend's sung narration. Having withheld the sound of a voice for a length of time causes something of an audience jolt (especially in the Quintophonic road show prints) when the first words, "Captain Walker didn't come home, his unborn child will never know him," issue from the screen. In that these words coincide with Nora opening the telegram, Russell hereby imparts a similar shock to the viewer, reflecting and communicating that shock felt by the character onscreen.

Up to this point the narrative has progressed in a straightforward fashion, but from this sequence on, Russell starts making broad chronological jumps, in this case directly to Tommy's birth on VE Day, a fairly elaborate sequence introducing the first use of synchronized song. Russell neatly sidesteps the very real possibility of the film's operatic nature becoming risible (a problem which had completely defeated Norman Jewison in the screen's first rock opera, Jesus Christ Superstar), partly by simply brazening it out, but largely by investing the scene with an intentional humor, creating an aura of mocking operatic traditions. In establishing this original attitude, Russell bridges the gap into the actual opera of the film, and also sets up the viewer. When he later suddenly departs from the tone established here, the viewer is totally unprepared for the unleashed intensity. At the same time the scene neatly foreshadows much that is to come: the twin nurses suggesting the impending mirror images; the white-on-white decor of the hospital room establishing a visual link with Nora's white bedroom, in itself an indication of her innocence here, much as it later symbolizes her fall.

Taking a second chronological leap, Russell advances the action to Remembrance Day, 1950, with Tommy at age five. This little scene is important to the film, suggesting as it does Nora's self-imposed repression in the intervening years. Garbed in black, she is evidently still in mourning for Captain Walker. Grasping this is of the utmost importance as it helps to explain the mental conditions which precipitate her fall upon meeting the oily seducer, Frank Hobbs. Also it is the first indication of the type of picture she has painted of Captain Walker for their son. Here, too, Russell begins a carefully wrought textural pattern which raises the scene from being simply a Christ parable to a personal indictment of the modern world. Russell's criticism starts almost imperceptibly in the person of Reverend Simpson, who, in his bombastic self-importance as officiator of the memorial ceremony, points up the essential hollowness to which the idea of Remembrance Day has descended.

The element of social criticism prevalent in Tommy is strictly a Russell invention. The original album was set between the World Wars and had little relation in this sense to the period of its own origin. In restructuring the storyline to bring the film up to date, Russell strengthened its immediacy and broadened its scope. Unlike Russell's previous forays into the modern world, French Dressing and Billion Dollar Brain, Tommy works because it is about the modern world in a particular time frame--the Second World War through the early seventies--and does not attempt to give the impression of events occurring "now." Tommy is modern, but in such a way that it will still be modern twenty years from now. (French Dressing and Billion Dollar Brain are of a time as well, but they evoke a style of filmmaking prevalent in 1963 and 1967 respectively more than the eras themselves.) The social criticism in Tommy is quintessential Russell, though, on a broader level it is also intrinsically British. It is, after all, a primarily British notion to place a strong reliance on the Second World War in a way that is not readily comprehensible to the American mind, and Russell's view of a world going downhill after the war is in keeping with this national trait. Unlike the majority of successfully exportable English filmmakers, Russell has steadfastly maintained his Britishness, and his films are all the fresher for it.

Continuing in the slyly satirical manner of the Remembrance Day ceremony, Russell next embarks on an examination of that most curious of British institutions, the holiday camp, in a sequence ordered by Russell and not found in Townshend's original. (It is a perfectly logical development, especially as concerns the film's circular structure, of the climactic "Tommy's Holiday Camp" found in the original.) Highly choreographic, it is in this artificially ordered environment of organized activities that Nora meets Frank Hobbs. The sequence works beautifully as a counterpoint to Nora's natural relationship with Captain Walker. Opening by tracking backwards with the oncoming camp bus through the

entrance (flanked by fake and quite tacky palm trees) and
continuing to pull back as a camp instructor and his charges
pop into frame doing regimented exercises, we finally see
Frank, a beefy charmer, slicking back his heavily brillian-
tined hair, preparing to size up the newcomers. This first
collaboration between Russell and Oliver Reed since The
Devils is in many ways their greatest tandem effort in characterization, smoothly alternating broad strokes of carica-
ture (N. B. Shirley Russell's costume for Frank with its too
long sleeves and too short trousers showing off his ridiculous green socks and clumsy shoes), and subtler recognizably
human characteristics. Despite his name, Hobbs, which suggests some kind of link with the devil, Frank, as conceived
by Russell and Reed, never descends to cardboard villainy.
In fact, he is rather likable in a crude way, not in the least
because of the ineptitude he displays in nearly every respect
except opportunism. Significantly, the importance of Frank
grew with the film, indicative of the good working relationship of Russell and Reed. In the 1973 screenplay much of
the villainy in the film was intended to be in the hands of
Uncle Ernie. The metamorphosis of Frank as chief villain
takes little away from the character of Uncle Ernie, but adds
immeasurably to the complexity of Frank, rightly raising his
character to the level of that of Nora so that they are on
an even footing.

Never losing sight of the absurdity of the holiday camp
tradition, Russell chooses to play out the romance of Frank
and Nora against this background. At this point in the narrative Frank is an unabashed lecher, eternally letting the audience in on the fact that he considers Nora fair and desirable
game with an evil leer at the camera. Indeed, Nora's years
of repression make her easily susceptible to Frank's smarmy
charm, as indicated by the lyrics, "You don't know how much
I've missed, to feel a man again, to dance, to kiss." In no
time the opportunistic Frank finds himself going home with
the Walkers. His original view of Nora as an easy mark is
unchanged as he sees their comfortable suburban home. His
attitude is of one who, as Russell succinctly puts it in the
screenplay, has "struck oil."

Once inside the house Russell carefully blends image
and symbol to suggest an important impending development.
The tone is still mocking (Frank's ubiquitous green socks
which he seemingly retains in bed, his muscleman poses,
Nora's slightly nauseating admiration of him), but there are
undercurrents of something beyond this surface humor: the

watchful photograph of Captain Walker by Tommy's bed, the
model bomber suspended from the ceiling, Tommy's airplane
silhouette wallpaper, an amazing deep-focus shot of Frank's
reaction to Tommy's question as to whether "Uncle" Frank
fought in the war, the reflection of Frank and Nora in the
bedroom mirror. This buildup is more than justified by the
stark intensity of the events which follow. Returning to Tommy's bedroom, the camera focuses on the door in the background, which swings open revealing a silhouetted figure:
Captain Walker in a duplication of his image on the mountaintop at the beginning. He crosses the darkened room and
leans into the glow of Tommy's night light candle (burning
in front of his father's photo like a small shrine). In an unbearably tender moment his scarred face softens as his
fingers reach out for the child's face, but never touch so as
not to awaken him. Regretfully, he turns and goes from the
room, but his presence has been enough to rouse Tommy
from his sleep. The boy follows him down the hallway just
in time to throw open the bedroom door and see Frank brutally murder Captain Walker with a lamp after the boy's
father has surprised Nora and him in bed. Unleashing the
full fury of every cinematic device at hand--a white hot mixture of editing, music, playing, and camera movement, culminating in a tight zoom shot close-up on Nora which reduces the image to almost abstract hysteria--the murder and
its immediate aftermath achieves a gripping level of emotional communication transcending even Russell's not inconsiderable successes along these lines in earlier films. It
is, of course, imperative for this level to be reached as it
triggers Tommy's deaf, dumb, and blind state that is central
to the film.

    The murder of Captain Walker is the primary ideological point of departure between Russell and Townshend.
Judging from Townshend's remarks in The Story of Tommy,
his view of the murder is entirely symbolic--that it is simply
the replacement of the idealized father figure with Frank.
Russell, on the other hand, clearly approaches the murder
as an actual occurrence as indicated by the screenplay itself: "Nora is the first to realize that Tommy has witnessed
the murder."[30] This change in approach is probably attributable to the differences in the ages of the two, much
as the entirety of the social criticism is born of Russell.
As a real murder the event better fits Russell's concept of
the downward spiral of the post-World War II world, and
therefore works more successfully within the framework of
the film than Townshend's more psychological approach. (Also

the repetition of the first image of Captain Walker as a foreshadowing of the collapse of his world only works symbolically if the murder is real.)

The murder is a turning point in the film. Immediately after it Russell begins the inward exploration of his main character in the breathless "Amazing Journey" sequence. That Tommy, Nora, and Frank have now become a family is economically conveyed by their walk through the Greenwich Tunnel which opens the scene, where they are all clothed in outfits of the same material, a purposefully hideous fifties' space-age design. The balance of symbolism and sensation is well judged by the conveyance of Tommy's inner feelings spurred by the physical movements of the fairground rides leading into the symbolism itself. As the grown-ups enjoy the rides, Tommy is propelled into his own mind, envisioning riding with his father in an airplane and encountering the mystical sphere images that suffuse the film. Despite the fact that low light levels rendered a good deal of Russell's original concept impossible when large chunks of footage proved to be out of focus,[31] the physical sensation of movement is well captured with rhythmic editing, contrapuntal movement, and animation effects smoothly bridging the gaps of the first concept. The entire path of the film is indicated by the image of Captain Walker standing atop the mountain, holding out a sun-like circle of light to his son. The light fills and then whites out the screen in a foreshadowing of the closing shot in the film. Further, the climactic portion of the "Amazing Journey"--with its zoom into the iris of Tommy's eye (an effect similar to, but smoother than, the shots into Rex Harrison's eye in Preston Sturges' Unfaithfully Yours; it still looked fresh in 1975, but has since been bastardized and dulled by constant exposure in the Space: 1999 television series) and the subsequent trip through a barrage of airplane silhouettes turning into poppy crosses as a pinball strikes them, ending on the image of Captain Walker crucified on an airplane, which when struck transforms into a cross topped by a pinball--strikes precisely the right note for the film's direction as religious allegory.

From the cosmic to the mundane, Russell's next sequence takes place at the Hobbs' dismal Christmas celebration, full of prim middle-aged ladies sipping sherry and middle-aged men gulping ale. All the children, except Tommy, cavort with their new toys. In the midst of these festivities--staged with no hint of real happiness, choreographed like the regimented holiday camp--Tommy sits in a toy car, staring catatonically. Occasionally either Frank or Nora will attempt to penetrate his private world, but all they accomplish is to wear on each other's nerves, building a tension that carries the scene along to the point where, tired of trying, they slowly dance around the car. At this moment comes the film's first use of the famous "See me, feel me, touch me, heal me" theme as the thoughts of young Tommy are heard on the soundtrack. Coming in the middle of the celebration, the plaintive appeal for help seems doubly touching (the five-track prints had the additional advantage of the ghostly voice issuing from the rear of the theatre). Guilt overtakes the dancers and they make one more, nearly hysterical, attempt to reach Tommy before giving him his Christmas present--a Nativity scene, which Tommy fingers and then smashes to the floor. There has been some criticism of this aspect of the scene, but in view of the God-like aura with which his father has been invested, the crucifixion imagery of the preceding scene, and the action of the next, it is totally in keeping with the film. After all, for Tommy, God has been murdered.

With the next scene Russell propels the story headlong into the seventies, jump cutting from young Tommy to the adult Tommy. (There is a minor jolt here as Tommy's eye color abruptly switches from brown to blue, but this seems a small price to pay for the essential rightness of both Barry Winch and Roger Daltrey in the roles.) The scene itself, one of the most admired in the film, is an outgrowth of a scene in Russell's abortive screenplay The Angels. Much has been made of Russell's cannibalization of this screenplay in Tommy, but upon examination the similarities between the basic themes of the two stories are astonishing. It is almost as if in The Angels Russell had already conceived Tommy. The only real flaw in this complex scene is the stoned-out performance of Eric Clapton, who, though possessing a good physical presence, makes not the slightest effort to appear to actually play his guitar. Otherwise Nora's ill-advised attempt to have Tommy cured by a faith healer is a stunning scene, designed in such a way as to actually evoke the trappings and effect of this brand of spurious religion. The mesmerizing repetitiveness of the music combined with the hallucinatory visuals create an effect not unlike the mass hysteria of the genuine article. The rhythmic swaying of the Preacher in a telephoto shot causing him to blur just slightly as he moves; the focus shifts from a mirrored picture of the cult's deity, Marilyn Monroe, to the Preacher; the beautifully conceived multi-

Ken Russell and "Marilyn Monroes" on the set of "Eyesight to Blind" in Tommy. (Courtesy of Ken Russell)

image prism shots which, like the similar shots in Mahler, work because instead of relying on the prism effect alone they are combined with movement; even the sleeping pill and slug of Johnny Walker communion ceremony with its tightly rhythmic editing, all combine to reach this end. The very concept of a religious cult built around Marilyn Monroe is well judged in that it is an early portrayal of the same brand of false religion that will later be built around Tommy himself. It also has a direct bearing on Russell's stance on Tommy as a criticism of the modern age with its various forms of idolatory and hero worship. The climactic moment, where Tommy comes into contact with the giant Monroe statue (made to resemble her famous pose in The Seven Year Itch) and senses his vision in its circular mirrored base, hearkens back to the previous scene as he topples the statue and foreshadows his own fall later in the film.

There follows one of the most bizarre scenes in the film, and, like the preceding scene, one of the most critically successful, the "Acid Queen." For all that has been written about this scene, no one has ever successfully come to terms with either its meaning or its relation to the overall film. In itself this is not surprising as the very nature of a film like Tommy unfairly allows--even invites--the reviewer to break its structure down into segments or numbers without considering the film as a unit. To understand and to appreciate Tommy as a film, rather than some kind of phantasmagorical revue, it is necessary in evaluating those individual segments to place them within the entirety of the narrative. As a display of Russell's keen sense of the film as dance, or of technical bravura, or even of his ability to create something out of virtually nothing due to the limited time of Tina Turner and effects that just would not work, the "Acid Queen" is dazzling. Equally important, however, is its stylistic-thematic position in the fabric of the film. Largely it is the reverse side of Nora's attempted cure by the faith healer. In this instance, Frank--in his new position as owner of the Sin City Review porno house--tries to reach Tommy through a more materialistic approach: sex and drugs. This, in the end, proves as fruitless as Nora's dabbling in crackpot religion, but like the earlier experience it is not without its effects on Tommy. The similarities between the faith healer and the Acid Queen are strongly suggested in the meaningless rituals which surround both. There is little denying that much of the appeal to many people in drugs is the ritualistic manner in which they are approached, and the strong desire to "turn on" the uninitiated finds a ready counterpart in the recruiting of some religious groups. For that matter the aspect of Tommy being "reborn"--at least temporarily--through the Acid Queen (hinted at prior to the experience by the twin handmaidens who recall the twin nurses at his actual birth) is completely in keeping with the view of drugs as religion, as are the references to St. Sebastian and Jesus Christ. In order to better personalize the religious qualities of the scene, Russell includes visual references to Captain Walker (in himself a Christ figure) and Nora. Nora's appearance at the foot of the Acid Queen machine, dressed in her nightgown from the time of the murder, silently screaming, "You didn't see it," is a genuinely startling, but by no means arbitrary image that also ties the scene to her collapse in the munitions factory, her guilt in the murder, and her responsibility for Tommy's affliction. Interestingly, the idea of being stripped down to nothing and reassembled (Tommy progresses through stages of change under the Acid Queen's treatment--from himself to his war-scarred father to his unmarked father to his own form again

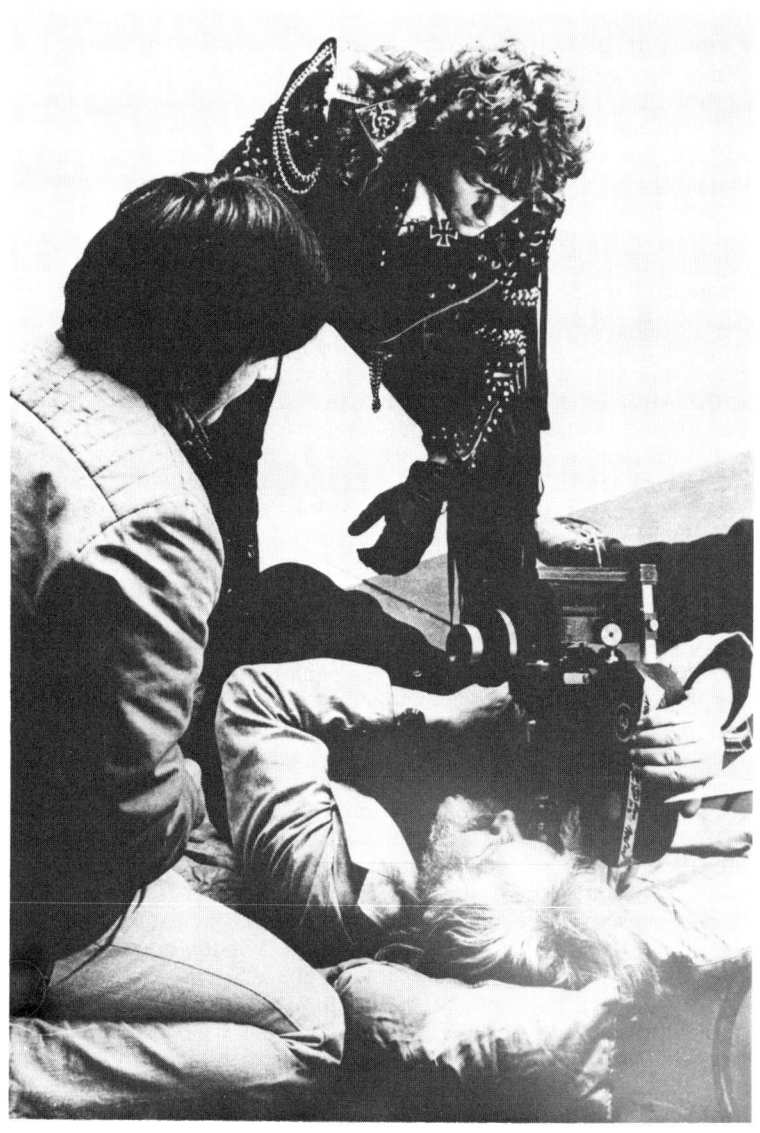

Ken Russell filming Paul Nicholas in the "Cousin Kevin" sequence for Tommy. (Courtesy of Ken Russell)

The Mature Films   267

to the idealized Christ figure to his skeleton and back to his
original state), achieving a kind of spiritual rebirth, forms
the basis for the ending of the much later Altered States.

As previously noted the Acid Queen's effects are purely transitory (though she does promise a cure if given "one
more night") except that Tommy now perceives a red monochromatic image of himself in the mirror (the sequence is
designed in red). It is with this image that Russell begins
his next scene, which is actually a series of three alternating
scenes. These scenes explore Tommy's growing neglect by
Frank and Nora, who have basically given up hope, his martyrization at the hands of others, and the onset of his journey to salvation. In constructing the scenes in a set of
three alternating occurrences Russell is using a typical compositional device, common to music where repetitions of
three frequently denote a mystical occurrence, and the final
scene more than bears this out.

The first of these scenes finds Nora and Frank preparing to go out for the day, though Nora has some misgivings about leaving Tommy in the care of his Cousin Kevin.
Nonetheless, Tommy has become such a burden to her by
this time that it is obvious her question, "Do you think it's
all right?" is scarcely a serious inquiry. As staged by Russell it is apparent that her real concern is her makeup, and
that by asking Frank if he thinks "it's all right," she has
done her duty and shifted the guilt should it turn out otherwise.

The alternating scene, then, is Tommy's encounter
with Cousin Kevin, with whom it was decidedly not all right
to leave him. Immediately upon the Hobbs' departure Kevin
proceeds to sadistically torture his charge. In a manic
series of extremely vicious vignettes, Cousin Kevin ties Tommy to a chair, puts a bag on his head, burns him, nearly
drowns him, hangs him on a hook, drags him by the hair
down a hallway, pushes him downstairs, turns a fire-hose
on him, and ultimately irons him dry so his transgressions
will go unnoticed. Boldly designed in vivid yellows the scene
is immaculately conceived and executed, and would be almost unbearably harsh were it not for the rich vein of humor
with which Russell has balanced it. A tremendous asset in
this is the presence of Paul Nicholas as Cousin Kevin (whose
participation here looks like a dry run for his role as Richard Wagner in Lisztomania). Nicholas is an electrifying performer in his Russell appearances, managing to convey bound-

less energy without a hint of the irritating hyperactivity that flaws many energetic players. The sequence also contains a number of pleasing surprises, such as Cousin Kevin's sudden appearance with a stocking over his head, and his handling the bathtub taps as if they were motorcycle handlebars, all of which helps impart a sense of freshness. In fact the only possible quibble with the scene is Russell's symbolism in the presents Nora brings the two upon her return--a ball for Tommy and a cricket bat for Cousin Kevin--which seems a bit obvious.

Returning to the alternating neglect motif we find Tommy now gazing at a monochromatic yellow image in the mirror alongside the red one, while the even less sincere "Do you think it's all right?" question is repeated as concerns leaving him with Uncle Ernie, who has "had a few too many tonight." Even Frank cannot regard Uncle Ernie without some suspicion, and certainly the audience has more than that. Regardless, he assures her that it will be all right, and they depart.

Comparing the "Uncle Ernie" sequence in Russell's screenplay with the one in the film, the viewer is immediately struck by the transformation of a facile scene of dubious humor into a creative one of genuine humor. Equally striking is the fact that "Uncle Ernie" retains its humor throughout, even though the idea of Uncle Ernie sexually assaulting the deaf, dumb, and blind Tommy is scarcely funny. At least in part this is due to the juxtaposition of this scene with "Cousin Kevin," which, by comparison, makes the sexual abuse seem relatively tame. Mostly, however, it is successful due to Russell's timing and sense of the bizarre. The scene is riddled with pleasant choreographic surprises--the visual pattern established by having the camera dolly in on Uncle Ernie, who drops below the frame line, followed by his upward movement in his trip upstairs--and numerous odd touches--the enema bag trailing behind him up the stairs, the fanciful moment where he "blows out" an electric light, his wild obsession with anything elasticized reminiscent of Roy Kinnear's Plastic Mac Man in Lester's The Bed-Sitting Room. Russell saves the best for last, though, in the return of Frank and Nora. To replace the weak gag in the screenplay where Frank returns having forgotten his keys, giving Uncle Ernie a false scare, Russell substitutes the whimsical image of Frank's Dashiell Hammett styled private detective impersonation. With his topcoat turned up and his hat shading his eyes, Frank's impression is perfect as he stealthily moves his head from side to side for potential danger. Upon finding Uncle Ernie in Tommy's bedroom reading the Gay News with a garter belt protruding from under his cap, Frank reaches inside his coat and whips out his cigarette lighter with which he ignites Ernie's newspaper. (The contrast of the warm-toned flame with the blue light of the scene is quite effective.) As outré as the private eye business seems it is far more rational than the silly business with the keys, fitting, as it does, with Frank's earlier apprehension about Uncle Ernie and taking excellent advantage of Oliver Reed's tough guy image. At the same time his furtiveness works as an indication of his deception of Nora. His expression shows that Frank does not really care what Uncle Ernie has done so long as Nora does not know.

The third and final use of the neglect theme is possibly the best of the lot. The fraudulent sincerity of the inquiry into Tommy's well-being has now degenerated to a purely mechanical function as Frank and Nora stare blankly at the soothing glow of a television screen throughout their well-worn "Do you think it's all right?" routine. Significantly, Nora reaches across Frank for a pair of dark glasses which she then puts on, and at the same moment, the images of Tommy in the mirror--including a new blue one from his experience with Uncle Ernie--merge into one full color image. This image turns and leaves the room, and like Orpheus in Cocteau's film, Tommy follows.

Once outside, the climactic mirror experience proper begins, as Tommy's mirror image leads him to a junkyard (a modern institution), but having brought him to the edge of a possible salvation, the image makes a full circle with his arms and disappears. Russell conveys this in a simple but effective manner by shooting the first portion of the junkyard scene with a great deal of supplemental light, inserting a black frame at the moment of the image's departure, and filming the remainder of the scene in much more subdued, low-key lighting, thereby externalizing Tommy's subjective experience for the viewer. Left alone and senseless in the junkyard, Tommy staggers through an obstacle course of old cars, television sets, stoves, and radios before finding a shining sphere like the one his father held out to him in the "Amazing Journey." Upon seeing this sphere Tommy's expression becomes elated (framed through a broken television set as a foreshadowing of his "star" status to come, and as a visual link with the broken picture glass on the framed picture of Captain Walker and the similarly broken glass through which we see Captain Walker in the cockpit of his bomber). Making his way through the junkyard, now with a purpose and meaning, he reaches out to embrace the sphere, and as he does so, Russell inserts a quick shot of a pinball with an eye on it being struck in a pinball machine. In a medium long shot we now see Tommy standing atop the junked car, excitedly playing pinball where the sphere once stood. It is in this state that he is found by a pair of Securicor guards, and Russell quickly shifts the scene from the mystical to the satirical, shooting Nora and Frank's recovery of Tommy in a handheld television news style. The guards then show Frank where the boy was found, and he is impressed by the astronomical score on the pinball machine--so impressed in fact that the first of Frank's great schemes for making money through Tommy is born. This phenomenal sequence, the only single part of the set of alternating scenes deftly mingling the religious-mystical qualities of the film with the satirical elements, is, like much of Russell, not designed for the strictly literal minded. The question of the exact symbolism of the three mirror images is a point that Russell's film prefers to leave mystically mute. (Intriguingly, though, the red-yellow-blue base colors are also the colors in Derek Jarman's Vortex set in Savage Messiah, as we have already noted, and the colors which form the tricolored ray that destroys Wagner in Lisztomania.) On the grounds of a literal approach the working pinball machine, complete with electrical hook-up, in the junkyard is ludicrous, but surely this is unimportant in relation to the film's thematic and symbolic construction. Russell's fantastic elements must be accepted in the offhand manner in which he presents them--as part of the separate reality of the film owing nothing to traditional naturalism--or the film will not work for the viewer.

Brilliant though the individual components of this part of Tommy may be, the actual importance lies in their strength as they relate to the entire film. (It is arguable that the "Acid Queen" sequence is a part of the unit of alternating scenes with the junkyard scene as the culmination of the two sets of three. This approach, however, does not entirely work when looking at the balanced nature of the film. The "Acid Queen" is appreciably longer and more complex than either "Cousin Kevin" or "Uncle Ernie," and has a more direct relation to the sequence with the faith healer thematically, stylistically, and structurally.) As a unit the musical approach of alternate variations on two basic scenes

Elton John as The Champ, with audience in Russell's technical tour de force "The Pinball Wizard" in Tommy. (Columbia)

is conceptually brilliant and creates a unique sense of unity in what would otherwise have been a very episodic framework.

Russell's narrative then takes a spectacular leap from this largely transitional section directly to Tommy's battle for the world championship at pinball, slicing away unnecessary buildup in a brief narration section where he humorously depicts the changed lifestyle of the Hobbses thanks to Tommy's pinball playing. Quite apart from the scene's ability to impart a maximum amount of information in a minimum of screen time in a witty manner, it also remains consistently logical in terms of character development. Frank, who has previously taken turns at playing uncle, lover, and father, is now embarking on his new role as a gentleman of leisure--a part he carries off about as credibly as his earlier ones. His unbelievable ineptitude in this department--his gauche attempts at creating his lower-class mentality notions of the upper-class--help to retain a measure of humanity for the character. He is almost lovable (even more so in the later visit to the Specialist) as he works so hard at being something he is not, and fails so miserably. Nora, on the other hand, begins to regain some depth here. Their new-found wealth has reawakened her genuine feelings of guilt, and she has taken to drink in a vain effort to numb those feelings.

As mentioned in the structural overview of the film the "Pinball Wizard" sequence is the technical high-point of the film--the most individually complex section in a very complicated film--and is positioned at the center of the narrative. It is also the best known part of the film in that it produced a popular single for Elton John, much as it had for The Who with the original album. Interestingly, it is also the one sequence least connected with the overall film--at least on the surface. The scene is so enjoyable on a purely technical level of sheer cinematic excitement, that its darker implications have all but been ignored. Russell has in this scene dropped the majority of the film's religious-mysticism and concentrated on the satirical. The satire, however, is so firmly woven into the story line that it almost goes unnoticed. To fully appreciate Russell's accomplishment in this scene one need only look at the rock sub-genre within which he is working. The rock film as a separate style of musical did not exist on any serious level prior to Richard Lester's invention of it in 1964 with A Hard Day's Night, a film which did not actually utilize anything particularly new in terms of cinematic language, but which did use a wildly eclectic, seemingly fresh, rearrangement of traditional structure and technique, giving the illusion of a new style. Unfortunately these stylistic elements were so readily discernible they were easy for lesser filmmakers to imitate with various degrees of success. Worse still was the fact that the film and its progeny were thematically suspect in the creation of a rock mythology. One only has to view the final Beatles film, Let It Be (1970), to understand how all-pervasive this "influence" had come to be. Let It Be is undeniably slower than its parent films--the direction by Michael Lindsay-Hogg looks for all the world like the work of a very lethargic Lester--but the style is still very much with us, and the myth is still being held together in spite of itself. This is especially questionable as Let It Be purports to be a documentary, which it is not, unless one considers

The Mature Films 273

it a documentary of a myth. The format established by
Lester proved commercially viable and no one bothered
about changing it either before or after Tommy. In the
"Pinball Wizard" sequence Russell tackles the Lesterian
principles head-on. Russell's sequence readily lends itself
to direct comparison with the climactic concern in A Hard
Day's Night. Where Lester presents the myth, Russell presents the reverse side of Lester's fraudulent innocence.
Like Lester, Russell zooms and tilts, rapidly cuts, and
edits to the musical and visual rhythms, building his scene
to a hysterical frenzy. The audience might almost be made
up of the audience from the Lester film, but they are no
longer the open-faced innocent fans. They are older, more
cynical, and more dangerous. Where Lester found something charming in their screaming and mindless adoration,
Russell finds something terrifying and chilling. As the scene
opens the audience is divided into two separate camps, Tommy fans and fans of the Champ (mysteriously referred to in
the credits as "The Pinball Wizard"). Each group cheers
lustily for its respective hero, but when Tommy defeats the
Champ all loyalty is gone. Russell's camera shows not one
remaining fan of the Champ, who is unceremoniously dragged
from the theatre by his oversized boots to the delight of all,
whether originally supporters or detractors. Tommy has
toppled the Champ much like the Marilyn Monroe effigy, or
even the Nativity scene, but for how long? In a world where
loyalty is an unknown quality, Tommy is, by implication and
the structure of the film thus far, ready for his own fall.

The transition into the next scene, the only really
controversial single scene in Tommy, is smoothly accomplished by a device that will come to have great impact within the text of the scene itself. Russell switches from the
cheering crowds carrying Tommy aloft in celebration to Nora
watching this action on television. Here Russell moves off
on a seemingly unrelated tangent as he inserts a garish television commercial for Rex Beans just before the beginning
of the song "Champagne," establishing an important visual-
aural pattern by marching the opening chords of the song with
the beans being poured out on a silver platter. (This song,
like the earlier "Bernie's Holiday Camp," is a Russell ordered Townshend composition unique to the film, though parts
of it are heavily reliant on existing themes, notably "Captain
Walker Didn't Come Home.") As the scene gets under way
it is apparent that Nora is already quite drunk on the object
of her song and becomes progressively so as the sequence
unfolds. Her inebriation combined with her resurfacing guilt

Ken Russell in an Ann-Margret t-shirt posing with the real actress in the white-on-white bedroom set for Tommy. (Courtesy of Ken Russell)

feelings triggers a fantasy in which Tommy's image on the television screen, with the accompanying first adult cry of "See me, feel me, touch me, heal me," refuses to be ignored. The television stubbornly reverts to the image despite Nora's constant attempts to change the channel. For a moment she will replace him with the Rex Beans advertisement, or one for Black Beauty Chocolates, or a laundry detergent, but then the television flips back to Tommy under its own power. The television that had so effectively numbed her in the third variation of "Do You Think It's All Right?" now turns on her, and in a fit of desperation, she throws the champagne bottle through its screen. This does rid her of Tommy's image and plea, but causes the television to gush forth with a torrent of soap suds, followed by baked beans and chocolate sauce. With a perverse fascination Nora begins to wallow in the mess, becoming increasingly filthy, corrupting everything she touches in her white-on-white bedroom, until the entire room is a sticky brown shambles, and she passes out in a fit of near orgasmic ecstasy. Once Nora loses consciousness Frank enters and surveys the damage. In a point-of-view shot we see the smashed television with the champagne bottle lying inside, but otherwise the room is untouched. Nora lies on the floor writhing unconsciously while Frank drunkenly staggers to the bed and collapses. Russell's detractors tend to feel that the scene is superfluous and simply a self-indulgent and excessive attack on television commercials, especially since Russell had made commercials for the very products which appear in Tommy before concluding that the work was too obscene. It is obvious that the choice of the combination of beans, soap, and chocolate was a conscious swipe at his own experiences, but the basic concept is firmly rooted in the satirical side of the film--and it is also inherent in Russell's thematic overview as far back as Women in Love. As a metaphor the scene works on two levels. Nora's guilt and self-pity are perfectly realized by the effect, and the combination of ingredients sufficiently resembles excrement to suggest the level of childish depravity to which she has descended. The very fact that the television actually floods and corrupts the room, on the other hand, makes her a victim of the age in which she lives. As a satire on television this brief segment is more vicious and unnerving than the entirety of Sidney Lumet's Network. A large measure of the effectiveness of the scene rests with Russell's unorthodox presentation. The sequence starts out as an objective occurrence and becomes subjective with no warning whatsoever. The world established in Tommy is just enough off-center that one is not quite certain, on a first viewing, if this is fantasy or reality. Russell certainly presents the scene as if it could be actually happening by the film's own definition of reality, and up to this point in the narrative he has not staged any lengthy fantasy sequences of this nature. It is not until we reach Frank's point of view that it is clearly established that the previous events have been what can best be described as an objective presentation of a subjective scene. Because of this presentation the scene is unusually disturbing, for in appearing to be real it causes us to more readily share the experience, unsoftened by the inherent detachment of obvious fantasy.

The "Champagne" sequence represents the low point in Nora's fall. From this scene, where she recovers her sense of guilt, her character continually, if laboriously, works toward redemption. The next scene establishes the pattern once again of trying to find a cure for Tommy. The bridging sequence to Tommy's trip to visit a specialist comes as a welcome respite from the foregoing fantasy and helps soften Frank's character as a lovable oaf. Shot very simply, Frank enters to the strains of Townshend's jaunty music, dressed in obviously brand-new country gentleman tweeds, carrying a shotgun, and sporting a brace of freshly slaughtered pheasants, as he jovially announces that he has found a doctor "who can cure the boy." The scene is nothing more than a means of introduction to the next scene--purely a transitional device--but even here Russell's attention to detail elevates the device to a level nearly equal to the most complex part of the film.

The visit to the Doctor accomplishes very little for Tommy as The Specialist is far more interested in seducing Nora than he is in the boy's condition. Nora, in fact, very nearly succumbs to his charms (and doubtless in the pre-fantasy sequence Nora would have done so), but her guilt, represented by Tommy's mental cries of "See me, feel me, touch me, heal me," and Frank's presence hold her back. The tone of the scene, though, is slyly humorous and almost impossibly light, as Russell blends snatches of Nora's inner fantasies about the doctor into the reality of the sequence with no visible seam. On the whole the scene really belongs to Frank in his ultimate hopeless attempt at being a gentleman. Dressed in the height of very proper fashion (complete with a monocle that refuses to stay in his eye), his first move is to bite the end off a cigar and spit the waste on the floor. More pathetic still is his attempt at an upper-class accent. Frank makes an ass of himself, Nora nearly gets seduced, and Tommy is left untouched. The only good to come of this visit to the Specialist is the information that there is nothing physically wrong with Tommy and that any hope for a cure must come from within.

There follows a very simple and touching scene of Tommy and Nora in the car on the way home. The scene is basically accomplished in one lengthy take, except for a brief cut-away to Tommy's reflection in the car mirror. Russell crowds his camera in on his actors, creating an almost uncomfortable sense of intimacy, while at the same time weaving it in and out and from one to the other to suggest Nora's increasing state of anxiety and drunkenness.

The scene to which the ride home is a buildup is a curious mixture of good and bad qualities, which ultimately succeeds through its carefully structured visual and aural unity and its sheer intensity. Back in Nora's bedroom Tommy stands staring into the gigantic circular mirror. Nora, having reached the end of her rope through drink and fear and guilt, reaches a fever pitch of desperation in her attempts to reach him. She blocks his view of the mirror with her body, and in a dubious move arbitrarily reminds the audience that the actress is a dancer by engaging in a brief bit of Las Vegas laden dance. Brief it may be, but as the only completely false move in the film, it stands out all the more. Russell quickly recovers, however, as Nora's nerves finally shatter. (There is a chilling moment following Nora's question, "How can the mirror affect you?" where a breathtaking edit is startlingly reinforced by the rise of the horns on the soundtrack, which is badly blunted in the monophonic mix of the general release prints.) Directly drawing from her hysteria in the "Champagne" scene, Russell has her pick up a vodka bottle and threaten to smash the mirror with it, stop just short of the impact, swing Tommy around by the hands and accidentally send him crashing into and through the mirror.

The crash through the mirror, like the buildup to it, deliberately recalls the "Champagne" sequence and is a reversal of it, so that it becomes a natural structural balance. Then again, it is also the objective presentation of a subjective experience. There is no break from the reality of smashing the mirror to Tommy's symbolic rebirth in his fall into the swimming pool. Apart from the fact that logic tells us that there is a wall behind the mirror, there is no pause from the objectivity of "Smash the Mirror" to the subjectivity of "I'm Free, " and in addition to creating an unbroken flow of events, this approach adds to the immediacy of the viewer's experience. It is with this sequence that Russell begins making significant changes from his original screenplay, which presented a more complex pattern of events, and introduced a helicopter. Thankfully, the helicopter (an uneasy evocation, particularly in the subsequent "Sensation" sequence, of the opening of Fellini's La Dolce Vita with its Christ statue being transported suspended from a helicopter, and Russell's own screenplay The Angels) has disappeared along with the unnecessary complexity. In its place Russell has substituted a series of intricately connected little scenes, which have far more bearing on the film's themes of religion and the modern age, as Tommy proclaims his freedom and newfound insight. Running through Russell's favorite field of mustard flowers, Tommy's exhilaration and the natural beauty are both blighted by pesticide-spraying technician-like gardeners. Similarly his efforts to reach a group of soldiers on maneuvers in the forest are met with apathy and hostility as one soldier tosses him over his shoulder and out of the frame. Undaunted, Tommy lands on his feet and keeps going in the following shot along a beach. Most people just stare at him blankly from behind their dark glasses--intentionally blocking out the natural wonders of the world in which Tommy is revelling. In a foretelling of events, only a few isolated fishermen casting their nets into the surf pay him any heed. At the climax of the scene Russell reverts to his screenplay, capping the scene as he originally intended to open it. Stated simply in the screenplay as a montage, where "Mountains spin by. Forests spin by. Clouds whizz by. The sun somersaults. Cities gyrate,"[32] the realization falls somewhat short of the obvious intent. Russell's idea of juxtaposing Tommy against what turns out to be backgrounds of natural wonderment is thematically consistent, and at least the last of his rear screen effects--"Clouds whizz by"--is effectively accomplished, but the approach is too much at odds with the real world exteriors and intimacy of the rest of the sequence to work well.

  The following scene exists neither in Townshend's original nor in the 1973 screenplay, but its content develops quite naturally from the scrapped material of "I'm Free. " In dropping the business with the helicopter and turning the sequence into an inward experience, "I'm Free" loses sight of Nora altogether. Furthermore, the significant change of events--in the screenplay it is Nora who crashes into the mirror, not Tommy--makes an additional sequence re-establishing Nora's position a necessity, and "Mother and Son" is that sequence. Its primary concern is therefore in smoothing out the story line, but Russell makes it into something more than this by exploring Tommy's reaction to the rush of memories brought about by his cure. Upon hearing the subconsciously familiar words, "Tommy, can you hear me?" and seeing Nora, his entire past up to the moment of his affliction floods over him. It is a brilliant moment, particularly in the dynamic editing pattern which is designed to blend past and present to unusual effect. The most startling of these cuts occurs at the moment when Tommy remembers the murder: he looks at Nora in the present and in the flashback footage she appears to acknowledge that look in her shocked reaction to Captain Walker's appearance in the bedroom. Similarly skillful are the cuts matching young Tommy's response to the murder and Tommy's painful memory of the moment. The force of the editing brings home Nora's original guilt, which Tommy's recovery can in no way relieve or absolve. Tommy, however, is prepared to help redeem her--"Those who love me have a higher path to follow now, and you, dear mother, too must be prepared," he tells her just prior to throwing away her jewelry, painfully ripping off her fake fingernails, and dragging her into the ocean to baptize her into his new ministration. The idea of Tommy as Messiah and Nora's baptism may seen odd at first, but both are consistent with the film's structure, and Russell's overall work. The Russell hero as potential savior is germane to his view of the moral significance of art in his creator biographies, and the visual symbolism in Tommy has been leading to this throughout the film. Nora's baptism, and its preparations (a literal stripping away of decadence), are the reverse of her orgiastic wallow in the "Champagne" sequence which depicted Nora's "baptism" into the materialistic world. At the same time this has a direct bearing on the film's heavy use of water symbolism in general: Tommy's conception in the mountain pool, his "baptism" into the horrors of the real world at the hands of Cousin Kevin, his rebirth as he crashes through the mirror into the pool. Nora's character is significantly changed through the experience. Through Tommy's cure and her baptism she finds a measure of redemption, but she pays a high price in being symbolically blinded herself. Her faith in Tommy is indeed blind and unquestioning, and at the very times when she might see the corruption gathering around his ministry, she is too preoccupied with gazing lovingly at her son to notice anything.

Russell, perhaps wisely, spares us the details of Frank's conversion, but by the very next shot, in the sequence entitled "Miracle Cure," it is evident that he has undergone a transformation, though one nearer adaptation than conversion. This leap in narrative is reminiscent of the earlier one in "Extra! Extra!" (in fact the music is the same) where Frank is suddenly playing at being a gentleman of leisure. The only difference is that now he is assaying the role of the religious zealot in charge of Tommy's new faith, a frightening idea that surely bodes ill. Imaginatively shot in a series of rhythmic pans, zooms, and cuts, the scene establishes Frank's position in the religion as he stands on a balcony looking down on his stepson. Throughout the final section of the film, Frank is seen in similar poses-- standing atop a tower balcony in "Sally Simpson"; looking out over the arriving converts from the top of a staircase in "Tommy's Holiday Camp"; perched atop the mountains of harbor floats when the converts reject the religion.

The screenplay indicates that the "Sensation" sequence should follow at this point, and for that matter so does the film's soundtrack album, but Russell asserts that the change in placing "Sally Simpson" next occurred prior to filming, and it is a good decision. In that "Sensation" has a close relation to "Amazing Journey," it better balances the film by coming later. Also "Sensation" is too musically similar to "I'm Free" to effectively come so near it, whereas the jauntiness of "Sally Simpson" seem to arise naturally from "Miracle Cure." Most importantly, however, the complexity of the "Sally Simpson" sequence makes it very much a part of the central set pieces of the film to which it is nearer in its final placement.

The sequence opens on a shot of the War Memorial from the Remembrance Day ceremony. Sally Simpson appears running from behind it, swinging a tennis racquet. Her father, Reverend Simpson, is nearby polishing his Rolls Royce. Russell clearly indicates the lack of depth in Simpson's religious views as, immediately after denying his permission for Sally to attend the Tommy revival meeting, he returns to polishing the grill of the car, manipulating his cloth to form the sign of the cross in his polishing. Reverend Simpson is a very modern man--so modern that when his daughter "picks up a book of her father's life," a self-satisfied looking volume entitled <u>A Soldier for Jesus</u>, and throws "it on the fire," she must be content with an imitation fire of glowing plastic coals in the grate--and, given the context of the film, this is no compliment. Sally's room is wallpapered with pictures of Tommy which recall the airplane pattern wallpaper of young Tommy's bedroom, making her decision to disobey her father and run off to the meeting something of a parallel with Tommy's journey down the hallway leading to his witnessing the murder. Sally's trip to the revival will have its repercussions as well.

At the revival Sally buys a Tommy button from Uncle Ernie and goes inside to await the appearance of her hero. There is a surprising moment as Frank appears to announce Tommy's arrival. Up to this point the sequence has been done entirely in narration and Frank's sudden completion of the Narrator's line with "Here we go!" is quite startling. Tommy's revival hearkens back to the Marilyn Monroe cult, especially with the other members of The Who forming his back-up band as they had earlier done for The Preacher.

Gary Rich as a rock musician "who came from California" marries Russell's daughter, Victoria, as Sally Simpson in the sequence of the same name in Tommy. (Courtesy of Ken Russell)

The police are present to keep order, but owing to her size, Sally is able to slip past them and hoist herself up on the stage in an attempt to touch Tommy. Frank, who has thus far sat to one side of Tommy on the stage having an exaggeratedly good time by moving with the music, scarcely misses a beat as he gets up, stomps Sally's hands, and sits back down, taking up where he left off. Tommy is so absorbed in his audience, and Nora so absorbed in her Tommy, that neither of them notices this. Sally's face is badly cut in her fall and she has to be carried from the hall, which Russell parallels by having Tommy actually leap from the stage into the audience.

Projecting events forward somewhat, Sally is next seen marrying "a rock musician that came from California," a bizarre Frankenstein monster sort. Now sporting a scar, she appears to have undertaken this marriage primarily to irritate her shallow father, whose church is reduced to a shambles by the show-business wedding. Finally, we glimpse her at one of her rock musician husband's concerts, where she sits distracted and bored, rocking a baby in a carriage while hordes of screaming fans are all around her.

The complexity of this sequence is in the great number of levels on which Russell is working at the same time--levels that the film's operatic structure make possible. First of all, the obvious parallels brought forth in the Tommy wallpaper between Sally and young Tommy make it clear that as a sequence "Sally Simpson" is Tommy in miniature. Russell stresses this in the shot where his camera zooms back and Sally appears split into three as she looks at herself in a triptych mirror--a reversal of the three Tommy's melding into one. Then there is Reverend Simpson, who as a "Soldier for Jesus" was decorated (his name on the book's dust jacket is followed by a "V. C. ") for the same war in which Tommy's father was thought killed, and who now conducts empty services for the dead of that war, is the reverse of Captain Walker. In searching for something to replace her obviously self-involved and cold father, Sally turns to Tommy, but the inherent flaws in his ministry cause this to fail. Sensing the similar fallacies in Tommy's gospel and her father's, she quite simply trades heroes--just as the fans of the Champ traded allegiances at Tommy's pinball victory, and the Marilyn Monroe followers who will do the same in the next scene. Her happiness in her new hero will also be short-lived because of its own unstable ground. Russell suggests, however, that Sally will be unaware of the real problem: the fact that as wife and mother she appears the same age she was at the onset of the sequence is evidence of her arrested development. Beyond these aspects of the sequence as being allegorical of the whole film--except "Sally Simpson" is almost entirely negative, while <u>Tommy</u> overall is not--the scene is notable because it sets up the pattern for the bulk of the film detailing Tommy's fall as a messiah, hinted at in his blindness to Sally Simpson's needs and, indeed, to her presence. These are attitudes which Russell begins to examine in greater detail in the very next sequence.

    The "Sensation" sequence is firmly rooted in the earlier "Amazing Journey," as previously noted, but is less fanciful since the journey is no longer an inward one, and it also draws on the satirical material of the film. Having already run a considerable risk in diverging from the main story line in the previous sequence, Russell here goes all out by starting off on a tangent and then linking the story to it. This, too, is a development not present in the original screenplay where "Sensation" was made up of a series of incidents observed by Tommy from the vantage point of the helicopter. In adapting this to the form of the final film, Russell opens with the idea of incidents of everyday life, develops a story, introduces Tommy into that story, and only then reverts to the incidental format. The most unsettling aspect of Russell's original is its final scene which equated Tommy with Captain Walker--a premature notion and terribly false track that Russell happily dropped. In the finalized scene it is Russell's desire to show a cross-section of humanity and the way in which Tommy can touch them, while concurrently undercutting his divinity to set the stage for the collapse of the Tommy cult.

    Russell begins his sequence with a montage of people going about their everyday business, finally focusing on two garbage collectors who find a "<u>Tommy Speaks</u>" newspaper amid a load of trash. Grasping onto this one detail (in a manner not unlike Buñuel's <u>Phantom of Liberty</u>), Russell proceeds to follow one of the trashmen, who turns out to be a "Black Angel" motorcycle gang member in his off hours. Suddenly we find ourselves in the midst of a gang war of uncomfortably violent proportion when the Black Angels attack another group of bikers. The effect is unbalancing and for a moment it almost appears as if we have landed in a Roger Corman motorcycle epic. (The violence in this scene is quite realistic, partly because, in looking for a biker jacket for Cousin Kevin, Russell ran into the Black Angels, who agreed

to appear as themselves in the film. Not being professional
stunt men they were unfamiliar with the tricks for faking a
fight, and resultantly the pummeling, kicking, gouging, and
slugging in the film are real. 33) Just as the scene reaches
a frenzy of action and the garbageman-leader is preparing
to shoot a rival gang member, the first triumphant notes of
the "Sensation" theme sound on the track and Tommy arrives,
flying over them on a hang glider. His very presence causes
them to stop fighting, and soon they are all dancing to the
song. From this Russell returns to the vignette structure as
Tommy reaches the blind people from the Marilyn Monroe sequence, and turns a group of slot-machine playing Teddy Boys
into converts. The sequence climaxes with him atop a ruined
tower addressing the new converts, flying off into the sun
claiming, "I am the light." The sequence is designed to
give an almost endless feeling of the freedom of movement.
Except where the blind carry him and his final perching on
the tower, Tommy is never seen not in flight and the effect
is exhilarating. Symbolically, however, the fact that Tommy
is dependent on the artificial means of the hang glider to
achieve this freedom sharply undercuts his divinity, and although his position on the tower places him on a high level
like his father on the mountaintop, Tommy's mountain is
artificial, transient, and already crumbling. Take away
Tommy's man-made wings and his personal divinity disappears
with them. Nonetheless, like Russell's depiction of the fraudulent Marilyn Monroe religion the attraction of the false religion must be apparent for the idea to work.

This same idea pervades the "Welcome" sequence
which follows. Starting on a close-shot of a smiling young
girl's face, Russell zooms back to reveal a group of people
(including Russell himself as a wheelchair patient) looking
up at Tommy, who once again addresses them from a manmade height. There is a splendid bit of time compression
as Tommy ducks into the house and immediately re-emerges
from the front door, which conveys a sense of the apparent
magical nature of his character. At first the converts are
well-mannered and orderly, but traces of their ability to become a mob are hinted at as an entire new group forces their
way into the already overcrowded dining room. In a composition reminiscent of Leonardo Da Vinci's "Last Supper,"
Tommy and his mother and "Disciples" (the fishermen from
"I'm Free") sit at the head table, where Frank warns him
that the extra people will cause the floor to give way. Tommy's answer that a new, bigger building is needed seals the
"Last Supper" idea as we see the look on Frank's face at

this idea--quite obviously he has just figured a way of making a profit on this. Once again, Nora misses the implication because she is too intent on Tommy. The single most telling comment on Tommy's divinity, though, is saved for the final shot, where he appears at first to walk on water as the converts jump around him into a pool in an act of baptism. As they cluster around him it becomes apparent that he is actually standing on a board overhanging the pool.

The next sequence was originally a quite complicated affair set to a song called "Deceived," which, according to Townshend, nobody much cared for.[34] In removing the sequence in its entirety Russell has tightened the flow of his narrative. Upon examination there is very little in "Deceived" that is not dealt with more succinctly in previous sequences. Its placement this late in the film would have tended to bog things down to no real purpose, and thrown the film off balance structurally. Townshend therefore cannibalized the song and turned it into the much simpler "T. V. Studio," which provides a smoother transition to the film's denouement.

"T. V. Studio" is another sequence, like "Extra! Extra!" or "Miracle Cure," that is essentially a bridge from one section of the film to the next, but Russell's treatment of it is every bit as assured and carefully executed as the film's large set pieces. Visually it is slightly reminiscent of "Miracle Cure," which opens with a rhythmic series of pans and zooms. Following the more stately rhythm of "T. V. Studio," Russell opens here with a group of elegantly slow zoom shots as Frank directs Nora's televised speech on Tommy's ability to "Raise your weary spirits high." The obvious sincerity of her speech is undercut by Frank's attitude which philosophically concerns itself with the fact that the needs and desires of the converts do not come cheaply--"But who am I to upset their dreams?"

That Frank has turned Tommy's simple teachings into an expensive show-biz religion is brought home in the next scene where the converts flock into "Tommy's Holiday Camp." High above the masses, Frank gazes down on the new arrivals, who are encouraged by Uncle Ernie (sporting a brand new set of teeth and riding about on a motorized organ cum cash register) to buy all manner of Tommy paraphernalia--stickers, buttons, records, shirts, mirrors to smash--in order to secure a passport to heaven. The take is good as they load down the converts with useless junk and charge a

three-pound entry fee to the camp, but there are signs of
discontent as more than one convert registers some disgust
at the cash outlay. (This scene has a long history. Russell's first condemnation of commercialized religion appears
in his amateur documentary on Lourdes in 1958. It was then
further polished in his unproduced screenplay for Gargantua,
and finally emerges here as an integral part of the motivation
of the converts.)

    Like the early portions of Tommy, Russell eschews
the sequential structure of the central part of the film for
the climax and instead builds one long scene. The action
cuts from the fleecing of the converts at the gate to Tommy
inside the Holiday Camp (in reality a junkyard) standing atop
the pinball-like mound of harbor floats, placidly giving instructions to a group of handicapped persons below him.
To further underscore his disassociation from what is going
on outside, Russell continually cuts back to brief shots of
the cash registers ringing up the converts' purchases and to
scenes of the growing disillusionment. The capper comes
as Tommy throws his arms out in a crucifixion stance and
Russell cuts to the leader of the Black Angels disgustedly
shoving his shopping basket at his companion and storming
off angrily. This action signals the beginning of the end of
the Tommy religion.

    In the very next shot the converts are seen marching
through the junkyard, demanding explanations and the promised enlightenment of their messiah, who confidently turns
from the handicapped to face them. At first Tommy regards
them with some amusement as his theme sounds on the track.
In a shot recalling the track-in on Uncle Ernie, and thereby
suggesting Tommy's corruption, Russell slowly zooms in on
Tommy as he explains his ministry, instructing the converts
on the use of the deaf-dumb-and-blind-goggles, and then
ducks below the frame line and out of the shot. Still skeptical, the converts nevertheless do as instructed. Tommy's
human frailty begins to creep through as Russell shows that
he is more than a little satisfied in achieving this reversal
of positions with Tommy the only unafflicted person in a
crowd of deaf, dumb, and blind followers. The converts are
then led to pinball machines which they proceed to play. In
an amazing shot combining tracking, panning, and zooming,
Russell moves along the rows of converts standing stock still
at the machines, numbly playing Tommy's game. At the end
of the track, Russell zooms in on Frank atop the harbor
floats, and then it happens. There is a quick shot of a con-

vert smashing his pinball cross through the glass of the machine, and protesting, "We're not gonna take it!" As soon as one person sends out the cry of revolt, there are others ready to follow, and the converts turn into a mob. The structure of the shots depicting the rejection of Tommy as messiah represents Russell's single most successful fusion of every element in the film into one overriding impression-- the shots themselves are abruptly edited to the jarring rhythms of the music, and the sounds of the smashing glass are so perfectly matched with the music that the two sounds become inseparable. Once again the hypnotic quality of the approach is invaluable since, like the similarly mesmerizing qualities of the Marilyn Monroe cult and the appeal of the apparent freedom promised by Tommy in "Sensation," the audience as a body is compelled to move with the rebellious converts; i.e., we have become one of them. Russell immediately slaps us in the face with our inherent guilt when he breaks the rhythm and forces us to see the horror of being part of the mob. Tommy, uncomprehending, holds out his arms in a repeat of his crucifixion stance. Frank tries to fight off the converts, but is stabbed by one of them, and Nora is struck over the head and killed by a bottle directed at Tommy. Tommy is himself kicked in the head and falls to the center of the pile of floats as the converts make their escape.

Here Russell departs from the apparent implication of Townshend's original album, which suggests that Tommy reverts to his deaf, dumb, and blind state, reiterating the "See me, feel me, touch me, heal me," theme. Russell's original screenplay retains the song in this form, but in the film, Tommy's hopeless appeal to his dead mother is changed from "heal me" to "hear me." Of course, Nora can no more hear him now than she could heal him earlier. If she had listened previously and not followed so blindly, ignoring everything wrong with his teachings and Frank's commercialization of them, all this might not have happened. Tommy's religion has failed because it was built on falseness--Tommy flies, but only with man-made wings; he walks on water, but only with the aid of a board; he scales heights, but only a decaying tower or a pile of junk. On the same basis the ability to communicate his religion to his followers fails because he can only artificially induce a state of deprivation, and cannot therefore possibly reproduce the moment of spiritual rebirth he experienced after years of actual affliction.

It would be completely wrong, however, to suggest

that Russell sees Tommy as either evil or consciously fraudulent, and by the same token neither attitude applies to Nora. Instead, Russell's central judgment on them rests more on their lack of insight and responsibility. At the same time Stephen Farber's complaint that Tommy "is just too good to be true"[35] rings false because Tommy is far from perfect. Farber is probably distracted by the fact that Tommy seems much better than he is in context, purely because of the corruption around him. Tommy is himself not free of this corruption. His sadistic baptism into the modern world by Cousin Kevin precludes this possibility, and like other Russell heroes before him, he is blind to what is going on around him. In reality Tommy is less a character than a symbol for the two contradictory aspects of modern man. On the one hand he chooses to ignore the horrors of the world or do anything about them. This is consistent with Russell's view of an audience so numbed to reality that their dinner is accompanied by graphic television news footage of wars and carnage, and no one takes any notice. Much like Richard Strauss in Dance of the Seven Veils urging the orchestra to play louder so as to blot out the sound of Jews being tortured by Nazis, Tommy retreats into a private world for similar reasons. And that private world lingers on after his cure in his inability to perceive Frank's commercialization, his ignorance of Sally Simpson's needs or existence, his frequent position above his converts, suggesting his disassociation from them. On the other hand, there is an essential goodness in Tommy--an inner and universal divinity representing the indomitability of the human spirit. Significantly, it is this aspect that emerges triumphant, and it is on this note that Russell climaxes his mammoth work.

Joining Frank and Nora's hands together, Tommy angrily throws away Frank's pinball cross, and still crying, "Hear me," runs from the burning holiday camp. His progression through the flames, past the disused relics of war in the junkyard, firmly links him with his father's experience in the airplane, and with Captain Walker and Nora's journey through a bombed-out London. It is at this point, with the introduction of the song, "Listening to You," that Russell begins the series of seven shots which mirror the film's opening. (Russell himself calls the sequence, "Reverse Prologue,"[36] in his screenplay.) Russell departs somewhat from his screenplay in that Tommy's goal--the mountaintop--is known from the beginning of his journey. Also, the opening and closing are altered. Russell's original intention to begin the sequence with elaborate special effects had been dropped in favor of a more stately approach. Escaping from the burning holiday Camp, Tommy drops into a lake and begins to swim toward the distant shore. Russell cuts without transition to his arrival there, and then to a close-shot of a waterfall from which he pans down to Tommy standing in the mountain pool from the film's opening with the purifying waters pouring over him as a kind of re-baptism into the natural world. With the new surge of life given by the waters, Tommy joins in singing with the chorus, and proceeds up the mountain. Just prior to his emergence on the mountaintop, Russell directly copies the film's second shot, so that Tommy appears in exactly that spot where Captain Walker and Nora had planned their day. Instead of stopping he continues forward into close-shot, his face colored by an orange glow, as his words build into a half-shouted, half-sung burst of exhilaration. Tommy pauses to catch his breath and Russell cuts to the film's final shot--the sun rising in front of him as it had earlier set on his father. As the song ends and the music rises in triumph, Russell zooms his camera past Tommy into the rising run and the screen floods with light. At first Russell had intended to have the chorus interject, "We shall all be saved," at the climax, but, in the end, he opted for this more mystical approach. Nonetheless, his meaning is clear. The spheres seen throughout the film are representative of the sun at the film's beginning, symbols of what Russell terms "Man's eternal divinity."[37] Since Tommy represents the hopeful transcendence of all people, Russell's final theme of a universal salvation is inescapable. As such the ending of Tommy, not despite, but because of, the dark nature of its interior themes, marks yet another progression in Russell's personal journey into the positive. In Russell's subsequent film, Lisztomania, much the same spirit will prevail, but to an even greater extent, as Liszt does not blind himself to the suffering around him, but instead knowingly sets out to transcend his limitations.

A great many hopes were pinned to Russell's Tommy, not the least of which was the idea that the film might in some way help to pull the British film industry out of its slump. Unfortunately, this did not happen, but the film was a watershed for Russell, who, with no major American distributor for Mahler (his first release in nearly two years), was in a perilous professional position. Tommy put his name back in the forefront as a major filmmaker.

Detractors of the film are fond of pointing out Russell's

supposed discrepancies in his assessment of the music, but apart from one obvious piece of publicity hype in which Russell ostensibly purported that Tommy was "the best opera written since World War II" (not that there is all that much competition for that accolade), there is little basis for this claim. For that matter, Russell might well have been in earnest with that remark, as his reservations about the music do not have anything to do with Tommy's final musical form. In his interview with David Sterritt in The Christian Science Monitor, Russell stated only that he "still doesn't care for the original album," which, as previously noted, has little to do with the film soundtrack. Beyond this, Russell put forth that it was the film he had made that "pleased me the most aesthetically."38 As a near perfect blend of music, dance, acting, theme, and stylization, Russell's judgment is quite sound. The critical attitude that it is a lesser work because of its rock music is sheer snobbery, failing to take into account the application of that music and lumping all rock music into the dustbin as being of a single quality. Similarly, claims that Tommy is really Pete Townshend's film and not Russell's have little weight considering the pure Russell vision of the work.

If there is a single major flaw in Tommy it does not lie with the creative end of the film, nor even with co-producer Robert Stigwood, whose primary contribution was an almost complete lack of interference. (Stigwood, a man not noted for his additions to cinematic art, now holds the unique position of having produced the best "rock film" to date with Tommy, and also the worst--Sergeant Pepper's Lonely Hearts Club Band, a film so dreadful that in time it might rise above its genre and qualify for the worst film of all time in any department.) The original road show prints of Tommy were beautifully made, effectively capturing every nuance of detail in a film running the gamut of exposure range. John Mosley's splendidly designed five-track sound system perfectly complemented the visual side of those prints and helped create a unique film experience. This, alas, ended abruptly with the general release prints with their indifferent monophonic mix of the track, and even worse pictorial values. The entire film seemed to have been printed so that the "Pinball Wizard" sequence would look good and everything else could fend for itself. The result was a combination of muddy-looking, greenish night scenes, c.f. parts of "Amazing Journey" and the latter section of the junkyard scene; and glaringly bright over-exposure in the white-on-white scenes in Nora's bedroom, which obliterated

The Mature Films 291

detail and reduced skin tones to a vivid pink. Those prints are but a pale shadow of the original film. (Oddly, the prints later struck for rental in 16mm were a decided improvement on Columbia's general release 35mm prints.) Fortunately, Tommy is a good enough film that this careless attitude could not obscure its impact or importance.

As the central piece of Russell's stylistic trilogy, Tommy is the most powerful of the three films in the set. It is also the most daring in scope. Freed from the constraints of the dialogue film, Russell allowed his creative powers free reign, and the resultant film not only justifies itself, but clarifies and supports much of what has gone before it. In calling Tommy Russell's most wholly successful film one runs something of a risk, but the richness and depth combined with Russell's realization of a difficult task, make the film impossible to ignore. Repeated viewings only serve to enhance the film, as subtle visual patterns become ever clearer, and the finely integrated symbolism emerges in sharp relief. It is a film of almost infinite variety and creativity, but, perhaps, the greatest of Russell's achievements in Tommy is the very fact that for all its complexity and daring it tells a coherent and immediately understandable story accessible to any member of the audience on any level the viewer wishes to perceive. Humane, witty, tender, savage, wise, vicious, hopeful--Tommy is all this for the viewer who approaches the film openly.

* * *

"Why is everyone so literal these days? I was speaking metaphorically."
 --Robert Powell as Mahler in Mahler.

Lisztomania, Ken Russell's most complex and misunderstood film to date, neatly rounds off and climaxes the stylistic trilogy begun with Mahler. In some respects it is a blend of its two predecessors, but the mixture is not so much that of the musical biography with the "rock" film as Gene D. Phillips views it. Taking that approach to the film, he is quite correct in assessing Lisztomania as a failure, albeit an interesting one. The fusion of elements from Mahler and Tommy has very little to do with the divergence of the musical styles or with the biographical narrative. After all, Tommy is essentially a biographical film of a fictional character in the sense that it tells a life story, and Russell had already mixed musical styles--classical and pop, if not rock--as far back as Isadora. The blending attempted, and to a great extent achieved, in Lisztomania concerns shaping the stylistic ingredients of Tommy and the thematic elements of both it and Mahler into a single structure. As bold a move as this seems on the face of it, Russell's execution of the idea is bolder still in that Lisztomania subscribes to no traditional form of narrative structure. Structure, as we have come to accept it, has been blasted out of existence, and therein lies the major difficulty in understanding Lisztomania. Gene Phillips may well be misreading the film, but he at least attempts to read it where most critics either become so engaged in attacking the obviously stylistic and metaphoric aspects of the film (that Wagner did not really rise from the dead as Adolf Hitler or that Liszt was not killed by voodoo) which they seem to believe Russell is presenting as fact, or like Joseph Gomez they largely ignore the film. In his frequently brilliant dissertation on The Music Lovers Gomez notes, "the demands made on audience by a film like The Music Lovers are incredible,"[39] and yet he fails to respond to those very same demands in the case of Lisztomania, which he tosses off in a scant three pages, and then borrows his final conclusion from Stephen Farber's article "Russellmania." (Gomez may have been pressed for time as Lisztomania was the last Russell film released at the publication of his book, but the Farber article appeared several weeks after that release, so this seems unlikely.)

Russell has not helped the cause of championing Lisztomania as he has expressed severe reservations about the film's effectiveness. His remarks about the film being underbudgeted and symbolically top-heavy[40] are reminiscent of his statements on The Boy Friend minus the personal remembrances of the difficulties encountered in making the film. And, as usual, when the filmmaker starts to publicly question his work, the general belief is that he ought to know. (Oddly, when a filmmaker defends an unpopular work the reverse does not hold true.) Some consideration must be given to the fact that Russell's reservations all seem to have come in the wake of the film's almost universal damnation. Perhaps the greatest indication of Russell's attitude suffering from outside pressures comes from the fact that a third Russell-Roger Daltrey project had been discussed and was discarded only after the denouncement of Lisztomania by friend and foe alike.

That Lisztomania was a doomed film now seems obvious. Having discovered a whole new, seemingly receptive audience through Tommy, Russell decided to create an original film with this audience in mind, and Lisztomania is that film. It is very easy to see that Lisztomania could scarcely succeed on those grounds, but it is impossible not to be touched by Russell's assumption that his youth audience would immediately be able to respond to and grasp a film that required a good knowledge of nineteenth-century musical history, as well as a strong sense of film history for complete appreciation. Russell's attitude here may be naive in the extreme, but it is also marvelously refreshing to find such an attitude in a world where most filmmakers feel their work must be geared to an audience with a collective mental age of ten. On the basis of intentions alone, Lisztomania is the grandest gesture of Russell's career.

If Russell's overestimation of his audience had not killed Lisztomania as a commercially viable proposition, Warner Bros.' advertising campaign might well have accomplished this on its own merits. The posters and lobby cards for the film all purported that it "out-Tommy's Tommy," which, translated into something like English, appears to indicate that Lisztomania is somehow more outrageous than its predecessor. The campaign further asserted that it was "erotic, exotic," and "electrifying," in a manner that made it look like Lisztomania might be some kind of classy porno film. And just in case anyone was in doubt about Warners' being at sea as to exactly what the film was, there was the pièce de résistance of asininity, the theatrical trailer. At least one theatre opted to run this just prior to the film-- possibly in an attempt to clarify the film for the audience. The high point of the trailer is certainly reached when the announcer informs the viewer, "You won't understand it, but you'll love every minute of it!" Warner Bros. may have viewed this as a challenge, but if so, it did not work. More likely they hoped to promote the film as just the sort of thing Stephen Farber had felt Tommy was: "movies to get stoned by."[41] The problem here, quite clearly, is that Hollywood is not comfortable with a film that cannot be categorized, and Lisztomania cannot. Since Lisztomania could not be effectively pigeon-holed, it followed that it could not be effectively marketed, hence the dubious and ineffectual ad campaign. (A few energetic exhibitors have since decided that Lisztomania, along with Tommy, might just be a cult item, and that by showing it at midnight, it might become the next Rocky Horror Picture Show. It is not, partly because it is too wholesome, and there is no way it either can or should become another Rocky Horror--a film whose only prerequisite is that the viewer check any moral sense at the door.)

Quite contrary to the ad campaign and the film's detractors, Lisztomania can and should be understood through detailed examination, and while an understanding of the film may not cause the viewer to "love every minute of it," it will reveal that there is much more to the film than the barrage of grotesque and outrageous images as is often supposed. Granting that Russell's approach to history and biography is extremely personal, Lisztomania is the logical outgrowth of this subjectivity. While it is fruitless and exceedingly difficult to divorce the filmmaker from the film in Russell's other works, it is futile and impossible in the case of Lisztomania, which can only be fairly evaluated in the overall text of the Russell filmography. As the culmination of the Mahler-Tommy-Lisztomania trilogy and as the full-flowering of Russell's structural experimentation and stylistic genius, Lisztomania is an exhilarating film of substance, shot through with keen perception and relevant implications--everything it ought to be. Falsely pried away from this milieu, however, it is at best that "sadly dangling, brilliant film in search of an audience that perhaps does not even exist,"[42] as Ross Care would have it.

Lisztomania opens with a fantasy sequence that sets the tone for the film, if only because of the great profusion of ideas hurled out at one time. The first image on the screen is a ticking metronome. The camera pans away from this onto Franz Liszt lying atop Marie D'Algout kissing her breasts in time to the beat, and on this image the Liszt symphonic poem "Battle of the Huns" rises on the soundtrack in eloquent comment. As the frenzy of the music increases so Marie continually causes the metronome (and resultantly Franz) to move faster until in a burst of passion the metronome is smashed to the floor. Apart from the establishment of Liszt as a womanizer, this opening poses a symbolic representation that recurs throughout the film--the abuse or misuse of art. The metronome put to use for purposes its maker never intended is simply a metaphor for Liszt's utilization of his musical prowess to an end *his* Creator never intended.

At this point Marie's husband, Count D'Algout, enters and catches the two lovers in this compromising position, the sight of which prompts him to engage Liszt in an impromptu swordfight, staged with all the panache of a Douglas Fairbanks swashbuckler and underscored with a Cat Ballou-styled country narration song. (Curiously, the music, the lyrics, and the performers of this song are not documented in the film's credits.) Right away Lisztomania's good-natured

The Mature Films

humor becomes apparent, and it should also be obvious that any attempt at reading the film as a straightforward biography of the composer is neither possible nor intended. (Surprisingly, though, the first three quarters of the film, stylized as they are and apart from some shuffling of chronological sequence, bear close scrutiny in regard to historical accuracy.) Throughout the swordfight Russell continues the symbolism of misuse as Marie substitutes a banana for her paramour, the Count's sword wobbles and droops ("... the swords supplied by Bendy Toys") as an indication of his impotency, Liszt parries the Count's attacks with a handy fireplace shovel, etc. Although none of these have any direct bearing on the abuse of talent theme, they serve to keep that theme in the forefront. Of greater interest is the design of the scene, which will become far more important as the film progresses, and, in fact, foretells the denouement where Liszt and Wagner have their final encounter and the point of the film is brought into focus. The climax finds Liszt and Marie imprisoned in a piano by the vengeful Count who has them set, in the best bound-and-gagged silent serial style, on a railroad track in the path of an oncoming train. The implication is obvious. By misusing his talents Liszt dies by his talents as equated with the piano. Through elemental crosscutting techniques, ably aided by a synthesized version of Liszt's Hungarian Rhapsody No. 13, Russell builds the suspense in a manner appropriate to its serial flavor, and then he slips us a surprise by cutting away from the scene to the film's opening credits just prior to the moment of impact.

Despite the brilliance of execution and design of this scene, it also represents the major difficulty with the film's structure as a whole. There can be little doubt that this is a fantasy sequence, but Russell has not given the viewer an anchor for the fantasy. To whom does the fantasy belong? This becomes even more difficult as the film proper begins and the viewer finds similar fantastic goings on. Later in this second scene the answer is supplied, though not in so many words. Admittedly, Mahler opens in a not dissimilar manner, but the point of view of the dream which opens it not only is immediately discerned as belonging to Mahler, but is discussed at some length in the ensuing dialogue. In Lisztomania such safeguards are discarded and the film proceeds along its own path, which is frequently a step or two ahead of the viewer. Whereas Tommy grew out of Mahler, taken from the same stylistic mold, but jettisoning the skeletal framework, it nonetheless quickly established its own norm so that the viewer could readily differentiate

from the film's fantasy world and the interior fantasies of
the characters. The single exception to this in Tommy--
Nora's fantasy where the television floods her bedroom with
soap suds, baked beans, and melted chocolate which is presented as an occurrence and not a fantasy until proved otherwise by the introduction of a second character who does not
share Nora's point of view--becomes the rule in Lisztomania.
Mahler worked in a series of carefully executed layerings of
memory, fantasy, and reality. Tommy repeated this process
to some extent without the concession to a traditional reality,
but with a carefully defined version of reality. Lisztomania
boldly layers fantasy upon fantasy with no clearly established
level of reality and leaves the viewer to fend for himself.
Russell has here taken a very large risk and, in some ways,
has failed. Working, as he has in the past, on the assumption that the film will be seen more than once, he has created a film that not only is enhanced by, at the very least,
a second look, but for which that second look is essential.
Actually, Russell has not failed his audience so much as his
audience has failed him. The viewer coming to Lisztomania
after Mahler and Tommy should have been better prepared
for such structural experimentation than seems to have been
the case.

For a film that is as seemingly self-indulgent and
chaotic as Lisztomania might appear to the casual observer,
Russell's structure of the film is beautifully economical.
There is scarcely a wasted frame in the film, and even the
main credit titles are not without their importance. Aside
from stopping the train crash in the pre-credit sequence,
and thereby providing a witty transition to the pre-concert
party, the music under the credits is of particular interest.
Musical legend has it that at the first rehearsal of Liszt's
First Piano Concerto, he played the first seven notes of the
piece and sang, "This none of you understands," in reference
to the composition's radical structure.[43] Significantly, these
seven notes are the music under the "Lisztomania" credit,
and are used as a recurring motif at various points in the
film as if they might be a reminder of its own radical structure.

Immediately following the credits we return to the
sound of the crash of the train, but the sound turns out to
be the report of a photographer's flash as a picture is taken
of Liszt, and we find ourselves in the party sequence, one
of Russell's most outrageous creations, and one of his best.
It is the old Hollywood biopic gone mad, taken to its logical

extreme. In one crowded, smoke-filled room Russell has amassed most of the musical talent of the nineteenth century. Recalling such Hollywood inanities as Devotion, the ostensible story of the Brontës, where a jolly Sydney Greenstreet version of Thackeray is seen showing Emily around London and is greeted by a bearded gentleman who says, "Good morning, Mr. Thackeray." Without batting an historical eye, "Mr. Thackeray" responds with, "Good morning, Mr. Dickens." (Devotion is full of this kind of authentic touch.) In keeping with the puckish tone of this brand of send-up Russell presses most of the members of his stock company of character performers--Otto Diamant, Murray Melvin, Ken Colley, Andrew Faulds, Imogen Claire--into service for the impersonations of historical personages in his film. Not surprisingly, Russell's scene is almost balletic in its execution, and not designed with any idea of lending an air of authenticity to the proceedings. The scene proper begins with a throng of screaming girls being held back at the door of the dressing room by Liszt's nineteenth-century "roadies," through the legs of whom Wagner crawls into the room, immediately crying out, "Where is my opera?" and slugging a bystander. Hans von Bulow informs Liszt, "It's the young man who wrote the opera about ancient Rome." Liszt decides to take the situation in hand, treating Wagner as if he might be some kind of animal, patting him on the head and saying, "Come over here," in the tone one might use to summon a dog. As they cross the room Liszt is accosted by a heavily bearded individual who is told, "Oh, piss off, Brahms," after which Wagner is informed, "I always feel that people who like Brahms would prefer to have no music at all." It would be easy to assume that Russell is here using Liszt as a mouthpiece to espouse his personal opinion, but there is more than a passing validity in giving Liszt this line since Brahms was one of the few people Liszt actively disliked, primarily due to the fact that when Liszt played his Piano Sonata in B Minor for Brahms, the young composer fell asleep. 44 Following some scene hogging by Wagner, who quickly maneuvers himself into line for a photograph with Liszt, Liszt delivers a crushing blow to Wagner's ego by telling him that Rienzi reminded him "very much of Mendelssohn," the main composer that Wagner feared might be superior to himself and helped spawn his rabid anti-Semitism. Wagner's outburst at this remark quickly leads him on a journey through the composers and other noteworthies present as it turns out that Mendelssohn is standing behind him. Russell's handling of this is notable and makes good use of Paul Nicholas' brilliant ability to move eccentrically and effortlessly on the screen.

At the beginning he rises into the frame shouting, "Mendelssohn!" When he turns from Mendelssohn he ducks down once again to point out passages from Rienzi to Liszt, who is being set-upon from the other side by Rossini, hawking a plate of chicken and expressing concern over Liszt's lack of weight and length of hair. Seizing this opportunity--"You're interested in opera. Meet Rossini"--Liszt rids himself of the pair of them as Rossini, preventing Wagner from introducing himself by grabbing his cheeks, turns his attention to "another boy who don't eat enough," leading Wagner to the similarly slender Hector Berlioz. This round, Wagner is prevented from announcing himself when Rossini thrusts a chicken leg into his mouth. Rossini, eternally eating (he magically produces an ice cream cone after polishing off the chicken), expounds on the musical legend that Beethoven kissed the young Liszt after hearing him play the "Moonlight" Sonata, verifying it as fact, but qualifying it with, "at the time he was as deaf as a post," just before dashing off after Robert Schumann. Wagner then mistakes a Strauss for Schumann, but Strauss turns out not to be Johann but "Levi Strauss," who pushes Wagner downward out of the frame in counterpoint to his earlier rising into the frame. On the floor he attempts to introduce himself to Chopin who is kneeling at the feet of George Sand, coughing tubercular blood into a handkerchief. At last Wagner gets his chance to announce himself to someone--"Madame Sand! An honor! I am Richard Wagner!" The top-hatted, cigar-smoking Sand peers at him through her glasses and answers in a man's voice, "Of course you are, dear boy."

Though the sequence is undoubtedly bizarre and extremely unlikely, it is in no way impossible, and everything in it has a firm basis in either historical fact or musical legend filtered through a personal vision. Russell's concern, however, is to entertain and delineate the film's two main characters, Liszt and Wagner. According to the sequence, Liszt is everybody's friend (save for Brahms), and the things that irritate or anger Wagner are just pleasantly humorous eccentricities for Liszt. Wagner, on the other hand, is loud, obnoxious, violent, and self-promoting, taking himself with a self-importance ("My opera, you thought it was a masterpiece?") and pompous seriousness ("Read this--'The Piano as an Instrument of Revolution'" as he produces one of his ubiquitous pamphlets), which renders him more than a little ridiculous. His "The Piano as an Instrument of Revolution" continues the theme of artistic misuse, but more importantly triggers the memory of the similar misuse of the piano on

The Mature Films 299

the train tracks from the opening scene for Liszt. This indicates that the opening fantasy belonged to Liszt and not to the film, whereas the presence of guilt feelings within the composer put forth the first signs that Liszt might achieve salvation since he recognizes his failings and shortcomings. There is nothing arbitrary about the scene, and in only one instance does it seem that Russell is using his characters to his own ends. When Liszt tells Wagner that the proceeds from the concert will go "to build a monument to your beloved Beethoven, which your beloved countrymen so belovedly neglected to build," the statement has the air of Russell's personal bitterness over the loss of the German financing on Mahler. Even so the statement gives the knowledgeable viewer a historical point of reference for the scene, as it clearly indicates that this is the concert for the Beethoven Memorial Fund, dating the scene as April 26, 1841.

Oddly, Lisztomania may well be Russell's most fact-filled biographical film, except toward the end where it becomes openly allegorical. As noted in the dubiously intentioned Playboy photo preview, the film's press kit contains a bibliography nearly as long "as its sixty-seven page screenplay."[45] This recalls Russell's stated intentions about the making of Dance of the Seven Veils in 1970--to create a film in a totally unrealistic manner and have it be more "real" than ever.[46] In fact, Lisztomania owes something of its attitude to the earlier work, but it is by no means a repetition of it, nor is the line of descent nearly as direct as some critics have suggested. Lisztomania is by far the better balanced of the two films. It is simply the difference between a mature work and an early one. On another level, it is the difference between a work by Wagner and a work by Liszt--both are touched by genius, but only one is tempered with humanity. Dance of the Seven Veils is an attack, possibly well-deserved and justified, but as an attack it is more limited in its aims. It is easy therefore to conclude that it is a more successful film than Lisztomania because its goals are more readily attainable. For this very reason it is the lesser film. A film does not simply achieve greatness because it accomplishes what it sets out to do. If that were the sole criterion for greatness, a film like Muscle Beach Party would have to be adjudged as nearly perfect. Lisztomania may well borrow some of its logic from Dance of the Seven Veils, but its direct relation is not deep. Whereas, attitudinally, The Music Lovers could (and did) come immediately after it, Lisztomania could not.

The climax of the party scene comes when Wagner, who has just been appalled that Liszt might "improvise a fantasy on some of your themes" to be included in the program, is equally horrified when he thinks Liszt has forgotten the music to do this. Not only has Liszt not forgotten the music, but he has instructed Hans to make Wagner a present of some money. The money completely drives the music from Wagner's mind as he cavalierly hands his manuscript to a roadie so that he can more easily count the money. So much for Wagner's high ideals of art.

The concert which follows is important to the development of the film, not so much because of Russell's witty allegorical association of Liszt with a pop star, but because of its broader awareness of the nearly impossible position of the artist in the commercial world. Liszt demonstrates this fact to Wagner by attempting to play some of Wagner's "little tunes" from Rienzi. Certainly Liszt is making fun of Wagner ("besides being German, Richard has something else in common with Beethoven. He's a bleeding genius. How do I know? You told me so yourself, didn't you, Richard?"), if only in an effort to puncture the man's pomposity. The real thrust, however, is that the audience will have none of it. They do not want Rienzi. They want "Chopsticks." Liszt's shoulder-shrugging look at Wagner indicates that this is by way of being a friendly warning to him that to achieve this kind of popular success there has to be some compromise. Russell's point is that Wagner will not compromise and that Liszt has compromised too much. Liszt's music is not being judged on its own merits, but by how flashy Liszt can be as a performer. What both men need, and for Russell Liszt ultimately achieves it, is the same sort of balance Russell is attempting to strike in this very film, something in between numbing self-importance and completely selling out to commercialism. Russell's attempt at achieving this balance is one of the factors that may account for the cool reception of the film by its youth audience. Despite the fact that this scene grows out of the "Pinball Wizard" segment of Tommy, which had been enormously successful with that same audience, Russell might just be getting too close to home here. Too many of the members of that audience have behaved in the manner of Liszt's groupies for the satire to be comfortably humorous.

Again nothing is wasted because Russell has telescoped events to introduce Princess Carolyn, who is among the women in the audience to whom Liszt takes a fancy.

The Mature Films

(The others are Georgina Hale and Izabella Telezynska as, one assumes, Alma Mahler and Madame von Meck, respectively, in an in-joke reference to Russell's own earlier work.) The choreographic feeling of the first two scenes is brilliantly continued here in a flurry of action, faultlessly timed to a condensed arrangement of Liszt's Hungarian Rhapsody No. 14, as Liszt dodges a woman with a baby (she claims it is his child) and searches the audience for potential feminine diversions, all the while giving a bravura performance, dancing atop the piano and tossing autographed silhouettes to the audience. As in the earlier scenes the tone is light and humorous, but not uncritical with the theme of artistic abuse very much in focus.

Unfortunately, Russell's narrative hits a bad patch in the following scene, but one that quickly rights itself. Curiously, Lisztomania is Russell's single most dialogue-oriented film in that many of his themes, which begin here to come together for the first time, are expressed in words; yet, it contains the most horrendous dialogue exchange in any of his films up to this point. The scene in the bedroom between Liszt and Marie is the only really false note in the film, living up to the firmly held notion that Russell is not at home with dialogue. Doubly unfortunate is the fact that the scene is immaculately designed. Phillip Harrison's set and Shirley Russell's costumes are among the best in an overall beautifully designed film, and the scene's placement leads gracefully into the Chaplin fantasy, but the words are abrasive and stilted. Further, Russell's handling of the scene betrays his own discomfort and the scene falls with a dull thud. The final impression is that it is a miniature version of the developmental section that had marred The Music Lovers. It is necessary as a buildup to the emotions expressed in the Chaplin fantasy since we have to see to what level the Liszt-Marie relationship has descended before we can understand his wistfulness. Nonetheless, one could wish that it were better done.

Once the ghostly voices from the past, reading the couple's old love letters, come into the scene, the film regains its balance, especially with the introduction of Cosima and the revelation that the voices are those of the children filtering down the chimney. Cosima is one of Russell's most unlikely creations, the total rejection of traditional realism in favor of psychological realism. Born of Sally Simpson in Tommy, Cosima's emotional stunting is boldly expressed by her complete lack of physical growth throughout

The "Liebestraum-Chaplin" fantasy in which Liszt and Marie bid farewell to their simple existence in Switzerland in Lisztomania. (Warner Bros.)

the course of the film. When first we see her in this scene she appears to be about thirteen years old. By the end of the film she is unchanged--the eternal spoiled brat.

The Chaplin fantasy, an outgrowth of the letter reading, is keyed by Liszt's own reading of one of the old letters after the other children have thrown them down the chimney (with a resultant burst of soot). No single fantasy within the text of Lisztomania has been so narrowly read as this one. If the sequence is approached solely as being patterned on Chaplin's The Gold Rush, as is universally the case, then Stephen Farber's conclusion that the scene presents Liszt "as a clown" is unavoidable.[47] If, instead of limiting ourselves to The Gold Rush as such, we broaden our view to take in Liszt as Chaplin in a way that extends beyond Chaplin's Tramp character, the scene takes on added meaning and relevance. The real Chaplin, after all, did share an idyllic existence with his last wife, Oona O'Neil Chaplin, in Switzerland, which is the setting for the fantasy in Lisztomania. Paralleling Liszt with Chaplin raises new issues altogether on the grounds of Liszt's longing for a lost innocence and idealized existence, and Chaplin's having achieved something along those lines. Then, too, despite Daltrey's exceptionally good imitation of Chaplin's Tramp, Russell's fantasy is not concerned with any direct quotations or murmurings from The Gold Rush. In fact the two strongest stylistic connections in the fantasy relate to the recalling of the metronome of the film's opening, and a direct reference to John Ford's The Searchers at the scene's climax where the door blows closed separating Liszt from the peaceful family world inside in the same manner that John Wayne is cut off at the end of The Searchers. (Strangely, this aspect of the sequence is generally accepted as an attempt to reproduce the iris-out technique of closing a scene in the manner of the silent film, but if this were the case surely Russell would have simultaneously faded out on the cabin's interior, which he does not do.)

The Chaplin fantasy is not an off-shoot of the main film as might easily be thought as it establishes a pattern about to be repeated in the next scene--the necessity of simply making money in order to survive. As Liszt and Marie cannot continue in Switzerland, so Liszt cannot "sit at home composing" and support them at the same time. This is a central concern in all of Russell's works on artists of any kind, finding voice in such similar incidents as Eric Fenby's job as a cinema pianist in Song of Summer, Tchai-

kovsky's position as a composition instructor in The Music
Lovers, Henri's art forging and clerking jobs in Savage Messiah, and Gustav's hopes to compose year round instead of
just in the summer and his "I conduct to live; I live to compose" line in Mahler. In fact Russell's unfinished screenplay, Music, Music, Music, was to have revolved around
this theme in total. Nonetheless, in Lisztomania it is a situation that Marie cannot grasp (though Liszt is certainly no
help with his lewd reference to not being cold "with all those
Russian muffs about") and it is the necessity of concert touring that drives the wedge between the couple. Russell has
here telescoped events somewhat, but in so doing he gives
Lisztomania a far more rational progression than it might
otherwise have had. Historically, the break with Marie and
the association with Princess Carolyn are separated by three
years, but in connecting the events Russell has created a
logical flow from the concert scene's "Princess Carolyn says
if you're ever in Petersburg to look her up, " to this scene's
announcement of a Russian concert tour, to the following
scene of Liszt "looking up" the Princess.

    The introduction of the fanciful voodoo element in this
scene is not nearly so ludicrous or arbitrary as has been
suggested. There is, of course, little point in arguing whether or not Cosima really did have a Franz Liszt doll on which
she could practice the art. As a symbol of the control she
could exert over her father there is nothing particularly ludicrous about it if the film's overall stylization has been digested by the viewer. (Then, too, the Liszt-pop star analogy
makes the existence of such a doll perfectly rational.) It
is undeniable that Cosima's later association with Wagner was
painful to Liszt, especially during the time when he was at
odds with the other composer, and, on this purely symbolic
level, the voodoo doll is a workable, albeit strange, choice
for Russell as the latter part of the film will clarify. All
of this serves to bring up the point that one part of Lisztomania cannot be judged until one sees how it relates to the
film as a whole.

    The sequence at Princess Carolyn's court continues
the film's high level of invention and consummate design, as
her servant (a cameo role for Oliver Reed) leads Liszt into
an antechamber, the walls of which are lined with plastic
derrieres. Liszt is locked in this room and "fumigated" by
smoke from these in a manner that evokes Aubrey Beardsley's
drawings for Lysistrata--an apt foreshadowing of the emasculating Princess. Most Russell films have their outrageous

woman character in them, and Princess Carolyn fills the bill here, except that the sexually voracious, cigar-smoking, free-thinking, art-crazed Princess is very probably the most outrageous of them all. In an effort to plug up the smoke gushing orifices, Liszt has stripped himself of nearly all his clothing. Having retained his sword belt, sword, and a small carrying case, he is immediately in the lesser position. Not only has the fumigating process saved the Princess from being "sickened" by the fresh air that her visitors "invariably stink of," but in so doing she has gotten the upper hand with Liszt, a position she manipulatively maintains throughout her scenes. Expounding her rather bizarre ideas on religion, sex, and art, the Princess immediately takes Liszt over, depicted by Russell in a symbolic fashion through one of his most infamous fantasy sequences.

After Liszt has expressed his desire to write "really great music," and Carolyn's subsequent promise that she can help him achieve this end if he will put himself "entirely" in her hands, she proceeds to literally engulf him. Reminiscent in some respects of the image of the Acid Queen in Tommy (that film's outrageous female) opening her mouth and swallowing the iron maiden in which Tommy is encased, Princess Carolyn swallows Liszt with her vagina as the fantasy begins. (In actuality the image of the predatory female swallowing up her victim dates back as far as French Dressing, at least in its incipient form.) Bold as this is, it is but one step toward the heights of outrageousness the fantasy ultimately scales. Skillful in its construction (as Liszt disappears over the edge of part of the giant mock-up vagina he drops back into frame, via a direct cut, in Carolyn's throne room), the sequence is designed to bring into focus the baser desires that plague the composer, and significantly, to climax them as this is the turning point in the film for Liszt's character. Once back in the throne room Liszt finds himself beleaguered by Marie, Lola Montes, George Sand, and the other women in his life. Calling on Carolyn for aid, Liszt soon finds himself swinging away from the ravenous women in a censer Carolyn has pushed in his direction, visually recalling his attempted escape from Count D'Algout on a chandelier. Carolyn presents Liszt with a lyre and he uses this to play music to soothe and tame his attackers à la Orpheus. The rhythmic cutting and gliding camera work combined with Daltrey's good-natured parody of Pete Townshend's "power-chord" guitar playing style helps produce a memorable series of images. Having thus used his musical gifts to save his skin and charm the women, Liszt finds himself weakened to his overly lustful state through the allure of this power, and as the women fawn over him, his penis grows to gigantic proportions. In a musical number, largely set to a comic version of Liszt's "Liebestraum" ("Dream of Love") No. 3, the ladies ride around on it, succumb to it as it passes over them on the floor, and ultimately turn it into a Maypole which they dance around entwining it with gaily colored ribbons, just prior to leading it off to be guillotined by Princess Carolyn. Drawn from Busby Berkeley's "Lady in the Tutti Fruiti Hat" number from The Gang's All Here, Russell has simply stripped away the symbolism of the giant bananas in that film and worked the situation around to his own purpose. Aside from that, the giant vagina and the giant phallus are visually linked to the plastic derrieres and the Beardsley-Lysistrata emasculation implications which they portend, and with which the fantasy quite logically concludes. Moving from the comic "Liebestraum" into the opening of Liszt's "Dante Symphony," the first notes of which are meant to evoke the words over the entrance to hell in Dante's Inferno, and which are here used as lyrics for the music, Russell stages Carolyn's execution of Liszt's member. When the Princess

Roger Daltrey mocking Peter Townshend's "power-chord" guitar style in the "Orpheus" fantasy for Lisztomania. (Warner Bros.)

guillotines the phallus her emasculation of him is complete, and this is the point toward which Russell has been leading the film.

True to the spirit of the film's opening, the guillotine dropping is stopped at midpoint, linking it with the train and the piano, and Russell employs his well-known penchant for the low joke (a factor which is as much purely British as purely Russell). Returned to reality, Liszt cries out in pain and then tells the concerned Princess that "the piano lid dropped and nearly cut off my ... thumb." Low the joke may be, but it still brings forth the overriding theme of artistic abuse in a verbalization of the preceding fantasy. The scene between Liszt and Carolyn, however, is one of those tricky transitional ones with which Russell often has trouble, especially if it is a dialogue scene. Fortunately, the dialogue here is quite a bit better than that of the bedroom scene, and Russell's cinematic invention does fail him as he brings off an astonishing little editing coup (switching from a long shot to a tight two-shot on Carolyn and Liszt as she sits next to him on the piano bench in a startlingly immediate manner), and effectively utilizing that most tricky film device, the focus shift, for the scene's climax. This encounter is essential to the narrative as it not only gives the viewer much needed information about the film's next move, but also crystallizes Carolyn's complete emasculation and control of Liszt as she prattles on about how promising a piece of music is that she has "suggested" Liszt write, and gets him to sign over the control of his children to her. The climax of the scene finds them readying to leave for Germany before the Tsar confiscates her property because of the unorthodox living arrangement she shares with Liszt and the publication of Marie's satirical biography, Lisztomania. Carolyn walks away from Liszt echoing the sentiments of Russell's first outrageous lady, Isadora Duncan, proclaiming that "art is so much greater than politics," but Liszt is worn down by his absence from the real world and his responsibilities, as guilt eats away at his soul for not supporting his friends in the Hungarian uprising.

This logically leads into the next scene in Germany where Liszt's guilt manifests itself in the song he sings set to his "Funerailles" composition. (Indeed this piece was written to commemorate friends who had died in the uprising.) As Liszt sings in his (literally) ivory tower, the revolution rages in the streets below, and he envisions his similar guilt in the spiritual damage to his wife and children. The very

Evil unleased by an eclipse of the sun as Wagner prepares to vampirize musical inspiration from Liszt in <u>Lisztomania</u>. (Warner Bros.)

fact that Liszt is seriously attempting to come to terms with himself and his failings is indicative of the direction in which the film is moving. As Liszt reaches the erroneous, guilt-ridden conclusion that the only thing alive in him is music, Russell reintroduces Wagner.

Unlike Liszt, Wagner has been actively involved in the revolution and is much the worse for it. When first glimpsed we see him shoot the guard outside Liszt's building to gain entrance and, in the process, kick a dog. (This seems to be a friendly jibe at Hitchcock's famous statement that a filmmaker can no longer show that a character is a villain by having him kick a dog and also seems to have overtones of Ford's The Searchers once again where Henry Brandon as the villainous Indian chief treats a dog in similar fashion.) Typically, Wagner is only seeking Liszt for a touch--and something more precious than money. The encounter between the two composers is one of Russell's most felicitous dialogue scenes, staged in intentionally anachronistic terms as Wagner assures Liszt that the money is "not for me. It's for the wife and kids. Unless I can smuggle them out of the country, we're all for the chop." His familial concerns, however, are quickly unmasked as he qualifies the price of their survival which will make them "homeless exiles, forced to suffer in some alien town where they've never heard of me or played a note of my music." All the while Wagner is setting up for his greater purpose by drugging Liszt's wine so that he can vampirize his musical talent. In an astonishing shot, taking full advantage of Lisztomania's wide-screen composition, Russell stages an eclipse through the window of Liszt's room while the lighting takes on sinister tones, and Wagner puts forth his belief that "I will write music that will fire the imagination of the German people, and bring to light a man of iron who will forge the shattered fragments of this country into a nation of steel." During the speech (delivered in a mock Boris Karloff voice) the camera moves in on Wagner, who has sprouted fangs and proceeds to vampirize Liszt in order that Liszt's musical talent might help him realize his vision. It is here that Russell begins his examination of Wagner's actual musical pilfering (the earlier reference to Rienzi being reminiscent of Mendelssohn, however, likely has bearing on the fact that Wagner's Flying Dutchman theme is partly a musical inversion of Mendelssohn's "Hebrides" overture[48]), and his relation to Nazism. Russell has received a great deal of criticism on this front, which is understandable, but not deserved. As concerns his linkage of Wagner and Nazism, there is little doubt that Wagner and the Nazi ideal are inseparable, and, given Russell's attitude on history as put forth in his previous works, there seems no way around his handling that connection in this way. Unfortunately for Russell there is a tendency to believe that death somehow sanctifies. This can be seen in so recent a serious book as Egon Gartenberg's Mahler, in which Gartenberg castigates a Mahler detractor for, essentially, not modifying his opinion on the composer's work upon the occasion of Mahler's death[49]-- an occurrence which certainly had no bearing on the quality of the music. A shift in this attitude, though, can be seen in Robert W. Gutman's Richard Wagner: The Man, His Mind, and His Music, where the author does not attempt to excuse his subject's more disreputable characteristics, except to postulate a theory on the possibility that Wagner was approaching some kind of humility and self-transcendence at the time of his death.[50] Film, however, as Russell pointed out in dealing with the response to The Devils, has a far more immediate impact than the printed word, and a no-holds-barred picture of Wagner on film is therefore less acceptable and more volatile. Too, the criteria for dealing with film and literature are distinctly different because, despite claims to the contrary, film is still generally regarded as being somehow intrinsically inferior to other art forms. Worse, the attitude on Russell's attacking Wagner for stealing from other composers is totally wrongheaded because it rests on the false premise that Russell is himself guilty of this on a filmic level. To misinterpret this is to misinterpret the differences between inspiration and plagiarism, or quotation and theft. Russell has quoted and Wagner stole. To this end one need only examine the facts. Russell is, and always has been, very open about his influences and sources. At the other end of the scale, we find Wagner asserting (in a letter to Hans von Bulow), "There are many matters which we are quite frank about discussing among ourselves (for instance, that since my acquaintance with Liszt's compositions my treatment of harmony has become very different from what it was formerly), but it is indiscreet, to say the least, of friend Pohl to babble this secret to the whole world."[51] Wagner's intent here is all too obvious and points to a nasty furtiveness, quite different from Russell's quotations and influences.

Having helped himself to Liszt's musical inspiration, Wagner quickly makes off with some of the Princess's jewelry and runs out, narrowly avoiding Carolyn as he thrusts one of his latest tracts ("Here! Read this pamphlet!") on Liszt. When we finally get a look at the pamphlet it turns out to be a Superman comic book--a clear indication of the direction of the film. Carolyn has returned to deliver the good news that her husband and the Russian government have at last agreed to a divorce that she might marry Liszt. "All we need now is the blessing of the Pope," she announces, and with this in mind prepares for the journey to Rome to attain said blessing.

Meanwhile, the fighting rages outside and it is in the middle of this battlefield that Wagner first meets Cosima. Russell is quite adept at communicating the situation in this one brief scene, which begins with Cosima calling Wagner, "the bum that's always begging favors off my old man," and ends with Wagner kissing her in front of her husband, Hans von Bulow. She is immediately fascinated by Wagner. One might go so far as to state that the implication of the kiss is one of infection. In any case the scene leaves little doubt as to Cosima's destiny and neatly encapsulates that period of time in which Hans was forced to play the cuckold for the two of them.

For one of Russell's composer biographies, the music in Lisztomania only reaches the level of cinematic invention we have come to expect from the filmmaker in these later portions of the film. The first, and easily the best, of Russell's scenes to really take advantage of his mastery in the utilization of preexisting music is the wedding rehearsal of Liszt and Carolyn in Rome. Recalling the film's opening scene the music is from "Battle of the Huns" once again, and Russell uses that section of the piece where Liszt practiced the musical equivalent of crosscutting. Liszt's intention was to counterpoint in musical form the prayers in the church with the assembling army outside. Russell's use of this is to counterpoint Liszt (the church music) with Carolyn (the troop assembling music). While Liszt quietly plays the church organ in the balcony, Carolyn is marshalling her own troops of priests, bishops, cardinals, nuns, attendants, and altar boys in the church proper. Her scenes are beautifully timed and executed with Russell's fine choreographic sense as she straightens robes, adjusts crosses, and shoots a look of disbelief at the camera as a Cardinal insists on having her kiss his ring.

Here Russell second guesses history as to the reason for the couple not receiving the Pope's blessing, but it is a soundly reasoned guess and does not depart from the facts as such. Musical historians tend to agree that the marriage was more desirable from Carolyn's point of view than it was from Liszt's, but Liszt was far too much the gentleman to have raised this point himself. In John Chancellor's almost absurdly sympathetic biography, Wagner (a work that goes so far as to drag in the deaths of Wagner's dog and parrot and the effects of these deaths on Wagner in an attempt to humanize the composer), the point is taken that this is a major character flaw in Liszt, i.e., the inability to discard a person when they were of no further use.[52] Be that as it may, Russell would have it that Liszt did bring about this dissolution, quite innocently, by telling his story to the sympathetic Pope, who appears incognito in the organ loft, and that this is the reason for his withholding the blessing on the marriage.

    Without the blessing the wedding cannot come off, and in one of the film's few exterior sequences, the Princess and Liszt decide to go their separate ways. Lisztomania is probably Russell's most studio-created film as befits its stylized nature, but in this scene Russell instead chooses to stylize Nature herself. This he accomplishes in a typically economical fashion by manipulating his soundtrack. Throughout their dialogue the Princess's laughter is continually mocked by a crow, and all of the pair's more dubious decisions are followed by the sound of a cuckoo in the distance. The scene is also the third of the film's major dialogue-oriented transitional sequences, and the best of them. Starting with Liszt and Carolyn engaging in a joke that smacks of the English Music Hall (Carolyn: "When is a veil not a veil?" Liszt: "I don't know." Carolyn: "When it's a shroud.") the scene proceeds with a deliciously nutty Goon Show logic of its own. The upshot of all this is that they will both get their revenge on the Pope. Carolyn will write a book exposing the Pope ("It shall be called The Interior Causes of the Exterior Weaknesses of the Church - in twenty-four volumes. That just about takes care of the rest of my life."), and Liszt will become an abbé and thereby be indirectly supported by the Pope. This, of course, is exactly the sort of thing Liszt has wanted to do all along, and his sudden leap into the river below--tossing his hat in the air and crying, "Praise the Lord!"--is consistent with much of Russell's water-purification baptism imagery. The idea of purification is apt in consideration of the final portion of Lisztomania into which we are now moving.

    In a composition of satiric thrust Russell cuts directly to the Vatican, where his camera pans downward from a re-

Ringo Starr as the Pope and Ken Russell on the set of Lisztomania. (Warner Bros.)

ligious painting to a crucifix and finally to Liszt cozily asleep in bed with a young woman. Sirens sound and the Pope rolls in on a propelled throne in a visual reference to the film's opening where the piano is rolled into the room. This immediately calls to mind the theme of misuse. Has Liszt misused his musical ability and his new position with the Church? Not exactly. At least not according to his explanation that is his music copyist, "Mr. Janine ... at least in her letter she said she was a mister," who has "entered the monastery disguised as a nun, and then forced me into bed at gunpoint." History verifies all but the last part of his story, which the Pope passes off good-naturedly as an example that "truth is stranger than fiction--we've kept going for two thousand years on that one." This sexual infraction of the rules is not the real reason for the invasion of Liszt's living quarters, however, nor is it at the center of Russell's scene. "You haven't heard the news, then?" he asks Liszt. "Your daughter's deserted husband, renounced her faith, and married Anti-Christ." Liszt is thunderstruck, "Cosima's left Hans and married who?" "Satan himself, Richard Wagner," the Pope tells him, and then further enlightens him that during his monastic period, cut off from the world, he has missed out on Wagner's development into "the Prince of Darkness, singing the praises of an obscene religion of his own creation." The crux of this is that Liszt is now Wagner's father-in-law, and "How can Holy Mother Church give her blessing to music written by the father-in-law of the devil?" This rationalization places Liszt at the lowest point in his life. Early in the film his music is judged by the marketplace rather than by its merits, but now it is not even judged as music, nor for that matter is Liszt judged as Liszt but as Wagner's father-in-law. This is a condensation and variation on the very real position of Liszt in music, with his originally popular works being viewed with scorn and his more important works being overshadowed by Wagner. The Pope, however, has a solution to the problem. "One of your orders is that of exorcist," he tells Liszt and proposes that Liszt exorcise Wagner, thereby redeeming his music, "and until such time it is tainted in the eyes of the world and will be put on the 'Index' and banned!"

With this the tone of the film changes dramatically and Liszt's reformation and transcendence begin. Just as Russell is concerned with creating a Wagner who is a total symbolic villain, he now starts shaping Liszt into the total hero. The first clear indication of his new heroic status comes when, in response to "Mr. Janine's" threat to shoot Liszt if he leaves her, he is given Humphrey Bogart's classic, "Go ahead, you'll be doing me a favor," line from Casablanca as he marches off "to drown Wagner in Holy Water." No Bogart hero is Liszt, though, for the lady does take a shot at him which misses. By implication Liszt is really touching bottom--his charismatic control of women fails him and he cannot even get himself killed.

The scene in the monastery is also the last one in the film to subscribe to any traditional form of realism. The remainder of Lisztomania is almost completely allegorical, and one suspects that it is this section of the film that has caused the greatest amount of trouble. Indeed this is surely the reason behind Gene D. Phillips' reference to Lisztomania as "in many ways a biopic."[53] This is doubly unfortunate for it is in this section of the film--wildly allegorical and completely stylized as it is--that Russell offers up the main reason for the film's existence, as well as the most clear-cut expression of his feelings on art to date. The final portions of Lisztomania are also among the finest technical achievements in Russell's filmography and are possessed of a joy of film and a joy of art in general unique to the film.

If it were not for the wide-screen, the color film stock, and the presence of Roger Daltrey, the first scene of the film's climactic section might well have come from Universal's golden age of horror films in the thirties. Liszt, complete with van Helsing-style vampire fighting kit (again the all-hero), arrives in, presumably, Bayreuth, and attempts to find the location of Wagner's castle from some Jewish peasants, who merely scream in terror and run the other way. After having this happen twice, Liszt manages to catch one by the arm and secure the information. Quite interesting is the manner in which Russell has filmed this scene. Once more he proves that he is quite capable of utilizing very restrained camerawork when the situation calls for it. Apart from some smooth but very elemental, functional tracking with Liszt there are no flamboyant tricks employed here, and the entire sequence is accomplished in one fairly lengthy take. Not surprisingly, Russell's restraint in this is no more arbitrary than his flamboyance at other times. The gliding tracking shot is reminiscent of the old horror films, and the deliberate pace and movement are clearly conceived as a breathing space prior to the Liszt-Wagner showdown.

Underlining the horror genre atmosphere and relatively stately cinematic attitude is the follow-up where Liszt attempts to gain entrance to the castle, but is refused admittance by Hans. Despite the fact that Hans has become a Wagnerite--according to the screenplay in order to be near Cosima and the children--he warns Liszt that Wagner's music is "an evil drug masquerading as a universal cure." Having been thus warned and his attempts at entry thwarted, Liszt resorts to climbing the side of the castle to a balcony. A lightning flash reveals that the top of the castle tower is in the shape of a World War II German army helmet and the wrought iron of the balcony rail is of a swastika pattern, so that once again the design of the film should clue the alert viewer on the direction of the narrative.

Once on the balcony Liszt observes a Wagnerian ritual, the visualization of the Pope'e statement of "singing the praises of an obscene religion of his own creation." The ritual, for all its fancifulness, is a fairly accurate representation of Alberich's theft of the Rhine Gold from Wagner's Das Rheingold. Choreographed to Wagner's "Magic Fire

Music," the Alberich-Rhine Gold ritual is Russell's attempt to represent Wagner's major preoccupations with sensuality and anti-Semitism. The paganistic ritual of the naked women worshiping a giant stone phallus, the head of which is the Rhine Gold, and the depiction of Alberich as the "Jewish Beast" is nothing more or less than Russell stripping away what is for him the thin veneer of Wagner's music and exposing what lies just beneath the surface. Undeniably, this is part fact and part personal opinion, but then the stylization and the subjectivity of the work as a whole should prevent any confusion on this point. Beyond that, Russell's visualization of the ritual is almost hypnotically Wagnerian in its execution--its giddy moving camera effectively capturing the heavily textured mysticism and mixture of personal horror and sexuality that is uniquely Wagner. This is not a grudging admiration for the actual genius of Wagner, but a warning. Russell's decision to present Wagner in this effective manner is much the same as his earlier evocation of the beauty of the Romantic Ideal in The Music Lovers. The point has little to do with Wagner's creativity, but the effect that creativity has on others--the manipulation of the little Superman suited Wagner-Hitler youth as they register delight over the beauty and terror over the rape of the Rhine Maidens, and even Liszt's own reflections of these same reactions as he watches from the balcony, are the real reasons behind the scene.

Also, by presenting the Wagnerian ideal in a straightforward manner it better stresses the sharp difference between even this perverted ideal and reality. Wagner is only effective prior to seeing the man himself--something that could be read as a summation of all of Russell's more critical biographical portraits. Once Wagner appears, brandishing his electric guitar-machine gun and singing of the coming of the Aryan Superman, Russell not only peels off the last vestige of the humanity of Wagner's work, but commences to make the work's creator appear foolish. Worse, the song that Wagner sings is not even of his own creation, it is the piece he stole from Liszt, and, as later dialogue makes clear, it is not simply the act of stealing the music that is important, but the perversion of the music to less than noble ends.

When Wagner finishes his ritual and dismisses the youth group and Cosima, he removes the curly blonde wig he has been wearing and changes into a leopard print zoot suit with a matching beret (of the type so beloved of the com-

The Mature Films

poser), again pointing up the large gap between the idealized Wagner and the real one. At this point Liszt makes his presence known, and after a brief moment of uneasiness on Wagner's part ("I thought it was the devil," he tells Liszt, suggesting an all too plausible familiarity within the text of the film), the final confrontation between the two begins. The attempted creation of the Wagnerian superman which follows is one of Russell's more difficult scenes in its combination of quite serious allegory and low humor. The creation is so rife with in-jokes (when Wagner drops a reference to Nietzsche's The Gay Science the feeling is that we almost might be in the midst of Woody Allen's Love and Death with its dialogue scene made up of a barrage of Dostoyevsky titles) that it becomes difficult to sort out the serious from the trivial for a time. The Siegfried creature, born of Wagner's philosophy and music (a battery of gramophones blare forth a deafening rush of messy sopranos, "Ride of the Valkyries," and a string of Jewish names), is a clumsy oaf devoid of a soul, who only manages to gulp a stein of beer (the request for which is immediately mistaken by Wagner as a predeliction for slaughtering Jews as his creature cries, "Stein!") and urinate in the fireplace, much to Liszt's delight. Wagner is not so easily dismayed as he pushes the creature back on the table with vows of streamlining "the features, modernize the clothes." Liszt is skeptical, though, because not only does Siegfried look "like a character out of a comic," but "what about his soul, Richard? What good is a leader without a soul?" Wagner is ready for this problem and was working in the belief that Liszt could supply him with the requisite soul--"That's your business, isn't it? Buying and selling souls." This idea only results in Liszt cataloging the items that Wagner has already appropriated from him: his money, his daughter, and his music, "there's not much left to steal." Wagner is not adamant at this point and bides his time by having Liszt make him an anachronistic Bloody Mary, which Liszt uses as an opportunity to slip Wagner some Holy Water. At first Wagner is horrified at having drunk this, but to a blast of the first seven notes of Liszt's first Piano Concerto, he downs the rest of the drink and smiles, exposing his vampire fangs. "And now it hasn't worked," he tells Liszt. "Have you lost faith, Franz? The Church has certainly lost faith with you." This statement, combined with the fact that the last remaining thing for Wagner to steal-- his soul--is at stake, forces Liszt to the realization which is the core of the film: "I put my faith in the wrong thing. I should've been praying to my music, not Holy Water." Wagner, however, has not lost faith in Liszt's music, "I need it to make my creation live, and if you will not give it, then I must take it," he tells Liszt while advancing on him. Liszt rises to the occasion, realizing that "your work is the creation of the devil, but my music will drive him out," and he proceeds to do just that by hammering away at his Totentanz (Dance of Death) on the piano. The effect is immediate as the piano whirls around, doors fly open, and high winds buffet Wagner about the room. Having thus reclaimed himself, Liszt finds his position a reversal of the film's opening. No longer abusing his musical ability or disregarding his real calling for a spurious one, the piano that had once been his coffin is now his ally, and it is Wagner ("The Piano as an Instrument of Revolution") who is attacked by the piano and who swings from the chandelier. The good art of Liszt is thereby able to destroy the evil art of Wagner for whom everything goes wrong as he is trapped in his own electrical machinery, a sword in his hand turns into a snake, and ultimately he is buried in the rubble of his pagan altars. The scene is breathtakingly conceived and wonderfully executed, full of Russellian invention--artfully timed flashes of lightning in the Bloody Mary portion; Wagner making his drinking glass ring with his finger just before attacking Liszt; the slickly elemental editing of Liszt hurling his case at Wagner and Wagner's unruffled catching of it; the flawlessly rhythmic bursts of flame from Liszt's piano, etc. The confrontation is not, however, the climax of Lisztomania, but only the first of two climaxes, and Russell immediately begins building the second of these.

The furor of their battle has summoned Cosima, who runs to the horribly burned and scarred Wagner, whereupon, in a masterpiece of understatement she tells him "Dearest, you look poorly." Wagner informs her that he is dying and wants to give her some final instructions. In the next scenes Russell implies that those instructions are the founding stones of Nazi Germany.

After torturing the imprisoned Liszt by sticking pins in her Franz Liszt doll, Cosima performs the funeral rites for Wagner, gravely intoning the opening words of the Rhine Maidens' song from Das Rheingold. The funeral itself is made to look like a Nazi rally, and Cosima's incantation causes lightning to strike the crypt and Wagner as a combination of himself, Adolf Hitler, and the Frankenstein monster rises from it. (Interestingly, this is echoed in the opening of Hans Jurgen Syberberg's Our Hitler: A Film from Germany, where Hitler materializes from Wagner's grave,

The Mature Films

Wagner rises from the grave as the Frankenstein Monster of his own making, Adolf Hitler, in Lisztomania. (Warner Bros.)

and there no one questions the validity of the allegory. Of course, Our Hitler has two distinct advantages over Lisztomania: no one would dare to question the seriousness of a seven-hour film, and certainly not a seven-hour film in a foreign language.) Wagner's Frankenstein monster-Hitler is still not the "Messiah" that the composer envisioned, but a perversion of even that ideal--an uncontrollable beast who turns his electric guitar-machine gun on friend and foe alike, hence the logic of the Frankenstein element. Wagner's ideology has given birth to something far worse than even he might have imagined. So warped is this creature that it is not far removed from the Jewish beast-Alberich figure, as it lumbers through a distinctly Hollywoodized ghetto, machine-gunning the stereotypical Jews (all of whom appear to be pawnbrokers) that Wagner would have expected to find there. With Cosima at his side and his youth followers (their blindness to his actions brought out by their blindfolds), the Wagner monster blithely murders one and all to the warped strains of an electronic "Ride of the Valkyries." Liszt watches the destruction from his prison through a swastika design stained-glass window. While watching Cosima paint a Star of David on the door of a Jewish dwelling, he attracts her attention, and she delivers the death blow by sticking a pin into the heart of the Liszt doll.

Bizarre and stylized as the sequence is, it is also very much to the point of the film and is defensible on both a historical and thematic level. The stereotyped Jews, for example, are not included simply to indulge Russell's penchant for Jewish humor (though anyone familiar with Mahler would know that Russell is attracted to this). Rather their inclusion is subjectively Wagner's--the Jewish race as he perceived it. The voodoo doll death of Liszt is another case in point. As previously mentioned in this chapter, the existence of this element is purely symbolic, and Liszt's death by it should not be read as a depiction of his literal death. Instead, it is simply a visualization of what Russell views as the final blow struck at Liszt by his daughter in following Wagner. In effect she has broken Liszt's heart. Viewed in this light it is entirely consistent with the film on its own terms.

There follows one of the most genuinely sweet-tempered scenes in any Russell film, where Liszt, Marie, Cosima, Carolyn, George Sand, Lola Montes, and two other women from the early part of the film play a straightforward rendition of "Liebestraum" No. 3 with Liszt on the harp and the others on various stringed instruments. The location is heaven, which in itself is another logical outgrowth of the Hollywood biopic tradition, notably the climax of The Adventures of Mark Twain where Twain's spirit goes to heaven and is met by Tom Sawyer and Huckleberry Finn no less. Russell's evocation of a dry-ice mist filled heaven is not so much a satire of that notion, but as something of an ennoblement of the idea. Unlike the earlier film, Russell's film has a purpose far beyond mere whimsy. By placing Liszt in heaven, Russell asserts that Liszt's virtues outweighed his vices in the final analysis. The presence of the women, particularly Cosima, may come as something of a shock at first, but this is consistent with Russell's growing optimism about the indomitability of the human spirit, as well as his central Catholicism, i.e. Cosima's line, "I at least had someone to pray for my soul, but he (Wagner) hasn't even got one to save, poor soul. " The overall design of the scene is likewise in keeping with the theme of transcendence. The dais on which the group is seated is simply the phallus columns from Carolyn's court painted white, which, while conceivably an economic measure, is nonetheless indicative of the characters having risen above their baser natures. The focus of the scene, being one of the major reasons why Lisztomania has little thematic relation in its overview to Dance of the Seven Veils, is the concept put forth in Marie's exchange with Carolyn, concluding with Marie's statement, "The bad is dead and buried--the best of us lives on, enshrined in his music, and that's for everyone to share ... forever. " Such a sentiment could scarcely have come from the filmmaker at the time of Dance of the Seven Veils, but it is perfectly at home with the mature Russell. The difference is all the more astounding when one realizes that only five years separate the two films.

The final sequence in Lisztomania is a reassertion and clarification of the theme expressed by the Liszt-Wagner confrontation. While in heaven Liszt muses on what Wagner is "up to now, " and a voice (presumably God) tells him, "He's already destroyed most of the world and now he's destroying Berlin. " With this in mind Liszt decides that it is time to "put him out of his misery, " because he is "giving music a bad name, " and in a sequence modeled on the Flash Gordon serial style of cardboard realism (the all-hero motif), Liszt returns to earth in a pipe organ rocket ship and blasts Wagner out of existence in a beam of tricolored light. (Wagner has by this time become a complete raging monster, machine-gunning everything in sight in an already fairly well destroyed and burning Berlin.) Liszt and his followers then return to heaven, while he sings "Peace at Last, " the final version of "Liebestraum" in the film. It is a wondrous moment where everything comes together in a near perfect blending of camera, performance, sound, and editing. "Peace at Last" is Russell's ultimate celebration of the positive aspects of creativity, an exhilarating and heartfelt paean of praise, which is obviously inspired by, but does not attempt to copy, the implicit salvation of "Listening to You" at the climax of Tommy. Although Russell's continued use of "Liebestraum" as the base for much of the music in Lisztomania might be called into question, there is an innate logic in both the choice and in the repetition. The piece appears on four occasions in the course of the film: first in the Chaplin fantasy, second in the Orpheus fantasy, third in the heaven sequence, and finally in the "Peace at Last" climax. "Liebestraum, " though not one of Liszt's greatest compositions, is certainly the most familiar, and as such is a piece of music with which the audience can readily identify. Also, it is thematically valid as an expression of Liszt's own search for this "Dream of Love." The four-time repetition of the piece is completely consistent with the Hollywood tradition on which Lisztomania is based. The various uses of it in various forms throughout the film pokes fun at the typical Hollywood biopic formula of restricting itself solely to the presentation of only the best known works of a composer, and is strikingly reminiscent of W. S. Van Dyke's film of Naughty Marietta in which "Ah, Sweet Mystery of Life" is continually fooled with in bits and pieces until reaching full-flower upon the final realization of the protagonists' love.

In the end, Lisztomania is Russell's most completely original work, which has unfortunately been denied the examination that might reveal it as the major film it is, and not the curious aberration it is frequently mistaken for. Part of the reason for the film's peculiar success on aesthetic grounds is Russell's use of old films as a basis for this one. On the surface this is not a particularly inspired notion, and it is assuredly not unique to Lisztomania in the Russell filmography, nor, for that matter, in films in general. Two distinct differences emerge immediately. Lisztomania uses preexisting films in much the same manner that Russell uses preexisting music--taking the familiar, ripping it out of its original context, giving it an entirely new application, and thereby creating something fresh, that is at once strikingly original and yet faithful to its source. Beyond this Lisztomania fuses the film building blocks into its overall structure in a way that is foreshadowed by both The Boy Friend and Mahler. To fully understand the importance of Russell's achievement on these lines, one need only look at the pieces of preexisting films that find their way into the films of Woody Allen, e.g. the completely arbitrary quotations from Potemkin in both Bananas and Love and Death. Very much to the point, Russell includes two references to Potemkin in Lisztomania, or, more correctly, in his search for a unified visual structure he uses the same quote twice--that of the unattended runaway baby carriage. (Incidentally, Allen utilizes this same quote.) In both cases, it is not a simple inserted gag, but is worked into the film and the meaning of the image owes nothing to Eisenstein's film. In the first instance it is the empty carriage which, during the concert scene, rolls off the stage and crashes onto the orchestra conductor. The scene is funny with or without a knowledge of Eisenstein's film, so that a knowledge of Potemkin only enhances the joke and is not the joke itself. The burning runaway carriage in the war sequence where Liszt sings of his guilt in the tower above the suffering gives back to Eisenstein the drama and tragedy that he originally intended, and still has as much, or more, bearing on Liszt's guilt as it applies to his shirking his responsibilities, i.e., is this the same baby in the same carriage that he earlier refused to acknowledge as his own? Ultimately, Russell has skillfully created a film with a language all its own, completely based on film, but the real achievement is that while it is, like the Allen films, very much a film for film enthusiasts, it is comprehensible to the casual filmgoer as well.

At this point Lisztomania remains Russell's most recent excursion into that area of film that is especially his, the musical biography, and in many respects it is his best. It is not as warm as Mahler, nor does it deal so extensively with the actual mystery of creation as that film had, but, as the ultimate celebration of the power of art to transcend and ennoble it is perhaps the more satisfying of the two films. That it was a resounding commercial and critical failure at the time of its release has no bearing on its importance to an assessment of Russell's career in terms of quality. Film history is littered with films that were considered disasters at the time of their release, and are now undisputed classics. Two prime examples, Leo McCarey's Duck Soup and Josef von Sternberg's The Scarlet Empress--both originally dismissed as too crazy, too nonsensical, and too outrageous-- are particularly relevant to Lisztomania, which contains elements of both. To use Mahler's words of consolation to Hugo Wolf in Mahler, "Some day our time will come," so too might the time for Russell's misunderstood masterpiece.

NOTES

1. Martner, Knud, ed. Selected Letters of Gustav Mahler. New York: Farrar, Straus & Giroux, 1979, p. 172.
2. Farber, Stephen. "Russellmania," Film Comment, 11 (Nov.-Dec. 1975): 40-47.
3. Barnes, Richard, and Townshend, Pete. The Story of Tommy. Middlesex, England: Eel Pie, 1977, p. 97.
4. Hauptfurher, Fred. "Wild and Wooly Ken Russell Finds the Golden Fleece Directing Altered States," People, Vol. 15, No. 12 (March 30, 1981), p. 69.
5. Gomez, Joseph. Ken Russell: The Adaptor as Creator.

London: Frederick Muller, 1976, p. 183.
6. Personal Correspondence with Ken Russell, November 1982.
7. Sterritt, David. "Whole Film Is 'One Flash' in His Mind," Christian Science Monitor, (June 2, 1975): 27.
8. Phillips, Gene D. Ken Russell. Boston: Twayne, 1979, p. 124.
9. Gartenberg, Egon. Mahler: The Man and His Music. New York: Schirmer Books, 1978, p. 281.
10. Simon, John. Review of Mahler. Esquire, 83 (April 1975): 58.
11. Gomez, Joseph. Ken Russell: The Adaptor as Creator, p. 191.
12. Gow, Gordon. "Shock Treatment," Films and Filming, (July 1970): 10.
13. Kalbeck, Max. Cited in Gartenberg, Egon. Mahler: The Man and His Music, p. 290.
14. Simon, John. Review of Mahler. Esquire, 83 (April 1975): 58.
15. Alpert, Hollis. "The Murder of Mahler," Saturday Review, 2 (February 8, 1975): 39.
16. Cited in Gomez, Joseph. Ken Russell: The Adaptor as Creator, pp. 190-191.
17. Gomez, Joseph. Ken Russell: The Adaptor as Creator, p. 191.
18. Gartenberg, Egon. Mahler: The Man and His Music, p. 180.
19. Gomez, Joseph. Ken Russell: The Adaptor as Creator, p. 190.
20. Farber, Stephen. "Russellmania," pp. 40-47.
21. Ibid.
22. Phillips, Gene D. Ken Russell, p. 128.
23. Barnes, Richard, and Townshend, Peter. The Story of Tommy, p. 93.
24. Phillips, Gene D. Ken Russell, p. 151.
25. Cited in New York Magazine, "Intelligencer," (June 21, 1982), p. 10.
26. Ibid.
27. Personal Correspondence with Ken Russell, November 1982.
28. Sterritt, David. "Whole Film Is 'One Flash' in His Mind," p. 27.
29. Personal Correspondence with Ken Russell, November 1982.
30. Russell, Ken. Tommy (unpublished screenplay, dated July 18, 1973), p. 12.
31. Barnes, Richard, and Townshend, Pete. The Story

of Tommy, p. 12.
32. Russell, Ken. Tommy screenplay, p. 41.
33. Barnes, Richard, and Townshend, Pete. The Story of Tommy, p. 37.
34. Ibid., p. 118.
35. Farber, Stephen. "Russellmania," pp. 46-47.
36. Russell, Ken. Tommy screenplay, p. 62.
37. Ibid., p. 63.
38. Sterritt, David. "Whole Film Is 'One Flash' in His Mind," p. 27.
39. Gomez, Joseph. Ken Russell: The Adaptor as Creator, p. 98.
40. Phillips, Gene D. Ken Russell, pp. 167-169.
41. Farber, Stephen. "Russellmania," pp. 46-47.
42. Cited in Phillips, Gene D. Ken Russell, p. 176.
43. Mordden, Ethan. A Guide to Orchestral Music. New York: Oxford University Press, 1980, p. 183.
44. Sitwell, Sacheverell. Liszt. New York: Dover, 1967, p. 191.
45. "Lisztomania" Photo Preview. Playboy, 22 (October 1975): 88.
46. Cited in Baxter, John. "The Television Films: Poet's London to Dance of the Seven Veils," Ken Russell, edited by Thomas R. Atkins. New York: Simon and Schuster, 1976, p. 35.
47. Farber, Stephen. "Russellmania," pp. 40-47.
48. Jacob, Heinrich Eduard. Felix Mendelssohn and His Times. Englewood Cliffs, N.J.: Prentice-Hall, 1963, pp. 203-204.
49. Gartenberg, Egon. Mahler: The Man and His Music, p. 166.
50. Gutman, Robert W. Richard Wagner: The Man, His Mind, and His Music. New York and London: Harcourt Brace Jovanovich, 1968, p. 454.
51. Sitwell, Sacheverell. Liszt, p. 199.
52. Chancellor, John. Wagner. Boston: Little, Brown, 1978, pp. 127-128.
53. Cited in Phillips, Gene D. Ken Russell, p. 176.

CHAPTER 9

TOWARD A NEW HORIZON

"Valentino"

Much admired by Gene D. Phillips and boasting a screenplay which Russell himself has termed the best he has ever worked from,[1] Valentino is a film that just refuses to attract many admirers. It is the least revived of all Russell works and the least discussed. Any number of reasons can be brought into play as to just why Valentino is unpopular. Trouble with Rudolf Nureyev is the most commonly cited defect, and even though it is undeniable that his lack of trust in Ken Russell compromised and badly mars the film, it is not the sole reason for the film's difficulties. Many of Valentino's problems are traceable to Russell himself.

To a certain extent all of Russell's mature works contain large bits of the filmmaker himself. In a sense they are autobiographical, if only due to the subjective nature of his approach to the subject at hand. Part of any Russell film entails his reaction to a given character or situation. Valentino is no different in this respect, but it goes beyond that reaction and strays for the first time into that realm of self-indulgence of which his detractors have been incorrectly accusing him for years. In no earlier work--including the almost overtly autobiographical Mahler--is there a strong feeling that Russell has grafted himself onto the story, but in Valentino there is the uncomfortable impression that Russell is doing just that. The film was made during a particularly troublesome time in Russell's life and seems to reflect those troubles in a manner that undermines the film in general and Russell's sense of humanity in particular.

Russell has always delighted in peopling his films with outrageous and not very admirable characters. This is especially true of his subordinate women characters, dating back to Hermione Roddice in Women in Love, who is herself

derived to some extent from Russell's Isadora Duncan. In
Valentino Russell presents Alla Nazimova as his latest incarnation of Hermione, but with a sinister difference--there
is little or nothing lovable about her outrageousness. In
Lisztomania when the Isadora-Hermione character in the shape
of Princess Carolyn plans to take revenge on the Pope by
writing a book entitled The Interior Causes of the Exterior
Weaknesses of the Church "in twenty-four volumes," there is
a lovable screwiness about the woman, brought out, not in
the least, by the ultimately ineffectual nature of her gesture.
Not so with Nazimova, who is portrayed with a viciousness
equal to her outrageousness. It is a markedly funny characterization, especially as handled by Leslie Caron, but undeniable though its humor is, the final result is more cruel
than amusing.

Russell's handling of the other women in the film is
no less vitriolic. There is some justification for his treatment of Natasha Rambova, but the characterization fails to
satisfy, in part through the ineptitude of Michelle Phillips in
the role, and largely because of the almost total lack of humanity with which she is presented. Rambova is not even
granted the token humor with which Nazimova has been tempered and emerges as a silly, pretentious, destructive,
grasping woman.

The minor characters fare no better. Starlet Jean
Acker (the first Mrs. Valentino) fails to register as anything
other than a rather cliched type. Valentino's first love,
Bianca de Saulles, is not fully developed, but emerges more
hysterical than sympathetic. Dance hall proprietress Billie
Streeter (played with a marvelous biting edge by Linda Thorson) is deceitful, manipulative and downright ill-tempered.
Valentino's legion of fans are personified in one girl named
Marsha, who comes off as something of a rehash of Tommy's
Sally Simpson, minus the depth and insight, so that she becomes a thoughtless, foolish groupie. Movie actress Lorna
Sinclair is shown as an empty-headed woman with sexual
fantasies that defy belief. None of these things would seem
out of place or irrational on Russell's part by themselves,
but when they are all combined in one film they stretch the
credulity of his judgment. There is no denying that he makes
his point through them--that Valentino was manipulated throughout his life by unscrupulous women, but the profusion and
repetition of the incidents undermine the message.

Few of the characters in Valentino display much of the

humanity one has come to expect of Russell. Screenwriter June Mathis, Valentino's manager George Ullman, and director George Melford are the most honestly human of Russell's creations, and they are scarcely sufficient to offset the mean-spirited quality of the rest of the film's rather large cast.

Exempt purposefully from this list of Russell characters is Valentino himself. Gene D. Phillips considers Valentino to best embody those attributes which Russell considers heroic and honorable.[2] This is true as far as it goes, but it fails to take the full picture into account. Valentino, as presented in the film, is simply too good to be true. Essentially he is possessed of the plastic purity which had so bothered Stephen Farber about Tommy.[3] The concept of Valentino as a saintly being poses two distinct problems beyond the factor of believability, and Russell is never quite able to surmount these difficulties. The less grave of the two problems is the possibility of Valentino's simplicity coming across as simplemindedness. On more than one occasion the feeling is that our hero is very nearly stupid. This, however, is far less damaging to the film as a whole than is the loss of the usual Russellian tension culled from the themes of sin, guilt, and redemption. Valentino is so blameless in the course of the film that there is no room for the development of these key themes.

It is undeniable that Gene D. Phillips is correct in his assertion that Valentino presents a kind of ultimate Russell hero. In this respect Valentino fits into the overall pattern of Russell's work--continuously progressing toward that more positive outlook. Valentino's innate resistance to anything that departs from his own beliefs makes him Russell's most positive creation to date, but it also makes him the least believable, interesting, and well-rounded.

As a film apart, Valentino also suffers from being a transitional work. Certainly for anyone dazzled by the cinematic fireworks of the three films that directly precede it, Valentino must come as something of a disappointment. Comparatively speaking, it is pretty tame stuff. This feeling is reinforced by the very subject of the film. Regardless of his qualities as human being the question of Valentino cannot help but appear considerably less significant than that of Tchaikovsky or Mahler or Gaudier-Brzeska or Franz Liszt or even Tommy Walker. The real shock, however, is less the significance of the subject matter and more the sharp change to a more straightforward presentation. It is not that Russell eschews experiment in Valentino. Rather, it is the subtlety of that experimentation in comparison with the more overt experiments in Mahler, Tommy, and Lisztomania. The full measure of Valentino's importance could not be fully assessed till one knew where this transitional film was leading. Now that Altered States has brilliantly supplied that information, Valentino needs a second look.

Valentino is a move toward a quieter, and possibly more mature, style of filmmaking. All things considered Russell had taken stylization and symbolism just about as far as they could go in Lisztomania. Not to have moved onward in another direction would have likely been just as deadly from an artistic standpoint as having settled into the rut of grinding out handsome editions of literary classics such as he might have done following the success of Women in Love. Without question Lisztomania is the more vital of the two films, but Valentino the more finely crafted. Symbolism and stylization are still present, but they are less overt. One could not really say that the stylization in Lisztomania was well integrated. Lisztomania was stylization. Valentino definitely not. The elements of stylization and symbolism are so well integrated into its basically realistic structure that they are all but invisible. It is perhaps Russell's single greatest achievement in Valentino, allowable largely because of the subject matter.

Valentino is a Russell film almost entirely devoid of fantasy sequences--a factor that comes as a double surprise considering its three immediate predecessors. Publicity stills indicate that fantasy sequences were indeed shot, but later eliminated. The only surviving fantasy sequence is a rather brief one in which June Mathis fantasizes Valentino as the Sheik whisking her away on his white horse in the desert. At least one of the aborted sequences appears to have been in a similar vein. The decision to dispense with such sequences was shrewdly conceived. Valentino does not need them because it has a built-in manner of making the same point. Where Russell would normally have utilized fantasy to comment on the actions and emotions on the screen, he is here at liberty to counterpoint these things by inserting large chunks of reconstructed footage from Valentino films. In this manner he is able to continually comment not only on the actions themselves, but to make his observations on a favorite theme: the curse of life imitating art instead of the other way around. The very nature of Valentino makes this possible in a manner that no previous work has afforded.

Comparatively sedate as it is, Valentino by no means refutes the fascination with using preexisting motion pictures as a base. It is not so diverse as Lisztomania, but the strong sense of film history and a love of films is there nonetheless. In this instance Russell has foregone the wildly scattered quotations that had proliferated in the previous film and settled on one film as a role model--Orson Welles' Citizen Kane. Russell has long been an admirer of the Welles film and frequently refers to it as a prime influence on his approach to filmmaking. In terms of style and structure, Valentino is Russell's homage to Citizen Kane, much as Lisztomania had been to films in general.

Similarities abound throughout the film. Its very structure resembles the structure of Citizen Kane--a series of flashbacks told from varying points of view about the life of one man as known by many. Russell even wittily includes a symbol of innocence, readily interchangeable with Kane's "Rosebud," in the orange, which like the snowball in Citizen Kane rolls out of the main character's reach at his death. Even the portraits of the two men, Kane and Valentino, are not dissimilar. Both are men searching for happiness and innocence. Both are willing to lose everything to satisfy their own principles and codes of honor. Thematically, of course, they are poles apart, since Kane's interests and principles become warped and distorted during his lifetime, whereas Valentino holds true to his beliefs throughout. This point of departure between the two men is not a flaw in Russell's logic. Using Citizen Kane as a base and then deliberately veering from its theme in this manner only serves to reinforce the admiration for those attributes in Valentino which Russell values.

As often seems to be the case it is necessary to look back to Russell's TV film Isadora in order to fully appreciate the influence of Citizen Kane on Russell's work in general, and why it is so apt that he should eventually make a homage to it. In Isadora, primitive though many of its aspects are, Russell begins quoting directly from other films in order to make his point. The first film from which he chooses to quote is Citizen Kane, which is neatly reflected in the breathless newsreel encapsulation of Isadora's life that opens the film. Russell has joked that this sequence is stolen from Welles' film,[4] but quoting and stealing are two entirely different things, and Russell's quotations are so open and apparent that the idea of stealing from someone else never enters into it. Taken in conjunction with Valentino, Isadora looks like a dry run for the later work. Both are the offspring of Citizen Kane. The primary difference being that where Isadora is influenced by Kane, Valentino salutes it. Russell as an artist is here paying his debt to his mentor. In this respect Valentino can be seen as a mature work that had to be made, the seeds of which were planted long ago.

Technically, Valentino is a marvel, a complete tour de force of filmmaking. Other Russell films may have greater elegance of imagery. The Music Lovers is almost suffocatingly beautiful, but its beauty is less photographic than painterly. Both Savage Messiah and Mahler are extraordinarily handsome productions as well, but Valentino has a truly great photographic beauty that is often strikingly reminiscent of the best work of the great still photographers of the era in which it takes place. One image in particular of Valentino cooking in his New York tenement apartment looks as if it might have stepped out of a book of beautiful period photographs. The image, however, is not arbitrary. It fits in with the rest of the film and works because Valentino has been designed in this style. Russell and designer Phillip Harrison have created a warm-toned film. Whereas Savage Messiah is a film leaning heavily on stone greys and whites and primary colors as befits its subject, and Mahler relies on a very natural palette in its pastoral approach, Valentino is a film of deep, rich colors with gold, black, red and dark wood tones pervading the film. Unlike many attempts at warn-toned films, Russell's film does not sacrifice the full tonal range of color in order to achieve his effect. The warm colors are not imposed on the film, but are inherent in the design so that the cool and bright shades do not suffer. Valentino has the look of the old three-strip Technicolor process, with its unbelievable saturation of colors. Cinematographer Peter Suschitsky had wanted to indulge in some soft-focus, pseudo-period-piece photography, but Russell was insistent on achieving a boldness of image,[5] and the final product certainly justifies his decision. Not only would such photography have detracted from the deep-focus style of the film's model, but it would have been at odds with most true period photography, which is usually pin sharp.

Russell starts his film with a bravura sequence, intermingling newsreel shots of Valentino's funeral with amazingly accurate reconstructed footage made in the studio. Fittingly the film is printed in sepia tone as a foretelling of the warmness to come. The final shot in this sequence--of Valentino in the coffin--produces the film's first truly startling effect as the image fades from sepia to full color. (There is a barely perceptible change from the last of the sepia footage to this shot of Valentino in the coffin, which indicates that it was done with careful lighting.) At only one point in the opening sequence does Russell's logic falter. Much as Gene Phillips has pointed out about the incorrect inclusion of June Mathis' fantasy in the sequence being told by Natasha Rambova, here the audience is presented with a front page newsphoto of Valentino and Rambova in a personal moment from the later tent sequence. If Russell's point here was to draw attention to Valentino's lack of a truly private existence then the inclusion is possibly justfiable. All the same one can't help but wonder, who was hiding in the tent with a camera?

The idea of using a flashback technique is not new or original, of course. Russell has often used it himself. Indeed Mahler, like Valentino, is structured as a series of flashbacks along a framing story. (Mahler, however, is quite the more adventurous of the films in its mingling of memory and fantasy.) Russell's model, Citizen Kane, also relies on the device and it wasn't new then. Aside from this there is a very valid reason for the structure of Valentino. Russell wants the audience to feel the waste of Valentino's death, but he does not want to turn it into grand tragedy as in The Devils. By structuring the film around Valentino's funeral he neatly avoids this, and it is a contributing factor in the film's overall positive outlook on its hero. Tragedy was a necessary element in The Devils, since Grandier's death was part of his redemption, but Valentino's death has no bearing on his qualities as a human being. His transcendence of weaknesses were part of his life, and tragedy would be out of place.

Unfortunately, Valentino not only repeats the structure of Citizen Kane, but the weakness of Welles' film as well. The problem being that, owing to the very nature of the concept, some of the remembrances are better than others. Russell does avoid the one major pitfall in which Welles descended--repetitive action. Doubtless the one sequence which Welles covered from two points of view was, in his mind, worthy of the repetition, but all the same it is the only truly slow portion of the film. In order to fully appreciate Russell's method of construction it is necessary to consider the individual sequences and the framing story in some depth.

Actually Russell's framing story is something of an

improvement over the one in Citizen Kane. At least Russell's framing story contributes something more to the film than a mere skeleton. This is not to say that Valentino is superior to Citizen Kane. Its flawed attitude precludes any such possibility in the first place, and it is rather unfair to compare the films in that Valentino has the entire body of Russell films to back it up, whereas Citizen Kane was Welles' first feature.

The opening sequence of Valentino works in part because it is an extension of ideas Russell has already put forth in Tommy and Lisztomania: the psychology of the mob. In this case the mob is at a funeral, but they behave no differently from the crowds in the other films. Russell has developed an almost Fritz Lang attitude and fascination with the collective mentality brought on by being part of a mob. Basically a mob is a mob, and the behavior of a mob is not radically different from emotional situation to emotional situation. Nowhere is this more clearly expressed than in Valentino. In fact here it is strengthened as it is treated by Jesse Lasky, Joseph Schenck, and, in particular, Richard Rowland as if the funeral of Valentino were some sort of grotesque premiere. Rowland can even be seen handing out free passes to the crowd as he makes his way to the funeral parlor. The established mood is pure Russell in its ability to imbue a comprehensible pattern of events into a scene that on the surface appears to be chaotic and frenzied.

Russell has been criticized for his portraits of the studio heads, and the criticism seems to rest largely on the opening scene which is unfortunate. Although it is true that of the three men only Joseph Schenck emerges as anything near a likable character, the ultimate characterizations of all three men are considerably more complex than this first scene might suggest. Particularly notable for a complete characterization is Jesse Lasky, played with tremendous vitality by veteran East Side Kid-Bowery Boy, Huntz Hall. Lasky is portrayed as greedy, vicious, and opportunistic, yet at the same time he is possessed of some not inconsiderable qualities. He, like Valentino, is true to an ideal up to a point, however disreputable that ideal may be. He is also possessed of an innate intelligence, knowing when to hold out and when to give in. Most significant of all, however, is the fact that he is openly contemptuous of Rambova's pretensions, offering her a job as a slave girl and consistently referring to her by her real name, Miss Hudnut. Basically Lasky is a well-rounded character, streets removed from the cardboard villain some critics have judged him to be. Certainly Russell treats him with more dignity and respect than he has treated others in similar positions, notably Shaw, the art dealer, in Savage Messiah.

Following the chaos of the first scene, where the crowd surges into the funeral parlor, order is more or less restored as coffin lids are nailed into place where the windows and glass doors have been broken. The mortuary has been turned into a circus, much like the church in The Devils, and the funeral into a mockery. Victims of minor mishaps and injuries are being treated on the spot and the press is having a field day. Out of this whirl of activity Russell moves in on the first of his flashback presentations, as one especially obnoxious reporter chances upon Bianca de Saulles, the first woman in Valentino's life. In order to retain her anonymity with the crowd she relates her story to the reporter.

It should perhaps be noted that Russell's reporters, against whom much has been written, are scarcely supposed to represent the genuine article. The reporters in Valentino bear no relation to reporters past or present. Instead, they might have stepped out of the Ben Hecht-Charles MacArthur world of The Front Page and must be viewed as such. Strict realism is hardly Russell's forte and there is no indication that it even very much interests him. Therefore, it is scarcely credible that the reporters in the film are meant to stand as an indictment against American journalism.

A flash from the reporter's camera plunges the viewer back in time for the first flashback (a transitional device not unlike the flash in Lisztomania, but with one difference-- here flashes abound throughout the film as a kind of visual punctuation mark). The audience is presented with the spectacle of Valentino dancing with another man, Vaslav Nijinsky. Based on the legend that Valentino taught Nijinsky to tango, Russell has carefully placed this scene early in the proceedings to establish the ambivalent attitude that the film takes as regards Valentino's sexuality. Rudolf Nureyev has put forth the view that Valentino was not homosexual, but almost asexual.[6] Whether or not there is any merit in this point of view, it is not born out by the film, which strongly suggests at least a latent homosexuality. Taking Russell's portrait of Tchaikovsky in The Music Lovers into account serves to strengthen this view. There is more than a slight thematic link between Tchaikovsky's marriage, designed to quell rumors about his sexual habits, and Valentino's tests of manhood. The operative difference between the two being that Tchaikovsky's marriage was destructive to others, where Valentino's boxing and drinking bouts are dangerous only to himself.

It is virtually impossible to fault this first flashback in terms of construction or technique, but it is not entirely in keeping with the bulk of the film. Russell gives the viewer a far more clever and resourceful hero in this scene than in any subsequent one. Unlike the honeymoon sequence in The Music Lovers where such a scene serves to make Tchaikovsky less pathetic and more sympathetic, Russell has here started his character as a man of some wit, only to increase his naivete as the film progresses. In the earlier film Tchaikovsky frequently seemed slow-witted and so self-pitying that the viewer was hard-pressed to sympathize with him, but then during the honeymoon he is humanized by his amusement at Nina's simplicity and by his outmaneuvering Count Chiluvsky's attempt to follow after the couple. This injection worked in The Music Lovers because Tchaikovsky's naive nature had already been established and explored by the time of this interpolation. It does not work nearly so well in Valentino because it is used to establish the character rather than enlarge upon him. As a facet of Valentino it would have been more than believable, it would have actually been welcome. Its placement so early in the film, though, promises a character who later fails to materialize.

This first sequence, although hardly extraneous, contributes little to the overall thematic structure of the film. Russell's development is a little too leisurely, as it is not until the following flashback that the viewer is really informed what the film is all about. True, Russell has established more subordinate notions about the point of the film, but his major interest in the film--or so it would seem from the amount of time given over to it--is Valentino's sufferings at the hands of manipulative people, especially women. Bianca de Saulles hardly falls into this category despite her hysteria. (To some extent Billie Streeter does fall into this group, but she is too much a supporting character to be considered much more than an incipient Nazimova.) In terms of theme the framing story has thus far been much more explicit. Perhaps Russell is trying in some way to link all the manipulation to Hollywood. There is some justification in this idea as Hollywood has indeed produced some pretty curious types and notions, though it seems unlikely that they have cornered the market on manipulation, even if that seems to be Hollywood's major stock in trade.

The second flashback narrative (by June Mathis) has all the technical panache of the first, as well as presenting Valentino somewhat in the less simple manner established by this preceding episode. It is superior to the first in that it does begin to shape the direction of the film via Valentino's partner's statement, "if you ever have anything worth taking, some bright bitch is gonna give you the ride of your life."

Here, too, Russell creates an atmosphere worthy of Josef von Sternberg. The draped light bulbs of Baron Long's beer garden, the stuffed bear, the tacky dressing room, the bead curtains, all contribute to the textural richness of the scene in a manner strikingly reminiscent of von Sternberg. Of course it is quite one thing to recreate the trappings of a Sternberg film, and something else again to achieve the charged atmosphere that marked his best work. Russell, fortunately, is equal to the occasion, not only evoking von Sternberg, but doing so in such a way that the scene integrates into the fabric of the entire film. Nothing else in Valentino has the same look and feel of this one sequence, and yet the sequence is not an appendage in any way. In fact it works better as a part of the film than the preceding scene or the much later jail scene, both of which are outwardly more at one with the film. The sequence works because Russell wisely never apes von Sternberg. Just as he never attempted to direct in another director's style in Lisztomania, he does not try to be von Sternberg here. It is always Russell directing a von Sternbergian scene as Russell, making the sequence first-rate Russell rather than imitation von Sternberg.

If any one aspect of the Mathis flashback jars, it is the question of Valentino's character. Once again Valentino is shown to be more in command of the situation than he will be in subsequent flashbacks. Here, however, Russell has some justification for this presentation, as it helps establish the same sort of attitude that will generate the boxing match. (It might be arguable that this is similarly foreshadowed by the events in the first flashback, but there Valentino is only really roused to action after he is fired.) Valentino throwing over his job because he is angered by the obnoxious Mr. Fatty is in the same mold as Valentino angered by the newspaper slur on his manhood. There is a certain unity also with Valentino's later self-imposed exile from the film world, but with a notable difference. The attack on Mr. Fatty and the boxing match are relatively noble and justifiable actions because they spring from Valentino's own desires and beliefs. His exile from filmmaking, however, is less sympathetic because the audience is never given any indication that Valentino himself even has an opinion on the quality of the films he is making, much less that under his own volition he would quit Hollywood rather than appear in inferior artistic works. The exile is the idea of Natasha Rambova and as such is not able to be viewed in the same light.

Following this sequence Russell embarks on the most outrageous and satirical section of the film. Starting from the moment when June Mathis repeats her line from the flashback, "Every day is Hallowe'en in Tinsel Town," Russell launches into the flamboyant Nazimova sequence. As if in response to Miss Mathis' line, Nazimova makes her grand entrance into the mortuary, wearing a huge cape made of camellias (as a reference to her role with Valentino in Camille) that is being carried after her by a procession of purple-veiled women. Her hair is arranged in the Aubrey Beardsley style of her Salome film, and she strides in perfect synchronization to Dies Irae played mockingly on the soundtrack. She carefully arranges the cape on Valentino's coffin (sending Mussolini's wreath crashing to the floor in the process) and immediately proceeds to pretend that she does not know where the body is. When its presence is pointed out Nazimova promptly faints, and then obligingly faints a second time for the photographers before launching into her part of the narrative.

Her story mostly concerns interrupting the shooting of Rex Ingram's The Four Horsemen of the Apocalypse in order to get a look at Valentino. Russell has so far drawn a vivid picture of her theatricality and fraudulence. In the flashback he carries her pretension further and lays the groundwork for her viciousness and complete lack of either loyalty or consistency. Upon first arriving on the set she rhapsodizes over Ingram's film, "What daring! What symbolism!" (Sentiments, the pretentiousness of which are roundly squashed by Rambova's, "What an awful lot of horse shit," which may or may not reflect a literal condition.) Once she believes, quite wrongly, that Ingram has played a trick on her, this attitude abruptly changes to one of derision. This may be a small point, but one that conveys the impression that the woman is, if not dangerous, then at least untrustworthy. Here, too, Russell introduces the character of

Russell recreates Valentino's electrifying tango from The Four Horsemen of the Apocalypse, originally directed by Rex Ingram, who, appropriately enough, is played by Russell in Valentino. (United Artists)

Toward a New Horizon

Rambova with one subtle line. Upon seeing Valentino her first comment is, "We'll have to do something about those awful eyebrows, " a statement that bodes ill for Valentino.

The scene is notable, aside from its humor and shrewd character development (significantly, since Nazimova is telling the story, Valentino enters into the situation almost not at all, and Russell is content to let his character lie for the moment), as the only time where Russell has taken over an active speaking part in a film by playing director Rex Ingram. It is a nice touch, and one that owes its existence to pure chance. Russell merely replaced the actor engaged to play the part when said actor showed up in a state of advanced inebriation. 7 Whatever the reason it is an adept little characterization on Russell's part and one that adds a personalized feel to the scene.

Russell's use of Dies Irae on the soundtrack during the framing section leading to Nazimova's flashback is one of two particularly well conceived uses of music in Valentino. Despite Russell's claims as to the importance of the music in the film, 8 Valentino simply does not present Russell's sense of combining music at its best. However, in these two instances Russell's approach to the music is masterful. Despite the addition of an orchestra in both cases, the music grows out of the perpetually droning mortuary organ. The viewer is so used to this incessant and generally nondescript music that the full force of the Dies Irae comes as rather a sharp blow, whereas the later use of Wagner's "Wedding March" neatly caps the satire of the moment. The "Wedding March, " though less spectacular, works better since Russell has the mournful music slowly turn into the lead-in to the march itself in so deft a manner that it is only after the march begins that the audience realizes what they have been hearing. The boldness of Russell's musical usage here is reminiscent of Edgar G. Ulmer's use of Schubert's "Unfinished" Symphony in The Black Cat, where a scene is constructed and choreographed to music not a part of the soundtrack, but coming from an explained source (in Ulmer's case a radio; in Russell's, the mortuary organ).

It is the next flashback that comprises the single longest portion of the film, and it is here that Valentino starts to lose ground. The story told from Rambova's point of view is just too long, though it might be argued that it corresponds to the length of the doubled opera sequence in Citizen Kane. It is also the sequence in which Russell starts altering the character of Valentino in the manner that refuses to fit his character in the earlier flashbacks. Part of the problem here is undoubtedly Michelle Phillips, who makes a striking Rambova, but is just not up to the part dramatically. Even considering the trouble with Nureyev, her performance is more damaging to the film in its final form than is his. To say that Michelle Phillips is a bad actress is unfair as this is not the problem with her Rambova. She simply does not belong in Valentino. Every other cast member from Nureyev and Caron on down are working in a particularly stylized manner while Miss Phillips insists on attempting a naturalistic performance. It does not fit in with the other players and does an injustice to Russell's floridly theatrical dialogue.

The sequence does contain a number of memorable moments, some of which are truly outstanding, but like the film itself, is better in parts than as a whole. One episode within this lengthy sequence which falls considerably short of the mark is the famous, or infamous, jail scene. It is an obvious and ill-advised attempt to recreate the intensity of

Rambova fastens a slave bracelet on Valentino on the wedding night, interrupted by a charge of bigamy against the groom in Valentino. (United Artists)

the railway carriage scene in The Music Lovers. It looks just that: obvious and ill-advised. At this point in the film the viewer is accustomed to the style of the film, and the jail sequence is at odds with that style and with the progression of the film. It looks, feels, and plays like the appendage it is. The scene comes across almost as if someone looked at the script and decided that the film needed a really intense sequence of the sort for which Ken Russell is famous. Stunning as individual aspects of the film are--notably the crosscutting to June Mathis watching the screen Valentino die in Blood and Sand while the real Valentino suffers a different kind of death in jail--the scene is largely superfluous.

On the other end of the scale the Rambova flashback includes the excellent "Sheik of Araby" scene wherein Valentino, Rambova, and Nazimova work on a photographic storyboard for Nazimova's proposed "history of the dance" film. As jaunty and sprightly as this scene appears on the surface, it is worth five jail scenes because Russell is so clearly attuned to its stylization. The scene also carries the film's characterization and plot forward in an economical and effective manner. In this brief space of screen time Russell conveys the full force of Valentino's ability to be manipulated; the inherent problem of pairing two people, Rambova and Nazimova, who both need to be in charge; along with a large chunk of the plot. An interesting point of comparison is the outcome of this scene--where Nazimova, jealous of her "protégé's" attentions to Valentino, sells the photographs "to the press as pornography"--with Chiluvsky's informing Madame von Meck of Tchaikovsky's homosexuality in The Music Lovers. In so doing it becomes clear why Valentino ultimately fails an an entire work. The situations are almost identical, but in the earlier film Chiluvsky's actions carried an undercurrent of sympathy, which is missing here.

Similarly admirable are the studio scenes where John Justin turns in a splendid bit as a frenzied Sidney Olcott trying against all odds to direct a scene with Rambova personally supervising Valentino's performance. It is a funny scene, beautifully realized, and yet one of the major instances where the overall feeling is that Russell is straying into an area that is perhaps too reflective of Russell's own troubles. The scene is briefly of interest also as the major instance in this portion of the film where something of the initially developed innate intelligence of the Valentino character resurfaces. Following his bizarre sexual encounter with his leading lady-- her approach to sex looking like nothing so much as Eddie

Cantor on the mechanical weight-reducing horse in A. Edward Sutherland's Palmy Days--and not under the eye of Rambova, Valentino actually makes a decision for himself. It comes across as a far more exhilarating moment than it really is, since it comes as an oasis by this point in the film. Unfortunately, it is too brief and too late to help solve the problem of Valentino's character.

Best of all, however, is Valentino's truly white-hot scene. Far superior to the jail scene because it is properly part of the film is the scene where Rambova conducts a séance to find out whether she and Valentino should "remain together" while hundreds of girls chant from Valentino's book of poetry on the lawn. Starting eerily and slowly the scene builds to a fever pitch as Valentino all but rapes Rambova on the dining room table (comparable in many ways to the scene where Nina turns on Tchaikovsky in The Music Lovers). The scene brilliantly captures a number of major points in the film, accurately registering Valentino's desperation, Rambova's hysterical obsession for control, and the mindless adulation of the legion of fans that Valentino neither comprehends nor desires. It is an altogether terrifying and succinct picture of a man trapped and embalmed in his myth as neatly conveyed by Russell's camera panning from the pair on the table to a statuette of Valentino as the Sheik on camelback.

The Rambova flashback ends with the séance and as such helps redeem itself. The return to the framing story where Nazimova re-ingratiates herself to Rambova, and the pair leave the funeral chapel to the "Wedding March" sums up Russell's attitude toward the two women. His contempt is understandable, especially in consideration of the manner in which he has presented them. Their exit from the film is complete. It is the last time either character appears in the film, and in terms of balancing things out this is of some help. The final flashback, told as a kind of joint memory by June Mathis and George Ullman, strains valiantly to counteract the problems of the Rambova flashback. Alas, the Rambova sequence is just too great an obstacle and the Mathis-Ullman sequence is engaged in a losing battle.

The flashback begins with what might have been a simple dialogue scene between Valentino and Ullman as they emerge from a movie house just having seen Rambova's film What Price Beauty? As the scene is handled by Russell it is something else again, splendidly evoking the feel of an old movie. The back alley in which their conversation takes place

Toward a New Horizon

Valentino and Rambova toast their decision to accept their new manager's offer of a lucrative dance contract promoting a line of cosmetics in Valentino. (United Artists)

looking like nothing so much as a beautifully lit studio set, makes the scene have a slightly unreal quality, quite in keeping with Russell's vision. Split into two parts (the middle section entailing the trip to the speakeasy and Valentino's discovery of the "pink powder puff" newspaper slur) the scene manages to convey a tired mood of resignation. This mood fits the transitional nature of the scene, and the only false note in the proceedings is that Nureyev's accent fails him at one point. His delivery of the line "Ridiculous? I'll tell you what is ridiculous..." sounds much less like Valentino and much more like Bela Lugosi.

The scenes in the alley, speakeasy, and later the press conference are little more than preludes to the film's major set piece, the boxing match. Like many Russell set pieces, the match is firmly grounded in reality, but not limited to realism. As presented in Valentino the boxing match never occurred (a private affair with a rather similar outcome, however, did), but it is nonetheless true to the character and the film more than any dry reading of historical fact could be. The change from a private boxing match to a public spectacle merely serves to reinforce the importance of the event in Valentino's eyes and to increase the dramatic validity of its inclusion as the last "big" scene in Russell's film.

The match itself is a gem of filmmaking, reflecting Russell's penchant for combining truth with legend and achieving a subjective truth. The mere fact that Russell has amplified the boxing match in the manner it appears on the screen attests to this, as do the faithful and steady trotting out of every screen boxing cliché imaginable and the character of Joseph Schenck. As concerns Russell's use of the cliché as a powerful filmmaking tool, the match is a prime example. By structuring the fight in a familiar, though not conventional, way Russell's comments--Valentino accidentally slugging one of his opponent's cheerleaders ("The great lover hit me!"); the couples dancing around the ring, switching to a very grave tango at one point; the crowd tossing pink powder puffs into the ring; the typically Russellian switching of loyalties (when Valentino wins the fight, most of his detractors are just as happy to cheer him as they were to cheer his opponent)-- stand out all the more clearly. This, of course, is exactly the point that Pauline Kael seems to miss in her assessments of Russell's work. Clichés of this sort are used precisely for their familiarity, so that the unfamiliar has a distinct reference point. Even Russell's clichés have a fresh look about them because of the boldness with which he uses them. When the camera closes in on Valentino gripping at his side the viewer knows what to expect, but it still carries an emotional punch, much as Tchaikovsky reaching for the glass of contaminated water in The Music Lovers, or the dialogue exchange--"Whoever wrote that should be shot"; "He was--last Thursday"--in Savage Messiah.

Given careful consideration, these are problems that must be faced by anyone working in the biographical format. The viewer, more likely than not, is aware that the character under discussion has died, and probably even knows how that death came about. This is all well and good, but the fact remains that the death is part of the story and must be dealt with in some way. In the case of Valentino the problem of presenting this with any degree of freshness is compounded by the fact that the framing story is built around Valentino's funeral, so we are obviously working toward the man's death. By taking the event at its face value, presenting it with wide-eyed enthusiasm for the story, Russell transcends the cliché by exalting it.

The boxing match is also notable in that it is the most intensely human of all the scenes in Valentino. It cements the innate decency of the relation of Valentino and his two real friends, George Ullman and June Mathis. Russell's portrait of their concern over Valentino's well-being and their uncontrolled exuberance over his winning the match is a glorious vindication of his overriding theme of decency and the indomitability of the human spirit. This one asset at least partly redeems Valentino from the more hateful outlook of the earlier scenes. Even Joseph Schenck comes off far better in this scene, though his characterization still owes less to reality than to the sort of fantastic creation dreamed up by Kaufman and Hart in the guise of Herman Glogauer in Once in a Lifetime. Valentino's noble, if ill-advised, fight in itself is a much more positive act than any we have thus far seen. As previously noted it is a positive statement because it is derived from the character's own sense of right and wrong and honor, and this is the note on which Russell has chosen to climax his film.

Only two short scenes follow the boxing match--the drinking contest and Valentino's death. Of these the death scene is the more important because of the final tie-in with Citizen Kane via its relation of the orange to the snowball in the Welles film, and also because it firmly cements the innocence of Valentino as viewed by Russell. Having proven to himself and the world his status as a man, the one thing that remains to him is the unattainable dream that at first motivated him, and the one thing that continues to elude him up to the very moment of his death as even the single orange rolls beyond his grasp.

Valentino ends on a curious shot of the body on a marble slab in a morgue. The shot appears to be the only vestige of an idea that Russell had considered for a time and ultimately dropped. It was his intention to utilize the legend that the body on display in the mortuary was not Valentino, but a wax effigy, and that the real body was kept refrigerated elsewhere. [9] Even though the idea was discarded, the final shot would seem to be based on it.

All things considered, Valentino must be judged as something of a lesser Russell work. The inconsistencies of the characterization, the overindulgence in quirky autobiographical undercurrents, the overall tone of the bulk of the film, all work against it. At the same time it is a good film, and coming from anyone other than Russell it might even be considered a great film, flawed as it is. In some respects it can be seen to be a retrogressive work. In its negative flavor it is less positive than three films that precede it, even though the character of Valentino and the manner in which Russell climaxes his film do much to dispel this negativism. Structured in this manner, Valentino is very nearly a microcosm of Russell's progression toward a powerfully positive outlook on humanity, as decency and humanity are what win in the end. As such it must be viewed as another step toward that outlook.

The commercial failure of Valentino coming directly after Lisztomania did untold damage to Russell's standing in in the film world. This was not altogether a self-induced situation. A good portion of the blame must rest on the advertising campaign for the film, which stupidly advised that the viewer might expect to see a film in the manner of John G. Alvidsen's Rocky! This unbelievable bit of barefaced huckstering was based entirely on the names of Robert Chartoff and Irwin Winkler, who produced both films, making it possible to say that Valentino was "brought to you by the people who gave you Rocky." The imbecility of this move certainly worked against the film in two respects. Viewers expecting to see another Rocky were bound to be disappointed, and viewers expecting a Ken Russell film in the grand Russell tradition might well have avoided the film altogether. It was scarcely the first time a Russell film had been poorly represented by the advertising campaign (consider Lisztomania), but it was likely the most damaging, especially since at five million dollars Valentino had cost more than any previous Russell film. The film put Russell right back where he was following Savage Messiah, and his persona non grata standing in the film industry must have seemed uncomfortably familiar by this time. The bleakness of this intermission in Russell's film career--it was to be more than three years before a new Russell film opened--must have been offset somewhat by the offer from Granada TV to bring his long expressed desire to make a small film about the Lake poets to fruition. Nonetheless, the comedown from international filmmaker to creator of a two-part television film must have been somewhat galling.

As things stand at this point, Valentino is pretty much a dead issue. Russell has openly voiced his own dissatisfaction with the film, and his constant companion and personal assistant on Altered States, Vivian Jolly, has said that he was "miserable" at the time of filming, "and he made a miserable film."[10] There is some justification for her attitude as Valentino all too clearly shows Russell's unhappiness, but the film itself is considerably better than miserable. Whether or not it will ever find a niche in the Russell repertory remains to be seen. Regardless, it cannot be considered a major work, even if it should be given the attention it has thus far been denied.

NOTES

1. Phillips, Gene D. Ken Russell. Boston: Twayne, 1979, p. 135.
2. Ibid., pp. 131-132.
3. Farber, Stephen. "Russellmania," Film Comment, 11 (November/December 1975): 40-47.
4. Gomez, Joseph. Ken Russell: The Adaptor as Creator. London: Frederick Muller, 1976.
5. Bland, Alexander. The Nureyev Valentino: Portrait of a Film. New York: Delta Special, Dell, 1977, p. 56.
6. Ibid., p. 30.
7. Phillips, Gene D. Ken Russell, p. 134.
8. Ibid., p. 134.
9. Bland, Alexander. The Nureyev Valentino: Portrait of a Film, p. 8.
10. Hauptfuhrer, Fred. "Wild and Wooly Ken Russell Finds the Golden Fleece Directing Altered States," People, Vol. 15, No. 12 (March 30, 1981), p. 70.

CHAPTER 10

INTERMISSION

"Clouds of Glory"

In 1978, when Ken Russell carried out his long held promise to return to television, conditions were far from ideal. The medium itself had changed, become far more unionized and expensive. Russell's position as an important British filmmaker was shaky at the moment and so he was scarcely in a position to rock the boat. Fortunately, producer Norman Swallow knew Russell, knew his work, and respected him, asking for economy, but in no way hampering his creative prerogative.

Working quickly with his usual handpicked crew of technicians--Shirley Russell, Dick Bush, and newcomer to the fold, editor Anthony Ham (who went on to edit Brideshead Revisited for Michael Lindsay-Hogg and Charles Sturridge)-- and a group of stock Russell players--Felicity Kendal, William Hootkins, Ben Aris, Imogen Claire, and Izabella Telezynska--left Russell room for two "star" name players, David Warner and David Hemmings, in the roles of William Wordsworth and Samuel Taylor Coleridge respectively. (Both men gave unreservedly brilliant performances under Russell, possibly the best of their careers.) The results leave little to be desired--two films, each whole in itself, yet each supportive of the other. In order to fully appreciate Clouds of Glory the films must be considered separately, but should both be known because of the light that the two films placed side by side casts on Russell's work.

William and Dorothy represents that side of Russell's nature that seems quiet and reflective. Rime of the Ancient Mariner would seem to have more bearing on Russell at his most outspoken and experimental. The films do not jar, however, and are both obviously the product of the same controlling voice, though the difference in the screenplay billing

(Melvyn Bragg is listed first on William and Dorothy, and Russell listed first on Rime of the Ancient Mariner) is indicative of the fact that Bragg's contribution is greater on the first film. What seems at first a dichotomy is really nothing of the sort, as we shall see. In fashioning the two films Russell simply followed the dictates of his feelings, and those feelings cause the two films to be unified. As with all of Russell's best work, Clouds of Glory is personal and true to the filmmaker. It is obvious that at no time did Russell say that the one film should be restrained and the other more daring, but that this grew out of his response to the subjects. The endings of the two films bear this out, for, interestingly, William and Dorothy has the more strongly stated climax of the two films, whereas the ending of Rime of the Ancient Mariner is very restrained and even stately. In any event the films merit careful and deliberate study on a par with that given to Russell's features, hence their inclusion with the theatrical work of which they are more a part than his BBC films.

"William and Dorothy"
(The Love Story of the Poet Wordsworth & His Sister)

> What fond and wayward thought will slide
> Into a lover's head!
> "O Mercy!" to myself I cried,
> "If Lucy should be dead!"

The excerpt above from one of Wordsworth's "Lucy" poems, "Strange Fits of Passion Have I Known," does not appear in William and Dorothy, and yet its presence is keenly felt. In dealing with the relationship of Wordsworth and his sister, Russell has opted, as so often in the past, to work from a central situation used as a framing story (in this case William's guilt and anxiety over Dorothy's possibly impending death), and build out from it in order to create an entire picture. It should be noted straight off that in fashioning William and Dorothy as "The Love Story of the Poet Wordsworth and His Sister," it was never Russell's intention to be outrageous or inflammatory, nor does he so much as imply that these feelings were ever acted upon. Instead of being an exploitative view, William and Dorothy is quite the most tender and fragile film in Russell's filmography. Even the comparative restraint of Song of Summer and Savage Messiah seem positively harsh by comparison.

It would be a great mistake, however, to lump William

and Dorothy into a group made up of these three films. Song of Summer is relatively formative, and Savage Messiah is Russell right on the brink of his full powers. William and Dorothy, on the other hand, represents him at the height of those powers. The fact that it shares the intimacy of approach found in the earlier films is misleading. Beyond the stylistic and thematic growth of Russell as a filmmaker in the years which separate the films, there is a recognizably different tone of voice at work here. Quite simply it is the work of a sadder but wiser Ken Russell--far more a reflective work than an active one. Resultantly, it is also a much sadder film. It is not the sadness that one finds in the tragic Russell of The Devils, nor that of the pathetic as in The Music Lovers. Rather, its air of melancholy has a more direct bearing on the bittersweet ending of Mahler, without the ironic undertones found in that film. In many ways it would seem that the Wordsworths have engaged Russell's sympathy more than any previous protagonists since William and Dorothy is his most openly affectionate film.

This sympathy that Russell finds for the poet is peculiarly interesting as there is little in common between the two men, save for their rather pantheistic view of life--something that both made communicable and real through the appreciation and use of the Lake District as its representative. To know the English Lakes through Wordsworth's poetry and to know them through Russell's films are very similar, yet unique, experiences, and this shared interest accounts for much. Other than this, however, the two are remarkably unlike each other. There is nothing in Wordsworth's work to suggest any common ground with Russell in other areas. Wordsworth is serious almost to the point of being humorless, and this is certainly at odds with the jokester side of Russell's nature. Still there is a bond here that goes beyond the Lake District, and it is the honest emotional integrity found in both men's works. Considering this and their shared outlook on nature it is perhaps little wonder that, as viewed by Russell, Wordsworth very nearly is poetry, not just one of its finest representatives.

Russell's approach to poetry (poetry being something he had only previously dealt with in Dante's Inferno, where it encompassed other art forms as well) is obviously drawn from the approach one finds in his musical films. Just as for Russell music never lies, poetry never lies, and so his approach is to examine Wordsworth and his sister through the truth of the poetry. Russell's evaluation of the poems and

Intermission 351

their relation to William and Dorothy (who is also drawn
from one of her few poetic endeavors and her famous Journal)
may be a bit too bold for some viewers, but even the detractors must admit that the approach has merit and Russell's
case for the readings is a strong one. Just as an example,
take the case of his use of "She Was a Phantom of Delight."
Wordsworth's only real comment about its subject was that
"it was written from my heart, as is sufficiently obvious."
The general consensus of critical opinion has seen fit to assume that it is therefore equally obvious that it is about Mary
Hutchinson, Wordsworth's wife. Russell places it within the
film as a poem given to Mary for their wedding, but by the
visual pattern of dissolves that lead up to and introduce the
poem he creates an intentional ambiguity as to the source of
its inspiration. It might just as well apply, Russell suggests,
to Annette Vallon, the French woman who bore his illegitimate
daughter, or to Dorothy--or perhaps to all three. Russell's
assertion is no more out of court than the idea that it must
apply to Mary. In fact it is a good deal more sensible since
we do not really know.

Russell immediately establishes the reflective nature
of the film by the application of the lovely and haunting
"Moonlight" section of Frank Bridge's suite, The Sea, over
the film's opening credits and first scene. Although not apparent on a first viewing, the image of William and Dorothy
frozen in time behind the credits is of great importance as
the establishment of a visual motif, the meaning of which becomes clear as the film progresses. Russell then sets the
tone, style, and approach of the film with William's recitation
of the original version of the poem "Louisa" (original in that
it includes the generally deleted second verse). The delivery
of the recitation is such that it comes across as half-wistful,
half-defiant, an effect enhanced by the visual construction of
scenes of memory intermingled with the present. The idyllic
scenes of William and Dorothy in the past are intercut with
scenes of William in a great state of excitement and apprehension, stalking about the grounds of his home. The attitude is that of a man at once sorrowful that the past is gone,
and defiantly angered over the situation.

Further, Russell establishes the idea that despite the
various names used in the poems the subject of them is
Dorothy:

> I met Louisa in the shade,
> And having seen that lovely Maid,

> Why should I fear to say
> That nymph-like, she is fleet and strong,
> And down the rocks can leap along
> Like rivulets in May.
>
> And she hath smiles to earth unknown;
> Smiles, that with motion of their own
> Do spread, and sink, and rise;
> That come and go with endless play,
> And ever as they pass away,
> Are hidden in her eyes.

In so doing the mood of the film is firmly anchored in this relationship. Beyond this there is the introduction of Russell's approach to a visual poetic device--the dissolve. As we have previously seen the dissolve is not a device that Russell generally uses wantonly as a simple transitional effect. Indeed it is only slightly more prevalent in his work as a transition than the fade-out/fade-in, so that its use in both Clouds of Glory films is a significant departure, marking not a stylistic change, but an evolutionary growth in Russell's cinematic vocabulary. By linking a series of zoom shots of Dorothy's facial expression accompanied by the second verse of the poem with a series of dissolves, Russell communicates a feeling of the seamless flow of thought inherent in a poem.

From this we are plunged directly into the film's actual present by the cries of "William! William!" coming from the house. Wordsworth turns and runs in, much to the amusement of the gardener and his assistant. In this case Russell creates a visual pattern which he will restate to different purpose at the film's end. In running from the yard at this moment Wordsworth narrowly avoids his first encounter with a visitor to the Lake District, who will eventually become a very important aspect of the film. Here, too, Russell puts forth the position in which William's wife finds herself as he rushes past her into the house, brusquely telling her, "I heard her call, " before she can say anything. With an air of complete resignation (evidently this is not the first such occurrence) Mrs. Wordsworth follows her husband inside.

Upstairs, after a brief consultation with the doctor who believes "there is little hope for recovery, " William stands by the bed of the ailing and aged Dorothy. In a bold implication of some mental link between brother and sister, her first words, "I heard the rain falling thickly, " seem to indicate the last image of the memory presented by Russell and the water imagery of the final line of the poem "Louisa"--

> When up she winds along the brook
> To hunt the waterfalls.

At first Dorothy's words are addled and incoherent. She cannot be sure of the passage of time, and seems more than a little disoriented. (It should, perhaps, be remembered that although Russell does not make much of this, Dorothy was quite mentally unbalanced in her later years.) This disorientation, however, serves as a structural foundation when Dorothy tells William, "I've been remembering so many different things about our lives. Jumbling them all up together till they all became a single dream, bound together by your poetry." And this succinctly sums up the approach of the Russell-Melvyn Bragg screenplay and Russell's handling of it: a flood of old memories, borne out of the distinct possibility that the link to those memories will soon be broken by death, "bound together" by Wordsworth's poems into a coherent narrative. "You've put all my life into your poems," she tells him. Wordsworth corrects her, "You have put your life into the poems. They're ours--not mine," and it is in this light that the poetry is explored by the film, for as the title suggests this is not a film about Wordsworth, but a film about William and Dorothy, and the unique--though possibly not quite healthy--bond that allowed the poetry to be what it is.

Much of what happens in these early scenes is not completely clear until the events are assessed within the context of the entire film. We have no notion as to the cause behind Dorothy's outburst, "Don't call me Dorothy! Dorothy's a name for strangers and forgetting your own poetry," though we have some hint in her reference to "when I was Louisa, Emma, Emmeline, or just plain Lucy." (This, too, prompts a start from William which is at this point mysterious.) Nor is there any way to judge the very singular importance of the first flashback with its recitation of "The Sparrow's Nest," in particular the poem's closing lines:

> Such heart was in her, being then
> A little prattler among men.
> The Blessing of my later years
> Was with me when a boy:
> She gave me eyes, she gave me ears;
> And humble cares, and delicate fears;

>   A heart, the fountain of sweet tears;
>   And love, and thought, and joy.

Once again we find that Russell is working on the assumption that the viewer interested enough in the subject, or just the art of filmmaking itself, will wish to see the film more than once in order to fully appreciate the beauty of its structural unity.

This first flashback, accompanied by George Butterworth's "Banks of Green Willow," performs a function not unlike the childhood memory scenes in The Music Lovers and Mahler in that by detailing the background of William and Dorothy we can better grasp the causes behind their deep relationship. First we see them in a literal depiction of the poem. From this Russell enlarges upon the meaning of the poem, and its suggestion of a childhood dependency as the two of them visit the grave of their mother. Finally, with the death of their father, we find the children forced to separate by an unsympathetic uncle, who packs Dorothy off to live with a "rich family at Halifax" and William off to school.

Russell then returns us to the framing story, where the events of the separation and their reliance on one another are discussed. Dorothy complains about the quality of life in that "good home" as being "cold as a convent." This is deftly blended into the next section of the poetic-flashback narrative by the utilization of rhyming dialogue, when Dorothy contrasts her life with William having "run the hills like a savage":

> William: Savages don't spend their days in schoolrooms with raw knuckles and sore eyes.
>
> Dorothy: Neither do they have holidays, I suppose, or roam about in tribes.

This dialogue then leads with a natural flow into a second flashback, again built on Wordsworth's poetry and Butterworth's "Banks of Green Willow."

It is with this flashback that Russell begins to draw on Wordsworth's mammoth autobiographical poem, The Prelude, and a good working knowledge of the poem is of immense help in understanding and appreciating the film. The actual amount of words drawn from this work is not very great, but the film draws many recognizable images and scenes from portions of it not directly quoted. In this manner we find something of a feeling of the line "I was the Dreamer, they the Dream" in the visual depiction of life at Cambridge, while on the soundtrack William recites:

> Thus while the days flew by, and years passed on,
> From nature and her overflowing soul
> I had received so much, that all my thoughts
> Were steeped in feeling; I was only then
> Contented, when with bliss ineffable
> I felt the sentiment of Being spread

And then, continuing with the poem, Russell spreads out to the real world of Wordsworth rather than the unreal self-enclosed world of the university as the words of the poem find their visual counterparts:

> O'er all that moves and all that seemeth still;
> O'er all that leaps and runs, and shouts, and sings,
> Or beats the gladsome air; o'er all that glides
> Beneath the wave, yea, in the wave itself.

Returning to the real world of nature, also returns Wordsworth to Dorothy, and their argument about his feeling that he must go to France is also drawn from The Prelude. It can be seen, therefore, that Russell's use of The Prelude is more as source material for the narrative of the film than for the poetry itself. Considering the intimate nature of the film, the little poems like "Louisa" and "To My Sister" and "The Sparrow's Nest" are far better suited.

The argument with Dorothy about France is of paramount importance in understanding the overall film, not for the argument iself, but for the visual pattern of its final shot. After deciding that he must go and be a part of what he then considered to be their glorious revolution, William sits face to face with Dorothy. As the camera zooms in on them, we can see this is the image that appears under the opening credits. Dorothy then promises William, "I'll wait for you," and Russell freezes the image on that promise. This is very significant if we realize that in no other film has Russell ever employed this effect as such, and therefore it is not applied as window dressing here. Rather, it makes a very important point as it singles out this moment in time, and because of it we know that Dorothy will wait for William-- not only for his return from France, but always.

Following this frozen shot is a dissolve onto a close-up of Annette Vallon, which is not without its meaning either, suggesting as it does the possibility of a breech between William and Dorothy by the advent of a third party. The subsequent zoom back from this close-shot, which reveals that she and William are asleep in each other's arms in a hayloft, tends to reinforce this view. There is a commotion and a band of starving peasants rush into the barn stealing and ransacking the food stores. William and Annette's argument over their right to do this is indicative of the gulf that separates them regardless of the fact that she is pregnant with his child. Whereas she concerns herself with their physical appearance ("Look at their faces, see how mean they are"), William is far more inclined to believe that they might be justified in their actions. In this we immediately see that not only is Annette totally unsuited to William (long before he does, one might add), but that she is a rather shallow human being on any level. The conversation which follows only serves to confirm this suspicion, when William proposes to do for Annette what he would not do for Dorothy by accepting his uncle's offer to become a vicar. (In the preceding scene he had told Dorothy that he would not do this as it would be done through no desire to be a vicar, but only to support the two of them.) Annette's refusal to accept him on these grounds is founded in good reason, but her assertion that she will "be married to a great poet, or not marry at all," casts severe doubt as to whether she cares about Wordsworth as a person. Further, the fact that she is unwilling to accept any hardship in order to be with William reflects badly on her, especially as contrasts with Dorothy, i.e., Dorothy tries to get William to stay in England by offering to "cook and clean and sew," promising that she "can manage on very little," while Annette's first question to William upon his asking her to return to England with him is whether or not he can support her. Underscoring William's naivete and simplicity in this matter Russell introduces an excerpt from Butterworth's melancholy "A Shropshire Lad" in the soundtrack during the final moments of their separation.

Returning to England William finds Dorothy acting as his conscience. In a beautifully detailed little scene where William and Dorothy, along with the other passengers, must get out of a coach and help push it out of a bad spot in the road, she encourages him to return to France. All of William's carefully thought out reasons on the impossibility and inadvisability of this are quickly countered by Dorothy, who only understands "a woman with your child waiting for you."

Intermission   357

(Once again we are confronted with the idea of waiting.) In
the end Dorothy wins out and William returns to attempt to
find Annette.

France, however, is not as he left it. In a scene designed to economically convey Wordsworth's disillusionment
with the French Revolution, he finds a country gone mad,
when, hiding behind a tree, he watches a group of peasants
torture and humiliate an aristocratic family after having apparently looted their house. Husband and wife are beaten
and made to pull a cart in which the peasants, decked out in
the tattered remnants of aristocratic finery, are riding. The
scene has distinct undertones of Isadora's visit to the new
Communist artists' party in Isadora, but it does not work
half so well here. As a depiction of Wordsworth's having to
face the difference between his ideal of the French Revolution and the reality of it, the scene is certainly valid and
even somewhat effective, but it jars as not being at one with
the overall film. Russell's approach to it (due, perhaps, to
the simple fact that his protagonist is only a spectator to the
events) is singularly uninvolving as his camera merely records the atrocities before it. Even the similarly out of
place jail scene in Valentino was distinguished by a technical
polish and sense of immediacy which is altogether lacking
here. There is, however, an effective unity of visual construction at the end of the sequence, as Russell shows Wordsworth fleeing the scene along the same path on which he had
previously parted from Annette.

>   I traveled among unknown men,
>   In lands beyond the sea;
>   Nor, England! did I know till then
>   What love I bore to thee.
>
>   Among thy mountains did I feel
>   The joy of my desire;
>   And she I cherished turned her wheel
>   Beside an English fire.

Russell once more uses Butterworth's "A Shropshire
Lad" in this case combined with the excerpt above from "I
Travelled Among Unknown Men" to stress the simplicity of
Wordsworth and his painful maturing process at the hands of
experience. The words and music are used to accompany
visuals of Wordsworth now back in England, at once relieved
and happy to be there, and yet saddened by his shattered
ideals about the Revolution. The construction of the scene is

such that it begins by concentrating on Wordsworth and in the second verse is expanded to actually picture the Cumberland mountains of which he speaks and Dorothy at her spinning wheel next to the hearth. In this way the poem becomes at once symbolic and descriptive. At first Dorothy's words of consolation offer William little comfort, and her insistence that he "must start writing again" is met with the dejected reply that "the critics scorn them or ignore them. I hate publishing them. I'm afraid to write them." Dorothy's voice now serves as William's creative conscience, when in response to William's questioning the value of the poems, she tells him, "They are worth fighting for." William's tender, "Oh, Lucy," as he takes her in his arms and kisses her lets us know that for William having one person who genuinely believes in him in this manner does make a difference. Dorothy's faith in his poetry assures its continuance.

On this remembrance of Dorothy's ability to help William through love and faith, Russell returns to the framing story, where William is finding himself unable to similarly help her. His feelings of helplessness in this are increased by Dorothy's statements (in part drawn from an actual letter she wrote), "Oh, yes, I confess, of all men I'm most partial to William. He never tires of comforting his sister. He never leaves her in anger; he prefers her society to every other pleasure. I've copied all his poetry; written them out in a fair hand." During this she clutches at her journal, and on the last line falls asleep. Unable to contain himself any longer William, near tears, picks up the journal and rushes from the room to go for a walk.

Once outside he is greeted by the still waiting Reverend Dewey, who is rather ill-humoredly invited to accompany him on his walk, "as long as you're in the mood for a stroll and not expecting a glorious sunset." Reverend Dewey is one of the most unusual characters ever to appear in a Russell film. Heavyset and wearing a voluminous black Inverness cape, sporting a longish walking stick and slightly foolish straw top hat, he stands out in marked contrast to the long, lean figure of Wordsworth, and it is unclear at first just how we are intended to take him. He looks like a figure of fun, and the sincerity of his praise is open to question by its very quality. This is perhaps significant as Reverend Dewey is the only person we have met who seems to honor William's work outside of those immediately connected with him, e.g. Dorothy and Annette. At first Russell uses him to bounce off dialogue. After a particularly flowery expression of his admiration Dewey is greeted by Wordsworth's curt, "If you were not a man of the cloth, I might suspect you of flattery, Reverend Dewey." A little later his clichéd assessment of the situation that "in this entire county of Cumberland not one volume of my works has been sold" prompts Wordsworth's suspicious, "You're not a missionary, are you?" The cheerfulness with which Dewey accepts Wordsworth's abuse is also something of a call to suspicion, but, then, as they wander across a hilltop, Wordsworth begins reciting from his "Lines Composed a Few Miles Above Tintern Abbey," and a change takes place in both men. The beginning of this is deceptively smooth as there is no break from dialogue to poem, and the first lines from the poem are interpolated as dialogue. It is not until Wordsworth stops in his tracks and Russell abruptly cuts from a medium long shot to a close-shot that the recitation becomes obvious. At this point, the lines of the poem take on the character of an artistic creed:

William reads an extract from Dorothy's "Journal" to the visiting Reverend Dewey in William and Dorothy, the first Clouds of Glory film. (Courtesy of Ken Russell)

> ... For I have learned
> To look on nature, not as in the hour
> Of thoughtless youth; but hearing oftentimes
> The still, sad music of humanity,
> Nor harsh nor grating, though of ample power
> To chasten and subdue. And I have felt
> A presence that disturbs me with the joy
> Of elevated thoughts; a sense sublime
> Of something far more deeply interfused,
> Whose dwelling is the light of setting suns,
> And the round ocean and the living air.
> And the blue sky, and in the mind of man;
> A motion and a spirit that impels
> All thinking things, all objects of all thought,
> And rolls through all things.

Visually Russell moves in a similarly poetic pattern into the mind of Wordsworth with a flow of thrillingly edited quick close-ups of the things of nature, flowers, fruit, dew-laden blossoms, animals, flowing water, until on the line, "And the round ocean and the living air," he zooms back to encompass these separate parts as a whole. In this manner Russell is able to convey the sense of the individual object as an integral part of the greater total, becoming more expansive and all-pervasive as the sequence progresses. This is due in no small part to the fact that Wordsworth's lines have very nearly as much bearing on Russell's artistry (none of the flow of images is in any way at odds with images in all of Russell's work) as they have on the poet's. At the climax Russell dissolves back from the thought to the man, and then moves back to encompass the Reverend Dewey, who appropriately caps the recitation with "Amen," and further adds, "You're something of a missionary yourself, sir." This sudden perception on Dewey's part deepens the concept of his character immediately. For Wordsworth, like Russell, like any artist interested in communicating, has more than a touch of the missionary in him. We find this concept running throughout Russell's work. It is voiced quite clearly in the "Torso" scene in Savage Messiah, in the "Creation" sequence of Mahler, in Tommy Walker's desire to convey his inner-peace and divinity to others in Tommy, and in Liszt's discovery that he has placed his faith in the wrong thing in Lisztomania.

Returning to Dorothy's sick room the film sets up (without seeming to do so) the eventual point and thrust of the scenes to follow and also indicates a slight shift in the narrative toward Dorothy's point of view. Here again what first appears to be an incoherent rambling--in this case Dorothy's cryptic outburst that she cannot die because "I'm dead already"--will prove itself to be considerably more in the final analysis.

That the specific interest of the proceedings is being narrowed down to concentrate on the relationship of brother and sister even more than previously where we were also concerned with a more broader-based outlook on Wordsworth's works is apparent early in the next scene. The sequence begins with Wordsworth and Reverend Dewey by the shores of a lake, where with a great deal of flourish Dewey recites the perhaps too familiar poem "I Wandered Lonely as a Cloud." In this we see something of a resurfacing of Dewey's role as an overenthusiastic dilettante, and there is more than a little too much "gee-whiz" to his pronouncement, "And to think these are the very shores that inspired those immortal lines." What is unique about the ambiguity of Reverend Dewey's character is that this style of presentation places the viewer in a position not dissimilar to that of Wordsworth. At one moment he seems to be a buffoon; the next, a man who might well be more interested in being able to lay claim to his "friendship" with William Wordsworth than in being a serious student of the poet; then again he seems at other moments to be an intelligent, perceptive man, who, as he claims, "loves the poems, but respects the poet." Just as Wordsworth cannot tell if there is some hidden motive in Reverend Dewey's interest, neither can we, and this is a point that Russell opts not to clarify until the end. In so doing he allows us the opportunity to understand a little better the plight of any person who achieves fame in his or her dealings with strangers, and in approaching the situation in this manner the plight does not carry with it the nasty undertones one finds in Alan Alda's latest complaint about having no private life due to his fame, or even in Woody Allen's encounters with fans in <u>Annie Hall</u> and <u>Stardust Memories</u>. We, like Wordsworth, may well be skeptical, but we are not prepared to reject Reverend Dewey out of hand, for while acknowledging the fact that a certain reticence is natural, even wise, in such an encounter, we also realize that not every admirer is a simpleton or a lunatic or a potential leech. Dewey continues in much the same key, going on about the happiness which Wordsworth's poem has given to "so many people ... myself included." Wordsworth's cheerless grunt and subsequent statement, "You have my eyes and ears to thank for that--and my heart," is misconstrued by

Dewey, who feels that he has given offense by possibly implying that anyone inspired by the shores of Derwent Water might have written the poem. This is not the case, however, as Wordsworth soon reveals by reading a piece of beautifully written prose describing the same scene as that in the poem. Dewey is visibly moved by this "rare privilege" and asserts that "an artist's sketches are often as exciting as the finished work. Your stamp is unmistakable." Here Dewey has fallen into an understandable trap because the Wordsworth "stamp" is clearly on the outlook, but it is that "stamp" which grows out of the almost collaborative bond of William and Dorothy, for as Wordsworth then tells him, "That, Reverend Dewey, was written by my sister." Wordsworth's apparent intentions in this are not so much to make a fool of Dewey, but instead as a kind of confession to an outsider of his creative dependence on someone outside himself.

This extract from Dorothy's journal leads naturally into a scene of memory from the same source, beginning with a charming domestic scene of William and Dorothy at home. The beauty of the opening lies not only in the tranquil nature of its presentation, suffused by gentle natural light and possessed of a marvelous ability to convey a sense of wellbeing, but also in the reality of the presentation. For the moment we might well be casual eavesdroppers to a situation that is at once supremely innocent, and yet tainted by a feeling of something not quite healthy just beneath the surface. As the scene opens Dorothy is standing at the kitchen window kneading bread in a large wooden bowl, while William sprawls in a chair composing "To a Butterfly." It is interesting to note how closely William's poem mirrors the extract from Dorothy's journal, which forms a sudden and rather unorthodox narration for this part of the film (indicative of the change in the point of view). Dorothy tells us, "The thought came to him as we were talking about the pleasure we both always felt at the sight of a butterfly. I told him that I used to chase them a little, but that I was afraid of brushing the dust off their wings, and did not catch them." Then William reads the poem:

> Oh! Pleasant, pleasant were the days,
> The time when in our childish plays,
> My sister Emmeline and I
> Together chased the butterfly!
> A very hunter did I rush
> Upon the prey:--with leaps and springs
> I followed on from brake to bush;

> But she, God love her, feared to brush
> The dust from off its wings.

The juxtaposition of Dorothy's words with the corresponding words of the poem is, of course, simply a reversal of the presentation of "I Wandered Lonely As a Cloud" in the previous scene and serves much the same function, reinforcing the idea in a less conscious manner. The scene, however, climaxes with William attempting to dissuade Dorothy from her work and go exploring with him--something he tries to achieve by reciting the closing lines of "To My Sister":

> Then come, my Sister! come, I pray,
> With speed put on your woodland dress;
> And bring no book: for this one day
> We'll give to idleness.

Dorothy's response to this, "You think all you have to do is say those few lines to me, and I'll follow you to the ends of the earth, " is intended humorously, and the tone, too, is humorous as William kisses her fingers and is rewarded by getting sticky bread dough stuck to his lips, but the following sequence attests to the basic truth that the innate innocence of William's approach does achieve the end of which Dorothy speaks.

The lakeside scene which follows is played without words and is suggestive of a relationship in which such are not needed for communication. As they wander along the shores of a lake, taking delight in various natural objects, the meanings underlying the actions are conveyed entirely through facial expressions and editing. At the end of the scene, where William slips a seashell over Dorothy's finger like a wedding ring, we know that regardless of what is to come Dorothy is William's natural bride. This is an aspect which Russell will explore in greater detail in the subsequent scenes.

The finality of their relationship is then depicted in a scene where brother and sister lie side by side in John's Grove and think "how sweet it would be to lie thus in the grave. " The scene has a striking pictorial quality, very reminiscent of Pre-Raphaelite painting. The feeling is more than a little morbid, but not in the sense of Tchaikovsky's unsuccessful suicide bid in The Music Lovers, suggestive here rather of a time when the painfulness of the feelings the pair have for each other will no longer matter. At the same time the scene is very cleverly designed to lead into the next, where the impossibility of their situation causes a breach in the relationship.

William is engaged in composition when Dorothy rushes up to him in a great state of agitation. She has come across his rough draft of "She Dwelt Among the Untrodden Ways," and in copying it out has run afoul of the last verse:

> She lived unknown, and few could know
>   When Lucy ceased to be;
> But she is in her grave, and, oh,
>   The difference to me!

Immediately we are reminded of Dorothy's original sickbed statement, "when I was Emma, Emmeline, Louisa, or just plain Lucy," and William's seemingly inexplicable start at this last name. Dorothy, considering this an attempt to rid himself of her ("I am Lucy. I know that. Amn't I?"), is quite understandably distraught at William's having "killed her off" and buried her. In this there is the distinct impression of the screenplay having taken a specific side in the matter, but upon examination it becomes clear that not only is this in keeping with William's feelings at this reflective time, but it is also far more complex than this simple idea.

Once having calmed Dorothy, protesting that "it's only a poem," William asserts that he will never marry. Instead of accepting the wisdom of this decision, Dorothy places herself more or less in the role of the martyr and suggests that he should marry, "I fear for us both if you do not." William, somewhat naively, takes her statement at face value, and, in a beautifully constructed sequence, the two of them set off to claim Mary Hutchinson, who it had long been said William would one day marry. The utilization of the poem "A Farewell" in this sequence is, perhaps, not of exact historical accuracy, though Wordsworth notes that it was composed "just before my sister and I went to fetch Mrs. Wordsworth from Gallow-hill, near Scarborough." It does have the merit of being presented in such a manner that it captures the feeling of underlying regret that is inherent in this ostensibly happy occasion. By playing scenes of memory of the making of Dove Cottage into a real home with scenes of the actual preparations for the journey to Mary Hutchinson, Russell grimly presents us with the picture of unalterable change. Apart from Wordsworth's poetic statement of how Mary will love and care for the cottage in the same way that he and Dorothy do, it is abundantly apparent that nothing will ever be the same once this action is taken. This is Russell's stance on the situation, which accurately reflects William's own feelings at the time of the film's framing narrative.

As if to underscore this fact Russell briefly returns the film to its framing story. It is a bold, almost supernatural move, as he cuts from brother to sister reacting in their respective locations to the thunder of a rising storm, linking the two in nature once again. The thunder then serves to move to a brief and sharply satirical scene in which he and Dorothy meet Annette and the child (again staged on the path from the two previous French sequences). On the thunderclap he commences a narrative recitation of an excerpt from "It Is a Beauteous Evening, Calm and Free":

> Listen! the mighty Being is awake,
> And doth with his eternal motion make
> A sound like thunder--everlastingly.
> Dear Child! Dear Girl! that walkest
>   with me here,
> If thou appear untouched by solemn thought,
> Thy nature is not therefore less divine.

Annette, in the intervening years, has become exactly the sort of person that we might well have feared she would become, and her influence seems to have extended to the child. William's ideas of what Annette was are here forever shattered, and she even proves to be too much for Dorothy, who had earlier (obviously inspired by William's idealized notions) championed her at every turning.

This then returns us to the framing story, where William muses, "She was a phantom of delight," indicating the large gap between the real and the ideal. The recitation of the poem follows, dissolving from William to Dorothy, and only then broadening out to include Mary as another "Phantom of Delight." The event being pictured in the flashback is William presenting Mary with the poem as a wedding present. The overall jovial nature of the situation is particularly painful to Dorothy, who must endure Mary's rather roughhewn relatives' crude statements about William being "fair champing at the bit" and the idea that "it's your turn next."

The movements in and out of the framing story are now becoming increasingly rapid, as Russell returns us to Mary taking care of Dorothy. As Mary wipes her fevered brow, Dorothy notices the wedding ring on her hand. "I had a ring like that once," she tells her, "I seem to have lost it. You haven't seen it, have you? It was mother's ring. I was married once, you know." As in the earlier instances this sounds like raving, but in the flashback we can see that the thought, if not entirely lucid, is firmly grounded in fact.

Dissolving from the ring on Mary's hand to the ring on Dorothy's hand, Russell pulls back to reveal Dorothy lying in bed on the morning of William's wedding. As suggested by this opening shot, the ring is the central issue of the scene. William enters and tells her that she must get up and dress for the wedding, but the emotional strain has proved too much for her, and Dorothy decides she cannot go. The situation quickly degenerates into a fight with recriminations on both sides. "You buried Annette and the child," Dorothy accuses, "and now you want to dispose of me!" William blurts out her name and is greeted with a reworking of her earlier outburst, "Don't call me Dorothy! Dorothy's a name for every day. Dorothy's a name for strangers." Nonetheless, she ultimately calms down and gives William the ring from her finger. In a restaging of the lakeside scene with the seashell wedding ring, William places the wedding band back on Dorothy's finger, only this time he removes it, and departs to marry another woman. In doing this William has dealt Dorothy a cruel blow, as the departure has the finality of a couple divorcing, but it should be noted that William's fall in this scene, his loss of innocence, is borne of innocence. He was unable to believe that Dorothy would tell him to marry Mary Hutchinson if she did not mean for him to do so. William is clearly in the wrong, and we recognize that Dorothy is correct that their lives will never be the same after this, but it is she who put William in this position. The entire situation is reminiscent of Alma's martyrization in Mahler--both parties are guilty and both are innocent at the same time. As is typical in Russell there are no easy answers.

This is reinforced by the next scene in which the wedding party returns to the house. Rushing out to meet them, Dorothy falls in a faint in William's arms, and it is she whom he carries across the threshold, not Mary. The handling of the scene is very adroit (does Dorothy really faint, or is it an act?) and in its presentation crystallizes the viewpoint that Dorothy is William's true bride.

Returning to the framing story we find that the advent

of the storm is drawing nearer, and Reverend Dewey suggests that Wordsworth should return home, "though it certainly does promise to be a magnificent spectacle." Instead of heeding this advice, Wordsworth heads out of the hills and down into the town followed closely by Dewey. The sudden recitation of the opening lines of the "Ode: Intimations of Immortality from Recollections of Early Childhood" seems a little abrupt at first, but closer examination reveals that it serves a twofold purpose and is exactly right. The opening of the poem clearly conveys the sense of loss, real or imagined, that Wordsworth is experiencing:

> There was a time when meadow, grove, and stream,
> The earth, and every common sight,
>   To me did seem
>   Apparelled in celestial light,
> The glory and the freshness of a dream.
> It is not now as it hath been of yore;--
>   Turn wheresoe'er I may,
>   By night or day,
> The things which I have seen I now can see no more.

In particular we cast our minds to Wordsworth's statement to the doctor early in the film, "If she were to depart my life would be robbed of a light that I have not the strength to contemplate." Further, the poem makes a transition from the purely mental to a more physical effort to recapture something of the past as, at its climax, we find ourselves in front of Dove Cottage. Wordsworth stares at it as if hoping that just being there, where he and Dorothy were once happy, will make a difference. It is of great significance that the "Intimations of Immortality" of the poem are those recalled from childhood, for as is common in Russell's work, salvation may only be achieved by the mystical idea of recapturing innocence. Standing in front of the cottage in this seemingly hopeless frame of mind, Wordsworth recalls one more memory as the sound of the rising wind comes up on the soundtrack.

    It is sometime after the marriage, and, as William and Mary play cards, Dorothy reads her poem, "Address to a Child," to William's son. The outward charm of this recitation is sadly undercut by the obviousness of the situation-- Dorothy has been relegated to the level of a baby-sitter. The tone is pleasant enough. Mary seems to happily accept "Auntie Dolly's" presence in the house, and Dorothy herself appears truly attached to young John Wordsworth, but it is different, and precisely for those reasons that Dorothy said it would be different. The end of the scene tells all. After John is packed off to bed, Dorothy, too, decides to turn in. She stands in the doorway, bathed in the soft glow of the firelight, and looks back into the room at the couple playing cards. Her expression tells us that she has become, in her own mind, an appendage--Dorothy will never feel a homogenous part of the family.

Russell dissolves from this image back to Wordsworth staring at the cottage. Reverend Dewey approaches him and inquires if this is the cottage where he once lived. Wordsworth's answer that he did, "when I could afford nothing better," is indicative of a man who has forgotten where true value lies. Similarly, his brusque response to Dewey's offer of assisting him in gaining peace of mind is that of a man who has grown distant. It is therefore left to Reverend Dewey, the enigmatic spouter of "I Wandered Lonely As a Cloud," to set Wordsworth to rights. "Then take heed of your own words. Words which brought me three thousand miles. Words you seem to have forgotten," he calls after him; then, surprisingly, he shows himself to be a much more serious student of the poetry than his earlier quotation would indicate. In rising conviction Dewey shouts the lines which begin the fifth section of "Ode: Intimations of Immortality":

> Our birth is but a sleep and a forgetting:
> The Soul that rises with us, our life's Star,
>   Hath had elsewhere its setting,
>   And cometh from afar:
>   Not in entire forgetfulness,
>   And not in utter nakedness,
> But trailing clouds of glory do we come
>   From God who is our home.

William shakes his head and continues to run on down the street. Dewey, the student who has remembered that which the poet has forgotten, can only look disheartened and mutter, "Poor man." His reminder has had its effect, though, and as William continues running, Russell indicates this by bringing Butterworth's "A Shropshire Lad," with its attendant suggestion of innocence, up on the track. In a marvelously atmospheric panning shot, William climbs over the fence at home and runs back toward the house, past the now smoldering pile of leaves that the gardener was working on in the opening, but calls out "those few words" to Dorothy that will cause her to "drop whatever I'm doing and follow you to the ends of the earth":

> Come my Sister, come I pray,
> With speed put on your woodland dress;
> And bring no book: for this one day,
> We'll give to idleness.

As he finishes his invitation to Dorothy, he arrives at the house to find her looking down from the window at him, and, in a series of reverse zooms from one to the other, followed by close-shots intercut, ending on Dorothy, the excerpt from "The Sparrow's Nest" is heard on the soundtrack:

> She gave me eyes, she gave me ears;
> And humble cares, and delicate fears;
> A heart, the fountain of sweet tears;
> And love, and thought, and joy.

Not only has Wordsworth here recaptured the innocence of childhood, but, as the closing credits attest, he has taken to heart, on faith, Dorothy's earlier promise to wait for him. The implication of the repeated use of the image of the two of them frozen at that moment in time when Dorothy promised to wait for William, which appears under the closing credits, is that William has finally come to realize that she would still be there waiting for him, when he returned. (Indeed, Dorothy lived on after him for some three years.)

The climax of William and Dorothy is, possibly, the single most beautiful moment to be found in any Russell film. It is apparent that for Russell William Wordsworth is not a complete person without his sister. (Surely it is no accident that in the second Clouds of Glory film, Rime of the Ancient Mariner, Coleridge likens a woman to Dorothy by telling her, "You are my Dorothy; you are my other half.") The ending, a kind of spiritual rebirth celebrating the relationship of the two, certainly has its roots in the climaxes of Mahler, Tommy, and Lisztomania. Its primary difference lies in the intimacy of the presentation, and as such it can be viewed as fitting in the progression of Russell's work, for its smaller scale (there are no hints of a universal salvation as in Tommy, nor does good art overcome evil as in Lisztomania) makes it more accessible, and its relative freedom from ironic undertones (the biting sting of Mahler's ending is nowhere to be found) adds to the optimism.

In the final analysis, William and Dorothy is a quiet, but not muted Russell film. Unlike Savage Messiah, which is intimate but not all that quiet, there is no feeling of self-enforced restraint. The film is quieter simply because that attitude is inherent in the material and the chosen approach. It is far more successful as a piece than its immediate predecessor, Valentino. Russell's decision to eschew the spectacular set pieces here pays off in the end. It matters not that the film lacks the flamboyance of a Mahler or a Lisztomania, nor that it has not the scope of a Tommy. What does matter in the end is the honesty and sincerity with which the film was made, and of those qualities and the consummate artistry of the manner in which these things were conveyed there can be no doubt.

"The Rime of the Ancient Mariner"
(The Strange Story of Samuel Coleridge, Poet & Drug Addict)

As might well be guessed from both the film's subtitle and its creator, Rime of the Ancient Mariner is no school history book version of the life of Samuel Taylor Coleridge, nor is it an orthodox reading of Coleridge's magnificent poem. Instead it is something of a character study of the poet as viewed in a very personal and passionate manner by the filmmaker. As such it is one of the most important works in Ken Russell's filmography and one of the most controversial. The brilliantly telescoped opening of the film so appalled Alistair Cooke that he immediately withdrew his interest in presenting the two Clouds of Glory films on Masterpiece Theatre. Says Russell, "He got to the part where Coleridge buries the anchor in his wife's breast and refused. Instead of dropping him, they dropped the movies."[1] Even after the films had been picked up by the more adventurous, but now sadly defunct, CBS Cable Network it was felt that it might be prudent to inform the unalert viewer prior to airing the film that this scene was of a symbolic nature and that "Coleridge did not kill his wife." As previously noted it is unfortunate that both of the Clouds of Glory films are less well known than they deserve to be, but in the case of Rime of the Ancient Mariner this is especially regrettable. Of the two films it is the more adventurous and the more personal--in fact it is one of the best things Russell has ever done for either television or theatrical consumption.

Like its companion piece, Rime of the Ancient Mariner goes far beyond the ordinary realm of image and sound, even for Russell. More than anything in his canon the Clouds of Glory films are almost obsessively British, and far from being chauvinistic this attitude works so well within the films that they are enhanced and freshened by it. These are great

British works of art by a great British artist about great British artists, and in addition to this they utilize a good deal of undeservedly obscure (and some not quite so obscure) British music. The soundtracks on the films are of particular interest in that they are one hundred percent Russell's contribution in regard to the choices and their placement. Russell has woven a textural richness of sound from a number of quite different pieces of music into a unified whole, which is all the more astounding when one realizes that the music is all from preexisting recordings as most of the music in Mahler had been. William and Dorothy with its complex interweavings of Bridge, Butterworth, Bax, and Ireland is the more musically diffuse of the two films, but Rime of the Ancient Mariner is the more successfully accomplished with its tighter blend of Ralph Vaughan Williams and Benjamin Britten. It would not be going too far to say that after Mahler, Rime of the Ancient Mariner--although not about a composer--is Russell's greatest achievement in the almost unique sphere of utilizing preexisting music so that both the film and the music are enhanced. Russell denies that the unparalleled brilliance of some sections of music-image matching in Rime of the Ancient Mariner would cause him to think twice before undertaking his oft proposed project on the life of Vaughan Williams, 2 but it is similarly undeniable that the repeated use of the music would automatically trigger certain visuals and feelings in the viewer familiar with the earlier film. (This, however, could be conceivably turned to an advantage, as we shall see, were it to be used as a direct point of reference, as are a number of repeat images from earlier works which are found in Rime of the Ancient Mariner.)

Russell starts his film with an excerpt from the third movement of the Vaughan Williams Fourth Symphony as the titles--in an odd and jarring mismatched lettering style-- appear over a sepia-toned print that we will later recognize as Coleridge's "painted ship upon a painted ocean." This then fades à la Valentino into color as Coleridge ransacks his rooms in search of a bottle of the precious laudanum. Russell follows these actions with an unsteady hand-held camera, which, like the very fact that we are as yet unaware of the point behind these hysterical actions, serves to transmit the feeling of Coleridge's own helpless panic to us. This is very important because it indicates the tone of the film, stressing a viewer-Russell identification with the character of Coleridge. It is this fact that helps to point up the difference of the mature Russell's approach with that of his more formative works. Surely, Samuel Taylor Coleridge is the most unsympathetic Russell hero since Tchaikovsky, and even though Russell spares no measure of cataloging many of the man's transgressions and shortcomings, the final portrait is an understanding and sympathetic one.

In common with its most logical immediate predecessors, Mahler and Lisztomania, Rime of the Ancient Mariner is firmly anchored in, but not stifled by, fact. Russell's decision to view Coleridge in terms of his most famous poem may be fanciful, but it is by no means fantastic. Assessing the man as artist and human being through his own words applied in a symbolic and allegorical fashion is, of course, perfectly in keeping with Russell's similar earlier approaches to getting at the truth or essence or spirit of a situation through a composer's music. With this in mind it is scarcely surprising that Russell has here--as he has done to an only slightly lesser extent in William and Dorothy--accomplished the feat of making the familiar seem fresh. By bringing a new--even slightly off-center--light to bear on a work that we are used to complacently accepting in one way, Russell opens our eyes and restores the immediacy and vibrance that may have been lost for years. When viewing Russell's approach to poetry one would do well to bear in mind his statement on the inclusion of the poem "Figs" in Women in Love that "Like all good poems it was about twenty different things at once."[3] In this it should be clear that Russell does by no means put forth the idea that his reading of the poem is the only correct one. In fact it should not be. Instead it should open our minds to other avenues of exploration of the work that might be just as profitable to examine.

Like music, poetry is a far more appropriate vessel for Russell's larger-than-life visions than mere dialogue, and the opening scenes of Rime of the Ancient Mariner bear this out. In both Clouds of Glory films there is a necessary amount of cinematic shorthand due to the relative brevity of the television format (not necessarily a bad thing when one pauses to consider the great number of films offered up today that are fifty-minute ideas padded out to two-hour feature lengths). Because of this, Russell plunges directly into the narrative in a manner that may at first seem overwhelming to some viewers--the mad scramble through the rooms; Coleridge's flight from the house; panning down from a statue of an albatross to Coleridge being blocked and impeded in his progress by a growth of tall grass (a direct reworking and grotesque variation on Rupert Birkin's escape from Hermione in Women in Love); Coleridge carelessly crushing his son's toy ship underfoot. All of this is hurled at the viewer with astonishing speed, but when the film's overall poetic approach becomes clear the effect is not in the least disconcerting. Like Russell's definition of a good poem, his film means many things at once on a series of levels. This is a factor that pertains to the entirety of Russell's filmography, but it is particularly cogent when dealing with Rime of the Ancient Mariner, a film which is the closest any filmmaker has come to creating a poem out of a movie. Therefore, the cinematic shorthand with its attendant use of symbols is a perfectly viable approach on a poetic basis. As usual Russell does not demand that the symbols be grasped on every level in order for the film to make narrative sense. In the case of the evocation of Women in Love, it is not essential that the viewer be familiar with Birkin's escape into the natural world in order for the scene to be comprehended on a simple level. It is necessary, though, that such knowledge be possessed for the scene's deeper meaning. Without that foreknowledge it simply adds to the panic and hysteria of the main character. With it we can see that where Birkin was at one with nature, Coleridge is at the opposite end of the stick. In fact he has become a most unnatural man, so that instead of offering him comfort and escape nature works against him.

Much as in the manner of telescoping time, Russell has also had to telescope Coleridge's poem, preserving its essence while only utilizing those parts of it that have particular bearing on the actions and situations as he has structured them. The reading of the poem commences directly with the encounter with Coleridge's brother-in-law, Robert Southey. The strength of Russell's utilization of the poem in this context does not become clear until the ambiguity of the approach is made apparent. Indeed, Russell does carefully work a choreography into scene and composition, so that the presence of Southey, Mrs. Southey, and Hartley Coleridge make up Coleridge's group of three with Southey as the "one of three" stopped by the Ancient Mariner. It is not, however, yet apparent that Coleridge is both the Ancient Mariner and the waiting Bridegroom of the poem, as, at this point, we are unaware of the constantly shifting levels of time on which the film works. Southey, obviously somewhat afraid of Coleridge and as viewed by Russell something of a fool anyway, attempts to calm the hysterical Coleridge as the tale begins. Here Russell's visual structure is such that he takes us from the opening hysteria with its crazily angled camerawork to a controlled medium long shot where Coleridge and Southey appear as in a theatrical tableau, to a shot which moves back revealing a statue in the shape of a ship's figurehead on the right of the frame as an indication of the commencement of the story of the Mariner's ill-fated voyage. There is some liberty taken with the appearance of Sara Coleridge as Russell first equates her with the "storm-blast" of the poem and thus alters the gender of the storm accordingly:

> "And now the storm-blast came, and she
> Was tyrannous and strong:
> She struck with her o'ertaking wings,
> And chased us south along."

Russell's decision to portray Sara first as the "storm-blast" and then as the Albatross (bearing in mind the poetic metaphor which attributes "o'ertaking wings" to the storm) is remarkable not only for its aptness within the text of the film, but because of the great association we already have of a certain type of destructive woman (Hermione Roddice, Madame von Meck, Nina's mother, Anna von Mildenberg, Princess Carolyn) with birds in Russell's work. Thus Russell's portrayal of Sara is distinctly consistent with his overview, and the significance of this fact is that, accordingly, Sara is no Nina Milyukova and should not be viewed in the same sympathetic light. This is visually apparent from her first appearance, furiously holding up the object of Coleridge's search-- a bottle of laudanum--as if to taunt him with it, and her subsequent lunge toward him, her arms outstretched ("her o'ertaking wings") does nothing to diminish our first impression.

Quite apart from any impression gained by this opening, the viewer is unprepared for the following scene, where Coleridge wrests the bottle from Sara and escapes onto the lake in a rowboat. Here, for the first time, we see the direction the film is taking and get a feel for its shape and structure which is astonishing even for Russell. Sara is still being viewed as the storm in the first part of this section. ("The ship drove fast, loud roared the blast," is accompanied by a shot of her urging Coleridge to return, enhanced by the use of a five-face repeat parallel filter, which is only slightly less effective than the prismatic filter effects in the Bush photographed Mahler and Tommy.) From this point on, the imagery becomes increasingly impressionistic with Coleridge and the boat blending into the water until the picture becomes so abstract that out of focus shots of sunlight on dappled water perfectly complement the mental visuals of the poem:

"The Lake Filmmaker," Ken Russell, on the shores of Derwentwater during the filming of the second Clouds of Glory film, The Rime of the Ancient Mariner. (Courtesy of Ken Russell)

> "And now there came both mist and snow,
> And it grew wondrous cold:
> And ice, mast high, came floating by,
> As green as emerald.
>
> The ice was here, the ice was there,
> The ice was all around:
> It cracked and growled, and roared and howled,
> Like noises in a swound!"

Russell shifts in and out of this impressionistic mold (all of which is heightened by the impeccable application of the ice music from the first movement of Vaughan Williams' Seventh Symphony, the Sinfonia Antarctica, a composition, it should be remembered, that the composer drew from his own film-score for Scott of the Antarctic) to the more literal image of Coleridge, having found solitude in a rocky inlet, drinking the laudanum. From this he moves to a similarly hallucinatory memory of the appearance of Sara in Coleridge's life:

> At length did cross an Albatross,
> Thorough the fog it came;
> As if it had been a Christian soul,
> We hailed it in God's name.

Sara then appears--her arms outstretched and waving in a bird-like fashion--through the "fog" of Coleridge's memory, accompanied by the haunting, wordless vocal of the Seventh Symphony. In an economical, yet effective and visually important, fashion Russell details their courtship: Coleridge engaged in some sleight of hand with an apple, which he makes disappear and then produces from behind Sara's head, as they laugh and jest together; their wedding, an affair controlled with great pomposity by Southey (the poem's Wedding Guest), in which we see that on this level of time frame Coleridge is the Bridegroom of the poem; and the first happy days of marriage. This pleasant memory is short-lived as the specter of Sara, all irritating piety and self-pity, appears to Coleridge in the boat. As if to throw the situation in her face, Coleridge downs the remainder of the drug, shows her the bottle is empty, and lets it drop to the floor of the boat. Russell underscores the dramatic impact by the sudden and quite unexpected introduction of exaggerated synchronized sound as the bottle hits (the first synchronized sound since the ransacking of the rooms at the film's opening).

> "'God save thee, ancient Mariner!

> From the fiends that plague thee thus!--
> Why look'st thou so!"--With my cross-bow
> I shot the Albatross!"

The steady building of the "murder" of Sara in this manner makes its finality all the more dreadful because of its inevitability. Russell uses sound (the monotonous, ever building, never climaxing repeated phrases from the third movement of Vaughan Williams' Sixth Symphony, combined with the sound of the empty bottle constantly hitting the boat's anchor--to Coleridge, the cross-bow--as it rolls with the movement of the boat), the predestined order of events as laid down by the poem itself, and the ever-present image of the "wronged" Sara to force the need for release. The release comes as Coleridge raises the anchor/cross-bow and plunges it into her heart, and the monotonous, unbearable buildup erupts into the sound of a bird screaming three times and a blast from the first movement of the Seventh Symphony, along with Coleridge's sudden outburst of dialogue (the film's first), "Well you say the Devil had mastered me! Southey calls it an indulgence. Well you bid me to rouse myself. It's easier to ask a mad paralytic in both arms to rub them together for a cure.... Once I was a poet. I walked among poets--Wordsworth, Southey ... Southey ... Southey. Ah, it was a dark and sorrowful day when he first introduced me to you--Sara. Southey! You pious fraud!"

Apart from the remarkable technical skill Russell demonstrates in this scene, one should bear in mind that the mixture of fantasy, memory, and reality is made as vague for the viewer as for Coleridge. Similarly, the need for release is communicated to our own feelings at the climax, which places us and the filmmaker in Coleridge's position, resulting in immediate empathy. In itself this is not atypical of Russell's approach--consider the train carriage scene in <u>The Music Lovers</u>, the subjective camera during the burning of Grandier in <u>The Devils</u>, etc.--but it does differ in two respects from these earlier scenes. In the first place it is of a piece with the more mature works in being a more objectively represented version of a subjective interpretation, i.e. very little is made of the idea of point-of-view camera to achieve the effect. Secondly, and more importantly, Russell has given us no distance from the character. This is in part due to the change in physical approach. Whereas both the train carriage sequence and Grandier's death in the aforementioned films achieve the thrust of their effect from the point-of-view camera, they are also, by virtue of this, broken down into parts, placing us in either the position of the character or the spectator, depending on the camera placement. In <u>Rime of the Ancient Mariner</u>, which does not rely on this device, it all becomes subjective so that our sensibilities and those of Coleridge never really part company. The importance of this development of Russell's over the years is part of his overall growth. To a great extent it is part of the process of maturing with age. Where once Russell was outraged and felt betrayed by the shortcomings of his main character (e.g., Tchaikovsky), he now is more saddened than angered, and instead of condemning the man and his flaws, prefers to attempt to reach a level of understanding.

This is both the strength and the curse of Russell's mature works. As his involvement with the characters has grown so, too, has the need for ever-broadening methods of presentation. All too often the reasoning behind these newer methods is lost on the critic who tends to believe that Russell is willfully blending reality with fantasy to no end. The very fact that in the mature films he slips out of reality and into fantasy without the trappings of an introductory transition (amounting to a flashing sign reading, "This is a Fantasy") is an advancement in getting at the core of the truth under the surface. That we should accept the fantastic as real for the moment draws us closer to the experience of the character, and the result becomes less intellectualized and more immediate.

It is unfortunate, but by no means unexpected, that the film tends to bog down slightly after this blood and thunder opening. Moving out of the poetic and into the more mundane world of a comparatively naturalistic flashback may well be a necessity given the manner in which the film is structured, but it is still something of a disappointment. To a certain extent this is obviously an intentional move on Russell's part, because it mirrors Coleridge's own disappointment with the way things were compared with the way he viewed them in his own mind. Russell's point here is to directly juxtapose reality with fantasy. On the one hand we have the sweeping poetry of the film's opening, and on the other the more mundane presentation of many of the same events and situations, designed to help us understand the causes behind the more fantastic representations.

This is not to say that Russell eschews stylization or has lost his wit in dealing with the realistic portions of the film. The first of these scenes in which Southey and his

friend, Robert Lovell, attempt to persuade Coleridge of the
viability of founding a Utopian society in America, is beautifully choreographic in its physical design and much of the
dialogue is witty, barbed, and entertaining.   Symbolically,
Russell photographs the scenes to represent Coleridge's intellectual superiority to that of his friend, as he has him
dart in and out a row of trees and hedges, while the others
try vainly to keep up with him.   There is a wonderful in-joke where Coleridge corrects Southey on the term Pantisocracy (a word coined by Coleridge), which Southey calls
"Pantocracy. " (The most ludicrous of their notions about
this Pantisocracy is the idea that "since it is a proven fact
that only one man in twenty does any physical labor" it will
only be necessary for each of their proposed group of twenty
to work one hour a day.) Admittedly, their recruiting process for this "new Eden" has not proven markedly successful.
The only ones who have agreed to it are, in fact, Lovell
and Southey--and as a bonus the three Fricker sisters, two
of whom are engaged to Southey and Lovell, with the third,
Sara, "as yet unattached. " Caring neither for the interests
of either Sara or Coleridge, it is the intention of Messrs.
Lovell and Southey to pair them off. The ultimately disastrous effect of this pairing is neatly foreshadowed in the fact
that Coleridge mistakes Edith as "the charmer at the end, "
and inadvertently introduces himself to her, ignoring the real
Sara.   Once this is set to rights, however, Southey and
Lovell and their fiancées exchange smug looks and set off,
leaving Coleridge and Sara to become acquainted.

Russell then briefly sketches in the decline of their
marriage in three scenes.   The first of these has the union
still fresh, at least insofar as Sara is concerned (the apple
she is eating being an indication of this, recalling the courtship conjuring trick of the poetic narrative).   Edith and
Robert Southey are upbraiding Coleridge for having failed to
appear and deliver a speech on Pantisocracy.   Coleridge
pleads illness, but Southey is not unaware of the fact that he
had, despite this illness, managed "to give quite a good
speech down at the Mariner's Arms. " The scene has certain overtones in common with the scene in The Music Lovers
where Nina sides with Tchaikovsky in his decision not to go
to the opera with Chiluvsky and Nina's mother, as Sara argues on her husband's behalf.   The operative difference in
this case is that Sara is not consciously trying to keep Coleridge by defending him, and after the departure of the
Southeys--and even more in the next scene--Russell makes
it clear that Sara would like nothing better than to have an
end to this dream of a Utopian society.

Russell directing Kika Markham, Patricia Garwood, and Ben Aris on location for The Rime of the Ancient Mariner. (Courtesy of Ken Russell)

Again like Nina, Sara is inept, but she is not inept in the same manner. Nina was disturbed, naturally clumsy, awkward, and ill-educated. Sara is quite simply careless, as demonstrated by her losing Coleridge's fishing rod in this scene, and in the next offering up "one burned mutton chop" for their dinner. Worse, in neither case is she the least concerned about her actions or the discomfort those actions cause Coleridge. As he sloshes into the river after his rod, Sara merely lies on the bank eating her apple, and smiling at him, asks, "Would you love me as much on the banks of the River Severn?" (as on the banks of the Susquehanna, where the Pantisocratic community was to be founded).

Russell counters her lackadaisical attitude with that of Coleridge, in whom we can clearly see the signs of estrangement--first in his expression following her question about the River Severn, and in the succeeding scene his beaten down irritation as Sara barges in, at the first pause, with a piece of unimportant news during his recitation of

"Frost at Midnight" to their child. Russell sums up the
state of their marriage when Coleridge is denied ale in favor
of a glass of water. In a reworking of his conjuring trick
with the apple, he produces a bottle of laudanum from behind
Sara's head to mix with his "fresh water." "The opposite
of fresh, alas," he says as he smells it, and the words are
broadened by the visual structure of the reworking in order
to make a statement on their relationship as well.

The real gulf between them occurs in the next scene
with the introduction of William and Dorothy Wordsworth, who
are much nearer being on the same emotional, intellectual,
and philosophical ground with Coleridge than Sara. The bois-
terous nature of the entrance of the Wordsworths, who have
been caught in the rain with Coleridge and burst into the Coleridge cottage unannounced and dripping wet, signals the beginning of the breakdown of Coleridge's marriage. One cannot help but feel a tinge of compassion for Sara upon finding
Dorothy coming back downstairs wearing one of Sara's dresses
in place of her soaked one ("I found these clothes in your
room, they fit quite well"), but her subsequent attitude is,
by contrast of the bright spirits of the others, just plain
shrewish. To begin with, Coleridge is excited by his companions' intellectual natures, where Sara is merely put out
by the intrusion and insists on treating Coleridge like a child,
ordering him to take off his boots and get out of his wet
clothes. Further, Coleridge has been fired up by Wordsworth's stories of the beauties and wonders of Cumberland
and cannot wait to go there. (This influence on Coleridge is
not dissimilar to the effect of Wordsworth's poems on Reverend Dewey in William and Dorothy, i.e., "Words that brought
me three thousand miles.") Sara, at the other end of the
scale, is unsympathetic to this desire, concerned only about
"those articles you have to write for the paper." In short it
has become altogether too obvious that Sara wants Coleridge
as a solid, upright, sober citizen--she wants him to be ordinary, and this is impossible from Coleridge's point of view,
and not particularly desirable from a historical vantage point.
(Would an ordinary man ever have written "The Rime of the
Ancient Mariner" or "Kubla Khan"?) The summation of the
entire sequence occurs when Dorothy notices that Coleridge's
boots have caught fire, and everyone, except Sara, who made
him take the boots off to dry in the first place, finds this
vastly amusing. Bearing in mind the similar situation in
Lisztomania when Wagner's Siegfried creation goes awry to
the amusement of Liszt and to the embarrassment and irritation of its creator, Russell, perhaps unconsciously, places
Sara very much in the wrong.

From this realistic flashback, we return to the boat with its attendant drug-hazed and mentally anguished version of reality. In so doing a pattern is formed whereby the structure can be seen as moving in and out of three interlocking but distinctly different levels--the poetic narrative, the transitional scenes on the boat, and the realistically designed flashback. Russell has started the film in a lead-in to the transitional, follows this by boldly utilizing the poetic narrative in an expository section culminating in a transitional scene which leads into the realistic flashback, which examines and explains the poetic narrative. The structure from this, however, is such that the realistic flashback goes beyond the point of examination and explanation and into exposition, leading back into the transitional and poetic narrative through which the expository portions of the flashback are examined and enlarged upon in those terms. This approach to the narrative structure of the overall film makes <u>Rime of the Ancient Mariner</u> as much like a musical composition as anything else. Not unlike the idea of a theme and variations compositional structure, Russell adds another layer of complexity to the approach by reversing the order, and at first offering the variations and then the theme.

"Love is the vital air of my genius, and love has deserted me, that was why I fell," says Coleridge upon dissolving from a close-shot of Sara and the baby to a close-shot of him in the rowboat. He continues, "Yours was the first to go with your temper and your nagging and stupidity, and your self-encouraged admiration of Southey." All of this is addressed to the dead Sara, who lies cruciform style at the prow of the boat. Like the Mariner's albatross (or like Tchaikovsky's Nina) he has "killed" her but is not rid of her. "William and Dorothy, they sustained me.... They realized that a man could be weak and not evil," he further states. The construction of this dialogue at first mirrors the activities of Sara in the preceding scene, and then sets up the dichotomy of the situation as portrayed in the subsequent poetic narrative.

Beginning with this recitation:

"Swiftly, swiftly flew the ship,
Yet she sailed softly too:
Sweetly, sweetly blew the breeze -
On me alone it blew."

Coleridge sets off in the boat, symbolically moving into the poetic narrative. The moody excerpt from the first movement of Vaughan Williams' Fifth Symphony eases the transition, which opens with Coleridge and the Wordsworths exploring the Lake District. Coleridge calls out, "Sara!" but the only answer (partly depicted in an interesting and unusual use of the zoom shot visualizing the word bouncing off the mountains) is the echo of his own voice.

> And I had done a hellish thing,
> And it would work 'em woe;
> For all averred, I had killed the bird
> That made the breeze to blow.
> Ah, wretch! said they, the bird to slay,
> That made the breeze to blow!

As these lines are heard on the soundtrack, we see the situation as it has come to be. Sara's "self-encouraged admiration of Southey" has led to an arrangement where she and the Southeys stand against Coleridge. Russell's handling of this scene is further evidence of the difference of approach he is using in dealing with Coleridge. The attitude is satirical, making the Southeys and Sara, in their attitude against Coleridge, more than slightly ridiculous. (The effect is enhanced by shooting various of them in close-shot with a wide-angle lens so that they appear monstrous, looming, and ludicrous in their self-righteous accusatory posturings.) The nature of this presentation is such that it is impossible for us to side with the Southeys and Sara, making Coleridge's exit (he simply turns and walks out of the room in which they have gathered) seem the only sensible move.

> Nor dim nor red, like God's own head,
> The glorious sun uprist:
> Then all averred, I had killed the bird
> That brought the fog and mist.
> "Twas right," said they, "such birds to slay,
> That bring the fog and mist."

Russell utilizes this verse of the poem to illustrate the support of William and Dorothy for Coleridge, and although it assuredly departs from the application in the original poem, it works brilliantly within the text of the film. It should be realized at this point that the killing of the Albatross/Sara is not an occurrence from the poetic section of the film alone. If we approach the film in such a manner that we attempt to afix a chronology of events (a somewhat arbitrary attempt at best) other than in the order in which Russell has designed them to flow one into the other, it becomes apparent that the fantasy killing in the boat during the film's opening is not meant to have a direct bearing on the footage leading up to it. The fantasy is not just a fantasy, but a fantasized memory. Sara is dead for Coleridge prior to the events depicted in the opening. Hearkening back to the imagery from William and Dorothy, Russell places Coleridge, William, and Dorothy on the hill, where in the previous film he established the "I'll wait for you" motif, and in so doing makes Coleridge an accepted part of Wordsworth's world. The elation of this camaraderie is short-lived as the recriminating figure of Sara--clutching the most powerful of her weapons of guilt, the child--appears before Coleridge. This then is mirrored by the continued recitation of the poem:

> "Down dropt the breeze, the sails dropt down,
> 'Twas sad as sad could be;
> And we did speak only to break
> The silence of the sea."

At this point in the narrative Russell begins the process of intertwining the various aspects of the film's levels of presentation so that, like the film's opening, these separate parts become one. The departure from the original presentation at the opening is simply that the procedure is now clarified, and this in turn serves to clarify the opening as well. Considered from this standpoint alone, Rime of the Ancient Mariner is the most advanced of Russell's films which experiment with new forms of structure. Unlike the layered structuring of Mahler, the circular building and descending of Tommy, or even the fantasy-on-fantasy linked in a logical scene-to-scene basis found in Lisztomania, Rime of the Ancient Mariner creates a continuous flow. The various levels of the film come at one time so that every aspect of the film, whether allegorical, symbolic, or historical, serves to develop the narrative as well.

The construction of the scenes forming this section of the film's poetic narrative is very shrewdly done. At the onset we find Sara standing next to the "painted ship upon a painted ocean," with Coleridge physically distanced from her at the other side of the large room (its size emphasized by the sparse furnishings). Russell then reflects the mental anguish of this situation in a brief scene of Coleridge in the boat drinking laudanum, but even the drug will not banish the image of Sara. Then, reverting to the same room where he was just seen with Sara, there is a sequence depicting the effects of his laudanum addiction in the past. In a superbly executed mixture of swirling camera effects and one of the few really effective and intelligent uses of slow-motion ever conceived (heightened by the eerie wordless vocal of the Vaughan Williams Seventh Symphony and exaggerated sound effects), Russell captures the feeling of lost control and mental collapse, giving greater power to the recitation:

> "Water, water everywhere,
> And all the boards did shrink;
> Water, water everywhere,
> Nor any drop to drink."

> "The very deep did rot: O Christ!
> That ever this should be!
> Yea, slimy things did crawl with legs
> Upon the slimy sea."

Coleridge's delirium and collapse brings Southey and the family into the room. In keeping with the earlier presentation of them, they are again photographed with the distorting wide-angle lens in a point-of-view shot as they hover over the prostrate Coleridge. Instead of expressing great concern over the situation, Southey offers Coleridge the rather cold comfort of draping Sara's arms around his neck--"Instead of the cross, the Albatross, about my neck was hung."

This image then dissolves to Coleridge in the boat with Sara as the slain Albatross at the other end. "There was a time when the thought of suicide was my sole comfort," he tells her, but like the Mariner of his poem, Coleridge finds himself "condemned to life," and beginning with a naturalistic flashback, Russell embarks on the strangest and most morbid section of the film.

The flashback starts with Coleridge and the Wordsworths during their trip to Scotland. This was a period in Coleridge's life when, as Wordsworth put it in the introduction to his poems from that trip he "was somewhat too much in love with his own dejection."[4] (This thought in fact finds its way into the dialogue here.) This naturalistic approach is of particular interest as it relates to William and Dorothy. As in the previous film, they are frequently given rhymed dialogue, and the charming quality of the bit where Dorothy offers advice on the composition of "The Solitary Reaper" ("How about 'overflowing'? 'Saturated' sounds soggy.") goes beyond mere charm to become a little statement on the collaborative nature of even such a seemingly private artistic endeavor as composing a poem. (This too is reflected in Wordsworth's rhyming statement on "The Rime of the Ancient Mariner"--"That's not true, I thought of the dead crew.") It is not Russell's intention to make mock of the creative act in any way through this (anyone with a working knowledge of his output knows better), but rather to point up the many different forms and levels through which the final work of art takes its shape. Within Russell's own work this is very apparent. It is well known that he chooses his actors and technicians on their ability to intuit his needs and desires, and it is also obvious that although the overall final film clearly bears his signature, he nonethless is open to suggestion and does not stifle other people's talent and creativity. (The simple fact that the film photographed by Dick Bush, and only the films photographed by Dick Bush, contain elaborate filter effects attests to this.) Each person who touches the artist or the work of art brings something to it that it might otherwise not have had, regardless of the controlling voice. It would be far afield to say that Dick Bush was responsible for the film at hand, and it would be equally absurd to say that Dorothy was the true author of "The Solitary Reaper," but both undeniably contributed something.

Russell conferring with cinematographer Dick Bush while filmming The Rime of the Ancient Mariner. (Courtesy of Ken Russell)

The peaceful collaborative nature of the poetry is at
once spoiled by the strained nerves of Coleridge, who only
feels all the more isolated by the bond shared by William
and Dorothy. His complaints of having "no dear heart to
read my verse" fall on rather unsympathetic ears as the
Wordsworths feel that they at least have tried to help and support him, and indeed this is the case. The important point
here is that Coleridge is a difficult man--difficult to know,
difficult to help, difficult to understand. As can be seen
from this illustration, Coleridge expects more than he can
ever hope to attain in any circumstance. Previously, he
wanted something in the relationship with Sara that just was
not there, and here he wants the Wordsworths to be more
committed to him than it is reasonable to expect. Similarly,
when the situation does not pan out as he would wish it, he
walks away from it. Deciding that he is "unfit for company, "
he leaves William and Dorothy just as he had earlier abandoned Sara, and even "escaped" into the false world of drugs--
this last being an escape from which there is no escape as
Coleridge himself realizes. Taking his leave, Coleridge tells
Wordsworth, "Well, you take the high road and I'll take the
low road. " Wordsworth's riposte, "The man who wrote that
line ended up on the gallows, " is countered by Coleridge's
cry, "Lucky fellow!" thereby introducing the morbid turn the
narrative is taking.

Russell immediately follows this with a sequence at
an inn in Edinburgh, where Coleridge, in a withdrawal delirium, awakes telling a servant girl, "I dreamed I was dying, " and then accuses her of having pilfered a bottle of
laudanum from his nightstand. In a bit recalling the rough
and thoughtless treatment of his beloved books at the film's
opening, Coleridge finds himself reduced to selling some of
his books in order to buy the drug. After the girl has been
dispatched on this mission he cowers in the bed, bemoaning
his fate, "He escapes at length, poor Coleridge, and without
screaming, he dies, as he had always lived--dreaming. "
This aspect of self-pity is one of Coleridge's least endearing
traits, remarkably consistent with Wordsworth's assessment
of his being "too much in love with his own dejection, " but
it is nevertheless portrayed as genuine pain and remorse,
quite different from Tchaikovsky's theatrical outburst that
nothing lives in him in The Music Lovers.

Russell's choice of the First Sea Interlude from Benjamin Britten's opera Peter Grimes to accompany the lead-in
to the poetic narrative here is brilliant. Not only is the mu-

sic perfectly suited to the mood, but the actions are beautifully choreographed to it, and there is some thematic justification as well. <u>Peter Grimes</u> is a work that climaxes with the suicide of its main character, contains a subordinate character who is addicted to laudanum, and it is not unlikely that Russell finds a peculiar humor in accompanying the delivery of Coleridge's laudanum with a piece of music which, in its original context, follows the lines, "Here is a friend. Here is a friend." The sequence begins with the precious bottle in sharp focus in the foreground and Coleridge out of focus in the back, eyeing it greedily. Dismissing the girl, he makes a desperate grab for the bottle, opens it, and is at once overcome by self-loathing at his dependence on it. Recapping the bottle, he decides to try to overcome the craving, and, in a fit of despair, hurls the bottle across the room (again with the attendant exaggerated sound as when he lets the empty bottle drop in the boat). Immediately he regrets this action and races across after it before it all spills onto the floor, where he then huddles in the corner holding the bottle. In a shot accompanied by the ice music from the Vaughan Williams Seventh Symphony we look down the blade of a bread knife. Russell interpolates this shot very smoothly, throwing us, like Coleridge, off balance. In the preceding shot he has Coleridge look up at something from his position on the floor. We therefore automatically assume that the shot of the bread knife is what he has seen, and in our own minds place the shot as immediately following in unbroken action. It is then a little surprising--and a good bit disorienting--when at the conclusion of the panning we find Coleridge's fingers already wrapping around the knife handle. Coleridge than rushes out onto the landing and leans over the stair rail with the knife poised in one hand and the bottle of laudanum in the other:

> "I looked to heaven and tried to pray;
> But or ever a prayer had gusht,
> A wicked whisper came, and made
> My heart as dry as dust."

From this Russell moves to a lovely composition of the boat in long shot, effectively evoking these lines:

> "Alone, alone, all, all alone,
> Alone on a wide, wide sea!
> And never a saint took pity on
> My soul in agony."

We have already seen how Coleridge is cut off from nature, and now he feels cut off from God as well. As the wordless vocal from the symphony comes up on the track, Russell reworks the preceding shots where Coleridge first saw the knife and began considering suicide. In this case he looks from the boat and sees another boat drifting toward him, first with only a woman hanging over the bow like a figurehead, and then with the figure of Death sitting in the back of the boat:

> "And is that woman all her crew?
> Is that a Death? and are there two?
> Is Death that woman's mate?"

As the poem goes on describing the woman, Russell combines the movement of the boat toward the camera with a zoom shot on the spectral woman, thereby creating a visual equivalent of Coleridge's suicidal thoughts rushing forth to meet Death. Intercutting this action with that of Coleridge attempting to decide between the laudanum and the knife on the landing, Russell leads into the woman's dice game with Death:

> "The naked hulk alongside came,
> And the twain were casting dice;
> "The Game is done! I've won! I've won!"
> Quoth she, and whistles thrice."

By pausing for the action after the line "And the twain were casting dice," Russell is able to heighten the suspense of the game, which has by intercutting also become the suspense of whether Coleridge chooses the laudanum or suicide. At the moment when the woman wins, Coleridge drops the bread knife, and, collapsing on the bed, gulps the drug. This Russell accompanies with the same blast of music from the Vaughan Williams Seventh Symphony that he had earlier used at the "murder" of Sara and adds to the impact by representing the three whistles with three bird screams, also recalling that earlier scene. This and the subsequent dissolve from a close-shot of Coleridge to one of the slain Sara/Albatross is suggestive of the idea that either choice represented death in one form or another. As was said in Mahler, "There are many kinds of death," and in deciding to live Coleridge has chosen but one of them.

> "There passed a weary time. Each throat
> Was parched, and glazed each eye.
> A weary time! A weary time!

When looking westward I beheld
A something in the sky. "

"At first it seemed a little speck
And then it seemed a mist;
It moved and moved, and took at last
A certain shape, I wist. "

Russell zooms back from the close-shot of Sara to reveal (in a strikingly beautiful composition) both of them in the boat, then dissolves to another close-shot of Sara designed to simulate the image of her dead in the boat. By so doing he restates the idea that, for Coleridge and for the marriage, she has been "dead" for some time. He then further mirrors the shot layout in the boat by zooming back from this to reveal the new surroundings, the room with the ship painting. The camera pans from Sara stretched out on the sofa to Coleridge at the far end of the room (again the emphasis on the distance between them) where he is looking out the window through a telescope. The "certain shape" into which the object he views transforms is that of a woman carrying a lantern, being followed by William and Dorothy. He raises the window and she steps into the room. An immediate empathy is noticeable between the two, while William and Dorothy enigmatically look on from outside. As the wordless vocal from the Vaughan Williams Seventh Symphony recurs on the track Russell dissolves to Coleridge standing in the boat.

Russell's camera moves around the boat in a rapid circle while Coleridge yells the woman's name, Asra, and offers us an explanation of who she is. The circling motion and the wordless vocal (associated with Sara and impending disaster) combine to form the idea that this is a doomed situation. The circular gliding of the camera foretells two upcoming poetic excerpts--"Around, around flew each sweet sound" and the line from "Kubla Khan, " "Weave a circle round him thrice, and close your eyes in holy dread"--as well as evoking the feeling of a circling bird of prey. Then, too, there is the character of Asra herself. In reality Asra, "the sister-in-law of William Wordsworth, " is Sarah Hutchinson with whom Coleridge became romantically entangled. By making her Asra (itself an anagram of Sara) Russell sidesteps the potential confusion of two Saras in the same film, but far beyond this he gives her a universal standing. Asra is a phantom creature (her physical resemblance to the woman specter in the boat underlines this). Less a person than

Intermission

an idea of Coleridge's, she is what he wishes Sara had been to him, hence the anagram and his shouting of her name which recall the unanswered calls to Sara in the mountains earlier in the film. This is also brought forth by the constant allusions to "Kubla Khan," a poem which Coleridge subtitled, "Or a Vision in a Dream." Addressing Sara's "corpse," he tells her, "Once I had a vision--a stately pleasure dome. You and Wordsworth destroyed it. Then I met Asra, sister-in-law of William Wordsworth. She with her symphony and song could restore my pleasure dome."

Dissolving from this to the image of a kite flying in the sky, Russell returns to the poetic narrative:

> "Around, around, flew each sweet sound,
> Then darted to the sun;
> Slowly the sounds came back again,
> Now mixed, now one by one."

We see Coleridge and Asra flying this kite in a field. It is the first occasion in which Coleridge appears peaceful and happy.

> "And now 'twas like all instruments,
> Now like a lonely flute;
> And now it is an angel's song,
> That makes the heavens be mute."

Reflective of this "angel's song," Russell introduces the beautiful lush theme of hopefulness from the first movement of Vaughan Williams' Sixth Symphony. He then dissolves from this idyllic encounter to Coleridge in the boat:

> "The self-same moment I could pray;
> And from my neck so free
> The Albatross fell off, and sank
> Like lead into the sea."

Zooming back from Coleridge we find the persistent image of the "dead" Sara is gone. Vaughan Williams' lyrical music mirrors the great relief of this seeming delivery as Coleridge rows the boat to shore. Coleridge's salvation, like that of the Mariner in the poem and that promised by this passage in the symphony, proves to be fraudulent. As he makes his way toward Dove Cottage, home at this point of Thomas DeQuincey, the craving for laudanum overtakes him, just as the terrifying opening theme of the symphony (hinted at in the film just prior to the slaying of the Albatross) returns and overshadows the hopeful theme. Collapsing in the street, he barely makes it into DeQuincey's house.

By effectively utilizing distorting wide-angle shots and tilting hand-held camera angles, Russell imparts the unworldly disorientation of Coleridge to the viewer as DeQuincey carefully doles out a measure of the drug to his stricken friend. (Played in a kind of horror film fashion, the scene has distinct overtones, with its angles and emphasis on the drugged drink, of Dr. Praetorius quieting the Monster with doctored Scotch in James Whale's Bride of Frankenstein.) The overall strangeness of the scene is enhanced by the fact that although Coleridge keeps up an almost nonstop philosophical dissertation on the nature of love, DeQuincey never utters a word. To some extent DeQuincey's distraction is explained as it turns out that he is keeping careful watch so as to warn Asra of Coleridge's presence. Unfortunately, Coleridge notices him signaling her, and bursts out of the house after her.

As he runs after her down the same street, Coleridge's pursuit of Asra calls to mind Wordsworth's flight from Reverend Dewey in the climactic moments of William and Dorothy. Russell reinforces this view when, upon catching up with her, he tells her, "You are my Dorothy." It is her intention, however, to leave Cumberland, to go "where you cannot find me." In his wildly disoriented state Coleridge has even forgotten what day of the week it is, and we see him here approaching the lowest point in his life as presented in the film. The break-off with Asra offers further evidence of the near impossibility of dealing with him, and this stems, in part, from the same problem found in his earlier relationships with Sara and the Wordsworths--he has built a fantasy image of what the person is or should be and cannot reconcile this with reality.

Following Asra to the Wordsworth home he has one final scene with her in which she knocks him to the ground. "You and your vile ailments," she screams. Leaving him huddled in a heap on the ground (recalling his crouching in the corner after retrieving the bottle of laudanum), she runs into the house, and his subsequent knocking brings forth only Wordsworth, who vainly tries to reason with him. The experience leaves Coleridge completely shattered ("But who will love me?"), and he staggers away from the house.

Intermission

In a masterful reworking of the climactic scene from Tommy, Russell brings Coleridge to the edge of the abyss. Shot from almost the exact same angle as the next to last shot of the earlier work, Russell gives Coleridge no inner peace from his trip to the top of the mountain. Considering the implications of a universal salvation in Tommy, the overriding feeling here is that Coleridge has digressed from the points where he was at odds with nature, even at odds with God, to a level where he is now at odds with these things and humankind as well. He has become one of the fantastic creatures of his own imaginings, and instead of finding salvation, he finds oblivion. Tommy Walker climbs the same mountain to find the actual innocence and hope that was lost in the post-war years of the modern age. Coleridge, in reciting the climactic lines of "Khubla Khan," is attempting to find and recapture that which never existed: "a Vision in a Dream." And yet the choice of these lines from the poem is indicative of Coleridge's own knowledge of his lack of humanity:

> And all should cry, Beware! Beware!
> His flashing eyes, his floating hair!
> Weave a circle round him thrice,
> And close your eyes in holy dread,
> For he on honey-dew hath fed,
> And drunk the milk of Paradise.

It is significant therefore that the scene presages his impending salvation at the hands of Dr. Gillman and his wife.

Utilizing the first of two lengthy excerpts from "The Rime of the Ancient Mariner," Russell introduces and establishes the Gillmans as an indication of Coleridge's potential deliverance, but carefully avoids the idea that all is immediately well:

> "The other was a softer voice,
> As soft as honey-dew:
> Quoth he, "The man hath pennance done,
> And pennance more will do."

Russell dissolves from this to Coleridge waking after a dream in Dr. Gillman's study, and it is in this scene that the structural pattern and thematic approach of the film is made perfectly clear. Coleridge is now a much older man, and the preceding events can now be seen to have been a dream, but this is far too facile. Regardless of whether the

viewer takes it to have been a literal dream (and this is
slightly untenable as the final section of the film utilizes the
same poetic-symbolic form) it is a dream with the stamp of
truth. In telling Dr. Gillman about the dream and its relation to the poem Coleridge says, "I wrote that so long ago--
nearly twenty years ago. Yet in some way it seems to contain the whole history of my life--my life before I wrote it--
after--then--now--perhaps to come. I am the Ancient Mariner." In that small section of dialogue, Russell makes clear
the idea that the use of the various levels and time frames
found within the film do indeed represent a blending of these
elements into a cohesive narrative. The characterizations of
the Gillmans and their relationship with Coleridge is also interesting in that it is the relationship of parents with a child,
which roughly parallels his earlier status with Sara. The
only difference here is that they are kindly paternal figures
where Sara was not. Russell's interpretation of Coleridge's
situation with them might appear a little too easily symbolic,
but it should be remembered that the idea is not a new one.
In his English Authors volume of Little Journeys to the Homes
of the Great, Elbert Hubbard notes, "So Gillman brought him
to his house at Highgate and took care of him as a child."5
This image of Coleridge as a child, hinted at throughout the
film, is brought home in this scene where Mrs. Gillman
gives him his daily ration of laudanum. Carefully giving him
a spoonful of the drug, she looks for all the world like a
concerned mother dosing a sick child with a cold remedy.
In her kindness, however, she gets Dr. Gillman's permission to give Coleridge a second spoonful, which causes him
to collapse in the floor.

> "Forthwith this frame of mind was wrenched
> With a woeful agony,
> Which forced me to begin my tale;
> And then it left me free."

> "Since then, at an uncertain hour,
> That agony returns:
> And till my ghastly tale is told,
> This heart within me burns."

Here Coleridge and Russell are concerned with the
nature of guilt, and its consequences. In making Coleridge
the Ancient Mariner of the poem, Russell presents him at
once as a soul redeemed and a soul cursed. This does find
a parallel in Coleridge's later years, where he took up the-
ology, and which under Gillman's care were decidedly less

turbulent. Also this is evident from Coleridge's own realization of his addiction and his decision to do something about it. In the letter to Dr. Gillman in which he accepted the idea of coming to live with him, Coleridge warned, "And now of myself. My ever wakeful reason, and the keenness of my moral feelings, will secure you from all unpleasant circumstances connected with me, save only one, viz., the evasion of a specific madness. You will never hear anything but truth from me: --prior habits render it out of my power to tell an untruth, but unless carefully observed, I dare not promise that I should not, with regard to this detested poison, be capable of acting one."[6] Coleridge, like his creation, has found a salvation, but the guilt of his deeds lingers on within him. By way of explanation and, if not justification, at least understanding, Russell offers up the film's final images, beginning with a memory of the wedding with Sara and its attendant statement to Southey:

> "O Wedding Guest! this soul hath been
> Alone on a wide wide sea:
> So lonely 'twas that God himself
> Scarce seemed there to be."

This is not offered so much as an apology to Southey, as of a clear statement of fact on his growing alienation under the influence of the drug. Now, like the Mariner, Coleridge finds comfort and consolation in God, though even this is blighted by his feelings of guilt, when, attending church, a golden statue of the Albatross looms up before him.

Nonetheless, the final image in the film, though slightly undercut by the presence of a stuffed albatross on a bookshelf above Coleridge, is a positive one of a man who has found redemption within his lifetime, and having learned from it wishes to impart that knowledge to his fellow man:

> "Farewell, Farewell! but this I tell
> To thee, thou Wedding Guest!
> He prayeth well, who loveth well
> Both man and bird and beast."

> "He prayeth best, who loveth best
> All things both great and small;
> For the dear God who loveth us,
> He made and loveth all."

From this Russell moves his camera up from Coleridge to a

close-shot of the stuffed albatross, which, in a reversal of the film's opening, fades into the sepia tone of an old print. It is at once one of the most uplifting, and one of the most shattering of Russell's endings, and a fitting climax to one of his best creations. The horror of it comes from the knowledge that even though Coleridge has found salvation and peace within the text of the film, he is no longer able to delude himself into blaming everyone around him, and the implied burden is therefore greater for him than for such an unredeemed Russell protagonist as Tchaikovsky, who can, even at the end, fool himself and take refuge in a dream.

In many respects Rime of the Ancient Mariner is Russell's most completely controlled work. There is not one aspect of it that rings false or appears arbitrary, and nothing is wasted. In the manner of the stylistic trilogy of Mahler, Tommy, and Lisztomania the film can be viewed innumerable times and not lose its effectiveness. Best of all, perhaps, is the fact that in drawing on a number of sources for his creative tools--the poems, the music, the man--Russell gives back what he takes. For those of us willing to use our eyes, our ears, and our imaginations, it becomes apparent that in no way does Russell merely trade on these preexisting creations. The elements used in the film are enhanced by their usage, not diminished by it. One can only fervently hope that the film and its companion piece, William and Dorothy, will find a place in the art house repertory and emerge from their relative obscurity.

NOTES

1. Personal correspondence with Ken Russell, November 1982.
2. Ibid.
3. Baxter, John. An Appalling Talent: Ken Russell. London: Michael Joseph, 1973, p. 169.
4. Wordsworth, William. The Complete Poetical Works. Cambridge Edition. Boston and New York: Houghton Mifflin, 1904, p. 294.
5. Hubbard, Elbert. Little Journeys to the Homes of the Great, Vol. 5., English Authors. Cleveland, Ohio and New York: World, 1928, p. 309.
6. Coleridge, Samuel Taylor. Letter to James Gillman. The Best of Coleridge. New York: Ronald Press, 1934, p. 659.

CHAPTER 11

A SUMMING UP IN HOLLYWOOD

"Altered States"

Following the financial disasters of Lisztomania and Valentino, Ken Russell desperately needed a hit movie to reestablish himself as a bankable director. Thanks to a producer willing to give him a chance, and the decision of the original director, Arthur Penn, not to do Altered States, Russell found a vehicle with which to prove himself once more. Conditions were far from ideal, however. The author of the screenplay and its source novel, Paddy Chayefsky, was already irritated that Penn had dropped out of the project and was not particularly well-disposed toward Russell as a replacement. Beyond this Russell was faced with the stigma of being a decidedly second choice, no matter how one looks at it. To further the anxiety he must have felt about the project, Russell was also working in Hollywood for the first time, and with none of his usual stock company of actors and technicians, save for editor Stuart Baird in his new capacity as associate producer.

Trouble with Chayefsky did not end with the start of filming. According to Russell, Chayefsky wanted to direct his directing. Tension grew between the two men until Chayefsky decided to put the continent between them and went back East. Afterwards Chayefsky demanded that his name be removed from the screenplay and the pseudonym Sidney Aaron be used. In a way it is surprising that the producer chose to back Russell over Chayefsky, but it was a commendable act. There is, after all, little point in hiring a unique talent merely to stifle it.

Chayefsky's claims that Russell was "scuttling" the script are, however, not without grounds.[1] The final product that is Altered States in its film incarnation bears much more relation to the Anglo-Catholic mysticism of Russell than to the two-fisted, very un-mystical, satire of Chayefsky. There are any number of basic differences between the two men, and Altered States points them out in no uncertain terms as an examination of the novel against the film quickly reveals.

In the novel, Chayefsky minimizes the visual and accentuates the dialogue. Russell reverses this approach. Chayefsky's attitude toward the characters is that of a cold observer. It is significant that he continually refers to them throughout the book on a rather gruff last name basis. In the film, Russell has made them quite personable. He responds to them and always identifies them by their first names. By far the most drastic difference between the source and the film, though, is Russell's use of design and symbol, which is admittedly something more viable for the visual medium of film than for the printed word. Working for the first time with designer Richard MacDonald, Russell has fashioned one of his most strikingly symbolic sets in the Jessup apartment in Boston. In choosing the Scottish Art Nouveau architect Charles Rennie Mackintosh as their inspiration, they have been able to create a setting that, although Spartan, still includes designs within it (N.B. the "Philosopher's Egg" designs in the stained glass windows) that have a bearing on the film's plot and theme. Beyond this, there is the question of Russell's judicious pruning of Chayefsky's screenplay. For two men so very much at odds with each other in terms of personality, Russell and Chayefsky are not terribly more incompatible thematically than were Russell and Pete Townshend. The thematic implications of Chayefsky's original are rarely at odds with Russell's central themes, and therefore it only needed some trimming of the more pretentious sections in order to be workable as a Russell film. Interestingly, Russell emerges as a more clear-headed writing craftsman than professional writer Chayefsky in this matter. In the novel, Chayefsky has Eddie Jessup tell his wife that he loves her (something he has heretofore been unable to admit) at several points in the dialogue prior to the actual climax,[2] thereby dulling the point of the ending. Russell's Eddie only says it at the very last of the film, which endows the line with the prominence it should have.

Do Russell's changes improve Altered States? In many respects the answer to that depends largely on whose camp one is a part of--Russell's or Chayefsky's. There is little denying that, dramatically, Russell's changes are valid, if only because his personal vision is broader than Chayefsky's

A Summing Up in Hollywood

(Witness the difference in the staging of the Hinchi Indian mushroom ceremony. Chayefsky's novel has it take place on a tumbledown front porch à la Carlos Castaneda.[3] Russell's film transports this to a mysterious, giant cave, giving the scene a grand, larger than life, mystical quality.) Russell approaches things in the film with wonderment, where Chayefsky approaches the same material with more than a little mockery and derision. Whether these aspects are viewed as improvements or not, they attest strongly to the fact that in its film form Altered States is almost pure Russell. Against all odds Russell has managed to turn a project which did not originate with him into a film that is as much a personal statement as any of his earlier works.

In many ways Altered States is a summation of those earlier films. With it Russell has come to the end of his long road toward a positive outlook. As each film has pushed a little more toward an unrestrained celebration of the indomitability of the human spirit, Altered States goes all the way through to become Russell's surest and clearest statement on man's redemption. Where Tchaikovsky was only redeemed (and then only in part) by his art; where Father Grandier could be redeemed only through a final heroic act that would cause his physical destruction; where Tommy had to lose all to find redemption for himself (and by implication for humanity at large); where Franz Liszt found redemption in his faith in his art, but left it too late to benefit in this life; Eddie Jessup finds this redemption without actually losing anything in the process. Significantly for Russell, Eddie's redemption comes less from the love that his wife has for him than from the love he has come to acknowledge that he has for her. The overt optimism with which Russell views the power of this love is his most glorious pronouncement on the human spirit. When Emily Jessup tells Eddie to fight the final transformation ("You made it real, you can make it unreal"), Russell views it as a challenge for that self-same human spirit to also turn the situation around--to make the loving, human part of himself real, and to make the inhuman, overly analytical, truth-seeking scientist part of himself unreal. Is it possible? According to Russell the human spirit can rise to almost any occasion, and so it does here. For the first time Russell's hero is victorious, not only unharmed, but better off than before his sins. In fact these very sins were necessary for him to attain this level of grace, which in Eddie's case is nothing more, or less, than accepting his own human qualities.

In terms of cinematic fireworks, Russell has concentrated his energies on the hallucinatory scenes, imbuing them with his complete bag of cinematic tricks and effects. The bulk of the film, however, is a reaffirmation of the approach he had earlier taken in Valentino. The approach works better with Altered States due in part to the film's set piece exclamation points, which Valentino largely lacked. Also Russell's more subdued approach to Altered States works better thematically and ties the film more with Savage Messiah than Valentino. Russell's earlier statement that the tone of Savage Messiah had dictated the style of the film is equally apt in considering Altered States. As previously noted, Savage Messiah is a film where the viewer becomes accustomed to a certain character's position on the screen to a point where that side of the frame is associated with that character. Russell has approached Altered States in a markedly similar manner. Russell almost invariably places Eddie on the viewer's left and Emily on his right in any major scene between the two of them. The impact of this move is underscored by the fact that there are very few close-shots of either character that do not place them on their respective sides of the frame, leaving dead space to the right of the viewer in Eddie's case, and to the left in Emily's. This is perhaps most noticeably applied in the scene in which Emily and Eddie decide to get married. As they discuss it in a hospital corridor, they are seated opposite each other on their respective sides of the screen. In the shot breakdown Russell always has an empty chair next to the character in the shot in the position where the other character would be if he or she were in the frame. When Eddie agrees to their marriage, he crosses to Emily and takes his place to the viewer's left, where he belongs, balancing the image. In this manner Russell stresses the need of one character for the other. They balance each other. One is incomplete without the other. In the film's climactic scene, Emily moves from the viewer's right to Eddie's side of the screen in her attempt to save him. The unleashed force propels her back toward the right, and, in order for Eddie to save her, he must move to Emily's side of the screen. This has come not too long after the single most isolating move in the film. After Emily has rescued Eddie in the tank room, she and Mason bring him back to the apartment and put him to bed. In one lengthy (perhaps the longest take in any Russell film) tracking-shot Russell follows her progression from one room to the next, moving laterally from the outside of the building, looking through the windows. Her progression is continually to the viewer's right. She is removed to the most possible extreme from Eddie, who would be far to the left if the shot could encompass them both. It is therefore necessary that they each cross into the other's space in order to set things right, after having been placed at their most extreme opposite points.

It would be erroneous to state categorically that Russell had carefully structured these moves in a purely conscious manner to convey this symbolic message, though he may well have done so, but it is apparent that he has some purpose in the placement of the characters, whether through conscious reasoning or simply because it was instinctively correct. This is also borne out by the fact that on the few occasions when these positions are reversed, it is only during moments of tension, uncertainty or because of a change in viewpoint.

Russell's handling of the dialogue in the film is also reminiscent of that in Savage Messiah. In this instance, however, it is as much for camouflage as from any desire to turn dialogue into a kind of orchestrated sound. In Altered States Paddy Chayefsky has constructed dialogue that is frequently so abrasive as to make the most awkward dialogue scene Russell has ever written--say, the bedroom conversation between Liszt and Marie in Lisztomania--seem almost poetic by comparison. Rather than rewrite the dialogue (and there is no indication that Russell was at liberty to do this in the first place) he has chosen to attack the problem by the speed, pitch, and volume of the speaker. It frequently matters very little what is being said in the film, but it is very important as to how it is said. Dialogue is spoken rapidly. Characters speak at the same time, trodding on each other's lines with a fury worthy of Howard Hawks. Dialogue is shouted, screamed, and bellowed. The final effect is akin to that of Savage Messiah in its orchestral, virtually musical sound, but there much of what was said needed to be understood. In Altered States it is often better when the dialogue reaches the unintelligible level of pure sound.

Aside from the handling of the dialogue, the thematic alterations, and the subtly psychological cinematic style, Russell's major contribution to the film in terms of pure creation are the fantasy scenes. In Chayefsky's novel these are not very detailed, and not particularly visually oriented. As structured by Russell they are exactly the opposite. Whether or not they convey the hallucinogenic effects in a realistic manner, they are among the most striking sequences in any

Russell film. The only possible flaw to be found with them is their placement within the structure of the film, but this is a flaw only if <u>Altered States</u> is approached as a strict horror film, which it is not. As structured the most terrifying of the fantasies is the first. The idea that this might be construed as a flaw is reinforced because of the vast number of strict horror films that have fallen prey to the main pitfall of the genre: the inability to live up to a real blood and thunder scene in the early portions of the movie. <u>Altered States</u>, however, does not attempt to become progressively terrifying as it goes. The later fantasy sequences are not designed to instill horror movie-type fear, and as such are not weaker than this first fantasy. They merely have different aims.

Because of the great volume of criticism that is designed to point out the similarities between Russell's later fantasies and the climactic "Star Ride" sequence of Kubrick's <u>2001: A Space Odyssey</u>, any study of <u>Altered States</u> needs to come to terms with the similarities between the two, if indeed they exist. It would be difficult to find two more opposing thematic viewpoints than those of the violently subjective Ken Russell and the detached, objective Stanley Kubrick. The only real similarity to be found is their shared technical mastery, but since both sequences under discussion rely on that mastery in no small way, this is one of the few instances in which a parallel may be aptly drawn. Obviously there is no relation to Kubrick in Russell's first fantasy sequence. Strong influences are at work here, but they are influences of René Magritte, Giorgio de Chirico, Salvador Dali, and, to a lesser extent, Jean Cocteau, not Kubrick. The same can be said of the Hinchi Indian ceremony, where once again the influence is largely that of the surrealist and metaphysical painter. It is not until the sequence in the tank room that a genuine connecting thread can be found. The sequence bears a somewhat greater similarity to the Kubrick work in that it deals with going back to the beginning in a manner not entirely unlike Keir Dullea's rebirth as the Star Child in <u>2001: A Space Odyssey</u>. Differences abound, however, and those differences are almost exactly the sort one might expect given the nature of the two filmmakers. These differences also make any but the most elemental surface comparison impossible. To begin with, Kubrick's is a pro-science positive experience, and Russell's is just the opposite point of view. In keeping with the analytical Kubrick, the "Star Ride" is devoid of the human element. Russell's sequence, on the other hand, not only contains the human element, but is, in fact, about that element. Perhaps the most outstanding difference, though, is the dependence of the Kubrick work on the special effects, as opposed to the relative lack of dependence in the Russell film. Even though Altered States is a great film, its greatness does not rise or fall on its special effects, brilliant though they are. On the contrary, 2001's effects are largely the reason for its greatness. They are an end in themselves and not merely a device for the presentation of the human drama at the core of the film, which is the function they serve in Altered States. This is in no way meant to detract from Kubrick's achievement, which is fine for Kubrick, but dead wrong for Russell. Rather it is intended to point up the lack of comprehension with which so many critics have approached Russell's film. Russell's work has never lent itself to mere surface examination, and Altered States' outward similarity to 2001 only serves to reinforce this.

Altered States is, however, an undeniably influenced and, to some extent, derivative work--both as novel and film. One cannot overlook the similarities to Arthur Machen's story "The Novel of the White Powder" in which a man is given a drug that turns out to be part of witchcraft ritual and ultimately reduces him to a kind of primordial ooze. For that matter Machen's "The Great God Pan" may have been an influence as well, with its story of a woman who deevolves in a manner not unlike Eddie Jessup. The whirlpool imagery in the film bears an obvious relation to John C. Lilly's sensory deprivation studies, as does part of the overall story itself. The influence of Carlos Castaneda's The Teachings of Don Juan is likewise very strong, but it appears to have been a greater influence on Chayefsky than on Russell. The Castaneda work appears in the novel in greater detail than it does in the film, and the parts of it that are in the film are also in the novel, e.g., the preparation of the "Devil's Weed" in the Castaneda work is duplicated almost exactly at the mushroom ceremony, down to the cutting of Eddie's hand, and Russell takes it directly from the novel. Chayefsky, however, remains much more faithful to Castaneda's anthropological account than does Russell, who merely uses it as a springboard. Chayefsky's Hinchi ceremony lacks the dramatic and symbolic connecting thread of the film in that it does not even mention Emily. Curiously, both Russell and Chayefsky make dramatic departures from Castaneda, though for different reasons. Chayefsky has lumped together images from two distinctly different Indian ceremonies--the "Devil's Weed" and the humitos or "little smoke"--and completely omitted the reasoning behind the use of the lizard, but does leap ahead of the "Devil's Weed" ceremony to the conclusive act of having Eddie eat the lizard. Chayefsky's changes appear completely arbitrary, serving no particular function, dramatic or otherwise. Russell's alterations on the other hand--departures from both Chayefsky and Castaneda--are shrewdly judged, working on both a psychological and symbolic level. His use of the lizard and its equation with Emily, and the lizard is later found dead, Russell has effectively and economically drawn the attention of the viewer to the idea that Eddie's blind search for the "ultimate truth" is both dangerous and destructive for Emily. Not untypically, Russell has picked up on a fragment of something (in this case a lizard) and magnified and adapted it to fit a dramatically valid point he is trying to convey.

Much of Russell's envisioning of the hallucinatory scenes are in fact built upon vague or passing references in the novel or the dialogue of the film. The first fantasy is drawn from part of the dialogue in the film's opening scene in which Eddie speaks of having experienced "a lot of religious imagery, mostly from 'Revelation.'" Using this as a base, Russell structures this fantasy quite literally on a portion of that book of the Bible as if viewed by surrealist and metaphysical painters. Not surprisingly he accomplishes the feat of terrifyingly depicting "Revelation" images in a sequence lasting well under five minutes much more successfully than such popular fiction apocalyptic claptrap as The Omen, The Chosen, The Final Conflict, and Fear No Evil manage to do throughout their feature-length running times. In part Russell's version works so well because it does not attempt to modernize or improve upon the already bizarre original. His images are drawn directly from "Revelation" itself and do not rely on drawing a modern allegory. This "Revelation" imagery crops up continuously throughout the film. In the later "hell" sequence Eddie's drug-induced mutterings contain quotations concerning the moon becoming "the color of blood" and the sun "as black as sack-cloth," along with references to the "bottomless pit." As religious allegory (and this is true of the novel as well, though for other reasons) it is not by any accident that Eddie speaks of having been redeemed "from the pit." This sequence is unique to the film. Essentially the "Revelation" fantasy does not exist in the novel, just the germ of an idea.

Calling the sequence the "'Revelation' fantasy" actually does it a disservice as it also has elements relating to Eddie's

A Summing Up in Hollywood

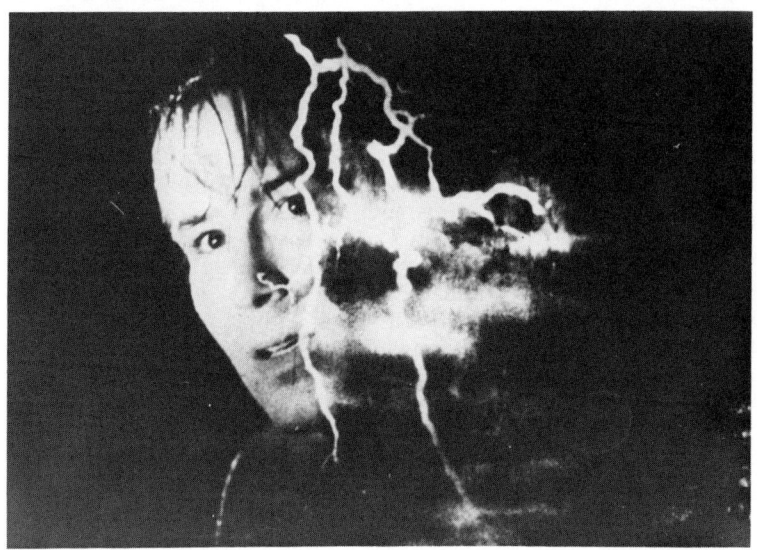

A symbolic moment from one of Eddie Jessup's fantasies under the influence of sensory deprivation and drugs in Altered States. (Courtesy of Ken Russell)

feelings about the death of his father, the rejection of religious beliefs (and the implication that such rejection is not possible for him), and Eddie's relationship to Emily. (This last being a depiction of the line Emily will later deliver about Eddie's sexual habits, "I sometimes wonder if it's me that's being made love to. I feel like I'm being harpooned by some raging monk in the act of receiving God.") The sequence's thematic relation with coming hallucinations and the later externalized experiences is also evidenced by the outbursts of circular, egg-like images that occur when the book of the Seven Seals is opened. The circular image of black rimmed with light has already been established by Russell in the intercut shots of the radiating heater in the scene between Eddie and Emily which immediately precedes this sequence. As a spherical image concerning the very beginning of life, it will be repeated throughout the film. Bearing Russell's previous films in mind--notably Tommy--and the overall tone of anti-science that clings to Altered States, the warm-rimmed sphere denotes less an idea of the beginning of creation, and more one of the apprehension brought about by the blacked out sun, as in the "black as sack-cloth" quotation. For Russell the sun has always been a constant image of life, even serving to keep evil away--in Lisztomania it is only during the solar eclipse that Wagner is able to vampirize Liszt. The image in Altered States then must be viewed as a false image of the beginning of life. In reality it is the negation of life. And, indeed, what Eddie ultimately finds is just that, "a hideous empty nothingness."

A weakness of the novel, which Russell deftly maneuvers around, is the Primal Man sequence. A central set piece for both film and novel, it is nothing more nor less than your everyday "ape-man-on-the-loose" schtick, already done to death in countless tedious films since the discovery of the gorilla suit and crepe hair. In the novel, Chayefsky manages to keep the material from becoming risible, though only just, because he cannot only record the events, but the thoughts behind those events. Given the nature of the presentation, Russell cannot readily do this. Happily, he has recognized the central flaw with such a sequence and avoided it with breathtaking technical skill and a decision to play the segment as much for humor as horror. Russell's approach is playfully mocking, with a good sense of Hollywood horror history, and a few surprises. In the best horror film tradition Russell blandly and brazenly utilizes several clichés, including the unlikely prospect that even the most cretinous of observers might actually mistake the Primal Man for "some kind of a monkey." At the same time, he has also studiously avoided other clichés, passing over such obvious chances for shock effects as the moment when the janitor opens the tank room door to be surprised by the creature. Yet he still delivers a full sense of brutality in the clubbing of the watchman, and surprises the viewer with a shock when the tiger swats at the Primal Man's hand as he reaches for the meat in the cage (an effect enhanced by the fact that the viewer is not given sufficient information by the shot breakdown as to just where the tiger is in relation to the creature). Similarly, the killing and eating of the goat is a bloody and bestial sequence, all the more so because of the lightness of tone that directly precedes it: the encounters with the rhinoceros, elephants, the gift shop animals, and the Mamoulian-like statuary of lions and a rhino. In terms of sheer technique, Russell's most bravura moment is undoubtedly the segment where the Primal Man is in the streets. His camera gliding along gracefully and swiftly, careening to and fro in a balletic manner, follows the creature's movements with

A Summing Up in Hollywood 407

seeming effortlessness. It is in the structure of this sequence that the film makes yet another departure from Chayefsky's novel, though this is a change with which Russell credits Chayefsky. 4 In the novel the Primal Man follows the wild dogs to the zoo, whereas in the film, he is pursued by the dogs and ends up there quite by accident. This works better on two levels as far as the film is concerned, as it not only sidesteps the issue of why he follows the dogs (again the novel has the advantage of explaining this in words), but it also makes Jessup's primal incarnation more sympathetic, more terrified than terrifying. Unfortunately, this change is not mirrored in the dialogue of the subsequent scene as Eddie tells Emily, "I followed a pack of wild dogs to the zoo," which is in direct conflict with what has just been shown. Considering the fact that these scenes were likely shot out of sequence and that the Primal Man scene has none of the same actors in it, this is perhaps understandable. A minor flaw to be sure, but it is a flaw all the same on an otherwise impeccable surface of logic.

The dialogue scene which shortly follows the Primal Man segment is, basically, just that: a dialogue scene, but even here Russell makes a few telling departures from Chayefsky. It is a seemingly casually handled scene, but this is deceptive. The traditional framing of the characters is reversed, with Emily on the left and Eddie on the right. This is Russell's most significant usage of this reversal of their usual positions, reflecting the change in attitudes. In the usual placement it is Emily who is on the offensive and Eddie on the defensive, and here, like their physical position, it is exactly the opposite. This in itself is not a change from Chayefsky, but the mood is altered. In the novel Emily is relieved to find Eddie in such an upbeat frame of mind for part of the scene. Russell instead has her apprehensive from the onset, slowly turning that apprehension into stark terror as it becomes impossible to dismiss Eddie's story as a hallucination. Interestingly, at this point in the scene she has retreated to the area of the front door, which in the climactic scene will come to represent the right side of the frame. In this case, however, she is still located on the left in the framing of her two-shot with Mason, stressing the uncertainty of her situation. The shot of Eddie, standing in the doorway at the far end of the hall in silhouette reflects the status of their relationship. It is a reversal of the first time she saw him (in the party scene) and as such aptly points up the virtual stranger he has become for her. One minor alteration that speaks volumes about the difference between Russell and Chayefsky also appears in this scene. In the novel, Eddie makes himself a cup of instant coffee before talking to Emily about his experience. Russell's Eddie is much less prosaic, cracking open a bottle of Mumm's Cordon Rouge champagne--a change of attitude that encapsulates much of the primary difference between the two men. Russell philosophically states about this change, "I hated Paddy's addiction to Sanka; Paddy hated my addiction to Cordon Rouge."[5]

At this point Altered States begins to share a structural unity with Lisztomania in producing a double-layered climax. The tank room scene and the final transformation roughly parallel Liszt's destruction of Wagner and his subsequent return to earth to end the evil Wagner created. Altered States, however, achieves a greater cathartic release in this respect than does Lisztomania, largely because of its smaller scope and tighter construction. Comparisons aside, the double climax is one of Russell's most impressive achievements to date.

The tank room scene (the opening of which has been done to death by constant exposure on television whenever a clip from the film was needed) is a neatly tailored bit of film that indulges Russell's penchant for elaborate cinematic effects, and even allows the typical, and pardonable, moment of visually referring back to his own earlier work: the reflections of the TV monitor gone berserk in Arthur's glasses calling to mind the similar reflections in Tommy and Valentino. This, after all, is the big scene, and Russell handles it as such.

Carefully building from a slow feeling of foreboding, as Russell's camera opens the scene tracking with a cadaver being wheeled around on a table, the sequence ultimately attains a level of white-hot intensity of the kind for which Russell is justly famous. In itself, the sequence is a series of seemingly nonstop climaxes, one on top of the other. Once the transformation begins, the scene builds to its first climax, where Mason opens the isolation tank and is blasted against the wall by the unleashed force. Russell holds this moment by then having Mason have to carry the hysterical Emily from the room. At this point he abruptly stops the sequence dead with one full second of silence on the track as the tank room goes dark, and then immediately starts rebuilding the tension as Emily reenters the room. This portion is then climaxed at the point where the observation window explodes, handled in such a way that both Emily and the

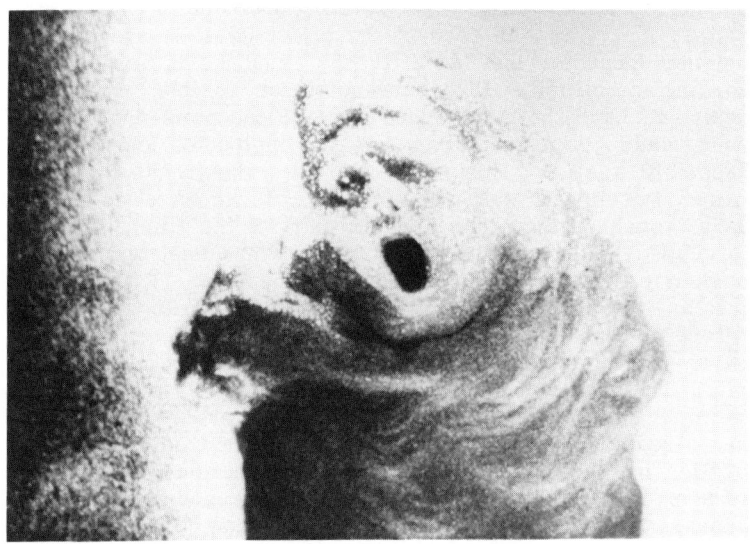

Eddie Jessup reduced to a pre-human state in the first part of Altered States' double climax. (Courtesy of Ken Russell)

viewer are unsure as to just what has happened in the tank room. Here Russell begins the climax proper of the denouement, as in a series of stunning images, some hearkening back to the earlier hallucinatory experiences, Emily pulls Eddie back from the destructive force of his experiment. The imagery of the actual rescue is one of the boldest bits of film in all Russell. It would have been very easy for this moment to topple over into the ludicrous, but Russell has approached it with such daring and beauty that this never happens, and Eddie's redemption "from the pit" becomes one of the most enthralling and touching moments in any Russell film.

The secondary climactic sequence--the final transformation--has the unique effect of not only bringing Altered States to a satisfactory conclusion, but also of bringing a kind of conclusion to all the Russell films which precede it. Essentially this second climax is a summing up of all the positive elements in Russell's films from the very beginning. It is fortunate that it is a sequence worthy of the position it holds in the Russell canon. Impeccably realized and wisely placed, it is the single most riveting moment in Altered States, and, yet, the seed of the effect itself is one of the original ideas for the "Acid Queen" sequence in Tommy. According to Russell's 1973 screenplay for Tommy, it was his desire to have the Acid Queen open at one point and Tommy's body would disintegrate into separate molecules and then reassemble itself.6 This effect did not make it into the final film. Possibly it was just too elaborate an effect to be used as a "touch" rather than a major part of the film, though it is echoed in the shot of the snake-entwined skeleton, which obviously draws its inspiration from the idea. It is perhaps just as well that it was not used, since it works so well in Altered States that it is doubtful it could have been used twice or that it would have been nearly so effective in Tommy. Ths idea would have been quite lost in Tommy, where it would have had no development. In Altered States Russell has already made a visual reference to the coming climax earlier in the film: in the "hall" hallucination Eddie's face is seen to dissolve into hundreds of tiny red dots and disappear. This quintessential Russell climax, like most everything in Altered States, works for the Russell novice as well as the seasoned campaigner, but in common with every Russell work means even more in connection with the films that

The end of the tank room scene--Emily "redeems" Eddie from "The Pit" in Altered States. (Warner Bros.)

surround it. As the ending of Altered States it is brilliant;
as the summation of Russell's progression toward a positive
vision it becomes phenomenal. For the student of Ken Russell's films it is an exhilarating moment, fulfilling every expectation. Indeed, it has been a long and sometimes difficult
journey to reach this vision, but there are few among the
travelers who would not consider it worthwhile.

   Altered States answers many questions about Ken Russell. One unavoidable question about any filmmaker naturally
arises from the communal effort that goes into the creation
of any film: how much of the film on the screen is actually
the work of the filmmaker? In Russell's case the question
was seriously compounded by the stock company of actors
and technicians with which he surrounded himself while working in Britain. The resultant films had a high degree of unified style, but from what source or sources? How much
must one credit editors Michael Bradsell and Stuart Baird?
Choreographers Terry Gilbert and Gillian Gregory? Even
set decorator Ian Whittaker? And, of course, the question
of taking Shirley Russell's contribution into account proves
an even thornier proposition, especially after her design of
Michael Apted's Agatha which captured something of the look
of a Ken Russell film, if not the dramatic tension. Based
on the evidence offered by Altered States one can assert,
with some significant justification, that Ken Russell is indeed
the prime force behind his films, despite the obvious contributions by those who have worked with him.

   The credits and publicity releases of Altered States
also show just exactly how low Russell's status as a filmmaker had dropped by the time of this film. It is perfectly
apparent that a conscious effort was being made to softpedal Russell's participation in the project. It is like a return to the days of Women in Love with its simple "directed
by Ken Russell" title, except that in that case the advertising
for the film was more explicit in its phrasing, "Ken Russell's
film of D. H. Lawrence's Women in Love. " It was only after the film had proven itself at the box office somewhat that
Russell's name was called into the forefront--an event which
could scarcely have been avoided when reviewers insisted on
referring to Russell as the creator of the film, and when certain controversies arose over alleged uses of "subliminal"
edits and "unorthodox sound procedures. "

   The patent silliness over Russell's "unfair" manipulations of his audience's emotions proves only one thing--a great number of people unfamiliar with Russell's earlier work were seeing Altered States. Altered States is no more powerful or intense than most other Russell films, and it is extremely unlikely that it could produce a physical reaction greater than The Music Lovers or The Devils, and no such allegations were made against those films. Anyone familiar with Russell's work would dismiss the idea of subliminal editing and "unorthodox sound procedures" (whatever exactly that might be) out of hand. This is scarcely Russell's line of country, and it is unthinkable that he should have to resort to this kind of technical jiggery-pokery in order to provoke a response from his audience. The answer to the problem is fairly simple. In part it does rest on the fact that Altered States was just seen by more people, but another factor does enter into the debate. Both The Music Lovers and The Devils were made in the early seventies, a much more intense period of filmmaking than any seen in recent years. It was, after all, a period in filmmaking marked, not always for the best, by the sudden freedom afforded filmmakers to deal with theretofore taboo subjects in an open manner. More often than not the films this time produced were neither really intense nor much of anything else, except tasteless, but they did give the early seventies an atmosphere in which truly intense films like The Music Lovers and The Devils seemed less odd and out of place than such works would seem in the comparative restraint of the latter part of the decade. It is highly unlikely that Altered States would have come under suspicion of unfair audience manipulation had it been made in 1970.

The soundtrack of Altered States does merit serious consideration. Not for supposed misuses, but because it is one of the finest soundtracks that has ever graced a Russell film. Surely something unique might be expected from the filmmaker who utilized the "Quintophonic" sound system on Tommy and was a pioneer in the use of Dolby sound recording for film tracks, and something unique is what Russell delivers. The soundtrack on Altered States not only continues Russell's filmic acquaintance with eminent composers of the day in the musical score by John Corigliano, but shows a keen perception on the actual recording process and the use of sound effects. The sound effects in Altered States are so much an integral part of the film that it is difficult to tell, in many cases, just where the sound effects leave off and Corigliano's musical score begins. In a way this is an advancement over the use of rhythmic orchestrated sounds used in Tommy to accent the musical track, e.g. the perfectly

A Summing Up in Hollywood

matched smashing of the glass in the pinball machines which very nearly melds and becomes part of the music. In Altered States a similar pattern is repeated, but the fine line between the music and the effect is all but obliterated. The result is a perfectly blended soundtrack where the music is neither more, nor less important than any other aspect of the track.

The score itself obviously calls for a comparison for Peter Maxwell Davies' score for The Devils as it most closely resembles that score in terms of style. Actually Corigliano's score is more generally accessible than Maxwell Davies' if, only because large portions of it contain memorable themes to a greater degree than the earlier score. Also, there are some notable differences in approach, for in The Devils the score fits the sound effects, which are less prominent in the first place. In Altered States the score and the sound effects fit each other. It is undeniable that a large portion of the film's effectiveness stems from its soundtrack, and Russell's statements about the difficulty in achieving some of those effects reflect the high regard with which he views the importance of the track.

When it was first learned some time ago that three of the most interesting and diverse filmmaking talents working in the present day cinema--Russell, Stanley Kubrick, and Peter Medak--were all embarking on the creation of horror films, few people could have imagined that it would be Russell who walked off with both the critical and popular applause. Medak's beautifully crafted but almost completely ineffectual film, The Changeling, bogged down in endless tracking shots of staircases (staircases having seemingly become a curious predeliction of Medak's) and showed none of the insight and inspiration that had marked his electrifying film version of The Ruling Class. Kubrick's film of The Shining started off on a brilliant note, but quickly collapsed under its own weight, and Kubrick's peculiar penchant for detailing the banal family interactions of everyday life, as well as failing to work up either tension or horror (except on sporadic occasions through its exceptional soundtrack). After these two long-awaited disappointments, Altered States emerged like an oasis--not only was it an excellent horror film, but it made for an excellent Ken Russell film, neither swamping the personality of its director as The Changeling had done, nor bearing the burden of having the director attempt to graft his personality onto the film in the manner of The Shining.

It would be a foolish idea to attempt to categorically state that any given Russell film is his greatest work. (Russell himself has a tendency to consider his latest film to be his best.) By the very nature of things some films will be more successful than others, and each is important in itself. It is, however, only in the overall filmography that the films can be fairly assessed. Some Russell works are more accessible than others, of course, and Altered States is one of them. In many respects it is Russell's most clear-cut work to date. Altered States does lack the inventive cohesion and scope of Tommy; it lacks much of the beauty and tenderness of Mahler; it lacks the unswerving satirical observation and stylization of Lisztomania. Altered States, at least partially, makes up for those things it lacks by virtue of its clarity and its resultant summing up of the overriding themes common to all Ken Russell films. It is a mature work by a serious and accomplished filmmaker--the work of a filmmaker who has stubbornly and correctly refused to stand still. Unlike any of Russell's characters, the director himself is in no danger of becoming embalmed in his own myth.

As with every other Ken Russell film the American commercial television broadcasting of Altered States was a travesty. The wholesale cutting of the film (which was by no means limited to the "censorable" parts) made a jumble out of the story, as ABC-TV hacked out the entirety of the love-making scene between Eddie and Emily which also removed the conversation about his religious background and beliefs, making much of the film's symbolism incoherent. For reasons unknown the editors then tried to salvage as much of the (now incongruous) "Revelation" fantasy as possible, making an unconnected mishmash of it in the process. No logic at all seems to have governed the removal of the dialogue concerning the sort of experience Eddie can expect from the mushroom ceremony, and the removal once more blurred the symbolism of the fantasy sequence that follows. There are also some odd cuts made during the Primal Man sequences, but the most unsettling and worrisome cut of all (in terms of the governing intellect of television) was undoubtedly the enlargement of the frame for the film's final scene so that Blair Brown's derrière would not show--and this done within a two-hour space in which ABC deemed it perfectly acceptable to show a piece of news footage of a murdered man lying in a pool of his own blood in living color during one of their "News Briefs"! This is not obscene, but Blair Brown's backside is. Even so, no film--no matter how good--can survive this type of treatment (as CBS and

PBS already proved with The Boy Friend and Mahler respectively), and until such time as broadcast television manages to mature somewhat, they would do well to leave a film on which they feel the need to cut--especially to the point of rendering the work senseless--alone.

NOTES

1. Hauptfuhrer, Fred. "Wild and Wooly Ken Russell Finds the Golden Fleece Directing Altered States," People, Vol. 15, No. 12 (March 30, 1981), p. 69.
2. Chayefsky, Paddy. Altered States. New York: Harper & Row, 1978, pp. 172-181.
3. Ibid., p. 47.
4. Personal correspondence with Ken Russell, November 1982.
5. Ibid.
6. Russell, Ken. Tommy (unpublished screenplay dated July 18, 1973), p. 22.

CHAPTER 12

THE MEDIUM OF THE FUTURE

"Madama Butterfly"

One would have thought that with the critical success of <u>Altered States</u>, Russell's stock as a filmmaker would have risen within the industry, but the film industry is a funny animal--and one which is far more likely to spit on its original and personal artists than embrace them. When Russell was first coming up through the industry the small film was a viable proposition. Not so now. The Hollywood film school whiz kids have taken over, making films which turn profits large enough to refinance Russell's entire filmography five times over, and they achieve this by the aesthetically dubious method of what can be charitably called corporate filmmaking. Lacking original ideas, and with little or nothing to say, they pore over box-office listings and come up with conglomerations made up of bits of historically successful formulas and devices. The process is not too different from ordering from a Chinese restaurant menu. As a result of this corporate thinking a film is no longer considered successful unless it grosses fifty-million dollars or better. This may bode well for the stockholder (though how one explains to the average person that something costing three million dollars which then takes in sixteen million is a failure is hard to fathom), but it is bad news for serious film.

    The year 1980 looked a glorious one for filmmaking on a serious level and a promising start for a new, exciting decade of film, with the releases of <u>Altered States</u>, <u>The Shining</u>, <u>Tess</u>, <u>The Elephant Man</u>, <u>Stardust Memories</u>, <u>Popeye</u>, and <u>Excalibur</u>, all films of genuine merit despite their individual flaws. That promise has not been borne out, though, and the corporate filmmakers have taken over. Russell has suffered in the pinch with the other serious film artists.

    In some respects Russell has fared better than others.

He was originally slated to script and direct Robert Stigwood's film version of Evita, but a flap over the casting of Eileen Page in the title role caused Russell to resign from the project.[1] (In light of the later announcements that everyone from Barbra Streisand to Olivia Newton-John would take the role and the general confusion surrounding the production, Russell may well have been wise to drop out.) There have also been rumblings of a Maria Callas biography for transmission on Home Box Office, a cable television program, but Russell has termed this something that might not come off. In the meantime he has been working on a television film of Gustav Holst's composition The Planets. Despite the fact that he has been unable to get either his adaptation of D. H. Lawrence's The Rainbow or his Beethoven film off the ground ("I'm constantly told that The Rainbow isn't commercial. I don't believe this."[2]), Russell seems far less the neglected filmmaker than the filmmaker who refuses to compromise any longer. If this seems unfortunate, think of the films made by Josef von Sternberg after his brilliant career at Paramount. Are we really better off because of the existence of Sergeant Madden or Jet Pilot? Or would we do better to consider The Devil Is a Woman--von Sternberg's last largescale uncompromised film--his last work for film? As Russell's filmography stands at the moment, Altered States is an amazingly satisfying climax, and there can certainly be little benefit derived from the prospect of a series of lesser, heavily compromised works in its wake.

In no way, however, is Ken Russell drifting about with no purpose. In assessing his present situation he says, "For a year and a half I tried to get Beethoven off the ground--nothing doing. Then two things happened at once. Lorin Maazel asked me to produce Eugene Onegin in Vienna ('85), and I was asked to produce Rake's Progress in Florence last May. Now I am doing Soldaten by Zimmerman in Lyons, February '83, Butterfly in U.S., May 20, '83, Tristan, Australia, '84. Doubtless there will be other dates."[3] (As of this writing one more is reported. The New York Times lists Russell as the director for Tannhauser in Geneva in 1985.) Judging by the initial response to the performance of The Rake's Progress in Florence, the world of opera promises to be more kind and more receptive to Russell's genius than the film industry. Michael Walsh's review of the production is indicative of the purity of the Russell vision as applied to opera--"Russell's great inspiration is to solve the paradox at the opera's core, that of a modern work in a courtly guise. If the music will not carry the dramatic load, then the action must. The director updates the splendid, rather literary W. H. Auden-Chester Kallman libretto from eighteenth century to contemporary England without altering a word of text."[4] This is certainly in keeping with the Russell approach through the years, as is his use of people with whom he is comfortable in a working relationship. Derek Jarman, who designed the sets for Russell's Rake, goes back to the designs for The Devils and Savage Messiah. The production of Madama Butterfly boasts the services of Ruth Myers and Richard MacDonald for costumes and sets respectively, both Altered States alumni. Walsh's review also indicates that Russell's concerns have remained unchanged in the transition: "There is certainly nothing boring about this Rake. For all its flashy images, the production captures the opera's cautionary moral spirit. Russell, however, is more concerned about a contemporary demon. Tom and Anne are watching TV as the opera opens, and the commercials excite his desire for the wealth flaunted by Nick Shadow. At the end, having fought off one devil, Tom gazes at the other--a TV screen--with fellow mental patients. In a chilling coup de theatre, the principals are led into the asylum, gibbering as they warn of the dangers of idle minds. All are pacified by the set's flickering light: the very picture of the modern family, at peace in front of the hearth."[5] Walsh might almost be writing about Tommy.

    Of course, it is difficult to conceive of Russell being no longer interested in filmmaking. Among other things the very nature of live theatre is oddly transitory for a director who left television primarily because of the inability of his work there to be seen more than once. It is extremely unlikely that were Russell given a free hand to make the films that he wants to make as he wants to make them, he would not return to the medium. For most of us, it seems a shame that a talent as unique as Russell's should be so lost to the majority of the world in this manner. Nonetheless, it is an outlet for that creativity in an uncompromised form, and as such is vastly preferable to a string of routine motion pictures. Russell sums up his feelings about opera with this statement: "The joy I experience in producing opera cannot be expressed. I have found the medium of the Future."[6] Film's loss is opera's gain.

* * *

Madama Butterfly (1983). Music by Giacomo Puccini. Libretto by Luigi Illica and Giuseppe Giacosa. Conducted by John

The Medium of the Future

Matheson. Sets Designed by Richard MacDonald. Costumes Designed by Ruth Myers. Lighting Designer: John McClain. Chorus Master: Glenn Parker. Choreographer: Robert Ivey. Directed by Ken Russell. An Opera in Three Acts. A Production of Spoleto, USA, Charleston, South Carolina. Gian Carlo Menotti, Artistic Director.

    Barry McCauley--B. F. Pinkerton
    Steven Cole--Goro
    Kumiko Yoshii--Suzuki
    Robert Galbraith--Sharpless
    Catherine Lamy--Cio Cio San (Madama Butterfly)
    Charles Damsel--The Imperial Commissioner
    Eric Halfvarson--The Bonze
    David Hamilton--Prince Yamadori
    Kathryn Cowdrick--Kate Pinkerton
    Cyler Applegate/Moultrie Townsend--Butterfly's Son

    Westminster Choir
    Spoleto Festival Orchestra

    Not a Ken Russell film, and therefore somewhat out of the range of this book, this landmark production of Madama Butterfly nonetheless needs consideration since it illustrates much of the direction that Russell is currently taking and shows that the transition from film to opera has indeed left his personal vision very much in tact.

    Despite an almost arctic atmosphere in the theatre (that left many of us with frozen noses by the end of the second act) due to an overzealous air-conditioning system, and a water fountain in the hallway that had obviously been installed by the Marx Brothers (at best) or the Three Stooges (at worst), which alternated between too little and too much water pressure (this, however, did afford much between-the-acts amusement), those of us present at Gaillard Municipal Auditorium on May 20, 1983, witnessed a remarkable event in Russell's American operatic debut. For nearly three hours Russell held us spellbound with his interpretation of Puccini's opera, and, at the end of that time, the audience rose in a thunderous standing ovation for the performers and the production, with an extra surge of applause and cheers when Russell himself (clad in one of those pull-over shirts painted to look like a tuxedo) appeared onstage. This was the scene as viewed by anyone in the audience. Then it happened. By Sunday morning Russell must have felt as if he had become enmeshed in his own film Savage Messiah. For while, as in his depiction of Henri Gaudier-Brzeska's ability to communicate with the public when he has the chance to do so, even if he is not the darling of the critics, Russell had very obviously connected with the public, the critical evaluation was such that one might have believed that he had coshed the Virgin Mary over the head with the giant plastic phallus from Lisztomania. One critic, imported by a local paper for (one assumes) the specific purpose of bringing a "New York sensibility" to bear on the events, went so far as to almost indulge in name-calling, insulting both Russell and the appreciative audience in the process. Just exactly how these critics can be so certain that they are in the right and the rest of the audience (those of us who were blissfully cheering in appreciation of having been entertained, involved, and made to think) are in the wrong is very mysterious.

Right from the start Russell made it clear that this was his personal reading of the opera, and that it was in no way intended to be "definitive" (any work that can be reduced to a single "definitive" interpretation is probably too narrow to be worth interpreting in the first place), but only the opera as he perceived it, presented as he himself would like to see it. This personal approach to the opera--in which, by the way, not one note of music or word of the libretto has been altered--results in a work that shows Russell at his best. His two previous forays into opera were a little less scandalous, in part because Stravinsky's The Rake's Progress and Zimmerman's Die Soldaten (The Soldiers) provided Russell with an already avant-garde base from which to work. With Madama Butterfly he crossed over into the realm of reshaping a very traditional operatic warhorse, and in so doing he unleashed the forces of traditionalism, all ready to lash out with cries of artistic rape. What the traditionalist point of view fails to grasp is that in this approach, Russell gives back much of the vibrance the work must have originally had. Like those moments in films where he has caused us to look at that with which we have become overly familiar (e.g., "Romeo and Juliet" in The Music Lovers, "The Rime of the Ancient Mariner" in the Coleridge film, etc.) through new eyes, he here forces us to reevaluate our position on a work that we think we know all about. Seeing Russell's Madama Butterfly is to be shocked into an awareness of the work's implications, and, as Russell views it, the almost mystically prophetic nature of Puccini's original. (It is a little unclear as to just how Madama Butterfly has reached its position as sacred in the first place. Most people only have the basic

The Medium of the Future

notion of the plot and are familiar with Cio Cio San's second-act aria, "Un Bel Di" [One Fine Day], which Hollywood has been representing for years, in films like Victor Schertzinger's One Night of Love and Henry Koster's First Love, with the implication that it climaxes the opera.   Beyond that it seems to mostly be approached as the operatic equivalent of a three-handkerchief "woman's picture," made somehow legitimate by its status as an opera.)

In the main Russell has stripped away the prettiness of the opera as we are used to seeing it and substituted a more forthright, satirical, and harshly cautionary tale. Where in the original Cio Cio San is a geisha, Russell makes her a prostitute who is palmed off on Pinkerton by Goro (changed from a marriage broker to a pimp who runs the brothel in which Cio Cio San works) as a geisha. In making this alteration Russell remains faithful to his own vision because he is dealing in the area of the illusion opposing reality, in which he is well-versed. The operative difference here is that the dream as opposed to the real works on a more complex level in Madama Butterfly than is common even for Russell. The illusion does not fool Pinkerton, who takes it all as a fine joke, but his acceptance of it as the truth on the surface does fool Cio Cio San, who comes to believe the situation as real, and, as usual in Russell's work, those who are beguiled by such dreams pay dearly for it. Cio Cio San as viewed by Russell is much like Nina in The Music Lovers--marriage to an "important" American naval officer represents a way out of her miserable life as a whore in the slums of Nagasaki, so she turns a falsehood (consider Nina's vows that her first kiss is reserved for Tchaikovsky) into her personal version of reality. Where Nina was helped in this by her own mental instability, Cio Cio San finds support of her dream existence through Suzuki and Sharpless, both of whom find they cannot bring themselves to tell her the truth about Pinkerton, and through her indulgence in opium. (Russell uses the opium pipe in the opera much in the manner of Nina's rocking motion in The Music Lovers, as something into which the character quickly retreats when the illusion is threatened by reality.)

Russell's view of Pinkerton's abuse of Cio Cio San may seem tinged with an anti-American bias (and as he points out there is an anti-American tone to Puccini's original which interpolates the "Star Spangled Banner" at any point in the proceedings dealing with materialism), but the production is not really so much anti-American as it is anti-materialism and anti-false dreams. At no point does Russell suggest that Pinkerton is an American "everyman," and, in fact, the presence of the sympathetic American Consul, Sharpless, precludes this possibility in the first place. Russell does deliver some rather unpleasant truths about America in foreign lands--all the more unpleasant because they are irrefutable and indefensible. His Pinkerton, for example, wants "the best" of both worlds, turning the monthly renewable Japanese marriage contract to his favor, accepting "one of the facilities of this house of pleasure--a pipe of opium,"[7] while at the same time installing such American institution items as a refrigerator, Coca Cola, and beer, as his shipmates come to celebrate the mock marriage.

So lost is Cio Cio San in her dreams of America and a life free from her poverty that she rejects her own religion and heritage (a grim foreshadowing of Russell's climactic point about modern Japan), taking on Pinkerton's faith and beliefs. This causes her to be cursed by her Buddhist priest uncle, The Bonze, thereby effectively cutting her off from both civilizations so that apart from the faithful Suzuki and Sharpless she is quite alone in the world, with only her opium dreams and visions of the American ideal as put forth in the advertising in American magazines to offer her comfort. Russell has frequently worked in this territory before, but, perhaps because of the utter naivete of Cio Cio San and the fact that she knows nothing beyond this false image--indeed she has no way of knowing anything more than this--the effect of the false promise of advertising on her life is by far the most pathetic and bitter in any of his works.

Russell's most trenchant statement on this dream world occurs at the climax of the second act, where he boldly replaces the traditional "waiting scene" with Cio Cio San's dream vision of "the happy life to come when Pinkerton carries them back across the ocean to his home."[8] What critics of this innovation (apart from one rather oddly minded reviewer who felt that it was in need of a scrim in front of the action to better underline its status as a dream[9]) do not seem to realize is that the images of Cio Cio San wearing an American flag for an apron, dishing up huge bowls of Kellogg's Corn Flakes, pouring out Coca Cola, putting a Mickey Mouse mask on her son, and giving Pinkerton the opium pipe to go with his breakfast, are supposed to be borne of a mind that has not the slightest grasp on American reality. As far as the truth of life in America is concerned Cio Cio San might as well be from Mars. She only knows it from advertisements she has seen and has therefore assembled a mental picture made up entirely of materialist American icons. She has no way of knowing that one does not (as a rule anyway) serve Coca Cola with breakfast or that a pipe of opium with the corn flakes is in the least bit untoward.

Of course, Russell's updating of the opera to the period of World War II has also been severely attacked, not in the least because of the improbabilities such a change incurs, i.e., what are Pinkerton and Sharpless doing in Japan during this time period? How does the Abraham Lincoln pull into Nagasaki harbor during the final days of World War II? The literal-minded attacks on this probability gap fail to realize that for Russell dramatic validity is always more important than realism, and in terms of drama the updating serves him well. Further, those of us familiar with Russell's approach to time and history are already aware that his concerns over the interrelation of one event to another regardless of the differences in the time factors of the occurrences make a literal reading of the work impossible. The events pictured here are obviously intended to be read on a symbolic level, not as literal depictions of the occurrences.

The first impression upon hearing of the updating was that Russell somehow intended to work in the atomic bomb, and he does not disappoint our suspicions in this matter. What could not have been foreseen, though, was the brilliance with which he interpolated it, the grand theatre with which he accomplished it, or the uncomfortable reality of the after-the-fact summation. At the moment that Pinkerton arrives back at the house, calling out to Butterfly, who has just committed hara-kiri after rejecting the "American" God, Russell bombards the audience with a blinding flash of light. Through an incredible piece of stage trickery, the entire two stories of Richard MacDonald's elaborate set are pulled away during this momentary white-out, except for the stairwell on one side of the stage which, with the set gone, proves to be a three story Coca Cola bottle, and a barrage of lighted signs for Toyota, Cassio, Sony, Sanyo, Nissan, etc., have been lowered, so that we see a vision of the Americanized Japan of which Cio Cio San had dreamed made manifest in the aftermath, once our view of the stage returns. (This is consistent with the original if we take it as a logical extension of the idea of Cio Cio San rejecting her own religion and heritage for Pinkerton's.) Typically for Russell it is a simple, yet overwhelmingly powerful, effect.

Critics of the production seem to feel that Russell has betrayed Puccini's original (something that we are all used to by now with critics and Russell), and, in a literal sense, there is some validity to this, but it is hard to decry any attempt at enlarging on our appreciation and understanding of a work that we take for granted. Hearing Puccini's music in this new staging makes us rethink our concept of it. His story takes on new shadings and meanings with undercurrents that have more relevance to us than the original fable, causing the work to connect with the audience in a way that is just not possible in a traditional staging. Best of all, it is very much alive and immediate, touching both our emotions and our intellects at the same time. What higher goal can art hope to achieve than this? Cio Cio San's heartrending "Un Bel Di" is, if anything, all the more effective coming from this prostitute in her dream world in the Nagasaki slums than it ever was from the traditional kewpie doll in her picture book cottage. With this in mind Russell's betrayal should be able to be viewed more as a revelation that removes years of stagnation and complacency.

As with all of Russell's work this production of <u>Butterfly</u> is not all flash and bang. There are many quiet moments in it, many tender ones, small touches scattered throughout its length, and a great sense of sheer theatrical excitement that should surprise no one familiar with Russell's films. When the curtain rises the first sight is of a drop with a gigantic Buddha painted on it, and, as Russell uses this at the beginning of each act, it becomes apparent that this is not merely a piece of exotica, but a symbol of the East-West clash that he views as central to the work. Behind this stands Richard MacDonald's overwhelming brothel set--two solid floors with stairs on either side and a third floor tower on the left. Russell's use of this set is one of the masterstrokes of his concept. Fully aware that many in the audience neither speak Italian nor are sufficiently well-versed with the libretto to know each and every word, he keeps action of one sort or another going on whichever floor is not central to the proceedings throughout most of the performance. This action is not distracting, but provides welcome visual excitement during those portions of the opera that are lengthy dialogue scenes of which most of us have only a general concept. Even so, Russell has so effectively worked out the actions and mime of the play that all of the action is perfectly lucid and would likely be so to the theatregoer who had never read the libretto.

Then, too, the performances he has gotten from his singers are almost completely successful. Of course, opera and the performance of opera is, by its very nature, something with which Russell can easily relate. In a New York Times interview Russell noted, "I admire opera singers because they're doing such a stylized thing. They're trying to be realistic while doing a stylized work of art, which is so bizarre! Operatic acting goes against credibility, but it transcends reality and goes to a super reality--a surrealism, a super consciousness. And that's what excites me about directing opera."[10] The same might be said for Russell's films, and the production we are dealing with here certainly bears out this search for, and to quite a large extent capture of, a "super reality." The performances of his players are quite up to the high Russell standard, with Catherine Lamy's tragic and pathetic Cio Cio San, Steven Cole's slimy villain Goro (whose mannerisms and outfit are particularly germane to a certain Japanese image of a Western hoodlum as any of the ersatz gangster sorts in countless American imitative Japanese movies will prove), Robert Galbraith's human and caring Sharpless, Kumiko Yoshii's intelligent and likable Suzuki; all are standouts. At no point is there a sense of mere posturing and singing, but a genuine feeling of acting within the stylized dictates of the form.

In the end the only regrettable aspect of Russell's Madama Butterfly, apart from the blindness of much of the criticism leveled against it, is that it is impossible to go back to it time and again, to savor this aspect and that. The complexity of its execution promises that renewed visits to it would be very rewarding indeed, if only they were possible. One can only hope that at some point in the future Russell will decide to have these productions put on videotape, which although unable to reproduce the original experience will at least give us a permanent record of them.

Inevitably Russell's Butterfly is bound to be directly compared to the recent Peter Sellars production for the Chicago Lyric Opera of The Mikado, which made similar use of the image of an Americanized Japan. (The New York Times reviewer has already made perhaps too much of this similarity, while completely failing to report the warm reception afforded by the real audience to both the production and Russell.[11]) In fairness to both men it should be noted that it is extremely unlikely that either knew of the other's intention. Even so it is quite one thing to approach a light work like The Mikado in these terms, and quite another when dealing with a serious opera like Madama Butterfly. The situation is much the same as that of comparing Russell's use of the in-joke and in-reference to that of Woody Allen--in Russell's hands these things become an integral part of the fabric of the work and not just a witty conceit.

Finally, it becomes obvious that Russell's works in this medium are going to be as fully worthy of exploration and examination as his work in television and film because their power still comes from his personal vision presenting the truth as he views it. Much as in his adaptation of Pete Townshend's Tommy, Russell is managing to create a work that is faithful to its source and the concerns of that source, while still bringing his personal view to bear on it, realizing an original product in the culmination. Typically, this approach is bound to anger and shock the traditionalists, as the critical response to Butterfly proves, but Russell's genius may win out after all. Even his artistic director, the man who hired Russell in the first place, Gian Carlo Menotti, was not without his reservations at turning Russell loose on Puccini's opera. Prior to the premiere performance he told a reporter, "Madama Butterfly is sensational. I was afraid of what that man would do, but he's done something extraordinary. I saw part of it already, and I was in tears."[12] Menotti's response is that of an artist to an artist, and as such should have more weight, along with the enthusiastic audience, than all the snide nay-sayers put together.

NOTES

1. Personal correspondence with Ken Russell, November 1982.
2. Ibid.
3. Ibid.
4. Walsh, Michael. "Rousing the Rake in Florence," Time, Vol. 119, No. 23 (June 7, 1982), p. 68.
5. Ibid.
6. Personal correspondence with Ken Russell, November 1982.
7. Madama Butterfly Program Notes.
8. Ibid.
9. McPhail, Claire. "Puccini's Music Survives Russell's 'Butterfly' Staging," Review, The News and Courier, The Evening Post (Charleston, S. C.), May 21, 1983, p. 5-A.
10. Gruen, John. "Ken Russell Shapes a New 'Butterfly,'"

The New York Times (National Edition), May 22, 1983, Arts/Entertainment Section, pp. 1, 24.
11. Henahan, Donal. "Opera: New 'Butterfly' Opens Spoleto USA," Review, The New York Times (National Edition), May 23, 1983, Arts/Entertainment, p. 16.
12. Anon. (Special to The New York Times). "Spoleto Festival USA Opens Seventh Season," The New York Times (National Edition), May 21, 1983, Arts/Entertainment.

CHAPTER 13

THE INFLUENCE OF RUSSELL

From time to time champions of Ken Russell's films will assert an idea about his influence on other filmmakers, but, rarely, if ever, do they clarify the question of whom he has influenced. The question put to Russell himself only produced a variation on one of the lines from Valentino, "Haven't thought much about it, and I don't go to many movies, " but he did note that there was "some very BAD Russell in that hideous film, The Wall."[1] True enough, but the "BAD Russell" in The Wall is not so much influence as it is derivation. Much like The Wall a quick sampling of the programming on the so-called video music cable network, MTV, makes one wonder whether the ridiculous, meaningless, symbol-laden claptrap passing for video music could exist if they did not have Ken Russell to steal from. There are more pirated images from Tommy than can be comfortably counted, all drenched in pseudo-Russell symbols that, in this usage, are devoid of all meaning. Even one of the network's logos consists of Russell images as a constantly shifting and changing "MTV" bashes itself back and forth against either side of a corridor before transforming into the standard "MTV" symbol, lifted directly from Altered States.

In terms of genuine influence, however, there are some rather notable examples. Certainly the most ironic of which is Fellini's framing train journey for his City of Women. The relation of this to Russell's Mahler seems a little too much for mere coincidence, though, unfortunately, Fellini captured neither Mahler's technical brilliance, nor its richness of structure in his film. Then, too, there is the aforementioned "Russell look" to Michael Apted's Agatha, which probably owes much to Shirley Russell's production design, especially when one considers that none of Apted's other work has this look. The contribution of Shirley Russell as costume designer on the recent, execrable version of D. H. Lawrence's Lady Chatterley's Lover is harder to assess, but the film certainly owes more to pilfered images from Russell's film of Women in Love than it does to Lawrence's novel.

On an altogether different level there is the case of John Boorman's Excalibur, arguably the best work of this interesting filmmaker. A quick study of Boorman's work reveals that there are many shared interests between him and Russell, especially as concerns a preoccupation with salvation and spiritual regeneration. These themes are prominent in Excalibur, but in Boorman's terms, not Russell's. Nonetheless, even though the film is almost pure Boorman, the utilization of Wagner on the soundtrack--indeed the whole inspiration of paralleling the Arthurian legends with the Wagner created myths--has a decidedly Russellian slant. Beyond this, the scenes between young Arthur and Merlin in the woods have more than a slight relation to those of young Mahler and Old Nick in Mahler. (Under the circumstances this last is a kind of Isaac Babel twice-removed influence.)

Best of all is David Lynch's The Elephant Man. It is impossible to tell just how profoundly influenced this promising filmmaker may be by Russell's work, as The Elephant Man is only his first "professional" film, but it is, to date, the best example of genuine influence with little hint of derivation. True to Russell, Lynch raises as many questions as he answers in his film, and not surprisingly there has been much misunderstanding of the film. What has been primarily misread about the film is Lynch's approach to the audience's first look at the Elephant Man--generally viewed as a horror film tactic. In reality, Lynch keeps us in the dark for such a lengthy stretch that he develops a severe audience curiosity about the appearance of his main character. Far from being a horror film technique, he uses this to slap us in our complacent and superior faces with our own self-knowledge that this curiosity makes us no better than the unenlightened types that want to gawk at John Merrick, the Elephant Man, as a sideshow attraction. Such an approach would be very much at home in a Russell film. Further, the film's very structure--its circular nature and its representative view of the soul of John Merrick set free at his death has much in common with Russell in general, and with Tommy and Lisztomania in particular.

Lynch's preoccupation with his film's soundtrack is also notable, and again we find the Russell-like brilliant application of preexisting music in the use of Samuel Barber's

"Adagio for Strings" as a predominant theme in the film. Lynch, like Russell, uses music to strengthen already strong material, not to prop up a weak scene at the expense of a blameless and hapless composer.

At this point in his career Lynch has much of Russell's technical mastery, more than a little of his mysticism, but sadly lacks the feeling of spontaneity one finds in the best of Russell. Whether or not he will prove a worthy successor to Russell in the years to come remains to be seen. At any rate, he has an exceptionally good start.

Derek Jarman, sometime Russell designer, has also made films of his own. The most notable of these has been his interpretation of Shakespeare's The Tempest, which provoked one reviewer to quarrel about the "ghost of Russell clanking" throughout the film, 2 but Jarman's work has thus far strayed too far beyond the boundaries of the commercial cinema to make much of an impact. Most critics also tend to find a greater similarity to Jarman's films in those of Fellini. For all that one can imagine that Russell would appreciate the gesture of climaxing a version of The Tempest with a large black blues singer wailing "Stormy Weather," even if the device itself might be too campy for Russell.

Old BBC colleague David Palmer, a strong supporter of Ken Russell, might well turn out to be the most directly influenced filmmaker of all when we finally see his mammoth biographical film, Wagner. Certainly, Palmer has the training, but he might shy away from anything too daring simply out of fear of being labeled a Russell impersonator. His documentary on Benjamin Britten, A Time There Was, was a satisfying, thoroughly warm, and even moving portrait of the composer, but it tells us nothing about Palmer's abilities as a dramatist.

In a slightly different vein we have the various and sundry parodies of Ken Russell that crop up in a good deal of British humor. This is not influence as such, but almost homage for only the truly original can be successfully made fun of. This type of humor is rife in the rather elaborate Russell jokes found in an episode of The Goodies, where the main characters take over Pinetree Studios. There is an ersatz Russell film, The Life of Pablo Casals, within the show (unfortunately, the film is a lot less like Russell than Fellini), and a good deal of sweet-tempered joking about Russell's flamboyant personality. (When, in due course, The

Goodies find it necessary to fire Russell--along with Fellini, Warhol, and Visconti--they quickly have to admonish him, "If you're going to cry, Russell, go outside.") Similarly, the Monty Python troupe members have had some fun with Russell in a generally far more cryptic--sometimes downright mystifying--manner; e.g., their "presentation" of Sandy Wilson's film of The Devils (consisting of a male chorus line in phone booths), and Ken Russell's Garden Party (a group of people in assorted strange outfits jumping into a flower bed for reasons that are anybody's guess). The single best example of Python humor applied to Russell, though, is found on one of the lobby cards for Monty Python and the Holy Grail, which shows a terrified group of knights supposedly reacting in horror to the fact that they have run into two of their number disguised "as the man who edited most of the Ken Russell films!"

It will be years before we can fully assess the impact of Ken Russell's influence on the film in general, but the rumblings are there. In the end it is likely that the areas of filmmaking he has opened up will be further explored by similarly adventurous filmmakers, who might one day inherit his mantle. It may be one of the filmmakers briefly touched on here, or it may be someone we have yet to hear from. In any case, these successors--if they exist --will be faced with a formidable task.

NOTES

1. Personal correspondence with Ken Russell, November 1982.
2. Kennedy, Harlen. Report on 1979 Edinburgh Film Festival, American Film, November 1979, p. 72.

FILMOGRAPHY

AMATEUR FILMS:

Peepshow (1956)
Amelia and the Angel (1957)
Lourdes (1958)

BBC FILMS:

Poet's London. (1959)
Gordon Jacob. (1959)
Guitar Craze. (1959)
Variations on a Mechanical Theme. (1959)
Untitled Film on artists Robert McBryde and Robert Colquhoun. (1959)
Portrait of a Goon (Spike Milligan). (1959)
Marie Rambert Remembers. (1960)
Architecture of Entertainment (John Betjeman). (1960)
Cranks at Work (John Cranko). (1960)
The Miner's Picnic (brass bands). (1960)
Shelagh Delaney's Salford. (1960)
A House in Bayswater. (1960)
The Light Fantastic. (1960)
Old Battersea House (Pre-Raphaelite Museum). (1961)
Portrait of a Soviet Composer (Sergei Prokofiev). (1961)
London Moods. (1961)
Antonio Gaudi. (1961)
Pop Goes the Easel. (1962)
Preservation Man (Bruce Lacey). (1962)
Mr. Chesher's Traction Engines. (1962)
Lotte Lenya Sings Kurt Weill (co-director with Humphrey Burton). (1964).

Elgar. (1962)

Watch the Birdie. (1963)

The Lonely Shore. (1964)

Bartok. (1964)

The Dotty World of James Lloyd. (1964)

Diary of a Nobody. (1964)

The Debussy Film. (1965)

Always on Sunday (Henri Rousseau). (1965)

Don't Shoot the Composer (Georges Delerue). (1966)

Isadora (Isadora Duncan, The Biggest Dancer in the World). (1966)

Dante's Inferno (Dante Gabriel Rossetti). (1967)

Song of Summer (Frederick Delius). (1968)

The Dance of the Seven Veils: A Comic Strip in Seven Episodes on the Life of Richard Strauss. (1970)

MAJOR RELEASES:

French Dressing. (1963). Produced by Kenneth Harper (Kenwood Films). Associate Producer: Andrew Mitchell. Screenplay by Peter Myers, Ronald Cass, Peter Brett, from an original story by Myers and Cass. Additional Dialogue: Johnny Speight. Photography: Ken Higgins. Music Composed and Conducted by Georges Delerue. Sound: Norman Coggs and Len Shilton. Edited by Jack Slade. Art Director: Jack Stephens. Directed by Ken Russell. Associated British Picture Corporation. Released by Warner Bros. / Pathé. Running time: 86 minutes.

James Booth--Jim
Roy Kinnear--Henry
Marisa Mell--Françoise Fayol
Alita Naughton--Judy
Bryan Pringle--The Mayor
Robert Robinson--Himself
Norman Pitt--Westbourne Mayor
Henry McCarthy--Bridgemouth Mayor
Sandor Eles--Vladek

Billion Dollar Brain. (1967). Producer: Harry Saltzman. Executive Producer: Andre de Toth. Screenplay by John McGrath, based on the novel by Len Deighton. Photographed by Billy Williams, B. S. C., Deluxe Color and Panavision. Cameraman: David Harcourt. Sound Mixer: John Mitchell. Production Design: Sid Cain. Edited by Alan Osbiston. Associate Editor: Willy Kempler. Art Direction: Bert Davey. Costumes for Françoise Dorleac Designed by Shirley Kingdon (Russell). Furs for Françoise Dorleac by Chombert of Paris. Production Manager: Eva Monley. Assistant Directors: Jack Causey and Jim Brennan. Location Manager: Robert Watts. Camera Assistant: Steve Clayton. Continuity: Angela Martelli. Casting: Weston Drury, Jr. Titles Designed by Maurice Binder. Music Composed by Richard Rodney Bennet, Conducted by Marcus Dods. Make-up: Freddie Williamson and Benny Royston. Hairstyles by Joan Smallwood. Wardrobe Supervisor: John Brady. Wardrobe Mistress: Maggie Lewin. Directed by Ken Russell. Released by United Artists. Running Time: 111 minutes.

Michael Caine--Harry Palmer
Karl Malden--Leo Newbegin
Françoise Dorleac--Anya
Oscar Homolka--Colonel Stok
Ed Begley--General Midwinter
Guy Doleman--Colonel Ross
Vladek Sheybal--Dr. Eiwort
Milo Sperber--Basil
Janos Kurtz--Latvian Gangster
Alexei Jawdokimov--Latvian Gangster
Paul Tamarin--Latvian Gangster
Iza Teller--Latvian Gangster
Mark Elwes--Birkenshaw
Stanley Caine--G. P. O. Special Delivery Boy
Gregg Palmer--1st Dutch Business Man
John Herrington--2nd Dutch Business Man
Hans De Vries--3rd Dutch Business Man
Fred Griffiths--Taxi Driver
John Brandon--Jim
Tony Harwood--Macey
Donald Sutherland--Computer Scientist
Michael Stayner--Scientist
George Roubicek--Edgar
Brandon Brady--Chief of Security
Alex Marchesky--Radar Operator
Peter Forrest--Radar Operator
Reed De Rouen--First Observer
James Woolf--Caller
Miki Iveria--Woman on Train
Susan George--Girl on Train
Jill May Meredith--Girl on Train
Dolly Brennan--Woman in Hut
Frederick Schrecker--Man on Train
Bill Mitchell--At Midwinter's House
Steve Emerson--Russian Plainclothesman
Mark Moss--Russian Plainclothesman
Max Kirby--Shoe Shop Assistant

Women in Love. (1969). Produced by Larry Kramer and Martin Rosen. (Brandywine Productions). Associate Producer: Roy Baird. Screenplay by Larry Kramer (and, uncredited, Ken Russell), based on the novel by D. H. Lawrence. Photographed by Billy Williams. Cameraman: David Harcourt. Assistant Cameraman: Steve Claydon. Sound Editor: Terry Rawlings. Sound Recorder: Brian Simmons. Sound Re-recorder: Maurice Askew. Music Composed and Conducted by Georges Delerue. Art Director: Ken Jones. Set Decorations: Luciana Arrighi, Harry Cordwell. Property Master: George Ball. Construction: Jack Carter. Edited by Michael Bradsell. Choreographer: Terry Gilbert. Production Manager: Neville C. Thompson. Production Assistant: Tom Erhardt. Assistant Director: Jonathan Benson. Production Controller: Harry Benn. Location Manager: Lee Bolon. Continuity: Angela Allen. Make-up: Charles Parker. Hairstyles: A. G. Scott. Costumes Designed by Shirley Russell. Wardrobe Supervisor: Shura Cohn. Directed by Ken Russell. Filmed on location in England at Derby, Sheffield, and Newcastle, and in Zermat, Switzerland. Deluxe Color. Released by United Artists. Running time: 129 minutes.

Alan Bates--Rupert Birkin   Oliver Reed--Gerald Crich

Glenda Jackson--Gudrun Brangwen
Jennie Linden--Ursula Brangwen
Eleanor Bron--Hermione Roddice
Michael Gough--Tom Brangwen
Norma Shebbeare--Anna Brangwen
Alan Webb--Thomas Crich
Catherine Wilmer--Christiana Crich
Sharon Gurney--Laura Crich
Christopher Gable--Tibby Lupton
Nike Arrighi--Contessa
Vladek Sheybal--Loerke
Richard Heffer--Loerke's Friend
Sarah Nicholls--Winifred Crich
James Laurenson--Minister
Michael Graham Cox--Palmer
Leslie Anderson--Barber
Charles Workman--Gittens
Barrie Fletcher--First Miner
Brian Osborne--Second Miner
Michael Garratt--Maestro
Richard Fitzgerald--Salsie

The Music Lovers. (1970). Produced and Directed by Ken Russell. Executive Producer: Roy Baird. Screenplay by Melvyn Bragg, based on the book Beloved Friend by Catherine Drinker Bowen and Barbara von Meck. Photographed by Douglas Slocombe, B. S. C. (Panavision). Camera Operator: Chick Waterson. Sound Editor: Terry Rawlings. Sound Recorders: Derek Ball, Maurice Askew. Musical Director: Andre Previn, conducting the London Symphony Orchestra. Musical Advisors: Michael Moores, Elizabeth Corden. Soloists: Raphael Orozco (piano); "Porgi Amor" sung by April Cantelo. Production Designer: Natasha Kroll. Art Director: Michael Knight. Set Decorator: Ian Whittaker. Edited by Michael Bradsell. Choreographer: Terry Gilbert. Production Manager: Neville C. Thompson. Assistant Director: Jonathan Benson. Unit Manager: Graham Ford. Make-up: George Frost. Hairstyles: Ramon Gow, Patti Smith. Costumes: Shirley Russell. Wardrobe Supervisor: Elsa Fennell. Filmed on location in England, and at Bray Studios, Windsor. Distributed by United Artists. Premiere: January 13, 1971. Running time: 122 minutes.

Richard Chamberlain--Peter Tchaikovsky
Glenda Jackson--Antonina Mikyukova
Max Adrian--Nicholas Rubinstein
Christopher Gable--Count Anton Chiluvsky
Izabella Telezynska--Madame Nadedja von Meck
Kenneth Colley--Modeste Tchaikovsky
Sabina Maydelle--Sasha Tchaikovsky
Maureen Pryor--Nina's mother
Bruce Robinson--Alexei
Andrew Faulds--Davidov
Ben Aris--Young Lieutenant
Joanne Brown--Olga Bredska
Imogen Claire--Woman in white
John Myers--von Meck twin
Dennis Myers--von Meck twin
Xavier Russell--Koyola
James Russell--Bobyek
Victoria Russell--Tatiana
Alexander Russell--von Meck child
Alex Jawdokimov--Dmitri Shubelov
Clive Cazes--Doctor
Graham Armitage--Prince Balukin
Ernest Bale--Headwaiter
Consuela Chapman--Tchaikovsky's mother
Alex Brewer--Young Tchaikovsky

Filmography

Principal Dancers, Swan Lake:

Georgina Parkinson--Odile
Alan Dubreuil--Prince Siegfried
Peter White--von Rothbart
Maggy Maxwell--Queen

The Devils. (1971). Produced by Robert H. Solo and Ken Russell (Russo Productions). Screenplay by Ken Russell, based on the play by John Whiting and the book The Devils of Loudun, by Aldous Huxley. Associate Producer: Roy Baird. Photographed by David Watkin. Cameraman: Ronnie Taylor. Assistant Cameraman: Peter Ewens. Lighting: John Swan. Sound: Brian Simmons and Terry Rawlings. Music Composed and Conducted by Peter Maxwell Davies, Performed by The Fires of London. Period Music Arranged and Conducted by David Munrow, Performed by The Early Music Consort of London. Art Director: Robert Cartwright. Assistant Art Director: Alan Tomkins. Sets Designed by Derek Jarman. Set Decorator: Ian Whittaker. Property Master: George Ball. Construction: Terry Apsey. Edited by Michael Bradsell. Assistant Editor: Stuart Baird. Choreographed by Terry Gilbert. Production Manager: Neville C. Thompson. Assistant Director: Ted Morley. Unit Manager: Graham Ford. Make-up: Charles Parker. Hairstyles: Ramon Gow. Costumes Designed by Shirley Russell. Wardrobe Supervisor: Tiny Nicholls. Directed by Ken Russell. Filmed at Pinewood Studios, England, and on location by Russo Productions. Released by Warner Bros. Panavision. Technicolor. Running Time: 111 minutes (GB), 109 minutes (US).

Vanessa Redgrave--Sister Jeanne
Oliver Reed--Father Grandier
Dudley Sutton--Baron de Laubardemont
Max Adrian--Ibert
Gemma Jones--Madeleine de Brou
Murray Melvin--Father Mignon
Michael Gothard--Father Barre
Georgina Hale--Phillipe Trincant
Brian Murphy--Adam
Christopher Logue--Cardinal Richelieu
Graham Armitage--Louis XIII

John Woodvine--Trincant
Andrew Faulds--Rangier
Kenneth Colley--Legrand
Judith Paris--Sister Agnes
Catherine Wilmer--Sister Catherine
Iza Teller--Sister Iza
James Mellor--Executioner
Oliver MacGreevy--Helper
Maggy Maxwell--Madame de Brou
Lawrence Trimble--Dream Grandier
James, Xavier, and Alexander Russell--Court Children

The Boy Friend. (1971). Produced by Ken Russell. Associate Producer: Harry Benn. Screenplay by Ken Russell, Based on Sandy Wilson's Musical, The Boy Friend. Music Arranged and Conducted by Peter Maxwell Davies. Musical Associate: Peter Greenwell. "All I Do Is Dream of You" and "You Are My Lucky Star" by Nacio Herb Brown and Arthur Freed. Choreography by Christopher Gable, Gillian Gregory, Terry Gilbert and members of the cast. Dance Captain: Peter Siniawski. Sets Designed by Tony Walton. Costumes Designed by Shirley Russell. Editor: Michael Bradsell. Production Manager: Neville C. Thompson. Production Associate: Justin De Villeneuve. Art Director: Simon Holland. Set Dresser: Ian Whittaker. Property Master: George Ball. Construction Manager: Charles Hammerton. Director of Photography: David Watkin. Camera Operator: Alan McCabe. Assistant Director: Graham Ford. Continuity: Sue Merry. Wardrobe Supervisor: John Brady. Costumes by Nathan's of London. Sound Recordists: Brian Simmons, Maurice Askew. Dubbing Editor: Don Challis. Make-up: Freddie Williamson. Hairdresser: Barbara Ritchie. Film Research: Philip Jenkinson. Hair Styling by Roger of Vidal Sassoon. Filmed in Panavision. Metrocolor. Directed by Ken Russell. Made at EMI-MGM Elstree Studios, Boreham Wood, Herts., England, and on Location by Russflix, Ltd., 26 Dorst Street, London, W. 1., England. Distributed by MGM. Running time: 123 minutes (GB), 109 minutes (USA)

Twiggy--Polly
Christopher Gable--Tony
Max Adrian--Max
Bryan Pringle--Percy
Murray Melvin--Alphonse
Moyra Fraser--Mme. Dubonnet
Georgina Hale--Fay
Sally Bryant--Nancy
Vladek Sheybal--De Thrill

Tommy Tune--Tommy
Brian Murphy--Peter
Graham Armitage--Michael
Antonia Ellis--Maisie
Caryl Little--Dulcie
Anne Jameson--Mrs. Peter
Catherine Willmer--Catherine
Robert La 'Bassiere--Chauffeur
Barbara Windsor--Hortense

Savage Messiah. (1972). Produced by Ken Russell. Associate Producer: Harry Benn. Production Associates: John and Benny Lee. Screenplay by Christopher Logue, based on the book by H. S. Ede. Director of Photography: Dick Bush. Camera Operator: Ronnie Taylor. Assistant Cameraman: Eddie Collins. Sound Editor: Stuart Baird. Sound Recorder: Robin Gregory. Sound Rerecorder: Doug Turner. Original Music by Michael Garret. Production Designer: Derek Jarman. Art Director: George Lack. Set Decorator: Ian Whittaker. Property Master: George Ball. Edited by Michael Bradsell. Artist: Paul Dufficey. Production Manager: Neville C. Thompson. Assistant Director: Graham Ford. Make-up: Freddie Williamson. Hairstyles: Betty Glasgow. Costume Designer: Shirley Russell. Song: "Two Fleas" composed by Dorothy Tutin. Wardrobe Supervisor: Tiny Nicholls. Directed by Ken Russell. Filmed on Location and at Lee International Studios, Ltd., London. A Russart Production. Distributed by Metro-Goldwyn-Mayer. Running Time: 103 minutes.

Dorothy Tutin--Sophie Brzeska
Scott Antony--Henri Gaudier
Helen Mirren--Gosh Boyle
Lindsay Kemp--Angus Corky
Michael Gough--M. Gaudier
John Justin--Lionel Shaw

Aurbrey Richards--Mayor
Peter Vaughan--Museum Attendant
Ben Aris--Thomas Buff
Eleanor Fazan--Mme. Gaudier
Otto Diamant--Mr. Saltzman
Susanna East--Pippa

Filmography

Maggy Maxwell--Tart
Imogen Claire--Mavis Coldstream
Judith Paris--Kate
Robert Lang--Major Boyle
Alex Jawdokimov--Library Student
Paul McDowell--Agitator
Claire Marshall--Maid
Howard Goorney--Gendarme
Henry Woolf--Gendarme

Mahler. (1974). A Goodtimes Enterprises-Ken Russell Production. Produced by Roy Baird. Executive Producers: Sandy Lieberson and David Puttnam. Director of Photography: Dick Bush, B. S. C. Production Supervisor: John Comfort. Assistant Director: Michael Gowans. Location Manager: Richard Green. Producer's Assistant: Brenda Dale. Choreography: Gillian Gregory. Camera Operator: Eddie Collins. Costumes Designed by Shirley Russell. Art Director: Ian Whittaker. Assistant Art Director: Roger Christian. Construction Manager: Peter Verard for F. T. V. Scenery, Ltd. Property Buyer: Gillian Quertier. Chief Props: Ron Lewis and Andy Andrews. "Chrysallis" Sequence Devised by Janet Deuters. Original Oil Painting by Paul Dufficey. Film Editor: Michael Bradsell. Assistant Editor: Stuart Baird. Sound Recorder: Iain Bruce. Dubbing Mixer: Gerry Humphries. Dubbing Editor: Ian Fuller. The Mahler Symphonies performed by the Concertgebuow Orchestra, Amsterdam, by Arrangement with Phonogram, b. w., Conducted by Bernard Haitink. Music Co-ordinator: John Forsythe. "In Stormy Weather" sung by Carol Mudie, performed by the National Philharmonic Orchestra, conducted by John Forsythe. "Sunset" arranged by Michael Moores. "Alma's Song" words by William Blake, music by Dana Gillespie, sung by Carol Mudie. Continuity: Kay Mander. Camera Assistant: Malcolm Vinson. Camera Grip: David Cadwallader. Make-up: Peter Robb-King. Wardrobe Master: Richard Pointing. Costume Designer's Assistant: Lenny Pollack. Special Effects: John Richardson. Sound Assistant: Charles McFadden. Hairdresser: Joyce James. Production Assistant: Clinton Cavers. Chief Electrician: Micky Thomas for Lee Electric (Lighting) Ltd. Filmed in Technicolor. Thanks to The National Trust for their cooperation of location shooting of this production in the Lake District, Cumberland. Made at Lee International Studios and on location by Goodtimes Enterprises, Ltd., 21 Great Titchfield St., London, England. Sound Re-recorded at Twickenham Film Studios, London, England. Written and Directed by Ken Russell. Running time: 115 minutes.

Robert Powell--Gustav Mahler
Georgina Hale--Alma Mahler
Lee Montague--Bernhard Mahler
Richard Morant--Max
Rosalie Crutchley--Marie Mahler
Miriam Karlin--Aunt Rosa
Gary Rich--Young Mahler
Angela Downs--Justine Mahler
Denny Lee--Uncle
David Collings--Hugo Wolfe
Dana Gillespie--Anna von Mildenberg
Antonia Ellis--Cosima Wagner
Ronald Pickup--Old Nick
Ken Colley--Siegfried Krenek
Elaine Delmar--Princess
Michael Southgate--Alois Mahler
Arnold Yarrow--Grandfather
Otto Diamant--Professor Sladky
Peter Eyre--Otto Mahler
Andrew Faulds--Doctor on Train
George Colouris--Dr. Roth
David Trevana--Dr. Richter

Sarah McLellan--Putzi
Claire McLellan--Glucki

Oliver Reed--Conductor

Tommy. (1975). Produced by Robert Stigwood and Ken Russell. Executive Producers: Beryl Vertue and Christopher Stamp. Associate Producer: Harry Benn. Screenplay by Ken Russell, based upon the rock opera by Pete Townshend. Photography: Dick Bush and Ronnie Taylor. Special Effects: Effects Associates, Nobby Clarke, Camera Effects. Special Photo Effects: Robin Lehman. Sound Recorder: Iain Bruce. Sound Re-recorder: Bill Rowe. Music by Pete Townshend, "Fiddle About" and "Cousin Kevin" by John Entwistle, "Eyesight to the Blind" by Sonny Boy Williamson, "Tommy's Holiday Camp" by Keith Moon. Music Director: Pete Townshend. Musicians: Elton John, Eric Clapton, Keith Moon, John Entwistle, Ronnie Wood, Kenny Jones, Nicky Hopkins, Chris Stainton, Fuzzy Samuels, Caleb Quaye, Mick Ralphs, Graham Deakin, Phil Chen, Alan Ross, Richard Bailey, Dave Clinton, Tony Newman, Mike Kelly, Dee Murray, Nigel Olsson, Ray Cooper, Davey Johnstone, Geoff Daley, Bob Efford, Ronnie Ross, Howie Casey. Music synthesizer programming: Pete Townshend. Theatre Organ played by Gerald Shaw; arranged by Martyn Ford. Vocal Chorus: Liza Strike, Simon Townshend, Mylon LeFevre, Billy Nichols, Jeff Roden, Margo Newman, Gillian McIntosh, Vicki Brown, Kit Trevor, Helen Shappell, Paul Gurvitz, Alison Dowling. Art Director: John Clark. Sets Designed by Paul Dufficey. Set Dresser: Ian Whittaker. Assistant Art Director: Terry Ackland-Snow. Sculptor: Christopher Hobbs. Property Master: Harry Newman. Construction Manager: Jack Carter. Buyer: Bryn Siddal. Music Recordist: John Nevison. Location Managers: Lee Bolon, Ricky Green. Camera Operator: Eddie Collins. Focus Puller: Malcolm Vinson. Continuity: Kay Mander. Hairdresser: Joyce James. Wardrobe Supervisor: Richard Pointing. Music Editor: Terry Rawlings. Gaffer: Bob Bremner. Lighting Contractors: Lee Electrics. Production processing: Rank Labs. Thanks to: Bill Churbishley, The Bluebell Railway Preservation Society, The National Trust - Lake District, City of Portsmouth, Birdman Sports Promotions, Ltd., and flyers: Ken Messenger, Dave Raymond. Costumes Designed by Shirley Russell. Editor: Stuart Baird. Choreography: Gillian Gregory. Production Manager: John Comfort. Assistant Director: Jonathan Benson. Make-up: George Blackler and Peter Robb-King. Made at Lee International Studios, Ltd., Kensal Road, London, W. 10, England, and on location by Robert Stigwood Organization, Ltd., 67 Brook Street, London, W. 1, England. Directed by Ken Russell. Released Through Columbia Pictures. Running time: 111 minutes.

Oliver Reed--Frank Hobbs
Ann-Margret--Nora Walker
Roger Daltrey--Tommy Walker
Elton John--Pinball Wizard
Eric Clapton--The Preacher
Keith Moon--Uncle Ernie

Jack Nicholson--The Doctor
Paul Nicholas--Cousin Kevin
Robert Powell--Captain Walker
Tina Turner--The Acid Queen
Barry Winch--Young Tommy
Victoria Russell--Sally Simpson

Filmography

Ben Aris--Reverend Simpson	Imogen Claire--Nurse
Mary Holland--Mrs. Simpson	Pete Townshend--Narrator
Jennifer Baker--Nurse	Arthur Brown--The Priest
Susan Baker--Nurse	Gary Rich--Rock Musician
Juliet King--Handmaiden to Acid Queen	Dick Allan--President Black Angels
Gillian King--Handmaiden to Acid Queen	Eddie Stacey--Bovver Boy
	The Who--Themselves

Lisztomania. (1975). A Goodtimes Enterprises Production/Visual Programme Systems. Produced by Roy Baird and David Puttnam. Executive Producer: Sandy Lieberson. Photographed by Peter Suschitzky. Special Effects: Colin Chilvers and Roy Spencer. Sound Editor: Terry Rawlings. Sound Recorder: Iain Bruce. Sound Re-recorder: Bill Rowe. Music by Rick Wakeman (Assisted by Franz Liszt and Richard Wagner). Lyrics by Jonathan Benson, Roger Daltrey, and Ken Russell. Performed by The English Rock Ensemble, The National Philharmonic Orchestra. Music Coordinator: John Forsythe. Solo Vocalists: Roger Daltrey, Paul Nicholas, Linda Lewis, and Mandy Moore. Instrumental Soloists: David Wilde (piano), William Davies (organ), and Jack Bruce (bass guitar). Art Direction: Philip Harrison. Set Decorator: Ian Whittaker. Edited by Stuart Baird. Titles and Opticals: Stewart Hardy Films. Choreographed by Imogen Claire. Fencing Master: Peter Brayham. Production Manager: Peter Price. Assistant Directors: Jonathan Benson and Terry Needham. Make-up: Wally Schneiderman. Costumes by Shirley Russell, "The Last Picture Frock." Jeans by Levi. Written and Directed by Ken Russell. Released through Columbia/Warner Bros. Filmed at Shepperton Studios, England. Running Time: 105 minutes.

Roger Daltrey--Franz Liszt	Peter Brayham--Liszt's Bodyguard
Sara Kestelman--Princess Carolyn	Rick Wakeman--Thor
	Rikki Howard--Countess
Paul Nicholas--Richard Wagner	Felicity Devonshire--Governess
Fiona Lewis--Marie D'Algout	Aubrey Morris--Opera House Manager
Veronica Quilligan--Cosima	
Nell Campbell--Olga Janine	Kenneth Colley--Chopin
John Justin--Count D'Algout	Ken Parry--Rossini
Ringo Starr--The Pope	Otto Diamant--Mendelssohn
Andy Reilly--Hans von Bulow	Murray Melvin--Berlioz
Anulka Dziubinska--Lola Montes	Andrew Faulds--Strauss
Imogen Claire--George Sand	Oliver Reed--Carolyn's Servant
David English--Captain of Hussars	Georgina Hale--Most Promising Actress
	Izabella Telezynska--Millionairess

Valentino. (1977). Produced by Irwin Winkler and Robert Chartoff. Executive Producer: Robert Chartoff. Associate Producer: Harry Benn. Directed by Ken Russell. Screenplay by Ken Russell and Mardik Martin, based on Valentino: An Intimate Exposé of the Sheik, by Brad Steiger and Chaw Mank. Photographed by Peter Suschitzky. Cameramen: Ronnie Taylor, Kevin Pike. Sound Recorder: John Mitchell. Music composed by Ferde Grofe and Stanley Black, performed by the National Philharmonic Orchestra. Musical Direction: Stanley Black. Production Designer: Philip Harrison. Set Decorator: Ian Whittaker. Property Master: Ray Traynor. Construction: Jeffrey Woodbridge. Edited by Stuart Baird. Choreographer: Gillian Gregory. Production Manager: Peter Price. Location Manager: Richard Green. Assistant Director: Jonathan Benson. Production Accountant: Len Cave. Production Secretary: Pat Pennelegion. Continuity: Zelda Barron. Casting: Maude Spector. Make-up: Peter Robb-King. Hairdresser: Colin Jamison. Costumes Designed by Shirley Russell. Wardrobe Master: Richard Pointing. Wardrobe Mistress: Rebecca Breed. Dialogue Coach: Marcella Markham. Stills Photographer: Barry Peake. Publicist: Brian Doyle. Filmed at EMI Elstree Studios, Borehamwood, England, and on location by Aperture Films. Released through United Artists. Running time: 128 minutes.

Rudolf Nureyev--Rudolph Valentino
Leslie Caron--Alla Nazimova
Michelle Phillips--Natasha Rambova
Carol Kane--Jean Acker
Felicity Kendall--June Mathis
Seymour Cassell--George Ullman
Huntz Hall--Jesse Lasky
Alfred Marks--Richard Rowland
David De Keyeser--Joseph Schenck
Linda Thorson--Billie Streeter
Leland Palmer--Marjorie Tain
Lindsay Kemp--Angus McBride
Peter Vaughn--Rory O'Neil
Anthony Dowell--Vaslav Nijinsky
Penelop Milford--Lorna Sinclair
June Bolton--Bianca de Saulles
Robin Clark--Jack de Saulles
William Hootkins--Fatty
John Justin--Sidney Olcott
Anton Diffring--Baron Long
Nicolette Marvin--Marsha Lee
Jennie Linden--Agnes Ayres
Percy Herbert--Studio Guard
Dudley Sutton--Willie
Christine Carlson--Girl in Tango
Don Fellows--George Melford
Bill McKinney--Policeman
Marcella Markham--Hooker
John Alderson--Cop
Elizabeth Bagley--Pretty Girl
Charles Farrell--Drunk
Hal Galili--Harry Fishbeck
Richard le Parmentier--The Sheik
Scott Miller--Ray C. Smallwood
Burnell Tucker--Assistant Director
Diana von Fossen--Make-up Girl
Ray Jewers--Electrician
Murray Salem--Vagrant
Mildred Shay--Lady at Maxim's
Deidre Costello--First Whore
Diana Weston--Second Whore
Mark Baker--Assistant Director
Amy Farber--Girl Friend
Ken Russell (unbilled)--Rex Ingram

CLOUDS OF GLORY: William and Dorothy (The Love Story of the Poet Wordsworth and His Sister). (1978). Production Manager: Roy Jackson. Production Assistant: Milly Preece. Floor Manager: Les Davis. Lighting Cameraman: Dick Bush. Edited by Anthony Ham. Sound: Phil Smith. Dubbing Mixer: John Whitworth. Electrician in Charge: Alan Longshaw. Make-up: Deborah Dufton.

Filmography

Graphic Designer: Jim Quick. Research: Margaret Watts. Costume Designer: Shirley Russell. Wardrobe Supervisor: Cathy Halloran. Associate Producer: Diana Bramwell. Casting Director: Doreen Jones. Design: Mike Grimes, Margaret Coombes, Alan Rutter. Produced by Norman Swallow. Written by Melvyn Bragg and Ken Russell. Directed by Ken Russell. Granada Colour Production. Thanks to the National Trust, the Calvert Trust.

Felicity Kendal--Dorothy Wordsworth
David Warner--William Wordsworth
Preston Lockwood--Dr. Carr
Amanda Murray--Mary Wordsworth
Robin Bevan--Young William
Susan Withers--Young Dorothy
Anthony Carrick--Uncle
Patricia Quinn--Annette Vallon
William Hootkins--Reverend Dewey
Thomas Henty--Jack Hutchinson
Freddie Fletcher--Tom Hutchinson
Bridget Ashburn--Joanna Hutchinson
Sally Adama--Mrs. Hutchinson
Trevor Wilson--John Wordsworth

CLOUDS OF GLORY: The Rime of the Ancient Mariner (The Strange Story of Samuel Coleridge, Poet and Drug Addict). (1978). Production Manager: Craig McNeil. Production Assistant: Milly Preece. Floor Managers: Les Davis, Bill Shephard. Lighting Cameraman: Dick Bush. Edited by Anthony Ham. Sound: Phil Smith. Dubbing Mixer: John Whitworth. Electrician in Charge: Alan Longshaw. Make-up: Deborah Dufton. Graphic Designer: Jim Quick. Research: Margaret Watts. Costume Designer: Shirley Russell. Wardrobe Supervisor: Cathy Halloran. Associate Producer: Diana Bramwell. Casting Director: Doreen Jones. Design: Mike Grimes, Margaret Coombes, Alan Rutter. Produced by Norman Swallow. Written by Ken Russell and Melvyn Bragg. Directed by Ken Russell. Granada Colour Production. Thanks to the National Trust, The Calvert Trust.

David Hemmings--Samuel T. Coleridge
Peter Dodd--Hartley Coleridge
Patricia Garwood--Edith Southey
Ben Aris--Robert Southey
Kika Markham--Sara Coleridge
Murray Melvin--Robert Lovell
Diana Mather--Mary Fricker
David Warner--William Wordsworth
Felicity Kendal--Dorothy Wordsworth
Annette Robertson--Servant
Imogen Claire--Spectre
Barbara Ewing--Asra
Ronald Letham--DeQuincey
Henry Moxon--Dr. Gillman
Izabella Telezynska--Mrs. Gillman

Altered States. (1980). Directed by Ken Russell. Music by John Corigliano. Special Visual Effects: Bran Ferren. Costumes designed by Ruth Myers. Associate Producer: Stuart Baird. Film Editor: Eric Jenkins. Production Designer: Richard MacDonald. Director of Photography: Jordan Cronenweth. Executive Producer: Daniel Melnick. Screenplay by Sidney Aaron, from the novel Altered States, by Paddy Chayefsky. Produced by Howard Gottfried.

Unit Production Manager: Dave Silver. Assistant Director: Gary Daigler. Second Assistant Director: Peter Schindler. Special Make-up: Dick Smith. Assisted by Carl Fullerton, Craig Reardon. Casting: Howard Feuer, Jeremy Ritzer. Additional Casting: Joel Thurm, Steve Kolzak. Music Doncuted by Christopher Keane. Camera Operator: James Glennon. First Assistant Cameraman: John Jensen. Second Assistant Cameraman: Carey Jones. Script Supervisor: Carilline Davis-Dyer. Special Effects: Chuck Gaspar. Assistant Special Effects: Larry Fuentes. Supervising Sound Editor: Michael Colgan. Music Editor: Don Harris. Production Associate: Jimsie Eason. Assistant Art Director: Jeff Howard. Illustrator: Joe Hurley. Set Decorator: Thomas Roysden. Lead Man: Ron Jacobs. Propmaster: Syd Greenwood. Assistant Props: Stan Cockerell. Sound Mixer: Willie Burton. Boom Man: Marvin Lewis. Stillman: Morgan Renard. Construction Coordinator: Roger Irvin. Gaffer: Gary Holt. Key Grip: Bobby Rose. Men's Costumer: Darryl Athons. Women's Costumer: Sharron Harrell. Make-up Man: Michael Hancock, CMA. Hair Stylist: Diane Taylor-Demsky. Assistant to Mr. Russell: Vivian Jolly. Assistant to the Producer: Christine Lear. Re-recording Mixers: Les Fresholtz, CAS, Arthur Plantadest, CAS, Michael Minkler, CAS. Assistant Editors: Thomas Penick, Arthur W. Forney. Apprentice Editor: Carl Coughlin. Location Manager: Paul Pav. Production Secretary: Lee Stitch. Transportation Coordinator: John Woodward. Sound Editors: Jay Wertz, Fred Stafford, Don Higgins, Colin Waddy. Assistant Sound Editor: Laurey Condon. Research Assistant: Susan Tarr. Technical Consultant: Scott Bartlett. Orchestrations: John David Earnest. Assistant to the Composer: Sheldon Shkolnik. Sound Consultant: Stephen Katz. Special Optical Effects: Robbie Blalack and Jamie Shourt. Macrophotography: Oxford Scientific Films, Ltd. Optical Effects: Cinema Research Corp., The Optical House, Inc. Time Lapse Photography: Lou Schwartzberg. Special Laser Effects: Media, Inc. Excerpts from Voile d'Orphée by Pierre Henry. Title Credits Produced and Designed by R/Greenburg Associates, Inc., Richard Greenburg. Technicolor. Recorded in Dolby Stereo. Filmed at the Burbank Studios, Burbank, California. Running Time: 103 minutes.

William Hurt--Eddie Jessup
Blair Brown--Emily Jessup
Bob Balaban--Arthur Rosenberg
Charles Haid--Mason Parrish
Thao Penghlis--Eccheveria
Dori Brenner--Sylvia Rosenberg
Miguel Godreau--Primal Man
Peter Brandon--Hobart
Charles White Eagle--The Brujo
Drew Barrymore--Margaret Jessup
Megan Jeffers--Grace Jessup
Jack Murdack--Hector Orteca
Frank McCarthy--Obispo
Deborah Balizel--Schizophrenic Patient
Evan Richards--Young Rosenberg
Hap Lawrence--Endocrinology Fellow
John Walter Davis--Medical Technician
Cynthia Burr--Parrish's Girl
Susan Bradhoff--Eccheveria's Girl
Larry Larroquette--X-ray Technician
George Gaynes--Dr. Wissenschaft
Ora Robinstein--Young Medical Student

Paul Larson--Charlie Thomas Martin Fiscoe--Graduate Student
Eric Forest--Mingus Olivia Michelle--Veronica
Adrian Shaw--Dr. Antonini M. James Arnett--Stuntman

Crimes of Passion (In Production). 1984. New World Pictures. Planet Productions Corp. A Donald P. Borchers Production of a Ken Russell Film. Directed by Ken Russell. Written and Produced by Barry Sandler. Co-produced by Donald P. Borchers. Executive Producer: Larry A. Thompson. Production Designer: Richard MacDonald. Costumes by Ruth Myers. Director of Photography: Dick Bush, A.S.C. Hair Design by Roger Thompson. Casting by Linda Francis. Edited by Brian Tagg. Make-up by Christie Ann Newquist. Production Manager: Bob Manning. First Assistant Director: Pat Kehoe. Music by Rick Wakeman (deal pending as of this writing).

Players: Kathleen Turner, Anthony Perkins, John Laughlin, Annie Potts, and Bruce Davison.

Just as this book wraps up comes word that Russell is once again helming a motion picture, and while it is not among the many cherished projects that he has long wanted to do, its basic storyline is one that appears perfectly at home with the films that precede it and in keeping with his progressions to date. The premise of the film is built very firmly on the Russellian themes of sin, guilt, and forgiveness, aligned with a liberal dose of the optimism and understanding one finds in his more recent work. The presence of Russell regulars Richard MacDonald, Ruth Myers, and the great Dick Bush (and the promise of Rick Wakeman on the musical front), plus the fact that the man who said not so long ago, "I'm on my way out as a filmmaker," is working in the medium again, is cause for celebration.

OPERA PRODUCTIONS:

The Rake's Progress. (1982). Igor Stravinsky--Italy.

Die Soldaten. (1982). Zimmerman--France.

Madama Butterfly. (1983). Puccini--U.S. and Italy.

The Italian Girl in Algiers. (1984). Rossini--Switzerland.

INDEX

ABC-TV 414
"Address to a Child" (poem) 367
Adrian, Max 38, 156, 157, 166
Adventures of Mark Twain, The (film) 320
Agatha (film) 428
Alexander Nevsky (film) 44
All at Sea (film) 42
All That Jazz (film) 221
Allen, Woody 317, 322, 361
Alpert, Hollis 231, 232
Altered States (film) 1, 2, 6, 10, 39, 48, 82, 92, 102, 107, 139, 179, 193, 256, 267, 329, 347, 397-415, 416, 417, 418, 428
Alvidsen, John G. 346
Amelia and the Angel (film) 16, 17
Angels, The (screenplay and proposed film) 218, 263, 278
Ann-Margret 143, 274
Antony, Scott 180, 182, 187
Apted, Michael 411, 428
Aris, Ben 348, 380
Armitage, Graham 165
Astaire, Fred 8, 151, 165, 170
At Long Last Love (film) 152

BBC-TV 15, 41, 53, 140, 180, 349
Babel, Isaac 82, 231-233, 245, 429
Baird, Stuart 397, 411
Bananas (film) 322
Band Wagon, The (film) 170
Barber, Samuel 429-430
Barnacle Bill (film) 42
Bates, Alan 54
Bax, Sir Arnold 371
Baxter, John 7
Baxter, Warner 159, 167
Beatles, The 272

Bed-Sitting Room, The (film) 268
Beethoven, Ludwig van 289, 299, 300
Beethoven (proposed film) 417
Beloved Friend (book) 81, 85, 99, 112, 253
Berkeley, Busby 150, 151, 152, 168, 170, 171, 174, 306
Billion Dollar Brain (film) 35, 42-50, 62, 95, 259
Binder, Maurice 48
Black Angels, The 283-284
Black Cat, The (film, 1934) 44, 339
Blake, William 10, 232, 239
Blood and Sand (film, 1921) 341
Blood and Sand (film, 1941) 97
Bluebeard (film, 1944) 44
Bogarde, Dirk 226
Bogdanovich, Peter 152
Boorman, John 429
Booth, Jim 43
Bowen, Catherine Drinker 85, 112, 253
Boy Friend, The (film) 2, 3, 6, 8, 18, 118, 121, 140, 150-178, 180, 196, 201, 218, 222, 227, 252, 322, 415
Bradsell, Michael 411
Bragg, Melvyn 92, 101, 349, 353
Brahms, Johannes 297, 298
Brandon, Henry 309
Bride of Frankenstein (film) 392
Brideshead Revisited (novel) 247, 252
Brideshead Revisited (film) 348
Bridge, Frank 351, 371
Britten, Benjamin 371, 387, 388, 430
Broadway Melody, The (film) 168
Broadway Melody of 1936, The (film) 168, 175
Brook, Clive 2
Brook, Peter 127
Brooks, Mel 152
Brown, Blair 414
Bruckner, Anton 82
Bryant, Sally 171
Buñuel, Luis 283
Burning to Speak (book) 199
Bush, Dick 20, 77, 180, 201, 222, 257, 348, 374, 386
Butterworth, George 352, 354, 356, 357, 368, 371

CBS Cable Network 370
CBS-TV 153, 414
Caine, Michael 49
Callas, Maria 417

Index

Camille (film, 1921) 337
Cantor, Eddie 342
Care, Ross 294
Carefree (film) 170
Carey, Joyce 200
Caron, Leslie 327, 340
Casablanca (film) 314
Castaneda, Carlos 399, 403, 404
Cat Ballou (film) 294
Catholic Film Office 10-14, 120
Catholicism 10, 11, 12, 13, 14, 221, 244, 245, 246, 247, 320
Chamberlain, Richard 83
Changeling, The (film) 413
Chaplin, Charles 154, 302, 303
Chaplin, Oona O'Neil 202
Chartoff, Robert 346
Chayefsky, Paddy 92, 397, 398, 401, 403, 404, 406, 407, 408
Cheap Detective, The (film) 152
Chopin, Frédéric 298
Chosen, The (film) 404
Christian Science Monitor, The 77, 290
Citizen Kane (film) 7, 20, 29, 330, 331, 332, 333, 339, 345
City of Women (film) 428
Claire, Imogen 297, 348
Clapton, Eric 263
Clockwork Orange, A 92
Clouds of Glory (films) 35, 43, 181, 187, 218, 348-396
Cocteau, Jean 257, 269, 402
Cole, Steven 425
Coleridge, Samuel Taylor 348, 369, 370-396
Colley, Ken 41, 297
Colouris, George 251
Columbia Pictures 291
Cooke, Alistair 370
Corigliano, John 82, 412, 413
Corman, Roger 283
Crawford, Jesse 172
Crist, Judith 118
Crosby, Bing 7, 148

Dali, Salvador 402
Daltrey, Roger 263, 293, 303, 305, 315
Dance of the Seven Veils (film) 39-41, 76, 245, 288, 299, 321

Daniels, Bebe 167
Dante's Inferno (film) 15, 35, 36, 256, 350
Death in Venice (film) 226, 250
Debussy, Claude 17, 18, 179, 195, 208, 216
Debussy Film, The (film) 17, 18, 49
de Chirico, Giorgio 402
Deighton, Len 42
Delerue, George 18, 51, 60, 63, 65, 70
Delius, Frederick 35-39, 57, 256
Del Ruth, Roy 175
DeMille, Cecil B. 131
De Palma, Brian 12, 179
DeQuincey, Thomas 391, 392
Detour (film) 44
Deuters, Janet 232
Devil Is a Woman, The (film) 417
Devils, The (film) 1, 3, 4, 10, 11, 13, 82, 116, 118-150, 169, 178, 180, 189, 193, 218, 223, 227, 247, 251, 252, 260, 310, 332, 334, 350, 377, 412, 413, 431
Devotion (film) 297
Diamant, Otto 180, 297
Dieterle, William 81, 82
Dietrich, Marlene 2
Director of Devils (short production film) 126, 149
Dolce Vita, La (film) 278
Don't Shoot the Composer (film) 18
Dore, Gustave 236
Dorleac, Francoise 44, 48, 95
Duck Soup (film) 323
Dufficey, Paul 232
Dullea, Keir 402
Duncan, Isadora 18-35

Ede, H. S. 180, 253
Eisenstein, Sergei M. 44, 163, 322
Elephant Man, The (film) 416, 429-430
Elgar (film) 18, 234
Ellis, Antonia 171, 246
Eugene Onegin (opera) 417
Excalibur (film) 416, 429
Exorcist, The (film) 81

Fairbanks, Douglas 7, 294
Farber, Stephen 178, 206, 242, 288, 292, 293, 303, 328
"Farewell, A" (poem) 364

Index   451

Faulds, Andrew 297
Fazan, Eleanor 180
Fear No Evil (film, 1981) 404
Fellini, Federico 6, 53, 278, 428
Fenby, Eric 37, 38, 39, 57, 303
Final Conflict, The (film) 404
First Love (film, 1939) 421
Fisher, Jack 51, 111, 150
Flash Gordon (film, 1936) 321
Flying Down to Rio (film) 151, 152
Ford, John 86, 179, 255, 303, 309
Forty-second Street (film) 150, 158, 159, 167, 168, 171
Fosse, Bob 221
Four Horsemen of the Apocalypse, The (film, 1920) 337-338
French Dressing (film) 18, 42, 43, 259, 305
French Lieutenant's Woman, The 18
Friedkin, William 81
Front Page, The (play) 334
"Frost at Midnight" (poem) 381
Funeral in Berlin (film) 42

Gable, Christopher 41, 165
Gallagher, Michael 11, 12, 14
Gang's All Here, The (film, 1943) 174, 306
Gargantua (screenplay) 286
Garrett, Michael 179
Gartneberg, Egon 225, 310
Garwood, Patricia 380
Gaudier-Brzeska, Henri 178, 179-219, 328
Gaudier-Brzeska, Sophie 179-219
Gay Science, The (book) 317
Gilbert, Terry 411
Gillman, Dr. James 393, 394, 395
Going My Way (film) 8
Gold-diggers of 1933 (film) 150
Gold-diggers of 1935 (film) 151
Gold Rush, The (film) 303
Gomez, Joseph A. 4, 34, 51, 73, 79, 85, 118, 119, 120, 142, 150, 180, 184, 190, 194, 197, 222, 226, 232, 234, 238, 292
Good Companions, The (book) 177
Goodies, The 430
Goon Show, The 312
Gough, Michael 180
Gould, Dave 151, 152, 175

Gow, Gordon 226
Grainger, Percy 37, 38
Granada TV 346
Grand Hotel (film) 2
Grandier, Urbain 4, 119-150
Grant, Cary 8
"Great God Pan, The" (short story) 403
Greenstreet, Sydney 297
Greenwell, Peter 8, 156
Gregory, Gillian 41
Gutman, Robert W. 310

HBO 417
Haitink, Bernard 225
Hakim Bros. (Robert and Raymond) 18, 19, 23
Hale, Georgina 8, 171, 301
Hall, Huntz 333
Ham, Anthony 348
Hard Day's Night, A (film) 42, 272, 273
Hardy, Oliver 7, 39
Harrison, Phillip 301, 331
Hart, Moss 345
Hawks, Howard 5
Hecht, Ben 334
Hemmings, David 348
High Anxiety (film) 152
Hitchcock, Alfred 5, 64, 309
Hitler, Adolf 137, 318, 319
Holst, Gustav 417
Hootkins, William 348
Hope, Bob 7, 148
Horse's Mouth, The (novel and film) 200, 202
Hubbard, Elbert 394
Hunchback of Notre Dame, The (film, 1939) 81
Huxley, Aldous 118, 119, 120, 127

"I Travelled Among Unknown Men" (poem) 357
"I Wandered Lonely as a Cloud" (poem) 361, 363, 368
Informer, The (film, 1935) 7, 86, 179
Ingram, Rex 8, 337-338
International House (film) 150
Ipcress File, The (film) 45
Ireland, John 371
Isadora (film, 1966) 4, 15, 18, 19-35, 37, 58, 166, 193, 243, 252, 292, 330, 331, 351

Index 453

"It Is a Beauteous Evening, Calm and Free" (poem) 365
Iturbi, José 111

Jackson, Glenda 8, 94, 167
Jarman, Derek 203, 270, 418, 430
Jazz Singer, The (film, 1927) 105
Jesus Christ Superstar (film) 258
Jet Pilot (film) 417
Jewison, Norman 258
John, Elton 271, 272
Jolly, Vivian 347
Jolson, Al 7, 245
Jolson Story, The (film) 152
Justin, John 8, 157, 180, 341

Kael, Pauline 8, 93, 344
Kalbeck, Max 229
Karloff, Boris 309
Kaufman, George S. 345
Keeler, Ruby 167
Kemp, Lindsay 180
Kendal, Felicity 348
Kern, Jerome 152
King of Kings (film, 1927) 131
Kinnear, Roy 42, 268
Kiss Before the Mirror, The (film) 143
Koster, Henry 421
"Kubla Khan" (poem) 381, 390, 391, 393
Kubrick, Stanley 7, 92, 268, 402, 403, 413

Lady Chatterley's Lover (film) 428
Lady with the Little Dog, The (film) 100
Lake District 3, 4, 5, 6, 350, 375, 383
Lamy, Catherine 425
Lang, Fritz 333
Lasky, Jesse 333
Laurel, Stan 7, 39, 245
Lawrence, D. H. 51, 52, 55, 57, 58, 64, 65, 66, 67, 70, 73, 75, 411, 428
Lee International Studios 180
Lester, Richard 42, 44, 268, 272, 273
Let It Be (film) 272
Let's Dance (film) 170
Lieberson, Sandy 222

Lilly, John C. 403
Linden, Jennie 54
Lindsay-Hogg, Michael 272, 348
"Lines Composed a Few Miles Above Tintern Abbey" (poem) 359-360
Liszt, Franz 4, 291-323, 328, 399, 401, 408
Lisztomania (film) 4, 5, 6, 8, 11, 12, 19, 39, 40, 43, 76, 107, 157, 170, 187, 193, 220, 229, 245, 255, 267, 270, 289, 291-325, 327, 329, 330, 333, 334, 336, 346, 360, 369, 370, 372, 381, 384, 396, 397, 401, 406, 408, 414, 420, 429
Little, Caryl 171
Little Journeys to the Homes of the Great: English Authors (book) 394
Logue, Christopher 180, 185, 187, 198, 199
"Louisa" (poem) 351, 355
Lourdes (film) 16
Love and Death (film) 317, 322
Love Me Tonight (film) 2, 234, 235
Lubitsch, Ernst 5
Lugosi, Bela 343
Lumet, Sidney 275
Lynch, David 429-430

MGM 3, 150, 153, 154, 168, 171
MTV Cable 428
Maazel, Lorin 417
MacArthur, Charles 334
McCarey, Leo 8, 323
McCarthy, Sen. Joseph 137
MacDonald, Richard 398, 418, 419, 424
McGrath, John 42
McGrath, Joseph 120
Machen, Arthur 403
Mackintosh, Charles Rennie 398
Madama Butterfly (opera) 416-426
Magic Christian, The (film) 120
Magic Town (film) 49
Magritte, Rene 402
Mahler, Gustav 5, 220-253, 328
Mahler (film) 4, 5, 6, 11, 24, 25, 40, 43, 77, 82, 127, 144, 163, 178, 180, 187, 201, 220-253, 254, 255, 289, 291, 292, 294, 295, 296, 304, 320, 326, 329, 331, 332, 350, 354, 360, 366, 369, 370, 372, 374, 384, 389, 396, 414, 415, 428, 429
Mamoulian, Rouben 2, 5, 76, 97, 105, 107, 234, 235

Index   455

Marat/Sade (play and film) 127
Markham, Kika 380
Marx Bros., The 7, 245
Masterpiece Theatre 252, 370
Maxwell Davies, Peter 122, 149, 152, 153, 172, 173, 413
Medak, Peter 93, 95, 413
Melvin, Murray 165, 297
Mendelssohn, Felix 297, 298, 309
Menotti, Gian Carlo 419, 426
Midsummer Night's Dream, A (play) 154
Mikado, The (Operetta) 425
Milestone, Lewis 179
Milligan, Spike 17
Miranda, Carmen 7
Mirren, Helen 180, 209
Monroe, Marilyn 263, 264
Monty Python and the Holy Grail (film) 431
Moon, Keith 8
Mosley, John 290
Murder by Death (film) 152
Murphy, Brian 165
Muscle Beach Party (film) 299
Music Lovers, The (film) 1, 2, 4, 5, 11, 12, 13, 40, 41,
   45, 55, 75-117, 118, 124, 126, 127, 131, 133, 135, 139,
   145, 149, 178, 189, 193, 218, 220, 223, 225, 229, 238,
   241, 251, 253, 292, 299, 301, 304, 316, 331, 334, 335,
   341, 342, 344, 350, 354, 363, 377, 379, 380, 412, 420,
   421
Music, Music, Music (screenplay) 252, 304
Myers, Ruth 418, 419

Naughty Marietta (film) 322
Neame, Ronald 200
Network (film) 275
Newton-John, Olivia 417
Nicholas, Paul 266, 267, 297
Nietzsche, Frederick 317
Nijinsky, Vaslav 334
Nijinsky (proposed film) 49
"Novel of the White Powder, The" (short story) 403
Nureyev, Rudolph 326, 334, 340, 343

"Ode: Intimations of Immortality from Recollections of Early
   Childhood" (poem) 367, 368
Old Battersea House (film) 17

Olympia (film) 21
Omen, The (film) 404
Once in a Lifetime (play) 345
Once upon a Honeymoon (film) 8
Our Hitler: A Film from Germany 318-319

PBS-TV 15, 252, 253, 415
Page, Eileen 417
Palmer, David 430
Palmy Days (film) 150, 171, 342
Paramount Pictures 168
Pearl, Elna 17
Peckinpah, Sam 12
Penn, Arthur 397
Peter Grimes (opera) 387-388
Phantom of Liberty, The (film) 283
Phillips, Gene D. 35, 73, 86, 150, 158, 220, 238, 252, 291, 292, 314, 326, 328, 332
Phillips, Michelle 327, 340
Pickles, Bivian 19
Pinter, Harold 18
Planets, The (film and composition) 417
Playboy 299
Popeye (film, 1980) 416
Potemkin (film) 7, 322
Powell, Robert 246, 257, 291
Prelude, The (poem) 354-355
Priestley, J. B. 177
Pringle, Bryan 42, 43, 171
Psycho (film) 64
Puccini, Giacomo 418, 419, 421, 424
Puttnam, David 222

Quadrophenia (record album) 254
Quadros, Mercedes 16
Queen Christina (film, 1933) 108

Rainbow, The (novel and proposed film) 73, 417
Rake's Progress, The (opera) 417-418, 420
Rambova, Natasha 327-343
Redgrave, Vanessa 19, 143
Reed, Sir Carol 5, 44
Reisz, Karel 18, 19, 23, 25, 28, 29, 34

Renoir, Jean 95
Rich, Gary 281
Rime of the Ancient Mariner (poem and film) 193, 257, 348, 349, 369, 370-396
Rocky (film) 346
Rocky Horror Picture Show, The (film) 293
Rogers, Ginger 8, 150, 151, 165, 170
Rosetti, Dante Gabriel 35
Ross, Herbert 152
Rowland, Richard 333
Ruling Class, The (film) 93, 95, 413
Russell, Shirley 221, 260, 301, 348, 411, 428
Russell, Victoria 83, 281
Ruthless (film) 44

Salome (film, 1922) 337
Sand, George 298
Sass, Eric 252-253
Savage Messiah (film) 3, 4, 5, 9, 13, 140, 150, 157, 177, 178-219, 223, 227, 229, 236, 251, 252, 253, 254, 270, 304, 331, 334, 344, 346, 349, 350, 360, 369, 400, 401, 418, 420
Scarlett Empress, The (film) 323
Schenck, Joseph 333, 344, 345
Schertzinger, Victor 421
Schumann, Robert 298
Scriabin, Alexander 179, 190
Searchers, The (film) 7, 179, 255, 303
Searle, Audrey 17
Sellars, Peter 425
Sergeant Pepper's Lonely Hearts Club Band (film) 290
Seven Year Itch, The (film) 264
Shakespeare, William 430
Shanghai Express (film) 2
"She Dwelt Among the Untrodden Ways" (poem) 364
"She Was a Phantom of Delight" (poem) 351, 365
Sheybal, Vladek 18
Shining, The (film) 413, 416
Siegfried (film, 1923) 7
Simon, John 179, 225, 231
Simon, Neil 152
Singer, Paris 22-24
Singin' in the Rain (film) 168, 176
Slocombe, Douglas 12, 77, 78
Soldaten, Die (opera) 417, 420
"Solitary Reaper, The" 385, 386

Song of Summer (film) 15, 35-39, 40, 57, 157, 178, 193, 196, 223, 256, 303, 349, 350
Southey, Robert 373, 377, 378, 379, 382, 395
Space: 1999 262
"Sparrow's Nest, The" (poem) 353, 355, 369
Stallings, Carl W. 168
Starr, Ringo 8, 313
Sterrit, David 77, 290
Stigwood, Robert 290, 417
Stokes, Sewell 19, 21, 23, 27, 31, 32
Story of "Tommy," The (book) 261
"Strange Fits of Passion Have I Known" (poem) 349
Strauss, Johann 298
Strauss, Richard 39-41, 76
Stravinsky, Igor 420
Streisand, Barbra 417
Sturges, Preston 5, 262
Sturridge, Charles 348
Suschitsky, Peter 77, 331
Sutherland, A. Edward 150, 342
Sutton, Dudley 143
Swallow, Norman 348
Syberberg, Hans Jurgen 318

Tannhauser (opera) 417
Tchaikovsky, Peter Ilich 2, 12, 71, 75-117, 126, 220, 223, 224, 227, 328, 334, 335, 342, 344, 363, 378, 379, 382, 396, 399
Teachings of Don Juan, The (book) 409
Telezynska, Izabella 8, 301, 348
Tempest, The (film, 1978) 430
Tess (film, 1980) 416
Third Man, The (film) 44, 47
Thorson, Linda 327
Till the Clouds Roll By (film, 1946) 152
Time There Was, A (film) 430
"To a Butterfly" (poem) 362-363
"To My Sister" (poem) 355, 363, 369
Tommy (film) 2, 4, 5, 6, 8, 9, 10, 11, 21, 28, 43, 48, 84, 107, 127, 139, 163, 180, 193, 204, 208, 218, 236, 253-291, 292, 293, 294, 295, 296, 300, 305, 321, 327, 329, 333, 360, 369, 370, 374, 384, 393, 396, 405, 408, 410, 412, 414, 418, 426, 428, 429
Top Hat (film) 165
Townshend, Pete 253, 254, 258, 259, 261, 273, 276, 278, 285, 305, 306, 398, 426

Index

Tristan und Isolde (opera) 417
Tuffano, Brian 20
Tune, Tommy 152, 161
Turner, Tina 265
Tutin, Dorothy 179, 198
Twiggy 155, 163, 165, 167
2001: A Space Odyssey (film) 402, 403

Ulmer, Edgar G. 44, 339
Unfaithfully Yours (film, 1947) 262
Universal Pictures 315

Valentino, Rudolph 326-347
Valentino (film, 1977) 6, 8, 11, 107, 139, 157, 193, 201, 241, 244, 326-347, 357, 370, 371, 397, 400, 408
Vampyr (film) 237
Van Dyke, W. S. 322
Vaughan, Peter 180, 188
Vaughan Williams, Ralph 371, 376, 377, 383, 385, 388, 389, 391
Vidor, Charles 85
Visconti, Luchino 54, 226
von Bulow, Hans 297, 310
von Meck, Barbara 253
von Sternberg, Josef 2, 5, 67, 85, 221, 323, 336

Wagner, Richard 76, 297, 300, 308-321, 408, 429
Wagner (film) 430
Wakeman, Rick 8
Wall, The (film) 428
Walsh, Michael 417, 418
Warner, David 348
Warner Bros. 168, 293
Watkin, David 77
Wayne, John 303
Weinstock, Herbert 81
Welles, Orson 330, 332, 333, 345
Wellman, William 49
Whale, James 95, 392
What Price Beauty? (film) 342
Whiteman, Paul 153
Whiting, Charles 118, 119, 120, 143
Whittaker, Ian 411
Who, The 272, 281

William and Dorothy (film) 193, 348, 349-370, 371, 372, 381, 384, 385, 392, 396
Williams, Billy 13, 51
Wilmer, Catherine 159
Wilson, Sandy 151
Winch, Barry 263
Windsor, Barbara 153
Winkler, Irwin 346
Women in Love (film) 2, 3, 4, 5, 13, 35, 49, 51-74, 75, 77, 78, 102, 116, 126, 139, 149, 150, 159, 182, 197, 275, 326, 329, 372, 373, 411, 429
Wordsworth, Dorothy 349-370, 381, 382, 383, 384, 385, 386, 390
Wordsworth, William 349-370, 381, 382, 383, 384, 385, 386, 390, 391, 392

Yeats, William Butler 200
Yoshii, Kumiko 425
Young Frankenstein (film) 152